Mandates and Empire

The League of Nations and Africa, 1914–1931

"The Mandates have always been somewhat of a mystery. The German African colonies made Mandates at the Paris Peace Conference were no exception. In this definitive book the meticulous research and critical analysis of Michael Callahan has brought clarity in the evolution of these murky mandates from the old imperial order to the acceptance of neo-imperial trusteeship at the beginning of the new. His scholarship will be rewarded as the source for students, their teachers, and those scholars of every nationality who seek to understand Africa in the lost but formative years between the two great wars of the twentieth century."

Robert O. Collins
Professor of History, Emeritus
University of California Santa Barbara

"Michael Callahan's marvellous book breaks new ground. The author not only explores the precise powers and complex workings of the Permanent Mandates Commission and the colonial bureaucracies involved; he also considers all of these institutions within the national, imperial, and international context for the crucial period between World War I and the Great Depression of the 1930s. This is a highly recommended piece of work; it is meticulously researched, well structured, clearly written. It will be of immense use for students of International and African history."

Andreas Eckert
Humboldt University, Berlin

Mandates and Empire

The League of Nations and Africa, 1914–1931

MICHAEL D. CALLAHAN

sussex
ACADEMIC
PRESS
Brighton • Chicago • Toronto

2 4 6 8 10 9 7 5 3

First published 1999, and transferred to paperback digital printing 2008, in Great Britain by
SUSSEX ACADEMIC PRESS
PO Box 139
Eastbourne BN24 9BP

Distributed in North America by
SUSSEX ACADEMIC PRESS
Independent Publishers Group
814 N Franklin St, Chicago, IL 60610, USA

British Library Cataloguing in Publication Data
A CIP catalogue record for this book is available from the British Library.

Library of Congress Cataloging-in-Publication Data
Callahan, Michael D. (Michael Dennis)
Mandates and empire : the League of Nations and Africa, 1914–1931 /
Michael D. Callahan.
p. cm.
Includes bibliographical references and index.
ISBN 978-1-84519-297-6 (pbk.: alk. paper)
1. League of Nations—Africa History. I. Title.
JZ4871.5.A35C35 1999
341.27′096′09042—dc21

99–20795

Printed and bound by CPI Group (UK) Ltd, Croydon, CR0 4YY
This book is printed on acid-free paper.

Contents

Acknowledgments

I could not have completed this study without the help of many people. Special thanks go to my mentor at Michigan State University, John W. Coogan. His extraordinary commitment, patience, advice, and encouragement over the course of my project was invaluable. I consider myself fortunate to have had his guidance and friendship for so many years. I am also indebted to Donald Lammers, David Robinson, and Gordon T. Stewart for offering constructive criticisms and asking difficult questions. I must also thank Martin Daly at Kettering University who read the original draft and provided many useful suggestions. Not least, I am grateful to my other friends and colleagues at Michigan State University and Kettering University for their much needed camaraderie, inspiration, and tolerance.

I thank the archivists and staff at the Public Record Office in Kew, India Office Library, British Museum, House of Lords Record Office, London School of Economics and Political Science, Cambridge University Library, Churchill College Library, Bodleian Library, Nuffield College Library, Rhodes House Library, the Scottish Record Office, the Archives du Ministère des Affaires Etrangères in Paris, the Service Historique de l'Armée de Terre, the Bibiothèque Nationale, the Archives Nationales, Section Outre-Mer in Aix-en-Provence, the National Archives of Canada in Ottawa, and the Michigan State University Library. I am also grateful that a portion of my research was funded by a New Faculty Professional Development Grant from Kettering University.

The jacket picture is an undated photograph of the *Bund der Deutsch Togoländer*, founded by Johan Kanyi in Accra, Gold Coast, *ca*. 1923–25; reproduced from the Nazi-era propagandist Paul Ritter's *Unvergessenes deutsches Land: 140 Bilddokumente aus den alten deutschen Kolonies* (Berlin, 1936).

Finally, I would like to thank my family, and most importantly, my wife, Christy, and our daughter, Mackenzie. Their love, laughter, and unwavering support are constant reminders of what is most important in my life. This book is dedicated to them.

Abbreviations

AE	Archives du Ministère des Affaires Etrangères, Paris.
ANSOM	Archives Nationales, Section Outre-Mer, Aix-en-Provence.
AP	Affaires Politiques.
BLO	Bodleian Library, Oxford University.
BM	British Museum.
BN	Bibliothèque Nationale, Paris.
CAB	Cabinet .
CC	Churchill College Library, Cambridge University.
CID	Committee of Imperial Defence.
Cmd	Command Paper.
CO	Colonial Office.
CU	Cambridge University Library.
Deliberations	Paul Mantoux, *The Deliberations of the Council of Four (March 24–June 28, 1919): Notes of the Official Interpreter.*
DKG	*Deutsche Kolonialgesellschaft.*
DO	Dominions Office.
FO	Foreign Office .
FRUS	United States, Department of State, *Papers Relating to the Foreign Relations of the United States.*
HLRO	House of Lords Record Office.
IOL	India Office Library.
JOC	*Journal Officiel. Chambre des Députés. Debats parlementaires.*
KAR	King's African Rifles.
LN	League of Nations.
LNU	League of Nations Union.
LSEPS	London School of Economics and Political Science.
MAE	Ministère des Affaires Etrangères, Quai d'Orsay.
MC	Ministère des Colonies.
NAC	National Archives of Canada.
NCO	Nuffield College Library, Oxford.

Papers of Woodrow Wilson	Arthur Link, ed., *The Papers of Woodrow Wilson.*
PCF	French Communist Party.
PMC	Permanent Mandates Commission.
PRO	Public Record Office, Kew.
RH	Rhodes House Library, Oxford University.
SG: Togo-Cam	Séries Géographiques: Togo-Cameroun.
SHAT	Service Historique de l'Armée de Terre.
SLOTFOM	Service de Liaison avec les Originaires des Territoires Français d'Outre-Mer.
SRO	Scottish Record Office.
WAFF	West African Frontier Force.
WO	War Office.

Africans: The History of a Continent.

For
Christy and Mackenzie

Introduction

The barter of colonies without regard to the wishes or welfare of the inhabitants or the welfare of the world in general is a custom which this war should put to an end, since it is a fruitful cause of dissention among nations, a danger to the status of civilized labor, a temptation to unbridled exploitation, and an excuse for unspeakable atrocities committed against natives . . . If the world after the war decided to reconstruct Africa in accordance with the wishes of the Negro race and the best interests of civilization, the process might be carried out as follows: the former German colonies with one million square miles and twelve and one-half millions of inhabitants could be internationalized. To this could be added by negotiation the 800,000 square miles and nine million inhabitants of Portuguese Africa. It is not impossible that Belgium could be persuaded to add to such a state the 900,000 square miles and nine million natives of the Congo, making an International Africa with over two and one-half million square miles of land and over twenty million people. This reorganized Africa could be under the guidance of organized civilization. The Governing International Commission should represent not simply governments but modern culture – science, commerce, social reform, and religious philanthropy . . . We can, if we will, inaugurate on the Dark Continent a last great crusade for humanity. With Africa redeemed, Asia would be safe and Europe indeed triumphant.

W. E. B. DuBois, "Memoranda on the Future of Africa,"
27 November 1918

It would be far better for Africa that the United States should take in hand the development of the great central and south-western block composed of the Belgian Congo and Angola, that France should take over the Cameroons and Togoland, and that we should develop a compact region in East Africa, than that Africa should be cut up into a number of disconnected minor colonial territories. From the point of view of British security continuous territory along the whole length of Africa from north to south would, of course, be a matter of the very greatest importance.

Leo Amery to Jan Smuts, 16 August 1918

The First World War transformed Africa and Europe. Nearly two million Africans served as soldiers and laborers in the many and difficult military campaigns in Europe, Africa, and the Middle East. The conflict brought considerable suffering to colonized peoples, caused enormous social and economic dislocation, and inspired increased resistance to imperial institutions.[1] For Europeans, the long and horrific bloodshed shook common assumptions about international order, left the colonial powers shattered or exhausted, and ignited widespread bitterness and fear. Germany lost its African empire to the victorious Allies. Britain and France survived the war as the world's two largest overseas colonial powers, but only after enormous carnage and expense.

This extraordinary loss sparked a far-reaching debate during the war about the purpose and future of European imperialism in the postwar world.[2] Some argued that the colonies were a source of strength, security, and pride. For them, empire had made the victory possible and would make recovery and peace easier. Many anti-imperialists and humanitarians passionately disagreed. Imperialism had drained resources, widened the European conflict into a global struggle, and had shamefully led to the deaths of countless European and colonized people. For this group, empire had made the war possible and would make recovery and peace difficult. This debate exposed the conflicting convictions within the culture of colonialism and made European imperialism a matter of serious national politics and international relations.

The fate of the conquered German and Turkish territories in Africa, the Pacific, and the Middle East pushed the problem of imperialism to the center of international attention during the Paris Peace Conference in 1919. The atmosphere was dominated by the competing pressures of revenge, anxiety, optimism, and intense skepticism. Since few of the delegates considered Africans capable of successful self-government, there was no discussion of either immediate political independence or a swift end of colonialism in Africa. Instead, the arguments hinged on how best to administer the former German possessions. Both Britain and France were determined not to return them. The British government wanted to ensure that Germany could never again attempt world domination while French leaders were desperate to demolish their former enemy as a military power. Eliminating Germany as a colonial power was a important part of this strategic planning for both. Britain's Imperial War Cabinet recommended in 1917 that "the retrocession of any African possession to the Germans should not be contemplated" because they posed a "grave political and military menace" to Britain's vital maritime connections with South Africa and India.[3] For a number of French leaders, the acquisition of the German African colonies of Cameroon and Togo was necessary "to ensure the unification of our African Empire" and to deprive Germany of a source of raw materials and manpower.[4] Many within the British and French governments assumed that annexation was the only practical choice.

These assumptions encountered stubborn opposition in 1919. Powerful and popular anti-imperialist sentiments in Europe and the United States rejected annexation of the German colonies and advocated new controls over European colonialism. The American president, Woodrow Wilson, was particularly unwavering in his rejection of crass imperial conquest. He remained an outspoken proponent during and after the war for the internationalization and reformation of European imperialism. Following a long, often angry debate during extremely trying circumstances, Wilson and the other delegates in Paris agreed on a compromise that placed the former German colonies, as well as the Middle Eastern Ottoman provinces, under the supervision of the newly created League of Nations. This plan gave the Allies control of their acquisitions, but as "mandates" within a framework of international accountability rather than as colonies under national sovereignty. Great Britain received the most mandates, including German East Africa, almost half of Togo, and a small portion of Cameroon. France obtained the other half of Togo and the rest of Cameroon. To the British and French ministers who had advocated transforming these territories into British and French colonies, the new plan seemed to make little practical difference. They left its details to others. The United States, a principal force in creating the mandates, never joined the League and thus had a limited role in the mandates system.

With the Germans out, the Americans disengaging, and the French and British cabinets preoccupied, the colonial officials in London, Paris, and at the highest levels of administration already established within the conquered possessions became responsible for implementing this new international system. They discovered that it was only a vaguely defined combination of established colonial practices and untested administrative theories.[5] Precedents from European rule in Egypt and Morocco, international treaties concerning colonial rule in Africa such as the Berlin Act of 1885, and the political and economic arguments of the British Labour movement, the League of Nations Union, and other groups all influenced the creation of the system. Its framers had divided the conquered Turkish and German territories, "inhabited by peoples not yet able to stand by themselves under the strenuous conditions of the modern world," into three alphabetically labeled groups according to European definitions of modernization. The "well-being and development" of colonized peoples formed "a sacred trust of civilization." Their "tutelage" was "intrusted to advanced nations," but "this tutelage should be exercised by them as Mandatories on behalf of the League." The Conference had decided that the Arab provinces were on the threshold of independent statehood and constituted the "A" category while the German islands in the Pacific and German South-West Africa could be "best administered under the laws of the Mandatory as integral portions of its territory" as "C" mandates.

All of Germany's colonies in tropical Africa fell into the intermediate "B" category.[6]

The British and French mandates in Africa reflected a mix of traditional humanitarian ideals and new political conditions. The mandates were to remain free-trade zones with the mandatory power reporting annually and sending accredited representatives to the League. For the first time, an international organization, through a permanent commission, had the authority to examine reports and question representatives concerning a colonial government's promises to protect indigenous peoples from "abuses" such as the drug and liquor trades, "forced or compulsory labor," and the arms trade. In addition, the B mandates included specific regulations concerning missionaries, immigration, the military, land alienation, and domestic slavery. The mandatory power was responsible for "the peace, order and good government of the territory" and had "full powers of legislation and administration." The mandate texts also required the mandatory "to promote to the utmost the material and moral well-being and social progress" of the inhabitants, though the meaning of this charge was not defined.[7]

The scholarly literature concerning the mandates is large.[8] A number of historians have examined the origins of the system in the context of British foreign policy and London's relations with the Dominions.[9] Others have studied the mandates in terms of French war aims and imperial expansion during and immediately after the First World War.[10] A few have offered a comparative approach to the partition of the German colonies in Africa while others have placed the mandates in the context of British foreign policy during the interwar period.[11] These works assert that British and French political leaders assumed "the 'mandates' in fact would differ only in name from other colonial possessions."[12] These studies all concentrate on leaders who had no day-to-day responsibility for making or supervising policies for the mandates and do not systematically examine British and French policy during the postwar period.

Many other scholars have studied British and French rule in individual mandates, but neither place the African mandates within an international context nor employ a comparative approach.[13] A few historians have attempted to measure the effect of the League on the administration of various mandates, but have done so without using diplomatic, colonial, or private papers.[14] In the early 1970s, Ralph Austen produced a useful sketch of the general characteristics of British and French rule in their African mandates during the interwar period, but relied almost exclusively on secondary sources and published League documents.[15] A more recent study by Dieudonné Oyono argues that the international status of Cameroon meant little for French colonial policy.[16] Peter A. Dumbuya says much the same about Tanganyika.[17] While Oyono makes full use of French colonial papers from 1919 to 1946, he does not use diplomatic archival materials and is concerned only with Cameroon. Dumbuya is equally limited in his focus and does not consult British Colonial Office files.

What the scholarly literature lacks is a fresh comparative study of the impact of the League of Nations mandates system on European imperialism at the point of intersection between the metropoles and the mandated territories where theories converged with practice. Historians generally have not examined the mandates system with particular attention to international relations as well as to national politics, the activities of pressure groups, and the way the foreign and colonial bureaucracies of the world's two largest overseas empires made specific policies. Further, few recent scholars have evaluated the mandates system with a sensitivity to international law, international organization, and the indirect and subtle powers of the Permanent Mandates Commission. Those who give some attention to these issues often assume that the PMC was ineffectual and that the League was unable to pressure the mandatory powers to alter their colonial policies or help to change the ideology of imperialism.[18] At worst, historians are content to declare that they have a "general feeling" that the PMC did not exercise "any close watch" over the mandated territories.[19] At best, others admit that the influence of the League on European colonialism in Africa "is shadowy and hard to detect."[20] Such suppositions reveal a failure not only to explore the precise powers and complex workings of either the PMC or the colonial bureaucracies, but to consider all of these institutions within the national, imperial, and international context of the crucial period between the First World War and the advent of the worldwide economic crisis of the 1930s.

The League was a product of international law. This type of law, which governs the relations between sovereign states, differs substantially from domestic or municipal law because it recognizes no ultimate authority higher than the individual state. International law was important to governments since it established greater predictability in the conduct of foreign relations and decreased potential conflicts. It also gave a form of legitimacy to colonial regimes in the eyes of the international community and was part of the legal institutions that Europeans extended to the wider world. The PMC used moral suasion, public opinion, sympathetic pressure groups, and the force of its own reputation to convince the mandatory powers that conforming to the letter and spirit of the mandates system was in their long-term national and imperial interests.

The Permanent Mandates Commission was never a harsh critic of imperialism bent on the destruction of the European overseas empires. Rather, the PMC was dedicated to a progressive agenda of gradual reform and to a pragmatic paternalism in Africa. Officials in London, Paris, and in the mandated territories could not ignore the work of the PMC and had much to gain by taking that work seriously. The Commission discovered that the threat of criticism was far more powerful than actual public condemnation and took advantage of the specific requirements and ambiguities surrounding the mandates system to exert its considerable influence. Further, because of the international status of the mandates, the PMC was part of the international relations of the postwar period and had force because Germany, Italy, the United States, and others expressed sustained and occasionally intense interest in the system. Colonial officials had to consider how their decisions might be interpreted in Geneva and in the rest of the world. The mandates system did not always mean dramatic changes for policy. But, while this form of Wilsonianism in Africa was not as successful as its most idealistic supporters hoped, it was not the failure that its most cynical detractors claimed.

The PMC also had to contend with expanding and elaborate diplomatic and colonial bureaucracies of Britain and France. Close examination of national institutions and their bureaucracies is hardly fashionable among historians, but such study is essential for understanding the impact of international relations on European imperialism in Africa during this period.[21] Large bureaucracies are shaped as much by personalities as by impersonal constraints of finite resources and time, divided and overlapping responsibilities, rigid traditions, and institutional tendencies to delay, defer, and drift. European bureaucracies determined the degree to which ideas became policy; they solved African problems or made them worse. In helping to define the mandates system, the British and French diplomatic and colonial bureaucracies became as much a part of that system as any colonial administrator or the Africans themselves.

Yet, the mandates system ultimately must be understood within the broader context of the political and cultural importance of European colonialism in the postwar period.[22] Imperialism formed the core of the international order and was integral to the westernization of the modern world.[23] It tied the actions of political leaders in the metropoles with those of Africans and was shaped by a multiplicity of individuals, interests, and ideas. Each link in this imperial chain had an impact on others and all were changed by the First World War. The mandates system attached Geneva and the League of Nations to postwar colonialism in Africa. It represented not only a tacit criticism of the abuses of European imperialism, but also provided a response to such criticism by insisting that the protection of colonized peoples was "a sacred trust of civilization." The principle of "trusteeship" in Africa was not new in 1919.[24] What the mandates system did, however, was to internationalize and institutionalize this notion of trusteeship and to make it a formal statement of what the international community regarded as the minimal requirements for European colonialism in Africa. The League emphasized the protective obligations of the trustee and subjected the mandatory power to systematic supervision. The larger world now held the imperial powers hostage to their own rhetoric and pressed them to maintain their legitimacy by accepting international accountability in their colonial rule in Africa.

The present book is an effort to examine the British and French mandates in Africa within this historical context. Its conclusion is that the mandates system represented an evolving internationalization and reformation of colonialism that had an impact on both Europeans and Africans from 1914 to 1931. The system gradually reshaped the ideology of imperialism and had an economic, political, and cultural impact on Africans within the mandated territories. In this way, the mandates system not only reflected the changing face of postwar European imperialism, but played its own transforming role in its operation. The internationalization and reformation of colonialism also made European imperialism in tropical Africa more acceptable to the political left, particularly the British Labour Party, which was anti-imperialist. For French and British colonial officials who shared a common faith in imperialism and were often sincere in their desire to correct its flaws, the mandates came to symbolize what seemed best about modern colonialism and were a nagging reminder of its defects.

While Britain and France did not always react to the mandates system in the same way or for the same reasons, they both developed policies for their mandates that were more restrained and more internationally-oriented than those in much of the rest of their empires in tropical Africa. These policies gradually altered the relations between Europeans and Africans and reformed the way in which the colonial state exercised power within the mandated territories. But the mandatory powers did not always initiate such reforms in unambiguous or mutually advantageous ways. Binding the League to colonial administration in tropical Africa often had contradictory, unintended, and sometimes adverse repercussions for the Europeans and Africans within the imperial structure. Still, rather than merely providing an "elaborate fig-leaf" or "a front for Allied territorial expansion" masquerading as "imperialism's new clothes," the League of Nations mandates system attempted to resolve the persistent dilemmas that resulted from the importation of European institutions into Africa and the perpetual international competition over Africa's peoples and materials.[25]

1

The Great War and Imperial Expansion

With the outbreak of the First World War, the scramble for Africa entered a new phase. While effective European occupation in Africa was still incomplete in 1914, the imperial powers saw the war as a superb opportunity to extend their colonial empires. Some optimistic German imperialists hoped to create "a continuous Central African colonial empire" by annexing Belgian, French, Portuguese, and British colonies.[1] This hope was never fulfilled. Instead, Germany began to lose its colonies in Africa within days of the outbreak of the war.[2] British and French forces combined to invade the German possessions of Togo and Cameroon in West Africa while Lieutenant Colonel Paul Emil von Lettow-Vorbeck defended German East Africa against attacks led by the British. The Allies had neither the time nor inclination to reflect on their reasons for fighting for empire in Africa as part of a European conflict. Vague notions of security, unabashed opportunism, and a four hundred year legacy of treating overseas colonies as spoils of war made imperial expansion an expected, if not inevitable, feature of the first emotional months of 1914.

These expectations were increasingly challenged as the war continued. The growing anti-imperialist sentiments of the political left, particularly in Britain, opposed direct annexation of the conquered German and Turkish territories in Africa, the Pacific, and the Middle East. This mounting "anti-imperialism" symbolized a general hostility toward the principle of bald expansionism, but not necessarily to the existing empires. While the institution of imperialism had some harsh critics before and during the war, only a handful of radicals insisted they were "anti-colonialists," or opponents of overseas empire entirely.[3] Yet, as the shocking slaughter in the trenches continued, many deeply disillusioned Europeans questioned the fundamental purpose of the conflict and wondered if old colonial rivalries may have contributed to the outbreak of war in the first place. "Imperialism" increasingly became a pejorative term that threatened the war effort and helped to widen the gulf between the Allied governments and their critics. After the entry of the United States into the war in 1917, London and Paris had to cooperate with a government that was highly critical of European colonialism. Anti-imperialists, led by the Americans, successfully made the issue a matter of serious international political concern and debate. They pressured Britain and France to respect the interests of colonized peoples and to place the captured German overseas empire under some form of international control.

The two imperial powers reacted differently to these pressures, yet with very similar results. In late 1918, many British political leaders reluctantly adopted the language of the anti-imperialists and accepted the general principal of international supervision, but only for German East Africa. This qualified acceptance meant little since Britain was not committed to keeping the former German colony and hoped to secure continued Anglo-American cooperation in world affairs by convincing the Americans to administer the possession instead. Further, few of these British leaders assumed that the wartime rhetoric concerning overseas expansion would translate into postwar realities and that "international supervision" would mean few substantive changes for the Empire. France, on the other hand, did not accept any form of international control and remained committed to the annexation of both Togo and Cameroon. French colonial policy remained firmly in the hands of a tiny group of committed imperialists who largely insulated themselves from the political pressures of their critics. From 1914 to 1918, neither Britain nor France altered its conception of European imperialism. They did not seriously intend to change much about their rule in Africa or submit themselves to the systematic scrutiny of an international organization. Both imperial powers took African interests for granted and expected to extend their African empires much as they had during the late nineteenth century.

The New Scramble for Africa

Between 1914 and 1918, the Germans lost all of their nearly one million square miles of territory in Africa, the Far East, and the Pacific.[4] Britain and France seized more than half of this overseas empire when they began to rule the 11,000,000 people in Togo, Cameroon, and German East Africa.[5] Togo was by far the smallest of the three colonies, measuring only about 34,000 square miles and extending from the port city of Lomé that had a railway system that connected the hinterland with the coast. German East Africa was the largest of the three colonies with an area of approximately 384,000 square miles which included Mount Kilimanjaro, Africa's highest mountain, and the administrative center of Dar es Salaam on the Indian Ocean. Cameroon was about 190,000 square miles in size and had one of the best ports in West Africa.[6] Togo was the only one of the three that paid for itself, but the total trade between Germany and the possession was minuscule.[7] The other two colonies provided some valuable raw materials including rubber and sisal, but depended on hefty subsidies from the German government and usually ran at a deficit.[8] While Germany's place in the African sun was considerable, it was never particularly valuable in an economic sense.

The British and French attacked Togo, Cameroon, and German East Africa less for their economic value than for their strategic and symbolic value. On 4 August 1914 the French Colonial Ministry told Martial Henri Merlin, the Governor-General of French Equatorial Africa, that Germany had declared war on France and ordered him to take military precautions.[9] In less than a week, Paris and London agreed to joint operations in West Africa and sent British and French troops into both Togo and Cameroon to destroy the German communication lines and occupy the ports.[10] The British Cabinet decided the day after declaring war on Germany that German East Africa was a threat to the British navy and approved an immediate invasion.[11] The widespread assumption that the war in Europe would be short as well as completely successful precluded any prolonged discussion about the German overseas empire. The British and French wanted to secure victory and were in a hurry to defeat the Germans wherever they could find them.

Once Britain and France had agreed to dismember Germany's African empire, the two allies began to bicker over the pieces. Outside Paris, the Allies barely avoided defeat in October by halting the massive German advance in the Battle of the Marne, but failed to drive the Germans from northern France in a counterattack. Inside Paris, influential colonial interest groups were worried about the latest partition of Africa. One of the most powerful such interest groups in France was the "Union coloniale française," a group founded in 1893 by a number of businessmen and politicians interested in imperial expansion and colonial trade.[12] As early as December 1914, the Union told the French colonial minister, Gaston Doumergue, that France must have "all or at least the major portion of Togo and Cameroon."[13] In January 1915, the Banque Française de l'Afrique Equatoriale cheerfully notified the Colonial Ministry that it intended to establish an office in Duala, Cameroon's chief port and terminus for the two railway lines, to assist local French merchants and to "contribute to the economic victory which must follow the success of our arms."[14] The main colonialist newspaper in France, *La Dépêche Coloniale*, argued often and vehemently in early 1915 for France's acquisition of Togo and Cameroon.[15]

The British Colonial Office too was making similar plans for the future of the German possessions in Africa. Officials not only hoped to publish graphic accounts of "German atrocities" in Africa in order to convince the public that the Allies should never return the captured German colonies, but strongly resisted any suggestion for administering Cameroon with France under an Anglo-French "condominium."[16] Such a condominium would give France equal control over Cameroon. The idea of sharing the colony with France was particularly repugnant to those British colonial officials who were conscious that British troops were responsible for the larger share of the fighting and controlled more of the territory, but who were convinced that the French forces were "only a not very efficient auxiliary" to British troops.[17] Lewis Harcourt, the secretary of state for the colonies, was willing to consider giving certain portions of Togo and Cameroon to France for other concessions, but was determined that Britain keep the railroads, the best plantation lands, and the port city of Duala.[18] For these reasons, Britain declined an early French offer to send troops from Madagascar to help conquer German East Africa and tried to limit Belgian participation in the long and difficult conquest.[19]

Relations between the wartime partners within Togo and Cameroon were often strained and punctuated by moments of pettiness and open antagonism.[20] In Togo, British and French military officials agreed to a provisional partition in late August 1914 that gave Britain control of Lomé and the railways.[21] Local French administrators protested that this allowed British companies to dominate the economy and gave Britain too much power over taxation and currency policies.[22] In Cameroon, one French official reported his shock in late 1914 that British Brigadier General Charles M. Dobell was asking the African population if they wanted to be "English or French" in preparation for a partition of Cameroon.[23] France was also unhappy with the fact that the British collected all of the local taxes and customs duties while local French officials had to depend entirely on Dakar for their budget.[24] Dobell was just as irritated to discover that the French commander, General Joseph Gaudéric Aymerich, was "apparently senior to me in military rank since a 'Général de Brigade' is senior to a Brigadier General" and demanded that London make it clear that the British general was the superior.[25] Dobell was also upset that the French were trying to increase their control over Cameroon by sending officials into the occupied territories without his permission.[26] Merlin, who indeed was trying to increase French influence in the possession at the expense of the British, continued his disingenuous demands for a condominium.[27] Much of this sharp Anglo-French colonial rivalry did not soften until German troops finally surrendered in Cameroon in 1916 and the British Foreign Office, far more distressed by the multiplying catastrophes almost everywhere else, gave the French provisional control of most of the possession, including Duala, for the remainder of the war. This solution allowed the delighted French to abandon their "offers" for a condominium and to participate in the German East Africa campaign, but enraged British colonial officials who were left with only two strips of Cameroon that ran along the border of Nigeria.[28]

Not equally pleased with this temporary partition of Germany's West African territories, British and French officials still wasted little time in establishing colonial administrations in them. The Colonial Ministry in Paris immediately appointed Aymerich, a career soldier with no experience in civilian administration, as "Commissaire de la République Français au Cameroun" who served until replaced a few months later by Lucien Louis Fourneau, the lieutenant-governor of Middle Congo. The new commissioner of Cameroon was under the supervision of Merlin, who administered French Equatorial Africa from Brazzaville.[29] Not to be outdone, the governor-general of French West Africa requested that the Colonial Ministry create a similar administrative post for the French sphere of Togo.[30] In September 1916 lieutenant-colonel Gaston Léopold Joseph Fourn, a former colonial administrator and soldier who had been wounded at Verdun, became Commissioner of Togo.[31] Aymerich and Fourn had many of the same powers as the lieutenant governors of French West and Equatorial Africa, but had different titles since Togo and Cameroon could not be absorbed into the two large colonial federations until Germany formally renounced its claims to the possessions.[32] In London, the Colonial Office gave the governor-general of Nigeria, Sir Frederick Lugard, a commission to administer the British sphere of Cameroon.[33] This commission gave Lugard powers similar to those of Sir Hugh Clifford, the governor of the Gold Coast, who had been responsible for the administration of British Togo since late 1914.[34]

Once in place, these administrators immediately started to transform their respective spheres of Togo and Cameroon into British and French possessions similar to those in the rest of tropical Africa. In early 1915 France had established special funds for "political expenses" in Togo and Cameroon and the British had already been busy rounding up Swiss missionaries suspected of anti-British sympathies.[35] For the next two years, French colonial officials reported to Paris regularly on conditions in Togo and allocated money for health services, police, public works, and agriculture.[36] In Cameroon, French officials produced extensive studies of the administration, economy, and geography of the conquered possession and concluded that France had to keep the colony after the war.[37] France also hoped to absorb fully its portion of Togo into neighboring Dahomey, replace the German missionaries with French, and reorganize the judicial system in Cameroon to conform with that in French Equatorial Africa.[38]

The British made similar plans. In May 1916 Lugard informed London that most of the British sphere of Cameroon would be "temporarily constituted as a new province under the Lieutenant Governor of the Southern Provinces" while the rest would be administered by officers in northern Nigeria.[39] The Governor-General then submitted a detailed budget for the conquered possession which included expenditures for administration, police, public works, medical services, and posts and telegraphs.[40] The next year, Lugard produced an even larger budget for what he now called "Cameroons Province, Nigeria" and expressed confidence that "the finances of this province will in future years fully provide for its administration" and "in time will add to the wealth and revenue" of Nigeria.[41]

As the British and French extended their new administrations into Togo and Cameroon, they brought their various imperial interests, values, and assumptions with them. For them, Europeans had created modern colonial Africa and could divide territories such as the two former German colonies according to European priorities and fully expect Africans to conform to the new conditions. Thus, while British colonial officials in London and Lagos knew that the partition of Cameroon split various ethnic groups, imperial and foreign policy concerns remained more important.[42] Later the same year, the influential Governor-General of French West Africa, Joost van Vollenhoven, felt free to contemplate extensive territorial changes that would give France complete control of not only Togo and Cameroon, but Liberia and most of the British colonies in West Africa as well.[43] In Cameroon, the French tightened their control over the lives of Africans by imposing heavy travel restrictions on laborers wishing to work on the plantations around Mount Cameroon in the British zone.[44] Paris, insisting that the Empire had to serve the needs of the metropole first, wanted Togo to produce 3,000 tons of corn for the war effort in Europe.[45] The Germans may have lost their West African colonies, but little else had changed as Britain and France continued to rule them according to traditional European imperial perceptions and requirements.

At the same time the British and French had been struggling first with the Germans and then each other for control of Togo and Cameroon, Britain was engaged in a much more frustrating and protracted conquest of German East Africa.[46] Soon after the outbreak of war in Europe, the Germans under von Lettow-Vorbeck had taken the offensive against Kenya, Uganda, Northern Rhodesia, and the Belgian Congo. By early 1916 he commanded a force of over 3,000 Europeans and 12,000 Africans and was conducting a highly effective guerrilla campaign. Constant attacks by over 60,000 British Empire and Belgian troops prevented a German victory, but in late 1917 the German forces crossed into Portuguese Mozambique and did not surrender until after the European armistice in November 1918. In the end, the conflict required more than 200,000 Allied troops, half of them Africans, and caused widespread human and material loss in the region.

By late 1916, however, much of German East Africa was under British control and the local military commanders, hoping to project at least the impression of final success, agreed to transfer authority to civilians. The Colonial Office promptly selected Horace Archer Byatt as administrator of the occupied territory.[47] Byatt had spent six years in Nyasaland before serving in various capacities in British Somaliland from 1905 to 1914.[48] London also selected Alfred Claud Hollis, the colonial secretary in Sierra Leone, as secretary to the administration.[49] The East Africa Department, the Colonial Office division directly responsible for supervising the civil administration, quickly began to advise Byatt in shaping policy for the territory.[50] It and the Colonial Office War Trade Department successfully petitioned the Privy Council in late 1916 to allow German East Africa to receive a trade license, "as if such territory were a British Possession or Protectorate."[51] Further, even though the War Office insisted that Byatt remain "technically subordinate to the military authority," the administrator and his staff began to rebuild some of the infrastructure destroyed by the war, appoint new administrative staff, create a police force, and solidify the remnants of the customs and medical services.[52] From late 1916 to the end of the war, Byatt managed to extend civilian rule despite limited resources, disgruntled subordinates, and stubborn local military authorities.[53]

Lloyd George, Wilson, and "Self-Determination"

While these various men of empire now responsible for ruling the conquered German colonies were certain of the future of their new acquisitions, others outside the Colonial Office and Colonial Ministry were not. At a meeting in February 1917, the British War Cabinet decided not to comment publicly on the fate of the possessions. While keeping in mind "the general arrangements with our Allies," the Cabinet stressed that "no definite decisions should be taken in regard to rearrangement of territory" until after the war.[54] This cautious policy continued as the American president, Woodrow Wilson, whose nation entered the war against Germany in April, rejected the notion of annexation and declared that the United States would not fight for "conquest" or "material compensation," but rather to make the world "safe for democracy."[55] In May, the British prime minister, David Lloyd George, remained unwilling to commit to annexation because "it might be necessary to make a bargain with Germany for evacuating Belgium in return for the restoration of her colonies."[56]

The next month, the French Chamber of Deputies held a secret session to debate war aims.[57] French ministers, frightened that the army might not hold out until the arrival of American troops and faced with increased demands from socialist deputies for a negotiated peace, claimed that French war aims did not include annexation or conquest. In a motion adopted at the end of the debate, the Chamber said nothing about the German colonies and insisted that France was fighting for the return of

Alsace-Lorraine, reparations for war damages, and a system of postwar collective security.[58]

By summer 1917 the war in Europe was going very badly for the Allies and the growing anti-imperialist mood made the case for territorial annexations increasingly unpopular. The Allies had suffered millions of casualties and the French army was on the verge of collapse. Those who had always been uncertain of the war's purpose now demanded assurances that they were not fighting for remote pieces of Africa or to protect narrow overseas investments. Socialists, including many from Britain and France, planned to debate belligerent war aims during a conference in Stockholm, and some members of the British League of Nations Society openly questioned the objectives of European imperialism in Africa in general.[59] Britain's Anti-Slavery and Aborigines Protection Society was particularly appalled by both the widespread use of African troops to fight in European battles and the apparent blatant disregard for African concerns in the former German colonies. In July the group held its own conference to discuss the "wishes and interests of the inhabitants" and "the advisability of international control" of the conquered African possessions as a way to protect Africans as well as prevent territorial annexations after the war.[60]

One organization that was most harshly critical of the war and of the nature of European imperialism during these difficult days of 1917 was the increasingly influential Union of Democratic Control. Founded in Britain by radicals including E. D. Morel and comprising members of the Labour Party, dissident Liberals and intellectuals, the UDC strongly advocated open diplomacy, a liberal settlement of the war, and "no annexations" of any sort.[61] In May, Morel published *Africa and the Peace of Europe*, a book that advocated a system of international government in tropical Africa. In an argument that directly linked European imperialism in Africa to the origins of modern war, he offered a proposal:

> The neutralization of the non-colonisable area of Africa, the internationalization of European commercial activities within that area, and such a distribution of territorial sovereignty as would secure Germany a participation commensurate alike with her past achievements in Africa, and with her economic needs – these, one would suppose, are the aims which an enlightened statesmanship might be expected to pursue if it desired to attain . . . the disappearance of one of the most potent causes of international ill-will, coupled with a real effort on the part of the powers to safeguard the interests of the native races of Africa.[62]

The book had widespread appeal among members of the Labour Party and with Ramsay MacDonald, Sydney Webb, and Arthur Henderson, the Labour member of the War Cabinet. Later, after he resigned from the War Cabinet in August 1917, Henderson, MacDonald, Webb, and others were responsible for drafting Labour Party policy on war aims and, like Morel, sternly condemned the "imperialist idea" and recommended that all of tropical Africa be administered as a single unit under an international authority.[63] Such suggestions offered an attractive and lofty war aim that would internationalize and reform European imperialism in Africa. A multiplying number of vocal anti-imperialists hoped that such a departure from the prewar colonial pattern would serve to prevent another catastrophic global conflict while protecting Africans from militarization and exploitation.

The War Cabinet was compelled to contemplate this anti-imperialist mood while preparing a speech for Lloyd George to deliver in Glasgow in late June 1917. The speech would have to invigorate civilian morale as well as somehow please as many on both ends of the political spectrum as possible. The Cabinet took some comfort in knowing they could delay discussion of the future of German East Africa since all final settlements would have to wait until the "Peace Conference," but agreed that "the inhabitants ought to be consulted as to whether they preferred British or German rule."[64] In the final version of the speech, Lloyd George adroitly told his audience that "[a]s to the German colonies that is a matter which must be settled by a great international peace conference" and "[w]hen you come to settle who shall be the future trustees of these uncivilized lands, you must take into account the sentiment of the people themselves." How people of "uncivilized lands" would have their sentiments taken "into account" in order to best select their "future trustees" remained conveniently ambiguous. Further, while the prime minister did not claim that Africans would definitely choose British rule, he was prepared to suggest that they would "rather trust their destiny to others and juster – may I confidently say – gentler hands" than those of their former German rulers.[65] The patriotic listener was left to determine whose were the "gentler hands" that gave their prime minister such confidence.

The Bolshevik Revolution in Russia in November 1917 and the subsequent publication of many secret Allied wartime agreements concerning the redistribution of enemy territories posed new and embarrassing problems for Britain. The Bolshevik government also quickly announced that it wanted a "peace without annexations or indemnities" with the Germans and had already indicated that it favored the complete restitution of all of Germany's colonies.[66] To make matters more difficult, Lord Lansdowne, a former foreign secretary and prominent Conservative, published an open letter asking the government to consider possibilities for a negotiated peace that avoided punitive measures.[67] The division in the War Cabinet between those who wanted eventually to annex the former German colonies and those who wished to avoid conflicts with the political left or anti-imperialists began to widen. Some were also worried about the United States, which was sympathetic to the Allied cause but was pressing for peace and hostile to European imperial expansion. Walter Long, the colonial secretary, had already argued for the retention of the captured German colonies. He knew that South Africa would insist on annexing German South-West Africa and that Australia and New Zealand would demand to control the German islands in the Pacific south of the equator.[68] In a meeting of the War Cabinet in November, Long advocated that Britain announce it would not return German East Africa after the war.[69] The foreign secretary, Arthur James Balfour, worried that Britain would be accused of being "out for plunder," opposed the idea and suggested that

> the Cabinet should consider very carefully the proposal for the internationalization of the former German colonies in Africa, which would have the effect of preventing the creation of a naval and military menace, while at the same time the most valuable raw materials would be available for the factories of the world, and not merely of Germany.[70]

The following day, after a meeting of Balfour, Lloyd George, and Colonel Edward House, Wilson's confidant and advisor, the War Cabinet decided it was best to make "no announcement as to our aims regarding East Africa."[71]

This decision did not end the debate. Influential members of the War Cabinet such as General Jan Smuts, South Africa's minister of defense, and Lord Curzon, lord president of the council and former viceroy of India, condemned any idea of "internationalization" and insisted that Britain keep the German colonies for security reasons.[72] Philip Kerr, Lloyd George's private secretary, told Smuts that it was "absolutely fatal to suggest that the German colonies must be retained because they are essential to British communications. The U.S.A. won't look at that for a moment . . . " Kerr went on to argue that while he opposed returning the colonies to Germany, the possibility that the colonies "be internationalized" was better than "the purely British argument" for annexation.[73] A few weeks later, the Board of Trade proposed a commercial and economic scheme designed to "go a good way towards satisfying the Labour demand for 'internationalism.'"[74] By early 1918 the British political leadership remained split on the general issue of the fate of the German colonies.

In France, the rise to power of Georges Clemenceau as prime minister in November meant little debate on war aims or the German colonies.[75] Clemenceau dedicated himself to defeating Germany and his only interest in the empire was in the number of troops it could supply for the western front.[76] While French pacifist and labor groups continued to protest against the war, Clemenceau's government largely ignored them or imposed harsh restrictions on their public activity.[77] This left the Colonial

Ministry, now under the nominal direction of the relatively inexperienced Henry Simon, free to contemplate the future of the captured German colonies with almost no interference from Clemenceau's "Comité de Guerre" or outside anti-imperialist pressure groups. Colonial officials in Paris and in West Africa had already made it absolutely clear that they wanted to annex their occupied portions of Togo and Cameroon after the war.[78] The task for the Colonial Ministry after November 1917 was to maintain this goal despite criticism.

This task became more difficult after Lloyd George's speech on 5 January 1918 to the British Trades Union Congress and Wilson's "Fourteen Points" speech three days later.[79] The British prime minister declined straightforward annexation and advocated the "general principle of national self-determination" for Germany's colonies. The American president called for a

> Free, open-minded and absolutely impartial adjustment of all colonial claims, based upon a strict observance of the principle that in determining all such questions of sovereignty the interests of the population concerned must have equal weight with the equitable claims of the government whose title is to be determined.[80]

The two speeches were broadly popular, particularly within the Labour Party and among anti-imperialists. Both Morel and Henderson strongly endorsed Wilson's principles and many considered them honorable war aims worth fighting for.[81]

French colonial officials were far less impressed. On 22 January, the Colonial Ministry told the Foreign Ministry that while the Lloyd George and Wilson declarations could not cast any doubts on "the sovereign rights of the Allies in these possessions or those already established," they could, nonetheless, "influence" the larger debate about "the colonial problem."[82] The Colonial Ministry then asked to discuss the subject with the Foreign Ministry before the government determined an official policy. The result was the formation in early February of the "Commission d'étude des questions coloniales posées par la guerre" under Simon's chairmanship.[83] This inter-ministry commission included former foreign and colonial ministers, several politicians, and businessmen. It also included various civil servants not only from the colonial and foreign ministries, but from the ministries of commerce, the navy, and war.

Simon told the members of this new commission from the start that they constituted a "political commission" responsible for solutions to the colonial questions resulting from the war.[84] He then handed leadership over to Gaston Doumergue, the colonial minister during the early years of the war, who was also a former prime minister and foreign minister, influential member of the Senate, and longtime member of the powerful colonial lobby.[85] It did not take him or the rest of the commission long to agree that France had a civilizing mission in its overseas empire and that the colonies were vital for French industry and trade.[86] Thus, they concluded that Togo and Cameroon would benefit from French rule and that France needed the two German colonies for economic development.[87] The Commission also decided that, despite public statements, Great Britain would never abandon the conquered German colonies.[88] The problem was political opposition from the United States.[89] The Commission's solution was to compile evidence of German "misrule" in Africa as well as African preference for French colonial government to demonstrate the superiority of France's brand of colonialism and convince the Americans that France deserved to administer Togo and Cameroon.[90]

By late 1918 the Colonial Ministry and Foreign Ministry were committed to this policy. Paul Cambon, the French ambassador to Britain, told the foreign minister, Stephen Pichon, that he was confident that the British would ultimately reject Wilson's "abstractions" about the future of the German colonies since the security of the British Empire was involved.[91] At most, the Foreign Ministry would agree to voluntary pledges to protect Africans from certain abuses, but would not accept any limits on its control over the conquered colonies.[92] Paris was sure that once the war was over, much of the silly wartime anti-imperialist rhetoric would quickly dissolve before a united French and British effort to defend traditional colonial interests while letting the Germans take the blame for the world's ills.

The British Colonial Office largely shared France's general sentiment of nonchalance about the public statements of Lloyd George and Wilson concerning the German colonies. Long told the colonial officials in the conquered German possessions that Britain was "firmly convinced that for security of Empire after the war to retain possession of German Colonies is necessary." Because of "divergences of opinion among [our] allies," however, it was not possible to "secure general acceptance of this view."[93] He then asked the officials for "a statement suitable for publication if necessary" detailing the desire of the inhabitants to live under British rule.[94]

Like France's strategy for keeping the German colonies by discrediting their former rulers, Long was determined to produce appropriate illustrations of "the interests of the population concerned" that would convince the Americans that continued British rule was best. Lugard, however, seems to have misunderstood the purpose of Long's order. In early 1918, the governor-general provided the Colonial Office with evidence of Africans in Cameroon who preferred British instead of French rule.[95] He then embarrassed London further by sending testimony from a dead African chief.[96] Finally, after receiving enough of what the colonial secretary wanted from Lugard and the other colonial officials in the other captured African colonies, Long was able to report to the War Cabinet in October 1918 that Africans overwhelmingly preferred Britain to Germany.[97]

Both Britain and France took pains to gather such examples of the "self-determination" of Africans in the captured German colonies. The two colonial powers not only wanted this material to prepare to defend themselves after the permanent partition, but needed it to help legitimize their new authority within the conquered possessions. It was a seemingly narrow interpretation of Wilson's principle, but one that reflected common prewar perceptions of colonized peoples and empire. Many Europeans and Americans, including Wilson, understood that the general concept of "self-determination" meant different things when applied to the different regions and races of the world.[98] As a result, the testimonials from Africans, or from those who claimed to speak for Africans, tended to follow a similar pattern. Many sounded like the group of Africans from Togo living in Duala who told the British "of our joy in seeing the Union Jack flying over this country and our home" and thanking them for "saving us from the unexpected death which would have happened to us through our former protectors."[99] Local French colonial officials who conducted a "referendum" in late 1918 were able to produce thousands of signatures and "declarations," many of them in Arabic, from Africans electing French rule.[100] British missionaries in East Africa reported that Africans did not want the Germans to return and a large British trading firm in Cameroon wrote that it had "no hesitation in saying that the whole of the population north of the Nyong River are keenly desirous of coming within the British sphere of influence."[101] London also received reports that Africans in Duala had petitioned to have the entire colony handed over to Great Britain and that the French were forcing Africans to choose French rule.[102] These self-interested samples of "self-determination" reflected the larger interests of those gathering the information more than local realities, but were a problem that was not unique to the governments of colonial Africa.

Despite this effort to construct a flawless picture of African preference for British or French rule, a few blemishes did emerge. African elites who had benefitted from German colonial administration did not want to lose those advantages under new rulers. Among Fourneau's many reports on the attitudes of the chiefs in Duala, he admitted that there was at least one who wanted the Germans to return.[103] In late 1918 a British missionary told his superiors that while the Africans living in Togo's hinterland wanted British rule, "there is also no doubt that the townsfolk, especially the younger generation, would desire the German restoration." He went on to relate one pro-German demonstration in Lomé after the arrival of a steamer that the local Africans of the "educated class" thought was German. "The natives trooped down to welcome back their old masters with every display of joy."[104] The Bishop who received this letter sent excerpts to Balfour who in turn thought it of "sufficient interest" to have it circulated to the War Cabinet.[105]

Annexation vs. Internationalization

Despite the real or imagined preferences of Africans, British and French colonial officials held firmly to their imperial expectations. In London, Long continued to argue throughout 1918 that Britain had to keep the German colonies, but was increasingly aware of the distinct shift away from annexation among some of his colleagues. He was particularly alarmed by Balfour's tendency to mimic the anti-imperialist opinions of Morel, Wilson, and the Labour Party.[106] Long reacted forcefully to Balfour's suggestion in early May that the German colonies in Africa become "internationalized territories" and "placed under some form of condominium from which Germany *may* be, but *need* not be, excluded."[107] In July, Smuts proposed the creation of a multi-national "Development Board," composed of representatives from the various colonial powers, that would oversee international agreements concerning demilitarization and free trade in all of tropical Africa.[108] German South-West Africa remained conveniently outside the zone. This solution meant that British security interests would be protected even if Germany participated in this mild form of coordinated self-policing in Africa. Smuts's proposal was attractive to the members of the War Cabinet who did not want to see Germany regain its overseas empire, but who wanted to alienate the United States and their own political left even less. It was less appealing to those who dreaded outside interference in British imperial policy or distrusted ambiguous international arrangements.[109]

In August, Lloyd George met the members of the Imperial War Cabinet, a larger body than the War Cabinet that included representatives from India and the Dominions, and raised a startling question. He wondered if Britain might be able to keep most of its captured possessions in the Middle East and the Pacific, as well as deflect some of the attacks from anti-imperialists, if it gave "great slices of Africa" to the Americans. Lord Reading, the lord chief justice and acting ambassador to the United States, responded that "I should doubt if they would accept the proposal to administer East Africa." Lloyd George replied that the Americans "have millions of negroes, you know." Reading remained skeptical. (Sir Robert Borden, the Prime Minister of Canada, suggested that if the Americans "could be convinced that it was practical to ship all their negroes to East Africa they would agree.") With so much division within the Cabinet, Lloyd George decided not to press the issue, but did leave it open for future discussion.[110]

Leo Amery, an assistant secretary to the Imperial War Cabinet, was strongly opposed to handing German East Africa over to the Americans and told Smuts the following day that it would be better to give away British Guiana, British Honduras, Gambia, the Gold Coast, "or even Gibraltar."[111] For the next two months, British leaders continued to ponder the possibilities of giving the United States various new colonies from around the world and to argue over the relative importance of the German possessions without resolution. Finally, the War Cabinet came to a very broad consensus in October that helped to mask the deep divisions within the government. Like France, Britain decided that it could promise at the peace conference to protect Africans from abuses and economic exploitation. Yet, unlike France, Britain was willing to accept the possibility of taking "the directions or advice" of an international body in carrying out these promises in German East Africa and "[s]uch a solution, if found practicable, might equally be applied to Togoland and the Cameroons."[112] This "decision" was sufficiently equivocal to suit the purpose and let the leadership concentrate on more important matters.

The end of the war was an immense relief to the Allies, but particularly to those who had expectations for a formal expansion of empire as soon as Germany signed a peace treaty officially relinquishing its colonies. French officials assumed that Togo would either be annexed to Dahomey or become a separate colony within French West Africa by 1 January 1920.[113] French officials also drafted a budget for Cameroon "necessary to ensure the administration and development of the new colony" and were sure that "New Cameroon" would quickly be absorbed into French Equatorial Africa.[114] Clifford, who wanted to keep Lomé and the railroads in Togo, warned that the surrender of any portion of Togo occupied by Britain would "have the worst possible effect throughout the Gold Coast."[115] The Colonial Ministry repeated its unwavering opposition to any "system of internationalization" and did not rest in its campaign to convince the Foreign Ministry of the "necessity" of France's obtaining most, if not all, of both Togo and Cameroon for the "cohesion" and "consolidation" of the French Empire.[116]

The Armistice was particularly welcome to officials in the East Africa Department and in German East Africa. In early January 1919 Byatt and his staff worked to set up new headquarters in Dar es Salaam and to control the influx of non-British citizens wishing to return to German East Africa. He was adamant about denying the return of anyone who "would not exercise a desirable influence in this country in the future."[117] Long agreed and convinced the Imperial War Cabinet to approve the necessary legislation.[118] Byatt also asked, "by what name is German East Africa to be known in the future when it has definitely become a British Colony?" His answer included a long list of possibilities such as "Azania," "New Maryland," "Bantuland," "Eburnea," "Victoria Province," "South

Kingsland" (if British East Africa were renamed "North Kingsland"), "Windsorland," and, perhaps somewhat whimsically, "Lululand."[119] Hollis began work on the new budget for the territory. It included allocations for reorganized districts, added staff, and more money for prisons, police, transportation, customs, and medical services as well as for new departments of education, agriculture, forestry, and public works.[120] The civil administration was clearly planning an extended British rule in the former German colony.

While British and French colonial officials continued to assume that their governments would annex the German colonies, political leaders in London and Paris were growing increasingly uncertain about the future of the captured possessions. Wilson, who was now wildly popular in western Europe, was the cause of most of this uncertainty. Despite numerous opportunities, the American president had never clearly defined what he meant by an "impartial adjustment of all colonial claims" or explained what, if anything, would eventually replace German rule in the colonies.[121] He told Sir William Wiseman, a British intelligence officer, that he would be "well content" to see Great Britain administer the German colonies, but not as "a sovereign part of the British Empire" and only "in trust" for the League of Nations.[122] But according to the "Official American Commentary on the Fourteen Points" by Walter Lippmann and Frank Cobb, generally endorsed by Wilson in October 1918, it was possible that Germany could make an "equitable" claim for the colonies along with the Allies and become the "protecting authority" acting "not as owner of its colonies, but as trustee for the natives and for the interests of the society of nations." Further, the colonial administration of this new trustee would be "a matter of international concern and may legitimately be the subject of international inquiry" subject to "a code of colonial conduct" drafted by the peace conference.[123] In early November, the Colonial Ministry was astonished to learn that Wilson had mentioned to the French ambassador in Washington that the German colonies should be administered by "a small State" acting under the supervision of the League of Nations as "some sort of trustee."[124] Wilson repeated this view during his voyage to Europe in early December and contended that the German colonies must become "the common property of the League" and "given to one of the smaller states to administer as the mandatory of the League of Nations."[125] Lord Derby, the British ambassador to France, told Balfour that while Wilson had finally abandoned any idea of returning the captured colonies to Germany, the president's views on the matter were "of the haziest description."[126]

Without clear guidance from Wilson, British and French political leaders were left to sort out their own plans for the future of the German colonies. On the day of the Armistice, Lloyd George told William "Billy" Hughes, the Prime Minister of Australia, that he was determined to let the

Dominions have "the former German Colonies to which they are fairly and justly entitled, on the ground of their future security," but said nothing about the other captured German overseas possessions.[127] When the topic of the German colonies came up during a conversation with Cambon the next day, Lloyd George wanted to avoid any commitments about Germany's colonies in tropical Africa and shrewdly changed the subject to Alsace-Lorraine.[128] Cambon was worried that Wilson's "vague and utopian ideas" would add to "the general confusion" surrounding the upcoming peace conference and proposed in late November that Britain and France settle everything among themselves first and then present Wilson with "a united opposition and an accomplished fact."[129] London shared Cambon's anxiety about the uncertainty that surrounded Wilson's peace proposals, but rejected the suggestion to desert the Americans. For Britain, facing Wilson's "vague and utopian ideas" was necessary in order to secure the government's larger aim of Anglo-American cooperation in the postwar world.[130]

While many influential British leaders agreed that Anglo-American solidarity after the war was imperative, some worried that it would come at the cost of the captured German colonies. Long, who now represented a minority view, continued to urge the annexation of all the German colonies and argued that "internationalization in a mild form, and assisted by humanitarian consideration, has proved, on the whole, a dismal failure in Tropical Africa."[131] Amery was more distressed that Lloyd George was still intent on making the United States an imperial power in Africa and told Smuts that "we shall have to work hard if we are to prevent the P.M. giving away East Africa to the Americans."[132] Smuts agreed and hoped to find a compromise by revising his "Development Board" idea to include an American nominee.[133] Smuts remained committed to pressing for the "unconditional annexation of the German colonies to the utmost," but acknowledged in late November that it might be necessary to make "a small concession" and accept "the control of the League of Nations in regard to certain specified subjects" in order to placate Wilson.[134] Balfour, after learning of Smuts's proposals, was unimpressed. To make matters worse, the foreign secretary wondered if German East Africa and Togo might be too much of a financial burden for Britain to acquire at all.[135]

Smuts soon did influence the fate of the German African empire, but not the adoption of a "Development Board" as he had envisioned. Instead, he unwittingly helped to create what eventually became the League of Nations mandates system by publishing a treatise entitled *The League of Nations: A Practical Suggestion* in mid-December. The pamphlet coincided with Wilson's arrival in Europe and proposed that the League could maintain peace and stability in Eastern Europe and the Middle East by "nominating a particular State to act for and on behalf" of the League.[136] Smuts had no intention of applying this system to the

German colonies which, in his opinion, were inhabited by "barbarians who cannot possibly govern themselves."[137] Wilson, however, mixed the General's suggestions together with those of a number of American and British advisers to produce his own mandates system.[138] This latest version meant that a single power would administer a "mandate" according to stipulations laid down by the League of Nations. It was still unclear, however, precisely what these stipulations would be or how the League would supervise the mandatory powers. Still, London could not openly reject what was now an Anglo-American mandates proposal. In late December, the Imperial War Cabinet decided to accept the notion of "mandates" for "the whole of the German colonies conquered by the Imperial forces," with the exception of German South-West Africa (promised to South Africa) and the German islands in the Pacific (promised to Australia and New Zealand).[139] Lloyd George then informed his colleagues that he had told Wilson that Great Britain would "leave German East Africa at the disposal of the League of Nations and accept all the conditions imposed by the League if we are entrusted with a mandate for its administration." The future of the rest of the German colonies, however, "would have to be fought out at the Conference" in Paris.[140]

Preparing for the Paris Peace Conference

On the surface, it appeared that Britain had made an important break with its imperial tradition in accepting the mandates principle and "all the conditions imposed by the League" for the conquered German colonies in tropical Africa. Yet, despite what Lloyd George had said in public during the war or had told Wilson, the British had agreed to almost nothing. Political leaders in London knew that France opposed the mandates system and wanted to annex Togo and Cameroon.[141] The Dominions also had made it clear that they were determined to defy Wilson and annex German South-West Africa and the islands in the Pacific as well. The British government decided that "it may be best to leave France to take the leading brief at the Peace Conference in the case of the Cameroons and Togoland, and to do no more than give general support to the French claims."[142] This meant that Britain would yield to France's annexationist aims, in effect blocking the application of the mandates system to West Africa for both British and French claims. British leaders had adopted the anti-imperialist rhetoric that openly endorsed an internationalization and reformation of European colonialism in Africa, but had done nothing to let that rhetoric impinge on the prevailing ideology of imperialism that resisted such change.

Only German East Africa was left "at the disposal of the League of

Nations" in any meaningful way. The Imperial War Cabinet still wanted to give the United States "her share of guardianship" at the peace conference, but could not agree if they should let America have Armenia, Constantinople, Palestine, Mesopotamia, or a part of Africa. It was Lloyd George who argued that German East Africa was "the least undesirable alternative" as a future American "mandate."[143] Winston Churchill, the minister of munitions, wanted much of the Middle East to remain under British control and announced that he too was "strongly in favour of giving up German East Africa" in this way.[144] Smuts was the only member who adamantly opposed handing over any African territory. In Lloyd George's memoirs, published twenty years after these debates, he recalled that "[t]here was not only a readiness, but even an eagerness to bring in America and hand over to her a mandate in respect of some of these German possessions."[145] Further, he remembered that "I certainly inferred from the course of the discussion that with one exception the Cabinet would not be averse to handing over the Mandate for East Africa to the United States of America."[146] Lloyd George most wanted to avoid the charge of "land-grabbing" by convincing Wilson to take German East Africa.[147] Maurice Hankey, the secretary of the War Cabinet, noted in his diary after a meeting of the Imperial War Cabinet on 23 December that "[t]he P.M. flatly declined even to discuss the question of the German colonies. The fact is that he didn't mean to be bound in any sort or kind of way in his conversations with President Wilson. He has told me plainly that he means to try and get President Wilson into German East Africa" in order to keep Palestine for Britain.[148]

On the eve of the Paris Peace Conference, the stage was set for a serious confrontation over the role of the League of Nations in pressing a "new" brand of European imperialism in the postwar world order. Germany's overseas empire was destroyed and Europe confronted daunting political, economic, and social problems. Wilson and the American delegation were convinced that all of Germany's former colonies would fall under the international supervision of the League of Nations as "mandates" and many of the abuses that Africans suffered before and during the war in those territories would end. He was sure that the mandates system would help ease the emotions of the war and would work to prevent another. Defenders of the League's objectives and members of the political left shared this vision of a break from the old culture of colonialism. They looked to the Paris Peace Conference to make Wilson's plan real and to help give meaning to the horrific devastation and sorrow of the previous four years. Lloyd George had agreed in principle to a "new" imperialism, but only as it applied to the one conquered possession that he wanted to give away to the United States. France was not willing to apply the mandates system at all and had no desire to give away anything. The colonial officials in London, Paris, and the highest levels of colonial administration within Togo, Cameroon, and German East Africa expected to annex their conquered territories as soon as the peacemakers proclaimed the formal end of the German empire. These widely conflicting forces prepared to meet in Paris and before a watching world to determine what the "mandates system" would mean for postwar European imperialism in Africa.

2

Reforming European Imperialism, 1919

The Paris Peace Conference formally opened on 18 January 1919. Despite much more pressing European problems, the delegates agreed to determine the fate of the captured German and Turkish territories early. Wilson was determined he would keep his promises to internationalize and reform European imperialism by appointing mandatory powers to administer the conquered possessions under the supervision of the League of Nations, but had not explained how this plan would function in practice. French colonial officials and the leaders of the British southern Dominions of South Africa, Australia, and New Zealand rejected any international control over their captured German colonies and were willing to defy the American president. Britain intentionally led many to believe that it was committed to Wilson's system, but Lloyd George assumed that it would probably never apply to British colonial rule in Africa anyway. He intended to defend the colonial claims of the Dominions and to keep much of the Middle East under British control while persuading the United States to administer German East Africa. Despite four disastrous years of war and a sharp mood of anti-imperialism on the side of a popular American president, many leaders of the two last great European overseas colonial powers seemed fixed in their prewar perceptions of Africa and in their assumptions about imperialism in the postwar world.

Few anticipated the contentious arguments or protracted problems that followed. At one point, Wilson's relentless drive to establish a "new" colonialism in Africa threatened to rupture the entire Conference. Even after he and the other delegates forged an uneasy and imperfect compromise under extremely difficult circumstances, the resistance to genuine change was tenacious. The Americans never accepted any mandates, but struggled to protect the system. Britain assumed a mandate for German East Africa, but was a willing accomplice in the French Colonial Ministry's efforts to undermine the system. Throughout 1919 the Allies argued over the meaning of the mandate texts and colonial officials in

London, Paris, and within the conquered German colonies were often left divided, confused, or defensive. Those concerned with Togo and Cameroon managed to escape international accountability altogether. Those responsible for German East Africa, however, discovered that the new League system challenged their imperial assumptions and had an early impact on the possession. A few among the African elite also understood the international character of the mandates and used it to contest aspects of European rule. Still, at the end of this eventful and trying year, the future of the mandates system remained almost as uncertain as ever.

Wilson and the Fight for Mandates

Before the Paris Peace Conference convened, French and British officials tried to prepare as best they could for Wilson's attitude toward the distribution of Germany's empire in Africa. Given Clemenceau's lack of interest in colonial matters, decisions concerning the French Empire were left to Henry Simon.[1] He and other French colonial officials continued their strategy of rejecting internationalization and preparing to demonstrate the superiority of French colonial rule in order to convince the Americans that France deserved to annex Togo and Cameroon.[2] Britain, on the other hand, formed a new special committee on Africa.[3] In the instructions drafted under the direction of Smuts, now South African prime minister and a member of the British Empire delegation in Paris, the delegates were to insist on "unconditional annexation" of the German colonies first, but as "a second line of argument" to accept some "general limitations" enforced by the Council of the League of Nations.[4] Privately, Smuts had not given up on the hope that the Americans would eventually accept a mandate for Constantinople so that "they may be willing to give us a free hand in respect to the German Colonies and Turkish possessions claimed by us, either outright or as mandatories."[5]

In mid-January, Lord Robert Cecil, the head of the League of Nations section of the British delegation and president of the influential League of Nations Union, held a meeting of the committee on Africa in order to "consider the application of the mandatory principle to territories in Africa and the Pacific." The Colonial Office representatives, led by Sir Herbert Read, an assistant under-secretary, agreed that a mandatory power should prohibit slavery, end forced labor, forbid the sale of "trade spirits" to Africans, and "raise no native troops other than those required for the maintenance of local order."[6] This last stipulation reflected not only the wartime fear of Germany's creating "a large native army" for use in Europe, but the desire to avoid any charge of "militarism" in Africa.[7] The committee discussed the question of "complete neutralisation," but found it raised "insuperable difficulties" and decided to postpone any decisions concerning fortifications. The group did agree to the principle of commercial equality for all members of the League of Nations, but opposed the League's appointing "a Commission for the comparative study of problems of tropical administration." The members also argued against applying the mandates system to "mere strips of territory" like Togo and Cameroon. Further, they wanted no systematic international supervision. All agreed that the League's power of "inspection" be "understood to mean the verification of complaints that specific covenants are being ignored by the mandatory power, not a general right of supervision."[8] Thus, the committee had merely recommended an extremely limited as well as casual form of international accountability over a finite set of conditions applied only to German East Africa. Still, Cecil was pleased with these modest results and somewhat surprised to find that the Colonial Office civil servants were "much more ready for reform and League supervision than I had expected."[9]

In late January, the delegates of Great Britain, France, the United States, Italy, and Japan met to discuss the fate of the German overseas empire. While Lloyd George announced that he could accept the mandates system if necessary, he argued that the Conference should accept the demands of the southern Dominions for unconditional annexation.[10] Japan requested the same for itself.[11] Wilson, angered by what he regarded as examples of naked imperialism, immediately halted the proceedings. In a long defense of his intention to reform European imperialism and end the worst abuses of colonized peoples in the former German overseas empire, he declared that the guiding principal of the League of Nations mandates system was not to "exploit any people" or "exercise arbitrary sovereignty over any people." Instead, "[t]he purpose was to serve the people in underdeveloped parts, to safeguard them against abuses such as had occurred under German administration and such as might be found under other administrations." Wilson had no wish to destroy European colonialism and argued that there would be "no administrative difference" between his plan and annexation. Further, the League of Nations would not subject the mandatory power to "constant irritation and constant interference" as long as "the mandatory performed his duties satisfactorily."[12]

Wilson envisioned a practical plan that would restrain imperialism by subjecting it to international accountability. This "new" colonialism would serve to end imperial rivalries as well as to confront the problems of the economic disparity between Africa and the outside world. He told the delegates that the mandates should be open to the trade of every League member. The League might even bear some of the cost of administration if a mandated territory became a financial burden. "The fundamental idea," according to Wilson, "would be that the world was acting as trustee through a mandatory, and would be in charge of the whole administration until the day when the true wishes of the inhabitants could be ascertained." The mandatory power would be accountable to the world and "would be so much in the view of the world that unfair processes could not be successfully attempted."[13] Nothing less than the future of the League and a lasting peace depended on this internationalization and reformation of European imperialism:

> If any nation could annex territory which was previously a German Colony, it would be challenging the whole idea of the League of Nations . . . If the process of annexation went on, the League of Nations would be discredited from the beginning. Many false rumors had been set about regarding the Peace Conference. Those who were hostile to it said that its purpose was merely to divide up the spoils. If they justified that statement in any degree, that would discredit the Conference.[14]

It was clear that Wilson would not abandon his mandates system. When the British delegation gathered later in the day, it immediately retreated to its "second line of argument" and began drafting a proposal that divided the mandatory principal into three classes. The first would permit the southern Dominions to annex their captured German possessions. The second would give "sovereign rights" to the mandatory powers of territories in tropical Africa subject to the same general limitations adopted by Cecil and the Africa committee the week before. The third would encompass the Middle East and the peoples who could "speak for themselves" and needed only "assistance in government."[15] Cecil then met with Colonel House, now a member of the American delegation in Paris, and told him that this proposal "would secure a very real supervision of the League of Nations without any dangerous interference with sovereignty" since the League could act when a mandatory power violated the limitations. House bluntly replied that the British plan "did not go far enough."[16]

Having failed to find a compromise with the Americans, the Allies next tried simply to bully Wilson into acquiescing. Lloyd George forcefully repeated the "special case" of the southern Dominions and Simon demanded that France have Togo and Cameroon without League supervision.[17] Wilson was not pleased. He exclaimed that "the discussion so far had been, in essence, a negation in detail – one case at a time – of the whole principle of mandatories." The delegates "had been brought to a point where it looked as if their roads diverged." The entire Conference was now in serious jeopardy. Lloyd George, fearful of a break with the United States, reaffirmed his willingness to accept the mandates system if it was "merely a general trusteeship upon defined conditions." The League would have "the right to interfere" only when those conditions were "scandalously abused." This interpretation of the League's powers was the same as that held by Cecil and Smuts. Lloyd George then gave Wilson an opportunity to demonstrate the depth of his devotion to the mandates system by accepting the administration of German East Africa. The prime minister deftly observed that

> as regards German East Africa, if Great Britain was not the mandatory, it had a big force there now which it would not wish to keep there . . . They could not withdraw and leave the people to massacre each other. They would be compelled to hand the country to some one.[18]

Wilson sympathized, but made no offer to relieve Britain of German East Africa. Instead, he suggested postponing the discussion of the German colonies altogether. This was not the response that Lloyd George wanted to hear and the meeting ended without any agreement.

For two days, the members of the British Empire delegation fought over the question of mandates.[19] After many bitter exchanges between Lloyd George and Australia's prime minister, the delegation agreed to draft another proposal that closely followed the previous three-tier division of territories, later designated A, B and C mandates.[20] This time, South-West Africa and the islands in the Pacific were placed in the "C" category since they were "best administered under the laws of the mandatory state as integral portions thereof" subject to limited safeguards. The Arab provinces were still in the "A" category and the colonies of "Central Africa" in the "B." The definition and stipulations of the B mandates remained largely unchanged from the earlier versions, yet the draft did contain a prominent addition that vastly increased the supervisory power of the League. It proposed that "[i]n every case of mandate, the mandatory state shall render to the League of Nations an annual report in reference to the territory committed to its charge."[21] Smuts showed this revised proposal to House who thought the British had made "great concessions from the position they took yesterday" and accepted the draft.[22]

The following morning, Lloyd George presented the British proposal to the Conference.[23] Wilson replied that the proposal was "very gratifying" since it made the administrations in all of the former German colonies accountable to the League, but wanted to delay the selection of the mandatory powers until after the League was fully functioning in order to avoid accusations that the great powers had divided the spoils among themselves.[24] Lloyd George said that the request "filled him with despair," but Wilson prevailed. The Prime Minister may have accepted this delay because Wilson hinted that the United States might actively participate in the "new" postwar imperialism and act as a mandatory if he had time to influence public opinion. While Wilson admitted that the American people "would be most disinclined" to accept a mandate, he boasted that "[h]e himself had succeeded in getting the people of America to do many things, and he might succeed in getting them to accept this burden also."[25]

While Wilson seemed to have succeeded at least in getting the Allies to bend to his terms concerning the conquered German and Turkish possessions, the delegates quickly fought over the meaning of his mandates system for the proposed B mandates. In particular, the practice of recruiting Africans into the military emerged as a confusing and controversial issue. The Canadian prime minister, Sir Robert Borden, suggested changing the clause for the B mandates in order to make a prohibition against fortifications more precise and to specify that Africans would have no military training except for "police purposes and the defence of territory."[26]

Wilson was pleased with the change, but the French foreign minister said that "France could not renounce the right of raising volunteers in the countries under its administration, whatever they might be." Lloyd George argued that "so long as M. Clemenceau did not train big nigger [sic] armies for the purposes of aggression, that was all the clause was intended to guard against." Clemenceau accepted this interpretation and Wilson thought it was "consistent with the phraseology" of the mandatory principle. In truth, the issue remained unclear. The French maintained that "defence of territory" referred to the territory of the mandatory power while Wilson and a number of British officials asserted that the intention of the clause was to provide for the defense of the mandated territory only. The conflict was the first of many such arguments and was an early indication of the difficulties facing those who hoped for colonial reform in Africa.

By late January, the Conference had established a broad theoretical framework for the mandates system, but there was no consensus as to what it meant or how it would work. A number of British observers were sure that mandates had damaged London's relations with the southern Dominions.[27] House considered the results a success and was pleased that the British had "come a long way" and had shown a "willingness to meet us more than halfway."[28] Philip Kerr, Lloyd George's private secretary, thought the mandates system simply reflected the "practical experience of the British Empire" and was an example of the needless complications of the Conference.[29] An anonymous letter to the editor of *The Times* warned that the system could "dislocate or jar the delicate fabric of the Empire" while another press story praised Wilson's "bold common sense" in championing a system that gave "an aspect of much-needed reality to the League."[30] Smuts told a family friend that "[t]he mandatory business is finally accepted, and I hope a great seed finally planted in the soil of our international life. May it be not too stony soil."[31] Balfour, told the press that mandates were only an experiment that might have "interesting results," but if "the colonies administered under mandate were found to compare unfavourably with the others in organisation and economic results, there would be no reason why the old system should not be reverted to."[32] Count Ulrich Brockdorff-Rantzau, the German foreign minister, told the American press that the Conference had violated the terms of the Armistice.[33] In France, the "Commission d'étude des questions coloniales posées par la guerre" acted as though the framework did not exist and continued to demand that France annex its portions of Togo and Cameroon "in plain sovereignty." It readily produced letters from several French colonial societies that vociferously agreed.[34]

Milner and Simon

One of the most important officials responsible for working out the details of the mandates system was not even in Paris or involved in any of the discussions surrounding it. In mid-January, Lord Milner had replaced Walter Long as British colonial secretary, but he was still in London in early February settling in to his many new responsibilities. Milner, the high commissioner for South Africa during the Boer War and an impassioned defender of the British Empire, insisted that Leo Amery, another staunch imperialist, serve as his under-secretary.[35] Neither man had the slightest interest in abandoning German East Africa or in accepting untested forms of international accountability for British imperialism in Africa. Milner hoped that Wilson would accept a mandate for Armenia to demonstrate "a bond of union" between Britain and the United States, but also to keep the Americans out of Africa.[36] Amery did not want "anything implying even the shadow of an international government" in the captured German colonies.[37] Few policy-makers were more steadfast in their traditional conceptions of British colonialism. The new colonial secretary assumed that the mandates system was similar to Britain's administration of Egypt and was largely unconcerned with the matter.[38] It was not until late February that Milner even began working on the specific terms of the mandates in consultation with Cecil J. B. Hurst, the Foreign Office legal advisor.[39]

While Milner was still in London, however, the power of the League to supervise the mandated territories was increasing. In early February, American and British delegates under the direction of Wilson and Cecil drafted a number of versions of the League Covenant that significantly strengthened the broad supervisory powers of the League. On 3 February, they produced a draft that contained the earlier conclusions of the Conference as well as provisions giving the League "complete power of supervision" and the inhabitants "the right to appeal to the League for the redress or correction of any breach of the mandate."[40] The following week, Smuts offered a draft that required the League to establish "a

Mandatory Commission to receive and examine the annual reports of the Mandatory Powers, and to assist the League in ensuring the observance of the terms of all Mandates."[41] Leon Bourgeois, a French delegate, tried to block this expanding supervisory power of the League by suggesting that the Conference adopt a form of "moral protectorate" for each of the captured German colonies instead of the mandates system.[42] The Commission on the League of Nations, dominated by Wilson and Cecil, easily squelched the suggestion.

In Wilson's statement to the third plenary session of the Conference on 14 February, the mandates system survived as an integral part of the League Covenant. The fledgling international organization had now firmly attached itself to the lives of colonized peoples in the Middle East, the Pacific, and Africa. Wilson declared:

> To those colonies and territories which as a consequence of the late war have ceased to be under the sovereignty of the States which formerly governed them and which are inhabited by peoples not yet able to stand by themselves under the strenuous conditions of the modern world, there should be applied the principle that the well-being and development of such peoples form a sacred trust of civilization and that securities for the performance of this trust should be embodied in this Covenant.[43]

While the Allies still had to work out the specific terms of the mandates, the draft Covenant established the authority of the League to supervise the mandatory powers through a permanent commission. The drafters eventually sharpened this authority by eliminating the commission's vague power "to assist the League" and inserted the more specific phrase "to advise the Council on all matters relating to the observance of the mandates."[44] While this change made the commission responsible to the smaller Council dominated by the large powers and not the general Assembly, it established the commission as a permanent and relatively independent advisory body. This version eventually became Article 22 of the Treaty of Versailles.[45]

After the third plenary session, Wilson returned to Washington and Lloyd George appears to have abandoned the idea of an American mandate for German East Africa. There was little popular support for such a scheme in the United States and the British embassy in Washington told the Foreign Office in early February that a press dispatch from Paris stating that the United States would take part in the administration of the German colonies "raised a storm among Republican members of the Senate."[46] While Wilson was still considering accepting a mandate for Armenia and Constantinople in 1919, Lloyd George recorded many years after the Conference that "America refused to accept a mandate for any of the German Colonies."[47] With Wilson gone, Lloyd George also decided to leave Paris. As he prepared to leave, he told a close friend that

Clemenceau had little faith in the "new fangled" mandates system. "Wilson has gone back home with a bundle of assignats. I have returned with a pocket full of sovereigns in the shape of the German Colonies, Mesopotamia, etc. Everyone to his taste."[48]

While Wilson, Clemenceau, and Lloyd George turned their attention to more serious matters, others had to sort out the details of the mandates system. After several meetings, British officials representing the Colonial Office and Foreign Office drafted a "Mandatory Treaty for German East Africa" that would serve as a model for the B mandates.[49] The draft contained many of the conclusions of the Africa committee of 20 January and reflected the same assumption that the effective authority of the League to supervise the mandatory powers would remain limited. It also said nothing about West Africa since London did not want League supervision for the relatively small portions of former German territory might remain under British control. When Milner and Simon met to discuss the two former German possessions on 7 March, Simon too wanted to say nothing about mandates. While Milner "explained that these Colonies would be ceded by Germany to the Allied and Associated Powers, who would then confer them under Mandate on France or Great Britain, as the case might be," Simon immediately turned the attention to partition.[50] He exploited Milner's lack of interest in West Africa not only to get him to make the generous wartime partition of Cameroon permanent, but to insist that Britain hand over all of Togo as well.[51] Milner was not willing to make such a concession, but the two men agreed to put off final partition. The next day, a harried Milner finished a long memorandum for the British Empire Delegation that he had started a few days before that tried to sum up his understanding of the mandates system.[52] The result was a fragmentary, somewhat impressionistic, and often contradictory explanation of how he thought the mandates system would ultimately function in practice.[53] He did admit that the mandates were "a new chapter in International Law" since "sovereignty" within the mandated territory would be "in a sense a divided 'sovereignty'" between the League and the mandatory power, but quickly dismissed such issues as only important to "lawyers." He noted that the mandated territories would be "under the supervision of the League of Nations," but did not define what "supervision" meant. Instead, he concentrated on the mandate texts and insisted that the mandatory's obligations were similar to those that Britain placed upon itself in other possessions in Africa:

> It thus appears that under mandates of the "B" class, the position of the mandated territory very much resembles, if it is not absolutely identical with, that of certain existing British Protectorates such as Nigeria and East Africa, in which equality of trade conditions has already been established under existing treaties.

Having characterized the mandates system as superfluous, Milner then turned to his own imperial agenda. He explained that in order to "greatly simplify" British rule in German East Africa it would be best to "bring all of East Africa – the country already British and that now to be confined to us – under a single administration." As for the British portions of Togo and Cameroon, Milner insisted that "it would be somewhat ridiculous to have separate mandates for all these small and unimportant bits of remotest Africa." Milner said that the Allies should simply settle the borders of all the various German colonies in tropical Africa "out of court" and not as an official part of the Peace Conference, something he did not mention he had already started to do.[54] Milner had convinced himself, or was trying to convince his colleagues, that probably only one or two B mandates would ever exist and that they could be annexed or absorbed into other colonial possessions. Thus, the League would not represent any changes for traditional patterns of British imperialism or prevent Britain from doing as it liked in eastern Africa.

By mid-March, the Paris Peace Conference had become badly disorganized and overburdened.[55] Wilson had returned to Paris, but agreed in late March to begin private meetings with Lloyd George, Clemenceau, and the Italian prime minister, Vittorio Orlando, as an informal "Council of Four" in order to expedite matters. Yet, since the delegates were so overwhelmed by the many unresolved political and economic problems, only a few determined colonial officials had much interest either in Togo and Cameroon or the preparation of the mandate texts. The Council of Four found this lack of progress particularly vexing when they met twice in early May to allot finally the African mandates.[56] While the Council was prepared to assign German South-West Africa as a "C" mandate to the Union of South Africa and German East Africa as a "B," the problem was Togo and Cameroon. Simon attended both meetings, but Milner, who had once again returned to London, did not. When asked about Togo during the first meeting on 6 May, Simon admitted to the delegates that "[t]here is nothing in writing," but reported that Britain and France had reached a preliminary agreement on Cameroon.[57] When Wilson insisted that each portion of Cameroon must become a mandate, Lloyd George complained that "[t]hat would be very inconvenient, for it involves a relatively narrow strip of territory" for Britain.[58] Simon then made an unrelated point about Togo and managed to muddle the proceedings so that neither the delegates nor those taking notes seemed to know the difference between two possessions. The delegates finally told Simon to come back the next morning with a suitable Anglo-French statement about both of the former German colonies.

In the morning, Simon returned to say that the drafts were not ready.[59] Later that afternoon, he still did not have a comprehensive statement and even raised some new complications.[60] Further, while the colonial minister presented prepared comments about the possessions, the Council members did not seem to realize that his vague references to the "conditions specified in the Covenant of the League of Nations, Article 22, paragraph 5," which did not contain the word "mandate," meant that he was not even talking about mandates at all. In exasperation, the Council decided to announce to the public the distribution of the other mandates, but postponed any discussion of the future administration of Togo and Cameroon and ordered France and Britain to make a joint recommendation "to the Council of the League of Nations" once they agreed to the final wording.[61]

Lloyd George was deeply annoyed with Milner for his part in the whole mess and wrote to demand that he solve the mandates question without delay since "there can be no colonial business which more urgently presses for treatment than these affairs."[62] Simon was delighted with his ability to frustrate the extension of the mandates system to West Africa and immediately boasted to the French president, Raymond Poincaré, that Britain and France would merely recommend annexing the two territories and that France would have Cameroon "without mandate and directly."[63]

Simon's successful overt resistance to League supervision over Togo and Cameroon, however, owed as much to Milner's own passive resistance to the mandates system as to his absence from Paris. In late May, Milner told the Colonial Office that Simon was convinced that the Council of Four had "virtually decided that Cameroon, like Togoland, should not be mandated territory."[64] He said that he and Simon agreed that Togo should be annexed by both powers "without any question of a mandate," and that the British portion of Cameroon similarly should be annexed to Nigeria. Since Simon always carefully avoided using the term "mandate," but promised to adhere to the conditions of Article 22, particularly regarding commercial equality, without League supervision, Milner declared that "as far as British interests are concerned, it would be a matter of indifference whether Cameroons [sic] was formally a mandated territory or not."

To this end, Milner told the Colonial Office that he would separate the question of the partition of Cameroon from any discussion of the mandates system. This decision gave British colonial officials every reason to conclude that the mandates system would not apply to West Africa. Milner suggested his approach to Simon who quickly agreed.[65] By pretending that the mandates system did not exist, the two men easily completed their negotiations in early July and confirmed the wartime partition of Cameroon, but devised a final division of Togo that handed most of the possession over to France.[66]

"Nomansland," the Duala, and French Resistance

While colonial officials in London and Paris could assume that Togo and Cameroon would not fall under the supervision of an international organization, those in the East Africa Department of the Colonial Office could not. Some of these officials, including Sir Herbert Read and Sir Charles Strachey, had helped to draft the B mandate "treaty" for German East Africa knowing that Milner was using it as a model for all of the B mandates. While these officials did not know before the public announcement of the Conference on 8 May that Britain would definitely receive a "mandate" for German East Africa, they assumed that Britain would rule the possession either as a colony or as a mandate.

As early as March, however, the details of Britain's draft B mandate began to circulate in the East Africa Department.[67] It provided colonial officials with an early indication of what the new internationalization would mean for British colonialism in Africa. The draft stipulated that the mandatory power had to grant missionaries free access to the mandated territory and had to ensure, "subject only to any necessary limitation in the interest of public order or morals, complete freedom of conscience and religious toleration."[68] It also granted missionaries the right to hold property and build mission schools. Horace Byatt, the administrator of German East Africa, wanted to deny the return of a group of Swiss missionaries whom he considered as having ties with Germany, but one Colonial Office official feared that "it is probable that freedom of action in regard to missions may be limited by the mandatory system."[69] In May Cecil tried to revise the draft, but colonial officials continued to protest against its implications for administration within German East Africa.[70] William Cecil Bottomley, a principal clerk in the East Africa Department, complained bitterly about Cecil's proposed revision.[71] He was worried about "freak missions of the United States" and argued that

> [q]uite apart from the fact that [the draft mandate] will give ex-enemy missions or missionaries the same rights as anybody else when ex-enemy Powers become members of the League of Nations, I do not think that we can possibly maintain that the new form gives us power to exclude any Body or anybody.[72]

Other colonial officials agreed. An assistant under-secretary of state for the colonies, Sir Gilbert Grindle, lamented that "[i]n the long run American freak Missions and bodies such as the Ethiopian Church are likely to be far more dangerous politically than any German missionary would be. But it is hopeless to expect to get power to exclude them as a class."[73] Bottomley told Byatt, who was on leave in London, that the

League of Nations would compel them to change their colonial policy concerning missionaries in the former German colony whether they liked it or not.[74] This issue was a matter of serious controversy for the next two years. While the final version of the mandate gave the mandatory the power to maintain "public order and good government," Britain remained obliged to admit missionaries of any member of the League of Nations.[75]

In addition to the new problems surrounding the entry of missionaries, the draft mandate contained a similar stipulation concerning immigration. The nationals of every member state of the League of Nations had an "equal footing" to enter, travel, and trade within the mandated territory.[76] The Colonial Office realized in March that when Germany joined the League of Nations its nationals, even those Germans identified as "enemy subjects" currently being repatriated, would have the right to immigrate to German East Africa "under the mandatory system."[77] The mandates system was now beginning to have an impact on the perceptions of colonial officials and to demonstrate the implications that an international organization could have for local conditions in Africa.

Throughout the next several months, these shifting perceptions and implications caused increasing problems for officials in the Colonial Office and within German East Africa. Byatt learned from the Treasury that since German East Africa was neither a colony nor a protectorate, the colonial administrator was not entitled to any pension benefits for his over two years of service in the territory.[78] In May, while still in London, Byatt proposed a colonial judicial structure for German East Africa and discovered that the principal legal advisor to the Colonial Office, Sir John Risley, thought it better to wait since "it is useless to discuss legal machinery or which Court's system will be constructed in G.E.A. until our position there is defined and established . . . "[79] The mandates system even affected the issue of renaming German East Africa. Bottomley complained that "a mandated country might aptly be described as Nomansland, but the name has no other merit . . . "[80]

Since Britain did not yet possess the authority of mandatory power, colonial officials were unable to pursue permanent policies for German East Africa. The delay had certain ramifications for Europeans and Africans in the possession. In early June, the Colonial Office submitted a proposed budget that was "necessarily provisional as we have not got our mandate yet and cannot formulate definite plans."[81] The Colonial Office also decided that it was impossible to make any permanent staff appointments to the territory even though officials knew that Byatt feared "a breakdown" in his administration without added staff.[82] The requirement of the mandate to "eliminate all forms of slavery" also caused particular debate and delay.[83] In early February, Byatt had suggested abolishing the indigenous slave trade in German East Africa "as soon as the occupied territory becomes a British Protectorate." But Fiddes argued that it would be best to wait, since "we haven't yet got the mandate" and the B mandates would specifically address the issue of slavery.[84] Byatt, Bottomley and Amery all rigidly opposed setting a precedent of "our going to the League for instructions on details of administration."[85] Despite this opposition, Fiddes agreed with Grindle's suggestion to "leave it till we got the League and the mandate."[86]

The Council of Four was also troubled by the long wait for the final mandate texts and decided on 27 June to create a special commission to complete the task.[87] The Council appointed Milner to chair the commission and designated Simon, House, and representatives from Italy and Japan to work with him.[88] The commission met the following morning, but after nearly two hours of heated debate, never moved beyond a very preliminary discussion of the C mandates.[89] A frustrated Milner adjourned the meeting and immediately left Paris to watch the Allies and representatives from Germany sign the Treaty of Versailles that same afternoon.[90] By Article 119 Germany renounced "in favour of the Principal Allied and Associated Powers all her rights and titles over her oversea possessions."[91] The same treaty contained Article 22 of the League Covenant which established the framework of the mandates system and gave the League of Nations the power of systematic supervision over the mandated territories. While it was still unclear what would replace the German overseas empire, reform-minded internationalists, led by Wilson, had succeeded in making sure that it would not be straightforward annexations or the unrestricted extension of European national sovereignty into Africa.

The significance of the break with imperial tradition was not lost on officials in the East Africa Department of the Colonial Office or in Dar es Salaam. While they still were unsure what a mandate was and did not know what the final text of the mandate would be, the formal incorporation of the mandates system into the Treaty of Versailles increased the number of administrative problems surrounding German East Africa. Legal issues were a source of particular confusion. In late July, the East Africa Department circulated an old Foreign Office memorandum entitled "Concessions in Ceded Territory" which asserted that the laws of a ceding state were no longer in force once a territory was conquered by another country.[92] The principal legal advisor remarked that the guidelines did not apply to German East Africa since "German territories 'mandated' to some other state are presumably neither 'conquered' nor 'ceded' in the strict sense. This seems to form a new class of acquired territory . . . [and] I should think that the German law remains until altered by the Mandatory Power," a legal status that Great Britain had yet to attain.[93] This interpretation had serious implications for colonial policy since it meant that Britain had no authority to make new laws for German

East Africa. From a legal point of view, the territory was in limbo.

The future of the former German possessions in West Africa was in a limbo of a different sort. On 8 July the Milner Commission met in London to discuss the mandate drafts once again. As before, Simon prevented immediate agreement by insisting that France retain the unrestricted right in the territories to recruit Africans into the military.[94] Both House and George Louis Beer, the American adviser on colonial matters, strongly opposed what Simon argued was in complete conformity with what the Allies had agreed to on 30 January.[95] Since Simon had no authority to resist the mandates system on any other grounds, he made the most of this demand.[96] After a session of three days, House told Wilson, who was now back in the United States, that the Commission had agreed on a B mandates text, but Simon continued to refuse any limits on African recruitment.[97] The conflict provided Simon with an excuse to stop attending Commission meetings altogether and to tell Milner that further discussion of the B mandates was "useless."[98] Wilson told House that the B mandates text was satisfactory, but without French participation the Commission dissolved and the members, including House and Beer, went home.[99] In explaining the results to the Colonial Office, Milner reported that he and Simon had only agreed to the boundaries of Togo and Cameroon and that "[a]s to Mandate or no Mandate we cannot agree, so there is at present an *impasse*."[100] This apparent deadlock must have been welcome to those who opposed the extension of League internationalism in Africa and never thought such formal international accountability was necessary.

In Paris, Simon did not maintain any pretense that mandates were still a matter of serious negotiation. He continued to assume that France and Britain would simply make a joint recommendation to observe the principles of the mandate, but not submit to any international supervision from the League of Nations. Within days of his abandonment of the Commission, the Colonial Ministry informed the governor-general of French West and French Equatorial Africa, Gabriel Louis Angoulvant, that an Anglo-French agreement concerning both Togo and Cameroon would be sent to the League "shortly" and that the two possessions soon could be absorbed into their respective administrative federations.[101] This agreement would only bind France to provide commercial equality to all members of the League and would not include any accountability to the League.[102] In early August, Simon informed the Foreign Ministry of his intention to avoid the mandates system and proudly announced his policy in the Chamber of Deputies on 17 September.[103] The colonial minister appointed a special commission composed of colonial officials such as Albert Duchêne, the head of the African department of the Colonial Ministry, and Lucien Louis Fourneau, the commissioner of Cameroon, to consider plans for fully incorporating Cameroon into French Equatorial

Africa and making Yaoundé, the second most populous town in Cameroon, the new administrative capital of the entire federation instead of Brazzaville.[104] The idea was already popular with Angoulvant and a number of other French colonial administrators.[105] Such a unified French African Empire would contribute to the metropole's economic recovery and preserve much of France's prewar status as a world power. As far as Simon and a number of other French colonial officials were concerned, the League of Nations mandates system and what it represented were dead.

A small but important group of Africans in Cameroon were not so sure. Throughout 1919 few independent African voices concerned with the future of the former German colonies reached the ears of Europeans outside Africa.[106] The German-trained elite among the Duala of the French portion of Cameroon were a striking exception.[107] The commissioner of Cameroon had known for some time that the Duala leaders were not only antagonistic toward French rule, but wanted a "free state" where "all of the property rights acquired by the European powers" would be annulled.[108] In the summer, the group made a much more public protest. On 18 August, sixteen Africans who claimed to represent the "unanimous" opinion of all the "natives of Cameroon and their chiefs," addressed a petition to the "High Conference" of the Allied powers. Aware that the fate of Cameroon rested upon an international agreement, the petition, written in German, requested that the Allies "be kind enough to discuss whether Cameroon could not be considered as a neutral country." If this request was "contrary to the intentions of the Allies," the petitioners agreed that

> we would be prepared to submit to a contrary decision of the Conference whereby we would be entrusted to the protection of one of the Allied powers, but we beg that the right of choosing such a power may be conceded to us.

Either by clever design or remarkable coincidence, the Duala thus appealed to Wilsonian concepts of self-determination as well as the idea of "trusteeship" embedded in Article 22 of the League Covenant. Further, the petition insisted that Africans in Cameroon would only accept this trusteeship if the Allies guaranteed a number of "civil rights." Foremost among these was "the right of citizenship for the natives of Cameroon (Douala), particularly from the point of view of individual freedom and from the point of view of property." The petitioners also demanded "freedom of commerce," the right to select their own chiefs, compensation for war damages, and the recognition of the treaties concerning land that Germany had signed with the Duala in 1884 and 1913.[109] Presented with such an embarrassing example of African opinion, officials in

London and Paris dutifully registered, translated, and filed the petition, but did not inform Lloyd George or Clemenceau of the requests and decided to remain silent.

While London and Paris may have wished that the Duala petition had never appeared, some French colonial officials were greatly alarmed by its sharp political demands and the implications of such demands if Cameroon were ever formally attached to the League of Nations. In 1919, the Corps of Colonial Inspectors, the independent branch of the Colonial Ministry responsible for overseeing colonial administration throughout the empire, conducted an inspection of both Togo and Cameroon. The chief inspector issued a detailed report on the Duala admitting that the group was "especially hostile to the French" and that a few "intellectuals" had demanded total independence.[110] He was particularly worried about "young Dualas" joining the growing pan-Africanist movement and participating in an international pan-African congress similar to the one recently held in Paris during the Peace Conference.[111] He warned that "without doubt the Dualas are in the position to provide the personalities capable of taking their place in a Congress of this type." Most importantly, he told the Colonial Ministry that if France ever accepted the international supervision of the League of Nations in Cameroon,

> the Dualas will always have the ability to have their voice heard when the work of France in Cameroon is examined by the League of Nations; it is very possible that they are the only ones in a position in Cameroon to make known in such an instance their opinion, if not their demands.[112]

The Corps of Colonial Inspectors, always sensitive to how Africans maneuvered within the colonial context, understood how an international organization tied to the changing postwar perceptions of imperialism posed a serious threat not only to France's colonial legitimacy in Cameroon, but to France's image as an imperial power in the wider world. Internationalization was dangerous since it gave Africans a potentially powerful tool to challenge French imperial interests and attitudes, force administrators to consider issues they would rather ignore, and re-shape the complex connections between Europeans and Africans.

The Lone "B" Mandate?

As 1919 drew to a close, the mood among British and French colonial officials differed widely on the mandates system. Those concerned with German East Africa were growing increasingly exasperated with their inability to make permanent policies and irritated by the changes that the system caused for decisions concerning slavery, immigration, and missionaries. Strachey complained that Britain without the mandate had no more authority "legally speaking, in G.E.A. (say) than Japan has."[113] The legal advisors of the Board of Trade warned the Colonial Office that all laws and regulations of German East Africa would "presumably" require the approval of the League of Nations once the mandate was in place.[114] This possibility so horrified one colonial official that he declared the "suggestion that all laws in G.E.A. will require the approval of the League of Nations is intolerable. I trust that we shall not have to accept such a nightmare proposal."[115] In November, Milner himself complained directly to Lloyd George and Balfour about the problems that the mandates system presented to colonial officials.[116] Lloyd George decided to wait and hope that the League would transfer the mandates "at the first meeting."[117] Risley suggested that the only option was to begin work on a draft Order in Council that would give Britain clear legal and judicial powers in German East Africa as soon as the League issued the mandates.[118]

For most of the colonial officials responsible for the administration of Togo and Cameroon, the mood was quite different. In early November, the French Foreign Ministry announced that it was prepared to adopt Simon's suggested form of Anglo-French joint recommendation to the League only to bind themselves to the spirit of the mandates system, but not to apply it in practice to either Togo or Cameroon. The proposal found universal support in the Colonial Office. Only A. J. Harding, an assistant secretary of state, was worried that since Britain would still accept a mandate for German East Africa, France would take advantage of the new vulnerabilities that the mandates system would place upon the British imperial structure.

> The only danger for us would be that unless the French are themselves put into a glass (mandated) house somewhere, they will almost certainly amuse themselves by throwing stones at our mandated houses whenever they are annoyed with us or want something from us.[119]

Milner agreed, yet was willing to risk letting France take advantage of the international status of the mandate for German East Africa in exchange for avoiding the mandates system altogether in West Africa. In a long defense of his decision to accept the French proposal, Milner argued

> it would be a cheap price for us to pay for getting the whole business settled out of hand to allow France to escape from some of the conditions, which a Mandate would impose on her in Togo and the Cameroons, especially as we should equally escape from the inconvenience of a Mandate for our share of these Colonies.[120]

That same day the Colonial Office asked the Foreign Office to begin negotiations with Paris based on the French proposal.[121]

At the end of November, Milner left Britain to confront the growing independence movement in Egypt.[122] Egypt became Milner's consuming official responsibility and he rarely concerned himself with the problem of mandates again. Yet, the future of Egypt and the issue of mandates did overlap briefly for Milner. Before the Colonial Secretary went to Egypt, Lord Robert Cecil suggested that "the British Government should become the Mandatory of the League of Nations for the Government of Egypt" since "[a]fter all a Mandate would only be a formal avowal of what we know to be the policy the Government wish to carry out in Egypt."[123] Not surprisingly, Milner rejected the idea insisting that there were too many impediments to such a plan. Further, Milner said that

> I feel another greater difficulty. We really cannot go on playing at this game of mandates all by ourselves. Before I could agree to putting any portion of the world, which we at present control, under a mandate, I should want to feel much surer than I do that the mandatory system is going to work. At present, it is not too much to say, that nothing has been done to make it a reality except what we have done (I might almost say what I have done) and that we have not succeeded in imposing its restrictions on anybody but ourselves.[124]

Thus, in this one letter, Milner acknowledged that France did not accept international supervision, that the mandates system was something new and untested, and that the League did indeed place certain limitations on a colonial power. He knew that German East Africa would remain internationalized under the League, but that the mandate would remain delayed until all of the signatories had ratified the Treaty and the League of Nations had begun to function officially. Simon's recalcitrance over Togo and Cameroon not only served traditional British imperial interests, but made it easier for Milner to frustrate the establishment of mandates in West Africa. He left for Egypt insisting that there was nothing more he could do.[125]

3

Accommodating the League of Nations, 1920

After nearly two years of confusion and confrontation, both Britain and France finally found accommodation with the League of Nations in late 1920 and accepted its systematic supervision of all the conquered German colonies in Africa. Anti-imperialists and those determined to construct new international institutions in order to prevent old conflicts prevailed over the defenders of straightforward annexation and unreformed European colonialism. British and French leaders decided the larger rewards from submitting to the League outweighed the limited disadvantages. This achievement represented an internationalization and reformation of imperialism that came remarkably close to the Wilsonian vision of transformed relations between Europe and Africa. Historians who have studied the early development of the mandates system traditionally have ended their examinations in 1919.[1] The result is a distortion of the evolving conception and nature of the mandates after the war. While many within the British and French colonial structures had great success in attempting to defeat the whole notion of mandates in 1919, the champions of the emerging system proved more resolute. They managed not only to expand the reach of the League of Nations into Africa, but firmly embedded both the spirit and letter of the mandates system into the new international postwar order.

"The Tanganyika Territory"

For most of the first half of 1920, both of the two largest colonial bureaucracies in Africa continued to function under the assumption that the only "mandate" was German East Africa. Yet, even here the culture of colonialism was changing only slowly. In early January, one clerk in the East Africa Department noted that he hoped that the League would revise the military clauses in the B mandates since "[a]t the present moment three quarters of the G.E.A. battalion (6th KAR [King's African Rifles]) are actually in Somaliland in connection with the operations against the Mullah."[2] Using Africans to fight for the imperial priorities of Europeans was precisely what Wilson and the anti-imperialists wanted to reform. In France, the powerful colonial lobby never abandoned its demands for the complete annexation of Togo and Cameroon.[3] In July, Albert Sarraut, the new French colonial minister, declared in the National Assembly that "[t]he present Government has no reason to depart from the point of view held by Monsieur Simon in favor of a pure and simple cession of [Togo and Cameroon] to France."[4] Like Henry Simon before him, Sarraut was willing to adhere to most of the general conditions of Article 22, paragraph 5, which did not contain the specific word "mandate," but rejected any form of League supervision. In this way, neither Togo nor Cameroon would become a formal mandate at all. Also like his predecessor, he assumed that France and Britain would eventually make a formal joint recommendation to the League that would confirm all of this.

France's slippery use of semantics and Britain's willingness to go along caused considerable confusion in Geneva and the British Foreign Office in early 1920. Eric Drummond, the secretary-general of the League of Nations, and a few baffled British officials in the Foreign Office had managed to convince themselves for months that both Britain and France had accepted League supervision of every former German colony in Africa. Since a small group of British and French colonial officials had conducted most of the negotiations surrounding the specific terms of the mandates, it took some time for others to discover how little beyond basic agreement over partition had been accomplished. Yet, by summer even Drummond had realized that Britain and France had not fully embraced League supervision and that a comprehensive and effective mandates system was in serious jeopardy.[5]

Even though mandates seemed to many as if they were withering away in early 1920 and the solitary "glass house" in Africa continued to conceal old problems, the system did continue to challenge the assumptions, perceptions, and actions of British officials responsible for German East Africa and the larger empire. In February, the India Office declared that India, as a member of the League of Nations, would have the same rights and privileges in the mandated territory as all other members. Indians expected complete religious and commercial equality as well as protection against institutionalized racial discrimination in the mandate.[6] This new and potentially troublesome legal consideration prompted a Foreign Office legal advisor to note that "it is rather an odd result that India should be entitled to rely on these provisions against the Home Government who are holders of the mandate."[7] Lord Robert Cecil, a driving force in the League of Nations Union (LNU) and no longer a member of the Cabinet, increasingly turned his attention to mandates and asked embarrassing questions in the House of Commons about their status. Both he and William G. A. Ormsby-Gore, a young and active member of the Conservative party and the LNU, made a habit of asking the prime minister why the League had not issued the mandates and why the government would not publish the draft texts.[8] In June, Cecil raised many of these same questions in a pointed letter to *The Times* entitled, "Mandates: A Duty of the League of Nations."[9] He hoped that persistent public pressure would not only increase awareness of the many uncertainties that surrounded mandates, but save the system from perishing from neglect.

Colonial officials found the lack of formal mandatory power in German East Africa particularly irksome. They could not even rename the former German possession though Germany had formally renounced all of its claims. While German East Africa was no longer "German," the territory was not legally a British "colony" or "protectorate" either.[10] A "mandate" constituted a new, but indeterminate category. The mandates system had caused colonial officials to postpone their choice for a new name and, with the realization that the British government was committed to the system, forced officials to abandon all their original choices. William Cecil Bottomley, a principal clerk in the East Africa Department, was desperate to change the name since it was such a tangible way to symbolize the transfer to British rule. Taking his inspiration from Lake Tanganyika, he advocated the temporary name of "The Tanganyika Territory."[11] An assistant under-secretary, Sir Herbert Read, accepted the proposal on the understanding that, after receiving the mandate, the possession would probably become "The Tanganyika Protectorate."[12] London informed Sir Horace Byatt, still holding the title of "administrator" of the conquered possession, of the decision and "German East Africa" officially vanished after 1 February 1920.[13]

The new name solved only one problem. But many others continued to plague the colonial administration. Byatt found that the stipulations of the draft mandate text concerning immigration made it difficult for him to prevent the re-entry of Swiss citizens that he considered "undesirables" since Switzerland was a League member.[14] The requirement of the mandate pertaining to missionaries was even more distressful to the new governor who was afraid that "it will be impossible to refuse admission to Pan-Ethiopian Societies or 7th Day Adventists . . . "[15] The principal legal advisor argued that, with the exception of former enemies, "missionaries of any other nationality must apparently under the mandate be allowed to enter . . . "[16] The Dar es Salaam Chamber of Commerce complained about the indefinite status of Tanganyika and accused Byatt of letting the delay surrounding the mandate hinder local trade.[17] While colonial officials and businessmen still did not know precisely what a mandate was, many of them were now convinced that they did not like it.

Even though Great Britain had to wait until July 1922 to receive the official mandate for the Tanganyika Territory, events in 1920 allowed colonial officials in the metropole and Dar es Salaam finally to begin making long-term policies for the territory. Most officials assumed that much of the uncertainty surrounding the mandates system, not to mention the League itself, was largely owed to the Americans. In March, the United States Senate refused again to consent to the ratifcation of the Treaty of Versailles leaving the other wartime allies to work out the details of the new international organization for themselves. Within weeks of the Senate vote, the East Africa Department was at work on a draft Order in Council in order to "regularise our position in the Tanganyika Territory without waiting any longer for the issue of a Mandate."[18] Over the next few months, the draft Order in Council underwent at least three substantive revisions, and each time officials removed direct references to the mandate and the League of Nations. In July the Colonial Office submitted the draft to the Cabinet. The Order stated that Britain had received the Tanganyika Territory by "other lawful means" and would administer the territory "subject to and in accordance with the provisions" of the Treaty of Versailles.[19]

The Order in Council was similar in many ways to those for other British possessions in Africa, but it did reflect some noticeable changes in the perceptions of colonial officials. Sir Charles Strachey, recently promoted to assistant secretary, wanted to "avoid criticism" by removing all "objectional [sic]" passages from the draft, particularly those that mentioned the "acquisition" of "Crown Lands" by "His Majesty."[20] Risley insisted that the term "Territory" remain in the text since "I should prefer 'Territory' for all our mandated territories to mark their peculiar status . . . "[21] He also noted that the Order in Council had to conform with legislation such as the Foreign Jurisdiction Act of 1890, "which of course makes no mention of 'mandates.'"[22] Thus, in order to avoid having to revise existing legislation or adding to the confusion already surrounding the nature of mandates, colonial officials made no direct reference to mandates in the Order. The Cabinet approved the draft, and within a few weeks Milner informed Byatt that he was finally the official governor and commander-in-chief of the Tanganyika Territory.[23]

The impact of the mandates system on the Order in Council was indirect, but had a much more pronounced influence on the drafting of the Royal Instructions detailing the responsibilities of the new governor. The permanent under-secretary, Sir George Fiddes, was particularly worried about criticism from Lord Robert Cecil.[24] While avoiding direct reference to the mandates system solved certain legal problems, Fiddes recognized that ignoring the system entirely could present new political dangers. The parliamentary under-secretary, Leo Amery, quickly agreed and suggested altering the Royal Instructions to mention the mandatory principle of protecting "the welfare of the native population" and upholding the "obligations of Our Government as the Mandatory of the Territory in accord with Article XXII of the Covenant of the League of Nations."[25] Lord Milner, the colonial secretary, once again forced to acknowledge the unique conditions of the mandate, ended the discussion by stating that "I think these words should certainly be inserted."[26]

Milner was only admitting what many colonial officials tied to Tanganyika already knew. Despite the decisions of the United States Senate, Britain was committed to the League and had accepted a mandated territory. The international status of this territory required changes in legislation, a heightened sensitivity to outside criticism, and a particular aversion to charges of old-fashioned imperialism. By the time that Amery and Milner had decided to alter the Royal Instructions to reflect these postwar sentiments, officials had already begun finding accommodation with the League of Nations and had decided to adopt a postage stamp for Tanganyika that did not portray the King's head, the symbol of sovereignty and British rule in neighboring colonial possessions. According to Eric Mächtig, a clerk in the East Africa Department, "so long as we do not have on them the King's head or another symbol suggesting direct sovereignty over the Territory, there could surely be no objection . . . "[27] Undoubtedly to the shock of monarchists and the delight of philatelists, the first postage stamps for Tanganyika displayed a giraffe's head instead of the profile of King George V.[28] The Colonial Office also understood that the international commercial equality stipulations of the mandate meant that Byatt could not adopt Kenya's mining laws that authorized only British subjects to drill for oil.[29] London realized that these same stipulations meant that Britain could grant preferential import rights to goods shipped from mandated territory, but could not insist on reciprocity or other conditions.[30]

Strachey was among the most aware of the increasing impact of internationalism and League-inspired colonial reform on British imperial assumptions. He had been a member of the British delegation to the Paris Peace Conference, had participated in a number of international conferences before the war, and had spent the first thirteen years of his professional life in the Foreign Office.[31] He was particularly interested in land policy and was one of the few London officials to have traveled in Africa.[32] In September, he warned that Byatt could not always copy laws, particularly land legislation, from other parts of the empire for application in Tanganyika. In defending his contention that Byatt should not adopt two Indian acts concerning the transfer of property and land acquisition, Strachey insisted that "we shall have to walk very warily in matters affecting land (1) on general grounds (2) on account of our position as Mandatories."[33] Risley and Read agreed. Adopting the language of Article 22, the Colonial Office suggested to the governor that he not apply the acts:

> This is necessary not only on account of the importance of safeguarding the rights of the native inhabitants, but also as a consequence of the objections arising out of the terms of the Mandate.[34]

As a growing number of British colonial officials were adjusting to the mandates system in 1920, a few more Africans were doing so as well. In July, J. T. Mensah, a former clerk for a British trading company operating in Lomé, sent Lloyd George and Milner copies of the first in a series of petitions he had addressed to the secretary-general of the League of Nations.[35] Mensah claimed that he was a member of a committee that represented "the Togoland Natives" and complained that Britain and France had divided Togo in "complete disregard to our wishes." Yet, remarkably, he was also aware, thanks to "telegraphic news just arriving on the coast," that the Allies had not submitted the draft mandate texts to the Supreme Council of the League and that the League still had not officially confirmed the mandates. Mensah declared that "the present division of Togoland is utterly against the wishes of us, the inhabitants" and that "the safest way of solving the problem" would be to appoint and send "a mixed commission" to Togo that would "find out from the natives concerned their desire as to the Government they wish their own country to be administered by . . . "[36]

Presumably Mensah wanted Lomé to fall under British rather than French rule so that Anglophone Africans like himself would have greater access to local political and economic power. He hoped that the international status of Togo and the League of Nations would serve this end. The League had no authority over the partition of the former German colonies, however, and was still waiting for Britain and France officially to accept the mandates system in West Africa. The Colonial Office concluded that the Anglo-French decision to divide Togo "is taken [and] final [and] there is no more to be said."[37] Still, Mensah's petition demonstrates how Africans grasped the significance of international events and understood that decisions taken in Europe had implications for Africa. Mensah was also aware of the force behind the rhetoric of Wilsonian anti-imperialism and tried to use that force to challenge the culture of colonialism and to shape political relations between Africans and Europeans in Togo.

French Capitulation

By mid-1920 both the British and French governments were facing growing domestic and international pressure from those who were dissatisfied with the long delay among the Allies in producing draft mandates. These groups had no intention of watching the mandates system shrink or disappear and demanded to see the "new" imperialism emerge under the supervision of the League. Perhaps one of the most important such organizations was the League of Nations Union. The LNU created a special "Mandates Committee" in June that included a number of diverse and influential people under the chairmanship of Ormsby-Gore. The other members included Sir Harry Johnson, the explorer and former governor of Nyasaland; John H. Harris, the secretary of the Anti-Slavery and Aborigines Protection Society; Dr Norman Leys, socialist, publicist, and harsh critic of white settlement in East Africa; Leonard Woolf, the secretary of the Labour Party Advisory Committee; and professor Arnold Toynbee, historian and scholar of the Middle East.[38] The committee quickly drafted its own mandate texts and attempted to get the League to accept them instead of the drafts prepared by the Allied powers. The Committee and the LNU leadership hoped that the mandates system would help to preserve the postwar peace, reform European imperialism, and confirm the importance of an international organization in establishing global order.

Other influential pressure groups included the various German colonial societies which, for reasons very different from the LNU's, insisted that Germany's former colonies fall under League supervision.[39] The societies detested both the League and the Treaty of Versailles, but were determined to block the complete annexation of their lost overseas empire and wanted to hold the mandatory powers to the letter and spirit of Article 22.[40] While Germany was not a member of the League, it was grappling with enormous domestic and foreign problems while having to conform to what it considered the harsh terms of the peace treaty. If Berlin had to conform to these terms, it insisted that London and Paris do the same.[41]

The most important public pressure for making the mandates system a reality came from the League itself. In response to the angry complaints of a number of its own non-mandatory members, the League Council began to warn the Allies that if Geneva did not receive draft mandates soon, the Council of the League would have to draft them itself.[42] Knowing that Berlin and other antagonistic governments were prepared to call attention to any violation of the Treaty of Versailles, the League had a vested interest in making sure that it was taken seriously and the terms of Article 22 were carried out. Some in Britain worried that the League might assign itself greater powers to intervene in the mandated territories or adopt unacceptable terms if left to its own devices. Lord Curzon, now foreign secretary, was angry that Geneva was trying to "poke its nose into the question of Mandates" and told Balfour, who continued to serve as Britain's representative in Geneva, that Britain should "severely discourage, and if necessary veto" any such attempt.[43]

The Foreign Office, which previously had been content to leave the problems surrounding the mandates to the Colonial Office, was growing interested in securing mandate texts for all of the former German colonies before the League decided on the matter. Yet Foreign Office officials knew that France still hoped to escape the mandates system altogether. In early August, France once again proposed a joint recommendation to the League that would bind Britain and France to all of the mandatory principle in Togo and Cameroon, with the exception of restrictions on military recruitment, without any League supervision. As before, the Colonial Office agreed since it was not willing to "antagonize the French by 'insisting' on a Mandate."[44] These problems combined with unresolved objections from Japan concerning the C mandates in the Pacific meant the Allies were still unable to agree on any draft mandates to submit to the League.

In Paris, oblivious to the warnings from the League or the apprehension in the Foreign Office, the Colonial Ministry seemed prepared to fight for straightforward annexation until the end. Sarraut, a former governor-general of Indochina and the current president of the revived *group coloniale* in the Chamber of Deputies, a bloc of nearly two hundred loosely allied pro-colonial nationalists, continued to reject the contention that France had ever accepted mandates or had to have them. He told the Foreign Ministry that France should offer to accept "a type of mandate similar to a C mandate" for both Togo and Cameroon, but only if it contained no restrictions on military recruitment, did not prohibit the territories from being "attached" to French West and French Equatorial Africa, and assumed that France would maintain its "complete freedom of action" without any systematic or formal accountability to the League of Nations. He also recommended never using the term "mandate" in any of the agreements to describe the two possessions.[45] This suggestion was virtually identical to Simon's earlier proposals to accept most of the mandatory principles, but not the mandates system.

In early November, Paris ordered Aimé Joseph de Fleuriau, the chargé d'affaires in London, to settle the status of Togo and Cameroon. He was under instructions to avoid allowing the League to draft the mandate texts, but to resist the mandates system as well. But in "a spirit of conciliation and friendly accord," he was told he could offer to accept Sarraut's dubious "C type" mandate as a last resort.[46] When Fleuriau suggested that Britain and France bind themselves to the spirit of the mandate texts, but avoid the term "mandate" entirely in their joint-recommendation to the League just as Sarraut wanted, Curzon exploded. "*I object* entirely to allowing the French to escape from a Mandate and cannot for the life of me see why we should agree."[47] Curzon was resentful of the conspicuous disparity between the two nations in accepting international obligations, but must have been aware of the intense criticism that would certainly come from Geneva, Berlin, the LNU, and elsewhere if Britain did not coerce the French on this issue. When Fleuriau reported home that Britain insisted on a modified B mandate text with a special provision concerning military recruitment in the French mandates, it was Sarraut's turn to be angry.[48] On 12 November, he sent an eight-page memorandum to the Foreign Ministry announcing that he had no intention of having B mandates, even if France was exempted from the recruitment restrictions, since any genuine "mandate" would require accountability to the League.[49]

The Foreign Ministry was now caught between Sarraut's demands and the dangers of an open split with Britain at the first meeting of the Assembly of the League of Nations in Geneva on 15 November. Georges Leygues, France's prime minister and foreign minister, headed a coalition government of conservatives who did not share the political left's sympathy for Wilson and the League, but wanted full British support in tough enforcement of the peace treaties. French officials decided that cooperation with Britain and accepting a much wider interpretation of Article 22 were more important than the interests of the empire. On 14 November, the day before the Assembly met, the Foreign Ministry instructed the ambassador in London, Paul Cambon, to accept genuine C mandates, but only after impressing upon London that France was making "a considerable concession" in doing so.[50] Paris also told its officials in Geneva that since Britain would never agree to "renounce" the mandates system jointly, France had to accept it.[51] The Colonial Ministry's two year fight against subjecting French colonialism to the League's system of reform and internationalization was finally over. The assistant legal advisor in the Foreign Office grasped the legal and political significance of the reversal:

> This represents, I think, a substantial advance on the part of the French Government. They agree to accept a mandate, which is really the most important thing as it brings in the control of the League . . . [52]

France accepted the mandates system, but the Allies had not reached agreement on all of the outstanding problems surrounding it. For the next several weeks, British and French officials fought bitterly over the exact wording of the mandate texts and the composition of the future Permanent Mandates Commission.[53] Balfour, in Geneva, had the difficult task not only of securing a general agreement among the Allies on all of the mandate texts, but of bringing those texts into as much conformity with Article 22 of the Covenant as possible. He told the secretary of the Cabinet:

> I am seriously pre-occupied in regard to Mandates. It is really essential that this question should be settled during the present session of the Assembly and I am anxious to put all pressure I can on [the] French and Japanese as

> to B. And C. Mandates and I am prepared to do this by calling a special meeting of the Council if necessary . . . [54]

Complicating these already difficult negotiations were the loud and incessant demands of the various interest groups. The League of Nations Union, which had offered its own B mandate draft to the Assembly, as well as those of the League itself, worked in tandem to urge France and Britain to produce immediate results.[55] Further, the German government put mounting international pressure on Paris and London by submitting a detailed protest to Geneva in November that openly criticized the Allies' decision to make the Council of the League, not the Assembly, responsible for the mandate texts and for receiving the advice of the Permanent Mandates Commission.[56] Since three of the four permanent members of the Council were mandatory powers, the German government argued that the mandates system would be little more than an elaborate sham.[57]

> Seen as a whole, the system proposed by the Council of the League amounts to the almost complete elimination of the Assembly, and it reduces the role of the Council to a mere formality, and it thus invalidates the control vested in the League. The Mandatory system would therefore become a mere fiction, and we would find ourselves confronted, in fact, with the annexation of the former German colonial possessions, through a distribution carried out by the Principal Powers. The German Government, for its part, would be bound to consider such a solution of the colonial question as a violation of the Treaty of Versailles, of which the Covenant of the League of Nations forms an integral part.

This stinging indictment not only reflected a popular abhorrence for the peace treaty in Germany, but was designed to embarrass the Allies, anger the members of the Assembly, and turn public opinion against the League and the mandates system. The Colonial Office representative at Geneva, Henry C. M. Lambert, thought that because Germany had renounced its overseas empire and was not a member of the League, it was "difficult to see on what ground she could question our action."[58] A Foreign Office official admitted that the charges were "in the main well-founded," but insisted that "it was only on such conditions that it was possible to introduce the mandates system at all."[59] Sir Eyre Crowe, the permanent under-secretary, responded "[f]ortunately, we are not called upon to reply . . . "[60]

This combination of domestic and international political pressure finally forced Britain and France to embrace the spirit and letter of Article 22. British officials, realizing after the German protest that the situation was "quite unsatisfactory and even dangerous," pushed hard to get France to accept a modified B mandate.[61] Still, progress was excruciatingly slow.[62] Cambon was sure that the reason for these nagging "divergences" was Britain's enduring "preoccupation" with pleasing the United States.[63] But British officials were far more worried that the Assembly, under the influence of the League of Nations Union and the German protests, would draft its own mandate texts.[64] After secret talks with Japanese officials that forced Tokyo to accept the C mandates, the French were left alone in their objections to acceding to any form of B mandates.[65] British officials warned that they would have to submit their own version of the B mandates to the League without France if the two sides could not reach agreement.[66] Paris decided it had no choice but to finally relent. Despite Sarraut's protests, the Foreign Ministry instructed its officials in Geneva to accept modified B mandates that exempted France from restrictions on military recruitment.[67] Balfour accepted this compromise, but privately thought that the exemption was inconsistent with Article 22 and left the clause intact in the British mandates.[68] He also accepted France's demand to adopt a clause from the C mandates that allowed both mandatory powers to administer Togo and Cameroon "as an integral part" of its territory.[69] On the evening of 17 December, after having received sanction from Paris only a few hours before, Balfour submitted the draft B mandates for the Tanganyika Territory, British Togo and Cameroon, French Togo and Cameroon, and Belgian Ruanda-Urundi to the League Secretariat.[70] Lambert was tremendously relieved that "we have at least got all those wretched Mandates put in . . . "[71]

French and British colonial officials were variously comforted and angered by the results achieved in Geneva. Sarraut was extremely displeased and protested bitterly. He repeated the old claim that France had never accepted mandates, that the B mandates contained stipulations that were contrary to established French colonial practice, and that the PMC had too much power and would interfere in "delicate questions" and problems of "particular complexity" that it would not understand.[72] In London, Strachey was surprised to find a number of minor alterations in the draft mandate for the Tanganyika Territory. "It is rather a matter of luck" that nothing "objectionable" was added.[73] In the West Africa Department, Harding was just as surprised to discover that the mandates for British Togo and Cameroon "are not C mandates with bits of B – as the French proposed – but B mandates with bits of C."[74] He too was displeased with some of the mandate clauses, particularly the stipulation concerning missionaries since it would not "keep out . . . all missionaries from Mohammedan districts of the North Cameroons." Harding also thought it was now time to send copies of the mandate texts to the governors of Nigeria and the Gold Coast since "[s]o far they have been told nothing about the proposed terms."[75]

"There Is No More Annexation"

At long last, both Britain and France had accepted the mandates system before the international community. Yet, the German government's protest to the League had accurately exposed some of the serious limitations of this "new" imperialism. The Council was dominated by the mandatory powers and appointed the members of the Permanent Mandates Commission. It was not unreasonable to assume that the Council could easily undermine the League's power of supervision over the administration of the mandates. The various mandate texts were not in strict conformity with Article 22, the military clauses of the mandates for French Togo and Cameroon representing the most serious abrogation. This unvarnished hypocrisy struck at the heart of the concept of a reformed and internationalized structure of European imperialism in Africa. Much about the nature of the mandates system remained untested, ambiguous, and contradictory, fueling suspicion that it was a poorly crafted disguise for old fashioned European colonialism, "a subterfuge which deceived no one."[76]

Despite these cynical assumptions and suspicions, the mandates system by late December 1920 was much as Wilson had envisioned it in January 1919. The Council, in an attempt to invest the Permanent Mandates Commission with a degree of balance and impartiality, adopted a constitution for the PMC that required it have nine members, the majority of whom had to be nationals from non-mandatory powers.[77] Those members were barred from holding "any office which puts them in a position of direct dependence on their Governments." The Council decided that at least one member should be a woman, a tradition that continued throughout the Commission's history. The mandate texts as submitted to the League also reflected anti-imperialist and humanitarian sentiments of accountability and reform. The mandates system internationalized and institutionalized the principle of "trusteeship" and held the mandatory powers accountable to it. Most importantly, the League retained Wilson's version of systematic supervision and received as formal and binding a pledge from both Britain and France as possible under international law to honor their mandatory obligations.

Mandates emerged from the politics of the First World War as part of the international postwar order. They were a departure from the nineteenth-century pattern of extending European national sovereignty into Africa. The Wilsonian goal of systematic accountability and international supervision for European imperialism remained intact despite two years of powerful and active resistance by some Europeans and passive resistance by many others. A number of British colonial officials in London and the Tanganyika Territory understood that the system was not a disguise for annexation and that it challenged their established ideology of imperialism. French colonial officials similarly knew that mandates and League supervision were not annexation and struggled to defeat the system in order to preserve a traditional form of colonialism. African elites had also grasped the international nature of mandates and used it to confront the European culture of colonialism, exploit the gaps within the imperial structure, and test the limits of colonial power. Together, Europeans and Africans were absorbing the language of Article 22 into their shared imperial order and were exposing the shifting ideological foundations of colonial relations.

Many anti-imperialists and those on the political left had reason to feel satisfied by late 1920. The principle of "trusteeship" and the concept that "the well-being and development" of colonized peoples formed "a sacred trust of civilization" were no longer merely rhetoric, but were now grafted into the fabric of a global order designed to deter a return to warfare and colonial rivalry. Philip J. Noel-Baker, a young clerk in the League of Nations secretariat and active supporter of the LNU and Labour Party, was convinced that the mandates system was "an attempt to take the Governments a little faster along the path of enlightened and disinterested progress in colonial administration than they would otherwise be inclined to go."[78] During Wilson's long fight to convince Americans to participate in the League of Nations, the President explained that old-fashioned European imperial expansion was over and that the new mandatory powers were "trustees responsible in the forum of the world at the bar of the League of Nations:"[79]

> There is no more annexation. There is no more land grabbing. There is no more extension of sovereignty. It is an absolute reversal of history, and absolute revolution in the way in which international affairs are treated. And it is all in the Covenant of the League of Nations.[80]

After 1920 it was the challenge of Geneva and the Permanent Mandates Commission to help the fledgling system to make the full transition from paper to practice.

4

The United States, Germany, and the Permanent Mandates Commission, 1921–1925

Despite the worst intentions of some British and French colonial officials, mandates emerged in late 1920 as an integral part of the new postwar structure of imperialism. Still, this new system was little more than an assortment of half-hearted promises, untested theories, and nagging ambiguities. Leo Amery, the steadfast British imperialist and parliamentary under-secretary for the colonies, exposed the strong undercurrent of contempt for the internationalization of colonialism by telling the Colonial Office that "I trust that we shall drive on our coach and four through all this silly mandate business some day."[1] Yet, he and others like him soon discovered they were unable to prevent the mandates system from making its transition from theory to practice. International forces were crucial to this transition. Outside the League, both the United States and Germany continued to express a sharp interest in mandates. In late 1921, the League, through the Permanent Mandates Commission, finally began to supervise the colonial administrations of the mandatory powers. Making the most of its prescribed powers, the PMC gradually learned to use the power of international public opinion to press an agenda of progressive reform and pragmatic paternalism in ruling colonized peoples. Between 1921 and 1925, the shifting demands of foreign relations and the adroitness of the League merged to help transform the wartime ambitions of the Wilsonian anti-imperialists into a functioning system capable of carrying out an international supervision of the British and French mandated territories in Africa.

America's Departure and Demands

Even though Britain and France had accepted the mandates system in late 1920, the League of Nations did not ratify the mandate texts until July

1922. This time the Americans were the reason for the delay. After the US Senate had refused to consent to the ratification of the Treaty of Versailles, relations between the League and Washington began to drift. The United States had been a driving force behind the creation of mandates in 1919 and was expected to take the lead in their eventual supervision. According to Article 119 of the Treaty of Versailles, Germany had renounced "in favour of the Principal Allied and Associated Powers" all rights to its overseas empire.[2] The United States, as one of the "Principal Allied and Associated Powers," had legal claims to the German colonies and had already informed Geneva of its intention to protect American interests in the Middle Eastern mandates and those assigned to Japan in the Pacific.[3] Yet the failure to ratify the Treaty of Versailles meant America was not a member of the League and could not enjoy the specific benefits extended to members by the mandate texts. To complicate matters further, the American president-elect, Warren G. Harding, was intentionally vague and contradictory about future American involvement with the new international organization.[4] In order to keep the mandates system alive and at the same time avoid offending the Americans, Geneva asked the mandatory powers to submit their first annual reports to the League and to continue administering their territories without official mandates.[5]

For several months, officials in London and Paris argued over how to respond to the League's request and confront the United States. A Foreign Ministry suggestion not to submit any reports until the League ratified the mandates found little support in the Foreign Office, which considered the proposal an affront to the League and contrary to the stipulations of Article 22.[6] When British officials, under pressure from the Dominions, indicated that it might be necessary to risk Washington's protests and push the League to ratify quickly, the recently reshuffled French government of Prime Minister Aristide Briand insisted that continued delay was preferable to causing even further American estrangement from Europe.[7] Winston Churchill, who had replaced Milner as colonial secretary in Lloyd George's cabinet, suggested that Britain might even offer control of Mesopotamia and Palestine to the United States in order to reach a final settlement.[8] Lloyd George, wanting to hold on to Mesopotamia and having tried and failed in 1919 to purchase American cooperation with overseas territory, rejected the idea.[9] Sir Eric Drummond, the secretary-general of the League, finally convinced London to accept delay and to open direct negotiations with the United States. He argued that

> [b]oth from foreign correspondents and from Americans themselves, we learn that the question of Mandates exceeds in popular interest all other matters of American foreign policy . . . We are told on the best authority that the Administration intend to treat the Mandates question as a test of European friendliness. If the Allied Powers give heed to the American

> protests on the subject, America will agree to close co-operation – obviously greatly to British advantage – in Europe; but if no notice is taken of the American claims, she is likely to retire into isolation, and this time with full popular approval.[10]

This "close cooperation" with the United States was necessary beyond Europe as well. American approval of the terms of the mandates would help to confirm British and French imperial legitimacy in the eyes of the new postwar world. If Britain and France chose to ignore the United States, they invited an easy and potentially powerful condemnation of their rule. If nothing else, American cooperation with the mandates system, in any form, would give tacit support to Britain's role as a world colonial power. After "considerable discussion," the British cabinet decided that, "in view of the attitude of the United States," it was necessary to fall in line with the views of France and the League and begin discussions with Washington on the terms of both the A and B mandates.[11] The British also agreed, in a compromise with the French, to submit reports to the League, but only with the understanding that they were not subject to League supervision.[12] Until the League officially ratified the mandates, the mandatory powers would not consider themselves legally accountable to Geneva.

Negotiations with the United States were tedious and protracted. In the summer of 1921, London and Paris hoped that it would not take more than a few months to draft special treaties with America that would give it the same privileges in the mandates as if it were a member of the League. Instead, nearly four years passed before all sides finally signed the necessary conventions.[13] Throughout the many exchanges of notes, the US was primarily interested in securing commercial equality and in protecting American missionaries. While the Italian government worried that the United States was getting "better terms" than members of the League, London insisted that there was no cause for such concern.[14] Once the United States was satisfied with the wording of the treaties, Britain and France discovered that Washington insisted on only a few relatively insignificant changes in the B mandate clauses.[15] For example, the Americans demanded and received a minor alteration to Article 8, the stipulation establishing the "free exercise of all forms of worship" within the mandated territory, but British officials concluded that the "practical effect of this provision appears to be identical with that of the earlier draft of Article 8."[16] Washington also asked for the right to be "consulted" before any future change in the mandate texts and to have "a duplicate, not a copy" of each annual report sent to the League.[17] Colonial officials found such requests irritating, but not burdensome.[18]

By early 1925 the United States had successfully attained all of the advantages of League membership in the mandates without joining the

League. Yet this degree of success had a price. While Washington officially accepted the terms of the mandates, it had rejected the responsibility of supervising the mandatory powers through either the League or the PMC. Thus, the Americans had little authority to criticize British or French colonial administration before the League. After 1921 America's influence over the mandates became passive, remote, and increasingly irrelevant. As early as June 1921 the French ambassador to London, Count Auguste de Saint-Aulaire, told Paris that British leaders were now more concerned about criticism from the Dominions and the League of Nations Union than from the United States.[19] As officials in Geneva discovered that the mandates system would have to function without active leadership from the United States, they too worried less about protests from Washington. In July 1922, long before the British or French had concluded their final agreements with the Americans, the League of Nations finally ratified the B mandate texts.[20]

Germany's Protests

As the influence of the United States over the mandates diminished, Germany emerged as the most important force outside the League concerned with the new system. The German government's public protests to the League in 1919 and 1920 had put the mandatory powers on notice that Berlin would hold them to the letter and spirit of Article 22 of the Treaty of Versailles.[21] German leaders hoped that pressing Britain and France to observe all of their responsibilities under Article 22 and calling attention to every violation or example of hypocrisy would strengthen their demand for a general revision of the entire treaty.[22] Enduring wartime bitterness and the fact that Germany was not a member of the League, however, made it easy for the Allies to dismiss many of these early protests. In late January 1921, when the German government argued that the liquidation of German property in the mandated territory caused "a severe injury to the interests of the natives" and did not "correspond to the spirit of the Peace Treaty," one British colonial official remarked that the policy was entirely legal under the Treaty and "[i]t is a safe working hypothesis that all such German proposals are more or less clumsy traps . . . "[23] The Colonial Ministry was similarly unimpressed when it rejected a request to return some German monuments left behind in Togo and Cameroon.[24] Even when the German ambassador, in a conversation with a British foreign official, accused France of using Africans from Cameroon as occupation forces in the Rhineland, the Foreign Office responded that "it is none of our business" and refused any official investigation.[25]

Formal protest was not the only tactic that the Germans used to try to undo the colonial clauses of the Treaty of Versailles. In early 1921 a German trading firm, the *West Afrikanische Gesellschaft*, received the sanction of the German government to propose the creation of a French-British-German trading syndicate to operate in the West African mandates.[26] This new firm would purchase former German property in the territories and permit "a certain proportion" of German clerks to enter and work under British and French supervisors. The Colonial Office expressed considerable skepticism and when the astonished Colonial Ministry insisted that the scheme was "absolutely impossible," it evaporated.[27] The German government made a point of officially requesting copies of the annual reports sent to the League and often tested Anglo-French resolve to exercise all of their treaty rights including the power to exclude Germans from returning to their former colonies or to forbid German merchant ships from entering ports in mandated territories.[28] In Tanganyika Territory, the local authorities refused to relinquish their power to exclude the return of "ex-enemies," but did admit a handful after they agreed to formally renounce their German nationality.[29] French officials were less conciliatory. They exercised their rights under to the Treaty to forbid the return of any former enemy, regardless of nationality, and barred all German ships from entering ports in Togo or Cameroon.[30]

The most vocal German challenge to the mandates system came from the various colonial societies who were determined to refute the "colonial guilt lie," the contention of the victorious Allies that the Germans had committed numerous "atrocities" in their former colonies and thus were unfit colonizers.[31] The ultimate objective of these societies was to see Germany regain its lost overseas empire, particularly in tropical Africa. The most important was the *Deutsche Kolonialgesellschaft* (DKG), led by Theodor Seitz, a former governor of both Cameroon and German South-West Africa. Between 1921 and 1925, the DKG grew steadily in membership and was particularly active in producing propaganda. While most of the German colonial societies were small and generally represented only those who had a direct and material interest in the former German colonies, some, such as the DKG, had close links to influential commercial interests and members of the *Reichstag*. Dr Heinrich Schnee, the governor of German East Africa from 1912 to 1918, was perhaps the most prolific and effective German publicist in the service of the DKG.[32] He never tired of insisting that Germany had a long and distinguished history as an overseas imperial power and that its former colonies often suffered under mandatory rule. As a representative of the German People's Party, Schnee was a member of an interparty group in the *Reichstag* that regularly demanded a sweeping revision of the colonial clauses of the Treaty of Versailles.

London and Paris responded differently to German colonial propaganda during this period. The Foreign Ministry provided French colonial officials with a steady supply of detailed information concerning the activities of the German colonial societies and their apparent impact on public opinion both inside and outside of Germany.[33] In return, the Colonial Ministry was careful to refute all such "anti-French" criticism.[34] In Cameroon and Togo, the local authorities conducted a persistent search for German intrigue or covert contact between "pro-German" Africans and their former rulers and employers.[35] At one point, French officials in Paris were worried that German propagandists might try to undermine French rule in the mandates by working with followers of Marcus Garvey, the controversial Jamaican-born activist based in America, and his growing Pan-Africanist movement.[36] As early as 1922 the Colonial Ministry was preparing for Germany's eventual membership in the League of Nations by informing officials in Cameroon that they would have to increase expenditures for propaganda control, "strict surveillance," and tight visa policies.[37] London was far less preoccupied with German propaganda within the mandated territories, but did react when it seemed to influence American public opinion. In early 1923 the Foreign Office, after urging from colonial officials, asked the British ambassador in Washington to provide information on an American academic who had publicly defended a recent translation of Schnee's revisionist views.[38] British officials were determined to preserve the tacit support of the United States for British imperialism as the model for mandatory administration.

Between 1921 and 1925 Germany managed to achieve a few important successes in its campaign to recapture influence in its lost colonies by reminding Britain of the international status of the mandated territories. On several occasions, particularly when larger economic considerations were involved, Berlin was able to win tangible concessions in the Tanganyika Territory. The first came in 1921 when the governor of Tanganyika asked whether German merchant ships could call at local ports. Eric Mächtig argued that it was a mistake for the mandated territory to "neglect trade openings from whatever quarter" and that it "would indeed be more in consonance with the spirit of the mandate not to induce prohibitive trade restrictions against nationals of any country."[39] As a result, London told Dar es Salaam that, while it could still prohibit Germans from entering the territory, it should let German ships engage in trade.[40] The following year, the German government offered to send representatives to Tanganyika in order to settle the debts that Germany had with the African soldiers who had fought during the war.[41] While the British strongly suspected that Berlin only wanted to buy African goodwill and embarrass the mandatory government, the governor could not ignore the "large sum of money" that he thought was involved.[42] After much negotiation, a small German delegation finally arrived in the territory, made some payments, and made the most of the publicity.[43]

In late 1924, the British and German governments began negotiating a commercial treaty that Berlin insisted must eventually include the mandated territories.[44] The Germans argued that including the mandates in the agreement would serve as a sign of good faith and such commercial equality in the territories would be required anyway once Germany joined the League. London acquiesced and asked Tanganyika to abandon all of its laws that restricted Germans from entry or from acquiring property in the mandate.[45] The governor, Sir Donald Cameron, was extremely hostile to London's request and wanted to hold Germany to the strict letter of the Treaty of Versailles. But after reporting that his own Executive Council advised making no changes "until we may be compelled to make them by reason of the entry of Germany into the League of Nations," he finally agreed in order to placate the Foreign Office.[46]

Germany had similar success in the British mandates in West Africa. In 1923 the French commissioner of Togo, Auguste François Bonnecarrère, was shocked to discover that his British counterpart had decided to allow three German missionaries and their wives to resume their work in Togo.[47] He argued that the decision caused "very real inconveniences" and might inspire Berlin to pressure him to do the same. Bonnecarrère and other French officials relentlessly enforced their legal right to exclude Germans from Togo and Cameroon and hoped that Britain would do the same. Lomé worried that the entry of the German missionaries into British Togo was another example of the growing rift in Anglo-French relations. France was left increasingly isolated in its demands to hold Germany to the terms of the Treaty of Versailles as London retreated from its commitments on the Continent and concentrated on its empire instead.[48] Bonnecarrère's fears were confirmed when, after an official note from the French ambassador on the matter, the British refused to reconsider.[49] In British Cameroon, after the local government was unsuccessful in finding buyers for the large plantations seized from the Germans during the war, it allowed the original German owners to repurchase their estates in 1924 and take possession in 1925.[50] German planters quickly became the foundation of the local economy and were soon operating at prewar capacity. Within a year, Germans accounted for 136 of the 219 Europeans in southern British Cameroon.[51] Within two years, these large German plantations employed 13,000 African migrant laborers and produced bananas, cocoa, palm products, and rubber for export.[52]

Like the United States, Germany was not a member of the League of Nations in 1925, but had secured many of the same advantages in the British mandates. The British ambassador to Berlin, Lord d'Abernon, even hinted that allowing Germany to return to its place among the other colonial powers, "within due limits," would improve Anglo-German relations.[53] Compared to the Americans, Germany was far more engaged with the mandates system and was much more influential. Through persistent pressure and by working within the confines of the Treaty of Versailles, Berlin had coaxed concessions from the British while making the French increasingly apprehensive and guarded.

The most important non-mandatory League member during this period interested in the mandates system was Italy. During the war, the Italian government had anticipated large territorial annexations in the Middle East and "equitable compensation" in Africa if Britain and France acquired German colonies.[54] To Rome's bitter disappointment, the Treaty of Versailles did not satisfy its definition of "equitable compensation" and Italy had to settle for relatively minor border rectifications in North and East Africa. Having no mandates of its own and feeling cheated, the Italian government was quick to call attention to any violations of the mandatory principles, no matter how insignificant, in order to embarrass the mandatory powers and remind them of Italy's imperial frustrations.[55] By 1925 Italy was under Benito Mussolini's fascist rule and was still insisting on a mandate. After the Locarno Conference met that summer and eased tensions in Europe by guaranteeing the Franco-German and Belgian-German frontiers in exchange for the voluntary German agreement to demilitarize the Rhineland, Rome expressed an increasing sympathy for Germany's "right to have a mandate."[56]

Geneva and the PMC

What ultimately made the mandates system an important part of postwar international relations were the League of Nations and the Permanent Mandates Commission. Yet, for the first six months of 1921, Geneva faced a number of serious problems surrounding mandates. It had drafts of the B mandates and a constitution for the Permanent Mandates Commission, but until the Americans were satisfied, the League would not officially ratify the mandates. Without ratification, the mandatory powers would not recognize the PMC's right of supervision. Without recognition, the PMC had no reason to meet. Meanwhile, in addition to the many bitter official and unofficial protests from Germany, several special interest groups, including the influential Anti-Slavery and Aborigines Protection Society and the *Bureau Internationale pour la Défence des Indigènes*, were loudly demanding that the mandates system be put into immediate effect.[57] The League of Nations Union was already calling for sweeping amendments to almost every clause of the draft mandate texts.[58] The Italian government, still deeply offended at not having received any mandates itself in 1919, accused Britain of discrimination in the Tanganyika Territory.[59] British merchants in West Africa publicly charged France with violations of the terms of the mandate for

Cameroon.[60] By late summer, as negotiations with the United States continued to drag on, many League supporters were worried that the mandates system once again faced oblivion.

A solution to the League's troubles came from inside the League itself. Philip Noel-Baker, now a member of the League of Nations secretariat, earnestly sympathized with the anti-imperialist sentiments of the political left and was determined to save the mandates system.[61] He remained in close contact with Lord Robert Cecil. In August, Noel-Baker sent Cecil a copy of a memorandum he had drafted entitled "'A' and 'B' Mandates: A Possible Proposal for the Adoption of the Council" that would officially bind the mandatory powers to observe the terms of the mandate texts and recognize the supervisory powers of the PMC pending the conclusion of the discussions with the Americans and final ratification. Noel-Baker hoped too that the mandatory powers would find it impossible openly to reject the spirit of Article 22. He argued that

> [a]s is evident in such matters as Mandates, it is much more the free consent of the Parties, rather than a legal obligation, which is of importance[. T]he above plan would, for the purpose of public opinion and for putting the League right in the eyes of the world on the subject of Mandates, be quite as effective as the definite legal establishment of the Mandate system . . . [62]

Cecil replied "[b]y all means get the proposal put before the Council" of the League since "I am of the opinion that we should never let the League wait on the U.S . . . "[63]

To Noel-Baker's delight, Cecil himself raised the proposal in September before the entire League membership during the second meeting of the Assembly. Cecil, who was officially representing the Union of South Africa, itself a mandatory for South-West Africa, was one of the most powerful voices in the Assembly. He carried the respect of the membership and the prestige of the League of Nations Union with him.[64] Both A. J. Balfour, Cecil's cousin and the British representative to the Council, and his French counterpart, Léon Bourgeois, expressed their displeasure with the proposal, but did not reject it.[65] The League publicly blamed the United States for the delay over mandates and the Council, in adopting Noel-Baker's idea, expressed its "appreciation" to the mandatory powers for their "courtesy" in submitting reports in accordance with Article 22 "even before it had been possible to confirm their Mandates."[66] The League and its allies had successfully used the power of public opinion to win substantive concessions from Britain and France, but did not fail to compliment as well as shift blame away from the two mandatory powers in the process. This was not the last time that the League used such tactics in order to defend the mandates system. Noel-Baker, pleased with this show of subtle strength, explained that such success depended on understanding that "Mandates is an affair in which publicity is the essence of the matter."[67] In early October the PMC met and produced its first set of published minutes, memoranda, and reports.[68] All of the meetings were held in private with the proceedings and related papers distributed to the public after the Commission had submitted its final report to the Council of the League. After 1922, the opening meeting was public in almost every session during the interwar period. Among the records created during this first session was a lengthy "questionnaire" for the mandatory powers designed to "facilitate the preparation" of the annual reports. The document comprised more than fifty questions concerning slavery, labor, missionary activity, and other issues specified in the mandate texts.[69]

From the outset the PMC understood that much of its power was dependent on public opinion and the amount of information that it received from the mandatory powers. The questionnaire established a precedent for Geneva to ask routinely for "full and detailed" reports in order to "fulfil its duties of supervision."[70] Squeezing more information from the mandatory powers allowed the PMC to ask more specific questions about a wider variety of subjects. Further, all of this material would be published for anyone to see. Noel-Baker, after reading the minutes and questionnaire, considered the meeting a great success and declared that the PMC was "the most enlightened and most progressive body the Council has yet created. It is the only Commission which has consistently tried to run faster than the Secretariat suggested that it should."[71] Members of the League of Nations Union were also deeply impressed with the questionnaire and began a practice of using the answers in forming its own public criticisms of the mandatory powers.[72] The records of this first PMC meeting, and many of those that followed, also served as sources for several extensive contemporary scholarly studies that formed part of the public debate surrounding the nature of imperialism and the changing relationships between Europeans and colonized peoples.[73] Colonial officials in London, Paris, and in the mandates could not ignore this expanding international audience and had a vested interest in taking it seriously.

The published papers of the PMC, however, expose only one narrow aspect of the commission's influence and obscure how its most powerful members had intricate connections with their national governments, leading interest groups, and the numerous colonial administrations. Like any bureaucracy, the League had layers of formal and informal powers, many of which depended on the resolve, abilities, or luck of the individuals involved. It was principally through a variety of complex connections, tied often to the threat rather than the use of international criticism, that the PMC was able to exercise influence away from public view and have an impact on every level of the structure of European imperialism within the mandates.

The PMC itself was composed of a mixture of personalities, some of whom possessed a great deal of influence both inside and outside the commission.[74] While five of the original nine members represented non-mandatory states, all but one were from states with overseas empires including Italy, the Netherlands, Portugal, and Spain. Ostensibly, the League wanted to have members who were "Colonial experts of international reputation," but some colonial officials had made it clear that they were unwilling to take the advice of states with no imperial traditions. Further, as the British Colonial Office told the Foreign Office, some argued that is was "absurd" and even "dangerous" to have the League "placing those who have the actual experience of Colonial Administration under the supervision of fussy busibodies" since it would be "opening the door to German intrigue."[75] Perhaps because of such sentiments, the League asked Anna Bugge-Wicksell, a Swedish lawyer, to accept the dual responsibility of being the sole woman and the only national from a state without an overseas empire. The most important non-mandatory representative was Alberto Theodoli, Italy's former under-secretary of state for the colonies, foreign minister, and a delegate to the Paris Peace Conference in 1919. Partially in an attempt to appease Italian resentment for not receiving any mandates, the other members elected Theodoli as the chairman of the PMC and he served in that capacity for the next sixteen years.[76] Other influential members included Daniel François Willem van Rees, a former colonial official with long experience in the Dutch East Indies, and Pierre Orts, a career diplomat in the Belgian foreign service. Van Rees served until his death in 1934 and Orts sat for the entire existence of the PMC. For a variety of reasons, the least effective members were those from Japan, Spain and Portugal, who tended to contribute less to the debates and opinions. The Director of the League of Nations Mandates Section was William Rappard from Switzerland, a lawyer, university professor, and former director of the Institute of International Studies at the University of Geneva. He was responsible for many of the day-to-day functions of the commission and for collecting information about the mandated territories from official and public sources. He earned a reputation as an energetic and thoughtful man dedicated to colonial reform and international cooperation.[77] When Rappard retired as director of the Mandates Section in 1924, he was appointed an extraordinary member of the Commission. Finally, as stipulated in the constitution, the League also appointed a representative from the International Labor Organization to join the PMC in order to satisfy demands for added supervision of the labor clauses of the mandates.[78]

The French member of the PMC, Jean-Baptiste Paul Beau, reflected a combination of domestic political pressures and French conceptions of the importance of the League of Nations in foreign affairs. Paris, responsible for two mandates in Africa and another in the Middle East, did not like the mandates system and did not trust the League. Since late 1919, the French National Assembly had been dominated by members of the *Bloc National*, a coalition of royalists, right-wing republicans, and other conservatives, who argued that a strict enforcement of the Treaty of Versailles tied to a persistent defense of French national interests, including strengthening the overseas empire, was the best way to avoid another war with Germany. Aristide Briand, serving as both prime minister and foreign minister in early 1921, was a pragmatic moderate, but did not have the strong support of the *Bloc* and wanted to avoid any break with the imperialists and ultra-nationalists in his brittle coalition government. As a result, Briand's Foreign Ministry took no chances and nominated Beau, the sixty-four year old French ambassador to Switzerland, to the PMC.[79]

As far as the Foreign Ministry was concerned, Beau was an ideal choice for the PMC. The former ambassador had spent more than thirty years in the French foreign service, but because he had served as the governor-general of Indochina from 1902 to 1907, he could claim some colonial administrative experience.[80] While Beau may have adhered to the strict interpretation of the Commission's constitution, which stipulated that its members "shall not hold any office which puts them in a position of direct dependence on their Governments," he participated in interdepartmental meetings held at the Quai d'Orsay and reported directly to the Foreign Ministry after meetings of the PMC.[81] He also delivered notes prepared by French foreign officials to Geneva and defended French mandatory administration in accordance with instructions from Paris.[82] For the Foreign Ministry, the PMC represented an aspect of foreign policy, not colonial policy. In this context, Beau performed his job well. He was a cautious, often defensive man who was generally apathetic about colonial matters. In 1923 Beau reportedly told the wife of one of his PMC colleagues that he and the Commission spent most of their time "discussing matters that we are not competent to deal with" and complained that "no-one [on the Commission] really understands what he is talking about."[83]

In striking contrast and overshadowing the other members of the PMC were the two successive British representatives that the League appointed in 1921 and 1923. When British officials discussed possible nominees to the PMC in February 1921, an interdepartmental conference composed of foreign and colonial officials suggested Sir Frederick Lugard, the former governor-general of Nigeria.[84] Lugard, who had retired in 1919, had no diplomatic experience and had never been a professional politician, but he had made a profound mark on the development of colonial administration in Africa.[85] He had been born in India in 1858 and his father, a chaplin in the East India Company, and his mother, in the service of the Church Missionary Society, had instilled in him a high sense of public service and duty. As a soldier and adventurer, Lugard had participated in the partition of Africa in the 1890s. As a publicist, he had helped to shape British public opinion to support colonial expansion in Uganda. As an administrator, he oversaw the "unification" of Nigeria and had extended a system of "native administration" into the possession that was based upon British conceptions of indirect rule. By 1919, the doctrine of "Indirect Rule" had become synonymous with Lugard when he revised his "Political Memoranda," first printed and circulated to colonial officials in 1906.[86] The document quickly became a standard for instructing British administrators throughout Africa in the process of indirect rule. At the end of his career in the colonial service, after spending over forty years of his life as a man of empire, Lugard told the colonial secretary, Lord Milner, that he was "as full of energy and work as ever" and was waiting for a chance to continue to serve.[87] For Foreign Office officials in 1921, Lugard was a good choice for the PMC because they considered mandates as primarily a matter of colonial rather than foreign policy.[88] For colonial officials, his international reputation in colonial administration made him someone that they could both respect and trust.

While Lugard had the support of bureaucrats in London, other considerations proved more important in February 1921. On the day the interdepartmental conference recommended the former governor-general of Nigeria for the PMC, Winston Churchill replaced Milner as colonial secretary. Churchill, like Lloyd George, was a member of the Liberal party who, with his prime minister, was finding it increasingly difficult to maintain the Liberal-Conservative coalition government formed in 1918.[89] A nomination to the PMC, if useful for placating Conservatives and holding the Coalition together, had political significance inside government. Outside government, neither Churchill nor Lloyd George could risk provoking the League of Nations Union. The LNU, officially a non-party organization with no direct involvement in electoral politics, contained large numbers of Liberals and Labourites as well as a few important Conservatives such as Cecil.[90]

Within days of assuming his new post, Churchill dismissed the advice of his permanent officials and together with Lloyd George decided to nominate William Ormsby-Gore instead of Lugard.[91] Ormsby-Gore was a young and ambitious Conservative MP who considered the League and the mandates system as reflections of pragmatic internationalism and the highest ideals of the British Empire.[92] He rejected "international administration" and advocated national responsibility subject to international criticism and supervision:

> [t]he aim of the Mandatory system is to secure disinterested and progressive colonial administration by experienced European powers of the more backward races. Successful conduct of such an experiment may have far

> reaching influences upon the character of European administration throughout Africa, and the whole of the world will watch with interest what is, and can be done by the application of the spirit and letter of Article 22 of the Covenant to this great and growing problem.[93]

From the point of view of domestic politics, Ormsby-Gore was an excellent choice. In addition to having been a member of Parliament since 1910, he was chairman of the Mandates Committee of the League of Nations Union, attended meetings of the Anti-Slavery and Aborigines Protection Society, and had ties with the Liverpool Chamber of Commerce.[94] Yet, he was only thirty-six years old, had no colonial administrative experience, and viewed his appointment to the PMC as a means to higher political ends. The following year, when the Conservatives finally abandoned the Coalition and Lloyd George resigned the premiership, Ormsby-Gore quit the PMC to become under-secretary for the colonies in the Conservative government of Andrew Bonar Law.

Lugard and the League

With Ormsby-Gore's resignation from the PMC, British officials were free once again to consider Lugard. In many ways, the former governor-general was now in a much better position to contribute to the League's efforts than he had been earlier. In July 1921 he earned the respect of the League of Nations Union by serving as chairman of a special committee on liquor traffic in Africa.[95] In 1922, he impressed Viscount Grey, the British foreign minister at the outbreak of the war and avid supporter of the League, with a suggestion that Geneva should dedicate itself to ending the slave trade in Ethiopia. Grey sent the suggestions to Cecil who responded that the League would investigate the issue.[96] Most importantly, in 1922 Lugard published his monumental study of British imperial rule entitled *The Dual Mandate in British Tropical Africa*.[97] Using the details of his system of indirect rule in Nigeria, Lugard constructed a specific political doctrine for colonial administration in Africa. He insisted that Britain had a double obligation to develop the colonies economically to produce for the outside world while preserving African culture and protecting Africans from exploitation by governing through "traditional" African leaders and institutions.

> Let it be admitted from the outset that European brains, capital, and energy have not been, and never will be, expended in developing the resources of Africa from motives of pure philanthropy; that Europe is in Africa for the mutual benefit of her own industrial classes and of the native races in their progress to a higher plane; that the benefit can be made reciprocal, and that it is the aim and desire of civilized administration to fulfil this dual mandate.[98]

While Lugard knew that Britain was not the lone colonial power in Africa, he had no doubts that the British were the best since "it is the genius of our race to colonize, to trade, and to govern." Britain's task in Africa was to champion "the cause of liberty and civilization:"

> There will always be those who cry aloud that the task is being badly done, that it does not need doing, that we can get more profit by leaving others to do it, that it brings evil to subject races and breeds profiteers at home. These were not the principles which prompted our forefathers, and secured for us the place we hold in the world to-day in trust for those who shall come after us.[99]

The Dual Mandate combined the humanitarian, economic and political influences of Edmund Burke, Joseph Chamberlain, and Rudyard Kipling with Lugard's own patriotism, prejudices, nostalgia, and lifelong convictions. Lugard acknowledged the problems of late nineteenth-century imperialism, but argued soothingly that expert administration motivated by progressive principles offered a solution. *The Dual Mandate* was a justification of European imperialism that members from both the political right and left could find attractive. Missionary groups could see Lugard's work as a powerful case against white settlement and land alienation while commercial interests could use it to rationalize their continued economic penetration of Africa. Anti-imperialists in the Labour Party, advocates of Wilsonian internationalism, and defenders of the mandates system could consider the book an authoritative defense of the concepts of trusteeship, imperial reform, and nation building in Africa. Lugard himself saw no contradiction in holding all of these views simultaneously or in defending any one of them.

Sometime in late 1922 Ormsby-Gore asked Lugard to replace him on the PMC.[100] He accepted not only because it was an opportunity to do "useful work" in a subject that he was "especially interested in and [had] studied," but because he needed the extra income.[101] Like Ormsby-Gore, Lugard did not support international administration in Africa and had admitted in public to "having some misgivings" about the mandates system and its impact on German and Italian foreign policy.[102] Still, he was convinced that the mandatory principles represented the highest aspirations of European imperialism and that expert advice from the League could help to make those aspirations a reality. After securing the approval of the governments of the southern Dominions, London formally nominated Lugard to the PMC in January 1923 and the League quickly appointed him.[103] Rappard, in offering his congratulations and expressing his regrets for Ormsby-Gore's resignation, told Lugard:

> [n]o compensation could have been more precious nor more encouraging

than the appointment of the author of "The Dual Mandate" which has been the bible of the Mandates Section ever since its publication.[104]

Ormsby-Gore was similarly complementary in a letter a few days later:

I am sure that you will do much better than I did. My experience was that the whole Commission took anything from the British member largely because he was the British member, and that you will find the same.[105]

Lugard served as British member of the PMC for the next thirteen years and the post gave him a means to expand his impact on African affairs. Between 1923 and 1925, Lugard joined several national and international committees, sat on company boards, and published a number of articles.[106] He continued to attend meetings of the Mandates Committee of the League of Nations Union, corresponded with Cecil about expanding the activities of the League, and tried to convince the Foreign Office to cooperate with Geneva in ending slavery in Ethiopia.[107] British merchants belonging to the powerful Liverpool Chamber of Commerce supplied Lugard with self-serving "details" concerning French policies in Cameroon that supposedly violated the forced labor and commercial equality clauses of the mandates.[108] By 1925 Lugard's web of connections with commercial concerns, the British government, interest groups, and the League of Nations combined with his international reputation in colonial administration to make him one of the most prominent and influential members of the PMC. He held few illusions about the authority of the PMC or his ability to exert influence through it:

The Mandates Commission must therefore rely on the individual knowledge and experience of its Members, aided by such persons or Societies as may make it their business to watch over the welfare of Backward Races, to read between the lines of reports, and to elicit full information from the accredited representative of the Mandatory Power.

The sole compelling power and driving force which the Commission can exert is the force of the public opinion of the world – and indeed in most cases the same may be said of the League itself. For this reason it is desirable to cultivate interest in the proceedings of the Commission and to circulate widely the Minutes of its Sessions, and its report to the Council, so that public opinion may be well-informed. The Secretariat is in turn charged with the duty of collecting and distributing to Members, the comments, suggestions and criticisms of the Parliaments and the Press of the World, to indicate to the Commission any points that may have escaped their attention, and to stimulate them in their work.[109]

The international context helped the mandates system make the difficult transition from theory to practice. Divergent pressures from the

United States, Germany, Italy, the League of Nations, and the LNU prevented the mandatory powers from quietly abandoning the international status of the former German territories in Africa. Once Lugard joined the PMC, the system had an authoritative, resolute, and practical advocate who insisted on steady colonial reform and a positive application of the principle of trusteeship in Africa. His various political, professional, and personal connections added to the informal influence of the PMC and mandates system in general. But the system was not merely supposed to exemplify an internationalization and reformation of colonialism, but was to advance such changes within all of the mandated territories. Caught between theory and practice, Europeans and Africans within the vast structure of imperialism still had to confront this novel product of international forces.

5

The British Mandates between Theory and Practice, 1921–1925

By early 1921, a few British colonial officials had already become relatively sophisticated in their understanding of the problems and possibilities inherent in international supervision. Those concerned with the administration of Tanganyika had known since early 1919 that it would remain attached to the League. The system made an earlier and deeper mark on the shared conceptions of colonialism of these officials and they pressed others to think of mandates as different from other British possessions in Africa. For example, in January, Charles Strachey, an assistant secretary in the Colonial Office, reminded the governor of the Tanganyika Territory, Sir Horace Byatt, that he could not require teachers to promise to make their pupils "good citizens of the British Empire."[1] Strachey remarked that "[i]t will make some of our L[eague] of N[ations] friends furious if they hear of it."[2] Tanganyika also had to return a small administrative outpost that had once belonged to Kenya since "[w]e can't very well hand over part of a British Colony to be included in Mandated Territory."[3] The East Africa Department told the Petroleum Department of the Colonial Office that, unlike in other British possessions, the commercial equality clauses of the mandate meant that Tanganyika could not restrict concessions for oil deposits to British subjects since "the Tanganyika Territory is not a British Possession or a Protectorate in the ordinary sense of the term."[4] These same officials tried to convince the Treasury that, "from the point of view of the relations of this country to other members of the League of Nations," Tanganyika deserved a larger grant-in-aid than the Exchequer was willing to give.[5]

In West Africa, officials familiar with Tanganyika had to enlighten colleagues who were only beginning to grapple with the new international status of Togo and Cameroon. The West Africa Department had to tell the governor of the Gold Coast, Sir F. Gordon Guggisberg, that until the League formally issued the mandates, he had no formal jurisdiction in Togo and had to stop drafting legislation for the mandated territory. This advice came from the assistant legal advisor, Henry Grattan Bushe. He chided the local government and noted that "[t]he Governor has forgotten that Togoland is not the G[old] C[oast]."[6] Officials in London had similar difficulties with Sir Hugh Clifford, the governor of Nigeria, who asked if the mandate for British Cameroon could apply "only to the Cameroons Province proper" so he could annex the rest of the territory to Nigeria.[7] A. J. Harding, an assistant secretary, had never bothered to tell the local administration about mandates since he thought they would not apply. Yet instead of blaming himself, he tartly remarked that "Sir H. Clifford is rather late in the day in giving his views" and had to tell him that "the whole of [the] British sphere will be included in [the] mandate" whether he liked it or not.[8]

It was not only British colonial officials who faced the increasing implications of the formal expansion of the mandates system to every former German colony under British rule. General Philip W. Chetwood of the War Office General Staff protested sharply to the Cabinet about the various military restrictions of the B mandates and demanded that they be removed.[9] A. J. Balfour, who had personally negotiated the final mandate texts under extreme pressure in Geneva just a few weeks before, coolly responded that "the B mandates could not now be modified in the sense desired by the War Office."[10] After much reflection, the Board of Trade announced that the mandates in Africa "cannot be regarded as part of the Imperial possessions of the Mandatory Power" since even granting preferential import rights to goods shipped from mandated territory, but not insisting on reciprocity, would infringe a number of international commercial treaties.[11] The Colonial Office agreed, but concluded that such a policy would damage British trade as well as the local colonial economy and decided to maintain the practice of "one-sided" preference anyway.[12] Even Maurice Hankey, the secretary of the Cabinet, realized that mandates were something other than typical colonial possessions. He told the foreign secretary, Lord Curzon, that "[p]ersonally, I have always detested the whole system of mandates, but the idea has rather a strong hold among the keen supporters of the League of Nations."[13]

This growing realization that the international status of the mandates made them different from traditional British colonies and protectorates had a direct impact on Africans. In January 1921 Clifford told London that he intended to end the system of Indirect Rule that Lugard had extended into the Cameroons Province when he was governor-general and abolish the "Cameroons Native Treasuries," merging their budgets into the provincial budget since "there are no chiefs capable of discharging the responsibilities."[14] The decision caused a long debate within the Colonial Office. Harding argued that while terminating the Native Treasuries was not a violation of the mandate, it would "look extremely bad" for the government to mark the start of mandatory rule "by abolishing institutions for local self-administration of natives which it had set up when it was a candidate for a mandate or even before a mandate was thought of."[15] With mandates finally fixed to British rule in West Africa, officials had to be wary of international opinion and criticism from the League. One of Harding's superiors disagreed and was not willing to interfere with Clifford's intention to end Indirect Rule in Cameroons Province.[16]

Harding did not give up. He persuaded the secretary for native affairs in Nigeria, Selwyn M. Grier, to oppose the opinion of his own chief and tell the parliamentary under-secretary, Edward Wood, that "the change was in the wrong direction."[17] Wood, who had already publicly demonstrated strong sympathies for the mandatory principles and the notion of "trusteeship" in Africa, was easily convinced.[18] He gave instructions to inform Clifford that abolishing the Native Treasuries could "afford an opportunity to hostile criticism" and would be "a step backwards in policy."[19] London was so anxious to "leave the existing system in force" that it told Lagos to use Nigerian funds if necessary to cover the extra costs of Indirect Rule.[20] Much to Clifford's displeasure, he had to keep Indirect Rule despite a lack of resources and an inability to identify many functioning indigenous state structures, particularly in the south where there was widespread political and social fragmentation.[21] British officials in several regions were forced to begin integrating diverse ethnic groups under single administrations and place immigrant populations into arbitrary districts.[22] When Clifford produced a draft annual report for the League in 1922 that made a passing reference to some of the local economic problems that this policy caused, Harding cut the passage before sending the final report to Geneva.[23] While in time Indirect Rule did create a certain degree of political stability in the region, conditions did not improve until the German planters returned after 1925 and began substantially to revive the local economy.

Slavery and Land Legislation

The international status of the mandates increasingly caused the Colonial Office to use its authority to direct policies within the mandated territories after 1921. In particular, the slavery and land legislation that the colonial administration in the Tanganyika Territory adopted during these years came from London, not Dar es Salaam. These two policy questions were the focus of close public attention and, because of the explicit stipulations of the mandate texts, fell under the supervision of the PMC. In both cases, the driving force behind drafting Tanganyika's laws was Charles Strachey. He was conscious of Britain's accountability to the League and routinely reminded his colleagues of the shifting culture of colonialism in the early postwar period. After becoming an assistant under-secretary of state in late 1924, he was an especially influential voice in the British colonial bureaucracy. He often used his position to defend and extend the mandatory principles.[24]

The Colonial Office had decided in 1919 to wait for the official mandate from the League before adopting slavery legislation for Tanganyika.[25] In early 1921 Strachey returned to the subject on the assumption that the wait would soon be over. He drafted two detailed memoranda on the question of slavery.[26] Both began with a recital of Article 5 of the mandate, which required the mandatory power to provide for "the eventual emancipation of all slaves, and for as speedy an elimination of domestic and other slavery as social conditions will allow."[27] In his second memorandum, Strachey reported that Byatt had enacted the Indian Penal Code a few months earlier, which punished anyone who "detains against his will any person as a slave." The principal legal advisor of the Colonial Office, Sir John Risley, told Strachey that the code provided "a substantial answer to any allegation that the Mandate had not been carried out," but did not "expressly abolish the legal status of slavery."[28] Strachey argued that the Indian Penal Code was insufficient and that Tanganyika should have a special ordinance that defined slavery as "involuntary servitude" and overtly ceased to recognize the legal status of slavery. In essence, he recommended adopting the "progressive" Nigerian approach in which, through "legal status abolition," slavery was slowly isolated and restricted while avoiding the social and political dislocation that immediate emancipation could cause, particularly among the "Arab masters" in Arab-Swahili communities.

In May 1921 Strachey sent Dar es Salaam his proposals for new slavery legislation.[29] Byatt agreed to Strachey's definition of slavery, which he admitted might apply to as many as 6,500 Africans throughout the territory.[30] Byatt's subordinates, however, did not agree. While Byatt was on leave in March 1922, the acting governor, Alfred Claude Hollis, along with the local attorney-general, L. H. Elphinstone, tried to dodge the Colonial Office ordinance. They produced their own draft that abolished "slavery" without defining it and expressly allowed persons voluntarily to "perform the duties of" slaves.[31] Strachey was infuriated. He called the ordinance "most objectionable" and complained that it was worded "so that the public would say that the whole thing is a piece of hypocrisy."[32] Strachey spoke directly with Byatt and convinced him to keep the original Colonial Office version. In May, the parliamentary under-secretary took Strachey's advice to send "a very brief note" to Dar es Salaam telling local officials that "they should enact the model sent out."[33] Within a few weeks Hollis did as London instructed and enacted the "Involuntary Servitude (Abolition) Ordinance, 1922" without alteration.[34] Strachey, concerned with public opinion and conforming to the mandate, was pleased and sent two copies to the PMC.[35]

Strachey confronted the more complex and controversial issue of land alienation in Tanganyika with similar determination and success. In August 1921 he produced another long memorandum that began with a citation of Article 6 of the mandate, which bound the mandatory power in framing laws "relating to the holding or transfer of land" to "take into consideration native laws and customs, and shall respect the rights and safeguard the interests of the native population."[36] Strachey argued that Tanganyika was "not a white man's country" and that the "mandatory conditions" were the most important consideration in drafting land legislation. He also noted that "the conditions of the Mandate forbid any differentiation against Indians or other subjects of States[,] Members of the League of Nations," but he wanted to avoid "Indian speculators in land," the creation of new European plantations that would place demands on scarce African labor, and duplicating "the difficulties which have arisen in Kenya" as a result of large-scale land alienation to whites.

> It is suggested that there is a strong case for consideration whether the land of Tanganyika should not be dealt with on West African and possibly Northern Nigerian lines, and this would seem very suitable to a Mandated country. The essence of the Mandate system is that the people are in 'tutelage,' and the recognition that the land really belongs to the natives, and that alienation on a large scale is inappropriate, appears to follow . . .

Since the Lugardian system in Nigeria was the model for most of British tropical Africa and represented the highest ideals of "trusteeship," it was entirely consistent for Strachey to argue that Nigeria should be the standard for a mandated territory. Strachey further strengthened this correlation by suggesting that the Colonial Office form a small committee to draft the land legislation for Tanganyika and invite William Ormsby-Gore, the British member of the PMC, to join it "in view of his position in connection with the League of Nations."[37]

Strachey had the strong support of George Fiddes, the permanent under-secretary, who did not see how anything like the land policy in Kenya "would be consistent with our position as mandatory."[38] The Colonial Office also knew that it could count on Byatt's backing. In early 1921, his government, "as trustees for native interests," had already proposed purchasing several former German properties in the Moshi, Arusha, Lindi and Usambara districts for restoration to Africans.[39] He had also prohibited the practice, common in Kenya and Uganda, of allowing members of the Tanganyika European Civil Servants Association to buy land in the territory.[40] This decision particularly satisfied one junior Colonial Office official, Charles J. Jeffries, who agreed that "the position in a mandated territory is not quite the same as in a Colony or Protectorate" and that "any suspicion of abuse would evoke much more widespread criticism than it would, say, in Kenya."[41] While not all of

Jeffries's superiors accepted this reasoning, Herbert J. Read, remarked that "I think that the extension of the privilege to mandated territory would certainly provoke criticism [and] we have quite enough difficulties at the present to deal with in connexion with mandated territory without creating new ones."[42] Perhaps most strikingly, Byatt had also rejected a request by a British company to construct a railway "conjointly with a land-settlement scheme."[43] Fiddes was gratified by the government's refusal. "I am dead against having anything to do with this scheme, apart from the fact that it could not be defended before the L[eague of] Nations."[44]

Strachey discovered that the greatest obstacle to his suggested land policy was not fellow bureaucrats, but the colonial secretary, Winston Churchill. For Churchill, the mandatory principles did not necessarily outweigh traditional concepts of empire. He knew that the decision in 1920 to transform the old East Africa Protectorate into the Kenya Colony and Protectorate had caused Indians, European settlers, and missionary groups to demand "self-government" within a greater "East Africa Dominion" that would include Kenya, Uganda, and Tanganyika.[45] In 1921 the colonial secretary was unwilling to make matters worse by formally adopting a land policy in Tanganyika that was so overtly contrary to the one in Kenya. His parliamentary under-secretary was aware of these particular political dangers, but decided to send his chief a copy of Strachey's memo in late August anyway. Wood agreed that the proposals would affect any "future consider[ation] of East African 'amalgamation' later on" and did not conceal "Mr. Strachey's reluctance to concur in the inclusion of Tanganyika under the suggested High Comm[issioner]."[46] Still, Wood defended the proposal for a committee while admitting that "its composition w[oul]d require careful consid[eration]." Churchill initialed the papers without comment, leaving an irritated Strachey to ask: "I do not want to worry the S. of S., but I wonder what is to be done on this. Nothing?" Yet, since Strachey was not willing to let his plan languish, he added a revealing and faintly threatening observation that "the L[eague] of N[ations] Union have got hold of the idea of the N. Nigeria system in Tanganyika. They did not get it from me."[47]

After several months of silence from Churchill, Wood finally gave instructions himself to create an "informal" committee to draft land legislation "in accordance with the mandatory system," using Strachey's suggestions as a guide.[48] On Strachey's recommendation, the Colonial Office asked Colonel Josiah Wedgewood, a famous war hero, humanitarian, anti-imperialist, and outspoken Labour member of the House of Commons, to participate on the committee.[49] As an MP, he had served on the formal committee that had approved Nigeria's land law and had at one time asked for a similar committee for Tanganyika, but agreed to compromise. The third member of the committee was Ormsby-Gore, who "attended as specially concerned in his capacity of Member of the Permanent Mandates Commission of the League of Nations."[50] In the end, Wedgewood and Ormsby-Gore gave their approval to a draft ordinance that Strachey was almost entirely responsible for composing.[51] After the draft was reviewed and approved by the principal legal advisor, it was passed to Churchill who, once again, was unwilling to comment and merely affixed his initials.[52] In early 1923, with only a few alterations, Byatt enacted the ordinance and Strachey sent copies to the PMC.[53] By 1925 local district officers were fully aware of the connection between Tanganyika's land legislation and the mandate and were using both to defend the land rights of the Wachagga in Moshi. The acting senior commissioner of the Moshi district, A. M. Clark, insisted that he was "convinced that the Government would be acting against the interests of the natives if any further alienation of land is permitted" and complained about Wachagga land that was being "exploited by European enterprise" by white settlers who seemed "quite oblivious to the fact that we had a mandate at all."[54]

Both the slavery ordinance of 1922 and the land legislation enacted the following year had a direct impact on Africans. While slavery as an institution had been in decline in East Africa since the late nineteenth century, British policy intensified the systematic pressure to end the practice.[55] The colonial state gradually managed to transform the remaining involuntary male slaves into either wage laborers or tenant farmers and peasant smallholders with greater autonomy.[56] While the survival of certain marriage customs and forms of "voluntary" servitude made it impossible for officials to claim that they had entirely "abolished" all forms of slavery during this period, the constraints of British slave law did alter the economic and cultural conditions of Africans living in the mandated territory. On Mafia island alone, some 1,225 men and 1,574 women severed their bonds with their masters in 1922 because of the Involuntary Servitude Ordinance.[57]

The impact of British land policy on Africans in the mandates was even more pronounced. By adopting land legislation based on Nigerian models, the Colonial Office distinguished Tanganyika from Kenya by actively discouraging European settlement to keep Tanganyika "primarily a Black man's country."[58] Under this legislation, the British alienated less than 400,000 hectares of land during the entire interwar period to bring the total to a peak of just over 1,150,000 hectares in 1937. While this total included some of the best land around Mt. Kilimanjaro, it accounted for only 1.31 percent of the country.[59] Even the British royal family was not exempt from this determination to limit land alienation. In late 1925, the private secretary to King George V, Lord Stamfordham, asked the Colonial Office if "one of the Princes" could purchase property in

Tanganyika since it "might be politically useful."[60] Strachey considered the suggestion ludicrous and remarked that "the special position of Tanganyika Territory as a Mandated Country (it is not a Colony, nor part of the British Empire) makes it very questionable whether the acquisition of property there by a British Prince would be politically advantageous."[61] The Colonial Office politely told Stamfordham that "we are inclined to deprecate" the offer.[62]

Rwanda and Religious Freedom

While mandates increasingly presented new limitations for British colonial administration in the early 1920s, they also created new opportunities. London's determination to draft slavery and land legislation demonstrated how international considerations, tied to the changing ideology of imperialism, served as a centralizing force that permitted the metropole to interfere more directly and consistently in local conditions. Yet, the same League system that forced colonial officials to adopt policies that were more restrained and internationally-oriented in the mandated territories also had important propaganda value and could even work to serve the traditional imperial priorities of the colonial state. For example, Byatt used the mandate principles to reject a request from the Bishop of Mombasa for government subsidies for his mission schools. Dar es Salaam argued that "in a territory governed under a Mandate," where there must be "equal treatment and equal opportunity for all nationalities," giving financial support to one mission would require similar support "to the educational efforts of all creeds, whether Catholic, Anglican, Non-Conformist, Mohamedan, Sikh, or Hindu."[63] The director of education in the Tanganyika Territory, Stanley Rivers-Smith, tried several times to expand his educational system by contending that "the education of the native is to be one of the first responsibilities of the Mandatory" and that League supervision dictated "a vigorous policy" that required more money from London.[64] The Colonial Office cited the mandate when it refused to grant a monopoly to the British East Africa Corporation to gin cotton in the Mwanza district of Tanganyika since such a monopoly would "keep down the price paid to the native grower" and restrict state trade and taxation revenues.[65] London also carefully edited the annual reports to the League and often changed or omitted passages from original drafts in an effort to control public information about the mandated territories.[66]

Still, the terminology and meaning of the mandates continued to press the guardians of the empire to reconsider old assumptions and new international conditions. When Geneva confirmed the mandates in July 1922, British colonial officials seriously debated abandoning the anomalous title of the "Tanganyika Territory" and formally converting the possession into the "Tanganyika Protectorate."[67] Once again, Strachey argued against the idea:

> Personally I doubt very much whether the advantages of such a course outweigh the possible disadvantages. It has generally been assumed by the public that Mandated territories form, and ought to form, a new kind of administration and will not become ordinary Protectorates. The French government have, I understand, taken this view as regards their shares of the Cameroons and Togoland, and even if the Protectorate were declared to be subject to the terms of the Mandate there would probably be a good deal of criticism, including some from the League of Nations.[68]

The name remained unchanged and the Tanganyika Territory joined the other B mandates in their peculiar place alongside the rest of the British Empire in Africa.

After the League's formal confirmation of the mandates in July 1922, the system was fully operational and the PMC could concentrate on prodding the mandatory powers to reform some of the more conspicuous examples of European imperial excess in Africa. One issue that particularly irritated Geneva was the Anglo-Belgian decision in 1919 to divide the African kingdom of Rwanda between British and Belgian mandatory rule. Lord Milner, the colonial secretary during the negotiations, had drawn the boundary to permit the eventual construction of a British "Cape-to-Cairo" railway through the region while the Belgian delegation, led by Pierre Orts, was interested in extending Belgium's African empire.[69] This apparent disregard for local African conditions appalled a number of the League's strongest supporters and remained a serious embarrassment for the PMC, particularly because Orts was now serving as the Belgian member of the commission. During its second session in August 1922, the PMC identified the partition of Rwanda as "the most important individual question" concerning the B mandates.[70] The PMC criticized the boundary as "hardly justifiable" in terms of the "well being, good order and political stability" of the local African community and, while admitting it had "no right to deal with the frontier question," asked Britain if it considered the boundary "gravely prejudicial to the welfare of the natives and likely to impede the progress of native civilization." Further, the members cited a local "neutral" missionary's report that detailed "the deplorable moral effect on the population of obliging the King of Rwanda to accept this arrangement." The PMC had chosen its first target well. Forcing the unification of Rwanda under a single colonial administration would not only enhance the League's reputation and demonstrate the power of international supervision, but would give the mandatory powers an opportunity to help repair the damaged image of European colonialism in Africa by seeming to place the priorities of colonized peoples above those of the colonial state. Further, unification could serve certain local African and European interests and create greater political stability in the ethnically fractious region.

The initial Colonial Office response to the PMC's criticism, however, was to suspect a Belgian plot and to dismiss the entire issue as being "outside their [the League's] province."[71] Both Eric Mächtig and Strachey read Belgium's annual report for the League without much comment and then sent a copy to Byatt.[72] It was not until the Belgian government, armed with the harsh criticisms of the PMC, combined with the arrival of Ormsby-Gore at the Colonial Office as the new parliamentary under-secretary, that British colonial officials were compelled to reconsider the revision of the Rwanda boundary. In early 1923 the Belgian chargé d'affaires asked the Foreign Office if he could meet with the colonial secretary, now the Duke of Devonshire, to "re-examine" the boundary question.[73] Strachey, worried about outside reactions if the issue became public, cautiously suggested dropping "the idea of the railway as a ruling factor" and opening new negotiations, but warned that this was "too complete a reversal of the policy of Lord Milner to be adopted without very serious consideration."[74] Both Read and the highest ranking permanent official, Sir James Masterton-Smith, advised that "we should go slow in this matter" since it could establish an uncomfortable precedent.[75]

Ormsby-Gore rejected this tepid advice and advocated speedy action. He argued that "I personally think the Belgians have a very good case [and] that we have a very weak one. The present boundary does divide the territory of the subjects of the Sultan of Ruanda [and] has caused him deep resentment." More importantly,

> I may say that the Permanent Mandates Commission were unanimous in their desire to urge a rectification of the boundary, but were most anxious not to do or say anything which might embarrass the British Govt. in the matter. As a procedure I suggest that the best 'face saving' device would be to get the Belgian Govt. to agree with the British Govt. to ask the Council of the League to appoint an independent investigator to visit the territory in dispute [and] report to the Council.[76]

The following day, Devonshire agreed to abandon all British demands concerning future railroad routes and to meet with the Belgians.[77]

While British and Belgian representatives began private negotiations to unite the kingdom of Rwanda by extending the border of the Belgian mandated territory eastward to the Kagera river, one member of the PMC used the threat of international criticism to goad the Colonial Office toward a quick agreement.[78] In April, Frederick Lugard decided to test his new authority as British member of the PMC by scolding British officials that "an injustice has been unwittingly done to the Native Kingdom of Rwanda by a partition which is opposed to the spirit of the Covenant."[79] He then began to badger his former colleagues with the threat of League disapproval:

> If, recognising the justice of modifying the present frontier, the British Government should see fit to take the initiative instead of awaiting any representations from the League of Nations, such a spontaneous recognition of the spirit of the Covenant would no doubt be very cordially welcomed in Belgium, and by the League of Nations.

Strachey, aware that formal Anglo-Belgian discussions had already started, suggested inviting Lugard to the Colonial Office to "tell him confidentially the present position of affairs."[80] Two weeks later, Strachey and Ormsby-Gore showed Lugard copies of the official correspondence with the Belgian government concerning the boundary changes.[81] Lugard was satisfied that the two sides were making a good-faith effort to "take the initiative" and stopped his threats. With the leading British member of the PMC fully informed and cooperative, London and Brussels decided that asking the League for an "independent investigator" was an unnecessary complication and formed a joint boundary commission in East Africa instead.[82] Still, the two governments were careful to request the Council of the League of Nations formally to amend the mandates according to an Anglo-Belgian recommendation.[83]

The PMC was pleased with the frontier revision and the explicit request to the Council, but Lugard and William Rappard, the Director of the League of Nations Mandates Section, still wanted more. Rappard wrote a private letter to Ormsby-Gore on 20 July, the opening day of the third session of the PMC, asking him to come to Geneva as the accredited British representative to defend the British annual reports for the B mandates and to make an official announcement.[84] Rappard argued that the boundary change "represents a signal success for the Mandates Commission" and "we are naturally very desirous that the announcement be made from Geneva." Lugard wrote a letter two days later making the same plea.[85] Ormsby-Gore acquiesced. On 1 August, he arrived in Geneva and told the PMC that the British and Belgian governments had responded to the League's criticisms and had agreed to alter the boundary accordingly.[86]

Ormsby-Gore's announcement, together with the request to the League a few days later, not only was a public-relations boon for Belgium, Britain, and especially the PMC, but had significance for East Africans. The British ambassador in Belgium complained that the Belgian press "seemed inclined to give all the credit for this arrangement to the League of Nations and to the Belgian officials who were at Geneva."[87] London quickly published the correspondence surrounding the boundary change as a command paper in order to get full credit for its sacrifice in "the interests of the inhabitants."[88] Lord Robert Cecil, still president of the League of Nations Union and now a member of Baldwin's Cabinet, publicly exclaimed that the boundary revision was "an excellent example of the value of the Permanent Mandates Commission" and "brought about an agreement which would undoubtedly be to the advantage of the native inhabitants of the two territories."[89]

These "advantages," however, were decidedly mixed. On 31 December 1923, British officials in Tanganyika began transferring to Belgian control a region of approximately 4,000 square miles comprising nearly one-half million Africans.[90] While this transfer reunified an ethnic community formerly under the consolidated rule of Musinga, King of Rwanda, and forms an area that is nearly one quarter of the present independent state of Rwanda, the indigenous population had to confront a colonial regime that was tied to the Belgian Congo administration and was adept at using local ethnic divisions to its advantage.[91] The Belgians, placing a high priority on mineral development and palm-oil production, were less interested in creating the form of political structures that marked much of British Africa. While one recent historian has suggested that international supervision did inspire certain reforms in the Belgian mandate, it still was placed under the control of a vice-governor-general who was responsible to the regime in Léopoldville, which often treated the region as a vast labor reserve for the mines and plantations in the Belgian Congo.[92]

The conclusion of the Rwanda border dispute depended as much on formal and informal pressure from the League as it did on the recognition by the mandatory powers that close cooperation with Geneva served a number of national and imperial interests. During this period, the PMC found that its ability to exert its influence over British policy in the mandates steadily increased not only because of Rappard's and Lugard's public and private activities in the service of the League, but also because the Colonial Office was willing to support Geneva's agenda of progressive reform and establish strong working relations with the PMC. Through "semi-official" communications, the Colonial Office supplied the PMC with information and resolved misunderstandings before they became public conflicts.[93] Colonial officials decided "on grounds of general policy to let the P.M.C. have [published] documents gratis which relate to the administration of mandated territories" in addition to the required annual reports.[94] London also made sure that Lugard knew about the continuing public activities of Dr Heinrich Schnee and other German colonial propagandists.[95] In return, both Rappard and Lugard kept the Foreign Office informed of unofficial "conversations" with German officials in Geneva, particularly a meeting in September 1923 between Rappard and Dr Julius Ruppel, a *ministerialdirektor* in the

German Foreign Office and an active member of the German colonial movement.[96]

In 1923 Lugard joined the Colonial Office's "Advisory Committee on Education in Tropical Africa" which brought him into direct contact with colonial-policy-makers and gave him the power to help shape educational policy not only in the mandated territories, but throughout British Africa.[97] Lugard also insisted on privately offering his unsolicited advice to reform a number of policies affecting British administration in the B mandates.[98] On at least one occasion during this period, Lugard met with the under-secretary of state to discuss land legislation in the mandates. According to one colonial official:

> Later he [Lugard] asked whether we would let him have a set of the Nigerian Laws, the Gold Coast Laws [and] Tanganyika Laws. A set of each is being sent to Geneva but Sir F. Lugard pointed out that it would be most useful to him to have a set of each for his own use as whenever a question affecting British Mandated Territory arises on the P.M.C. the other members looked to him for information. I think we might send him a set of each, if available, with compliments.[99]

The rest of the office agreed.[100] In late 1924 Lugard even offered advice on foreign policy by writing to Austen Chamberlain, the foreign minister, expressing his views on the impact of colonialism on Anglo-German relations. Lugard suggested expanding Germany's commercial access to the mandates and letting German nationals purchase property in all of their former colonies. According to Lugard, this change would ease Anglo-German tensions while working to strengthen the local economies.[101] Chamberlain remained skeptical.[102] Still, through these various informal channels, the members of the PMC had contacts and access to much more information than they could often admit. Further, the leading members of the PMC were able to operate on several different levels at the same time and use a wide range of techniques to internationalize and reform colonial policy in the mandated territories that went far beyond those specifically contained in the commission's constitution.

Perhaps the most effective way that the PMC increased its influence during these early years was the threat rather than the actual use of international criticism. As colonial officials discovered that Geneva would rely on public condemnation only as a last resort and genuinely wanted to cooperate with the mandatory powers to reform imperialism gradually, they learned to consider their international obligations before adopting a controversial policy. One such example was when Byatt asked to copy a practice adopted in Kenya and elsewhere that created separate "spheres of influence" for religious missions in Tanganyika in order to end the "religious jealousy and bitterness" between competing Protestant and

Roman Catholic groups. Byatt was aware that the subject was "one of no small difficulty and delicacy, more so perhaps in a mandated Territory than in a Colony where Sovereign rights exist," but he insisted that "the mandatory could not be held to contravene Article 8 were it to accord complete religious freedom within such limitations as would ensure the continuance of peace, good order, and goodwill."[103] Ormsby-Gore immediately objected:

> I see great difficulties in this. Of the nine members of the Permanent Mandates Commission five are Roman Catholics. My suggestion is that the Governor should include a chapter in his 1922 report on Tanganyika prepared for the League on the difficulties that have arisen and should make the suggestion embodied in this dispatch. The representative of the British Govt. could then take the matter up at Geneva this July. I doubt the Vatican giving way in a mandated territory . . . [104]

Ormsby-Gore, worried that Byatt's proposal violated the religious freedom clauses of the mandate, wanted to secure the approval of the PMC before provoking international criticism. The governor was forced to accept this decision and rewrite his annual report in order to point out that a "spirit of jealous rivalry and intolerance" among missionaries was causing an "undignified scramble" which made separate spheres necessary.[105] Still, Dar es Salaam did not commit itself to segregation and left itself room to retreat if Geneva protested. Mächtig was pleased that Byatt had followed the Colonial Office's instructions, but remarked that "I don't think that the trenchant paragraphs forwarded herewith will do at all for inclusion in the Report to the League of Nations: it would be likely to give offence all round."[106] Strachey and Read agreed and entirely rewrote the passages to eliminate almost all of Byatt's strong wording. The final version contained the essence of the governor's proposal, but hinted limply that it "might be adopted with general benefit."[107]

The reaction to the published annual report was swift. Despite a much softer tone and far more hesitant call for separation, the powerful Conference of Missionary Societies, based in London and representing a number of international Protestant groups, delivered a sharp protest to the Colonial Office. J. H. Oldham, the secretary of the Conference, was only moderately pacified when the Colonial Office told him that "the inconvenient zeal of certain Roman Catholic missionaries" was the cause of all the trouble.[108] The PMC was even less pleased. While Lugard expressed some sympathy for Byatt's idea, most of the other members would not accept the argument that the Roman Catholics posed a serious threat to the "public order and good government" of the mandated territory.[109]

While the PMC refused to comment on hypothetical policies or explicitly instruct British officials on how to resolve their difficulties, it easily convinced the Council of the League of Nations to accept its general "observation" that unwarranted restrictions on the freedom of missionaries was "contrary to the terms of the mandate."[110]

Geneva's cautious reaction matched London's purposeful hints and both sides achieved their desired results without an open clash. The Colonial Office, now aware of how contentious Byatt's plans would be if carried out, told Dar es Salaam and the governments responsible for the other British B mandates that "a system of spheres of missionary influence is not practicable" and issued instructions not to segregate any religious groups.[111] Without overt restrictions, Protestant and Roman Catholic missions continued to multiply and compete with one another in Tanganyika, often leaving local colonial administrators and African communities caught in the middle.[112] While the colonial state was able to exert some control over missionaries and mission schools after 1925 by instituting restrictions such as tying grants-in-aid to minimum teacher qualifications, colonial officials were still contending with disruptive interdenominational rivalries in Tanganyika more than ten years later.[113]

Cooperating with Geneva and considering the international implications of colonial policy eventually became routine for the Colonial Office. While Nigeria and Gold Coast administered Cameroon and Togo respectively, the Colonial Office was careful to adopt special machinery for legislating in the two mandated territories that "implied neither fusion nor incorporation" in order to avoid accusations of annexation.[114] This distinct legal foundation, combined with the yearly requirement to provide specific information on the two territories, gave the League just enough latitude to remind London of the international status of the mandates.[115] When officials suggested "deleting complaints about the Anglo-French boundary" from the annual report on Cameroon, it was Ormsby-Gore who insisted that the report should be accurate even if it raised embarrassing problems:

> This is a matter of grave importance. I see no reason why the report should not state the facts i.e. that the boundary does ignore tribal boundaries. I would merely tone down the adjectives and adverbs, and otherwise leave the report as it is.[116]

Ormsby-Gore was similarly adamant in rejecting Byatt's draft "Masters and Servants Ordinance" which allowed employers to fine Africans who "without reasonable cause" failed to appear for work:

> If we fail to get [a] satisfactory amendment I would suggest disallowing or suspending [the] ordinance until we have explained fully in [a] dispatch to the Governor that not even in a Colony but especially in Mandated

> Territory is it possible to make every employer of labor a judge in his own case. The Gov[ernor's] proposal is really indefensible.[117]

Byatt agreed to drop the provision of the ordinance that provided the legal sanction to punish laborers for deserting work, a common form of African protest against poor working conditions or inadequate pay.[118] After the PMC issued its third official report in late 1923, Walter Ellis, an assistant secretary in the West Africa Department, asked if "Mr. Ormsby-Gore would preside over a meeting of Heads of Depts. concerned with mandated territories to discuss what we are to do about their [the PMC's] recommendations."[119] The under-secretary readily agreed not only because he wanted to coordinate Britain's official responses to the League, but because he and the rest of the office were annoyed that Geneva had publicly praised the French annual reports for being more detailed and better organized than the British.[120] After reviewing the French reports, London distributed copies to Nigeria, Gold Coast, and Tanganyika with instructions to use them as models and increase the amount of information sent to Geneva.[121]

Military Recruitment and Africans

Yet even Ormsby-Gore's desire to avoid international criticism had its limits. At the same session at which the PMC expressed its delight over the reunification of the kingdom of Rwanda, the members recorded their distinct displeasure with the military recruitment practices in the B mandates. In its final report to the Council of the League of Nations, the PMC stated:

> The Commission was unanimously of the opinion that the spirit, if not the letter, of the mandate would be violated if the Mandatory enlists the natives of the Mandated Territory (wherever they may present themselves for engagement) for service in any military corps or body of constabulary which is not permanently quartered in the territory and not used solely for its defence or the preservation of order within it . . . [122]

It was not enough to forbid Africans who lived in the mandated territories from joining any military unit that might serve outside of the mandate. The PMC wanted to prevent the mandatory powers from recruiting Africans originally from Togo, Cameroon, or Tanganyika even if they crossed the border into a British colony to enlist. The members of the Commission, including Lugard, realized that mandatory powers could easily circumvent the military restrictions and had to accept the League's broad interpretation of the clauses in order to make them more effective.

This was especially true in West Africa where Africans living in the smallest mandated territories were vulnerable to exploitation by European recruiters. Ormsby-Gore's public response was quick and to the point. The former British member of the PMC said that he was "unable to accept the view" of the Commission which only had supervisory powers over the administration of mandated territories.

> To prohibit Mandatory Powers from employing a native of its mandated territory as a soldier if he applies for enlistment when outside that territory is to impose a disability upon the natives of the territory and to deny the essential rights of the Mandatory Power within its own Territory.[123]

Privately, officials in the Colonial Office were furious and decided that the PMC had gone too far. Mächtig called the commission's definition of the military clauses of the mandate a violation of Britain's "sovereign rights" and insisted that it should be opposed "as a matter of principle."[124] Yet, he admitted that more than a "matter of principle" was at stake since the Kenya battalion of the King's African Rifles had a history of recruiting "a considerable body of immigrants from the Tabora district of Tanganyika."

Harding drafted an "urgent" dispatch to the Foreign Office informing them that Devonshire "entirely agrees with Mr. Ormsby-Gore" and requesting that the British representatives to the League "take the same line when the point comes before the Council."[125] Mächtig complained directly to a British official in Geneva that the commission "have traveled outside their province" and expressed his dismay that Lugard had made the PMC view unanimous.[126] In late September, the standoff between the Colonial Office and the PMC forced the Council of the League to decide that "the matter should be further discussed between the Mandates Commission and the British Government, in the hope that agreement may be reached next year."[127] On 11 January 1924, Ormsby-Gore presided over a special meeting held in the Colonial Office to discuss the problem. He remained resolute and pledged that he would not give in to the PMC.[128]

A dramatic change in domestic politics prevented this impending confrontation between Britain and the League. A few days after Ormsby-Gore's final decision to stand firm against reform, the Labour and Liberal members of parliament combined to defeat the Conservative government led by Baldwin. The prime minister resigned, taking Devonshire and Ormsby-Gore with him. The King asked Ramsay MacDonald to form the first Labour government, with Liberal support. The new colonial secretary, James H. Thomas, had been an active union leader before entering Parliament as a Labour MP in 1910. His parliamentary under-secretary, Sydney Arnold, was a committed pacifist who had left the Liberals in 1922 to join the Labour party. In order to satisfy constitutional criteria, MacDonald made Arnold a peer.

While Thomas and Lord Arnold had no direct experience in colonial administration and were primarily concerned with domestic problems, they did share some common perceptions of British imperialism.[129] Both considered themselves anti-imperialists and along with men such as Leonard Woolf, Charles Roden Buxton, and E. D. Morel, represented the large moderate center of the party which fully embraced the Lugardian system of Indirect Rule, the principle of "trusteeship," and the role of international supervision in promoting progressive colonial reform. These assumptions mixed easily with the evolving postwar ideology of imperialism within the Colonial Office, where many permanent senior officials like Strachey were already treating the mandates differently from other colonial possessions. In the first days of the new government, Strachey produced a six-page "note" for Thomas and Arnold that explained the mandates system and how Tanganyika was "not, strictly speaking, a part of the British Empire. It is neither a Colony nor a Protectorate."[130] He also reminded his chiefs that "the very basis of the policy" in Tanganyika was that "the interests of the natives are the principal concern of the government."[131] From the start, Labour had no desire to provoke Geneva or undermine the mandates system. If anything, the new government was eager to demonstrate its support for the system by defending it more energetically than the outgoing Tories.

The controversy surrounding the question of military recruitment gave Labour an opportunity not only to reinforce the principles of the mandates system, but to prompt the reform of other colonial regimes in Africa at the same time. With the next meeting of the PMC only a few weeks away, Arnold asked Harding if British acceptance of the PMC's interpretation of the military clauses of the mandate would force France to do the same. Harding vigorously tried to convince Arnold that it would not and that Ormsby-Gore's previous policy was the only possible response to Geneva. In a minute that filled over twelve typed pages, he asserted that

> [h]owever we may bind ourselves not to recruit outside mandated territory, the French are not likely to bind themselves similarly, and as they have a representative on the Council of the League, they can prevent the Council from saying that they ought to do so . . . If we want to keep the French to the terms of their mandates, we should weaken our position by agreeing to submit for ourselves to something which the terms of our mandates do not justify. If we stick closely to the terms of our mandates and refuse to go beyond them, we shall be in a far better position to tell the French that they too must observe the terms of their mandates. Otherwise the French will say that they can attach no value to our interpretation of their mandates since we have shown by our acceptance of the absurd interpretation of our

> mandates which the Permanent Mandates Commission has put forward that we are incapable of correctly interpreting the terms of the mandates.[132]

Harding had wasted his time. After a private discussion with Thomas in early May, Arnold instructed the West Africa Department "to give way to the view of the P.M.C." and to ask the Foreign Office to inform the League of this decision before the PMC drafted the agenda for its June meeting.[133] Arnold also ordered the office to tell "the governors concerned" of the new policy which meant that in addition to Nigeria, Gold Coast, and Tanganyika, "Kenya and Nyasaland will have to be told also not to recruit T.T. natives in the K.A.R." The following week, Read sent a private note to Lugard to tell him that, even though the question "presents considerable difficulties," the British government had decided "to fall in with the views expressed by the Permanent Mandates Commission." Read then invited Lugard to meet Arnold at the Colonial Office to discuss "any question arising out of the last report" before the commission convened the following month.[134]

While Arnold may have thought that the administration of mandated territories in Africa was a matter for the Colonial Office alone, officials in the Foreign Office did not. They refused to inform the League of any change in recruitment policy until the Colonial Office secured the approval of the War Office.[135] Arnold was furious and on 29 May he telephoned one Foreign Office official "at great length and asperity" and insisted that Britain was adopting the new policy primarily "in order to be able to bring an end to the activities of the French who, in the furtherance of their policy of building up a vast army, are recruiting every native they can lay their hands on." He went on to declare that the decision was "of no interest to the War Office" and should be sent on to Geneva "without further ado."[136] The Foreign Office refused to budge. Sir Eyre Crowe, the permanent under-secretary of state for foreign affairs, appealed to MacDonald, who was serving as both prime minister and foreign secretary, for "higher authority" since "it is not the Colonial Office but the Foreign Secretary who has to bear the responsibility for what we say to the League."[137] MacDonald offered a convoluted response that ended with a vague indication – "I understand the matter is now settled," – but did not say how.[138] In early June, Arnold met Arthur Ponsonby, the under-secretary for foreign affairs, and urged him to leave the War Office out.[139] Crowe was now thoroughly confused and wrote to Ponsonby.

> I remain puzzled, and really do not know what to do. I gathered from the Prime Minister's minute that he had settled the matter with Lord Arnold but in what sense? Are we to write to the League as Colonial Office propose, or not?[140]

On 4 June, Ponsonby reported that Arnold and MacDonald had agreed to ignore the military authorities and to inform the League of the Colonial Office decision immediately.[141] Within hours, the Foreign Office dispatch was on its way to Geneva.[142] London's surrender had immediate results. The PMC was pleased and expressed its "special satisfaction" with the British government during the opening public meeting of the Commission.[143] Back in London, however, the mood in the Colonial Office was surly. Harding wondered if the new policy included the police forces because, if so, it would only add to "the legal tangle Nigeria has got itself into applying the Nig[erian] laws to the Br[itish] Sphere of the Cameroons."[144] Even Strachey was in no mood to discuss the larger implications of the decision. He grumbled:

> I should prefer to say nothing about the police in Tanganyika. It is true that they are armed, but because we have done more than we are required by the Mandate to do in the case of soldiers, it does not follow that we should do so in the case of police.[145]

The military authorities were much more annoyed. The Admiralty did not even hear of the policy until after the fragile Labour government had been defeated in parliament and MacDonald called for a general election in October.[146] After failing to convince the new Conservative government to reverse the decision, the Admiralty informed the Foreign Office that it had reluctantly issued orders that "the entry of natives from Tanganyika and the British parts of Togoland and Cameroons, for employment on H.M. Ships, is not to be accepted." This note to the Foreign Office ended with the admonition: "I am to add that Their Lordships would be glad to be consulted should the question of further limitation of employment of natives in the Armed Forces of the Crown be raised."[147]

Once again, the local administrations in the British mandated territories had to carry out this policy decision from the metropole.[148] While the governors of Nigeria and Gold Coast did not formally protest the changed policy in military recruitment and never reported any infractions, it was difficult to enforce in the best of circumstances. In Tanganyika, the British authorities promised that the Sixth battalion of the King's African Rifles (KAR), stationed in Dar es Salaam, would recruit local Africans who would not serve outside mandated territory.[149] For the rest of the decade, the Committee of Imperial Defense excluded the Sixth battalion from its calculations for defending British interests in India, the Middle East, and other parts of East Africa.[150] Brigadier G. H. Cree, a British officer serving in the Sixth battalion in the 1930s, recorded that the mandate limited his unit to internal work including road repair, famine relief, anti-locust work, and guarding tax defaulters.[151] Further, the Sixth never recruited or served in Zanzibar.[152] The British had to move the Second battalion of the

KAR, originally stationed in Nyasaland and composed only of Africans from that protectorate, to Tabora in central Tanganyika, but made Dar es Salaam responsible for its expenses.[153] This battalion was eligible for service outside Tanganyika if necessary. Tabora was a strategically located administrative and trading center and was the home of the Nyamwezi, one of the largest African ethnic groups recruited into the German military before and during the war.[154] While the Sixth included Nyamwezi, British commanders as late as 1939 insisted that the Second did not. Officers in the Second complained about the long distances that they had to travel in order to relieve the troops in Tabora and noted that Africans in the Second had longer tours of duty than those in other KAR battalions.[155]

British recruitment policies in Togo, Cameroon, and Tanganyika had political, cultural, and economic importance for Africans living in those mandated territories. Since local colonial officials had to justify their budgets and explain expenditures on the military to the League, they found that decreasing the number of Africans in the armed services was an easy way to save money and avoid accusations of "militarism" by the international community. While service in a colonial army was somtimes harsh, dangerous, and highly disruptive to the local cultural and political relations within some African communities, the military also provided one of the few means open to Africans to engage the structures of control and hierarchy within the colonial state. Service in the armed forces offered comparatively high pay, an escape from taxation, the promise of a pension or certain political rewards for extended service, a degree of prestige, meat and better food, and a chance to exercise a form of state-sanctioned power that Africans outside of the army or police did not have. In Tanganyika, the government officially maintained a total military force of only eighteen thousand "black soldiers," which was nearly 30 percent less than the Germans employed in 1914.[156] While the German figure reflects all of German East Africa before partition, half the British troops reportedly came from Nyasaland, effectively making the number of Africans from Tanganyika in the military only about nine hundred.

The British also dramatically decreased the size of the African police force by nearly one thousand men, claiming that this was more in line with the less obtrusive style of British policing, and conforming to the spirit of the military clauses of the mandate.[157] A circuit judge in Tanganyika in the early 1920s asserted that some Africans resented having fewer opportunities to join the armed services and police, particularly those unemployed veterans from the German colonial army who had lost power and prestige under British rule. He suggested that a few of these frustrated Africans, even when employed in other capacities for the colonial state, were responsible for a number of the more brutal crimes in the territory and posed a serious danger to public safety and order.[158] In British

Cameroon, one colonial administrator, Bryan Sharwood Smith, was sure that the removal of the battalion of the West African Frontier Force (WAFF) from Bamenda in 1924 was the cause of several "disturbances" in some of the outlying areas that were only quelled after a number of "skirmishes" with police.[159] Smith blamed the PMC:

> The departure of the troops from Bamenda was, before long, to cause trouble. They had withdrawn, not because the British administration thought that it could do without them, but because 'wise men' at League of Nations headquarters at Geneva felt that a military garrison in mandated territory was inappropriate, especially as the Bamenda people, who made very good soldiers, were enlisting in the Nigeria Regiment in considerable number. We who had the task of bringing under control the turbulent foothill people, whom even the Germans had never succeeded in weaning from their lawless ways, found it difficult to appreciate the force of these arguments.[160]

Police killed at least four Africans and arrested dozens more during this expedition to re-establish British control after the departure of the WAFF Smith had to use "special magisterial powers to try as many persons as the police could lay their hands upon from the long list of those wanted for homicide, arson, wounding, robbery with violence, slave-dealing, and other serious crimes."[161] Caught between theory and practice, Africans and Europeans found that fulfilling the wishes of the League of Nations had an often perplexing mix of beneficial and detrimental implications.

Cameron, Indians, and White Settlers

While many colonial officials in Europe and Africa, either by choice or coercion, had to take the mandates system seriously after 1921, perhaps the one who did so the most was Byatt's replacement as governor of Tanganyika in 1925, Sir Donald Cameron.[162] Cameron had demonstrated remarkable administrative skills during his eleven years in Nigeria during Lugard's governor-generalship. As the chief secretary in Lagos from 1921 to 1924 he was responsible for the administration of British Cameroon and oversaw the preparation of the annual reports to the League.[163] He was an outspoken proponent of the "progressive" doctrine of Indirect Rule and was the Labour government's choice in 1924 to govern Britain's most important mandated territory in Africa.[164] While Byatt had taken a few preliminary steps toward establishing Indirect Rule in Tanganyika, Cameron pushed the policy with an intensity that verged on obsession.[165] He argued that the Lugardian model as practiced in Nigeria contained a number of serious flaws that his own system of "Native Administration" would fix. In his campaign to bring his version of "guardianship" and

African self-government to Tanganyika, Cameron never failed to appeal to the mandates system to defend his policies. Even years later in retirement, he wrote:

> Let me revert to what I have described as the primary factor; the primary factor that the guardianship is not a permanent and absolute one and is to be exercised only until the people 'can stand by themselves.' That being so, it is clearly, I submit, the duty of the Mandatory Power to train the people so that they may stand by themselves . . .

Anything less would mean allowing "our obligations under the Covenant to go by default; a policy which no British Government would care to declare to the world."[166]

These were not empty words for Cameron. He was convinced that the theories of the mandates system reflected the best practices of British colonial administration and that he needed both to ensure the success of his political reforms. He also had convinced himself by early 1925 that he faced determined enemies in the Colonial Office and in East Africa, particularly after the new Conservative colonial secretary, Leo Amery, appointed Sir Edward Grigg governor of Kenya in order to defend the interests of the local white settlers.[167] In an effort to circumvent these enemies, Cameron enlisted a number of allies, the most important being his old chief and current British member of the PMC. Two months after arriving in Dar es Salaam, Cameron wrote privately to Lugard that:

> I am at present not happy about the future of the country [Tanganyika] because I see all round me this dreadful spirit which places the economic development of the country before everything else . . . The paramount interest to me is the welfare *and future* of the people and economic development must be slightly behind the former problem and not far in advance of it.

He went on to complain that "we are leaving people to die from famine" by training Africans to grow cotton instead of "food crops." Cameron argued that "the biggest problem of all" was determining the place that the African would take in the political future of "what is, after all, his own country." He ended the letter with a request. "I wonder if you could, gently and without their perceiving it, influence the view of the Mandates Commission to turn in this direction of the political future of the people."[168]

Before the year was out, Cameron and Lugard were carrying on an increasingly candid correspondence concerning the Colonial Office, the mandates system, and informal cooperation. In October, Cameron asked Lugard to keep their exchanges to himself and not mention them to any of the officials in the Colonial Office.[169] He also let Lugard know that the Colonial Office was restricting his access to information from Geneva by not sending him PMC documents:

> Will you please help me in the following. You write that I will see in the Minutes of the Mandates Commission so-and-so. I have not received them although the Editor of the weekly rag published here has had them direct from the League Secretariat for weeks. It is shameful that the C.O. should keep them back from me in this manner and I trust that you will recollect the incident when the Commission meets again.

The following month, Cameron was still complaining to Lugard about not having enough copies of the minutes of the PMC.[170]

The governor also began a practice of privately consulting Lugard on a few policy questions, which strengthened their productive alliance. In November 1924 Cameron noted: "it seems rather ridiculous to keep the King's head off the stamps because we are Mandated territory. What do you think?"[171] When Lugard did not protest, Cameron successfully pressed the Colonial Office to adopt the change and the PMC did not complain since the new stamps still bore the phrase "Mandated Territory of Tanganyika."[172] For Cameron, Lugard was someone who could exert influence in London and Geneva as well as protect and strengthen the governor's agenda for Tanganyika. For Lugard, Cameron was another inside source of information about mandatory administration and an effective collaborator in his own campaign to press for gradual reforms and a pragmatic paternalism in Africa. This relationship tied the League of Nations even more tightly to the larger imperial structure and was a symbol of the subtle way that the mandates system contributed to the changing face of European colonialism.

In addition to men like Cameron and Lugard, this larger imperial structure also included other groups outside of the colonial bureaucracies and Geneva whose lives were shaped by the mandates system and tried to use it to recast their position within the colonial system. In Tanganyika, one group that had some success in exploiting the force of international supervision was the Asian merchant class. Since India was a signatory of the Treaty of Versailles and the stipulations of the B mandates safeguarded commercial equality, immigration, and religious freedom, the Asian population of the mandated territory dramatically increased during the 1920s.[173] Throughout this period, Asian leaders cited the mandate and threatened to complain to the League of Nations in order to combat perceived examples of discrimination in Tanganyika. In 1921 the Indians Overseas Association, based in London, accused the governor of slighting a deputation of local Indians, which was "particularly unjustified in regard to a community whose members belong to a country that is an equal Member of the League."[174] A few months later, the same association successfully forced Dar es Salaam to end racial segregation in railroad travel in Tanganyika by insisting that the policy was a blatant violation of the mandate.[175] In early 1923 the Indian Association, the largest organization of Asian merchants and professionals in Dar es Salaam and with branches throughout Tanganyika, relied on formal protests addressed to the League of Nations combined with widespread shop closings to resist a tax ordinance that seemed to discriminate against Asians.[176] Colonial officials in London did not want to send the protest to Geneva since it did not meet all the specific definitions of a "petition."[177] Ormsby-Gore overruled his permanent officials:

> It is clearly contemplated by the Mandatory system that aggrieved persons have a right to petition the League through the Mandatory power on a question such as this, and as the exact procedure decided by the Council of the League has probably not yet been communicated to the Indian Association in Tanganyika I don't think we should be meticulous but we should forward the petition with our reply and such of the Governor's observations as we think necessary to the Governor General.[178]

The petition went to Geneva and after a series of similar complaints from the Indian Association, including angry threats from the Indian Legislative Assembly in India "to seek immediate redress" before the Council of the League for "Indians in mandated territories, especially Tanganyika," Cameron finally abolished the offending tax ordinance in April 1927.[179]

In addition to Asians, white settlers were subject to the internationalization and reformation of European imperialism and tried to use the mandates system against the colonial state. Instead of calling on the international status of Tanganyika as a source of protection, however, local Europeans tried to use its ambiguities as means for gaining the sympathy of political leaders in Britain. A number of settlers hated the mandate and wanted to rid themselves of it. A few weeks after the Conservative electoral victory in late 1924, a group of settlers calling themselves the "Arusha Conservative Association" wrote a letter to Prime Minister Baldwin demanding that he immediately transfer northern Tanganyika, including Arusha, to neighboring Kenya.[180] In the letter, bearing the commemorative date of 11 November, the association called the mandates system a bitter betrayal of the heroes of the Great War that cruelly cut them off from the British Empire:

> We do not belong to that glorious Empire of which we are so proud, and for which every member of the Association fought during the late War. We are political outcasts belonging to no country, with no voice in the conduct of our affairs, ruled as we are by the League of Nations. Our children are destined to grow up without nationality or patriotism. Never before has a

> European population been placed in such an ignominious position.

The association attached additional papers listing all of their problems including the fear that the League might eventually hand Tanganyika over to Germany, the contention that the economic development of Tanganyika was suffering, and the claim that "owing to mistrust of the future new capital is scared away." The members insisted, however, that they had no complaints with the local British colonial administration "which has helped us in every way as far as the Mandatory policy allows."

The association was largely met with ridicule in the Colonial Office. Strachey described the complaint as "mostly tosh."[181] A second official, H. F. Downie, exposed how much the Colonial Office had come to consider mandates as distinct from other British possessions when he minuted:

> Even if the Northern part of T.T. were to be administered as part of Kenya it would still be administered as mandated territory and the settlers of Arusha would not be relieved of the disabilities (real or imaginary) referred to in this letter.[182]

Only Amery took the protest seriously. The next summer he tried to put the settlers at ease by announcing that Tanganyika was "essentially a part of the British framework, as any other protectorate." This awkward phrase, however, only angered the German colonial movement, alarmed British imperialists, and made the settlers even more irritated with the mandate.[183]

"Mandated Territory and League of Nations Stupidities"

One of the more revealing assessments of the impact of the League on British colonialism during these first years after the war came from Sir Hugh Clifford. As governor of Nigeria, he was responsible for the administration of British Cameroon. In a private letter to his friend William Gowers, one of Nigeria's lieutenant-governors, Clifford not only expressed a deep resentment at having to remain under Lugard's influence, but painted himself as part of the newer generation of reformed colonial rulers in Africa that did not need the League. Still, the governor exposed a realization that Geneva had a direct impact on his administration and could not be ignored. In explaining why he could not allow a subordinate, John Thomlinson, to leave Lagos and serve under Gowers in the southern provinces, Clifford wrote:

> I have given your request for Thomlinson the most careful consideration and much regret that I cannot comply with it. At the moment, and for some time to come, we cannot spare him, as he is required here at Lagos in connection with Mandated Territory and League of Nations stupidities which despite their folly, have to be treated seriously. (To me, the idea of Lugard, blood-stained to the collar-stud with the slaughtered Hadeijas and Egbas, colloguing with two similarly empurpled ex-tyrants both recently emerged the one from the Portuguese, the other from a French tropical shambles, and subjecting honest John Tomlinson to a cross-examination of seven mortal hours' duration, [as accredited representative before the PMC] with the amiable object of discovering some hint of maladministration on my part in the Mandated Area of the Cameroons, would be comic if it were not so blazingly indecent).[184]

The years between 1921 and 1925 marked an important transition period for both the mandates system and European imperialism in Africa. The PMC made the difficult transformation from an idea into an entity and Britain gradually incorporated an international organization into its vast colonial system. Mandates symbolized the changing nature of European imperialism and made their own contribution to that complex change. The leading members of the PMC succeeded in building a variety of mutually beneficial alliances that gave the League a great deal of formal and informal power. By 1925 the mandates system had fully internationalized and institutionalized the principle of trusteeship and had altered the lives of Europeans and Africans on every level of the imperial hierarchy. As the British imperial structure slowly absorbed the mission and language of the mandates, it made internationalization and reform more a matter of practice than theory.

By the time Germany joined the League of Nations in 1926, the mandates system had penetrated deeply into the British culture of colonialism as individuals such as Strachey, Byatt, Wood, Ormsby-Gore, Lugard, Arnold, Cameron, and others saw in mandates something more than a propaganda opportunity. Together, they ensured that the League would have an economic, political, and cultural impact on Africans living in the mandated territories. Despite sometimes widely differing motivations, the British imperial ideology and the ideals of mandatory administration were becoming fused. Defending one meant supporting the other, even if this meant assuming restraints on colonial power, accepting unwanted advice and seemingly wasteful procedures, or implementing reforms that had highly ambiguous or paradoxical results. Mandates were emblems of Britain's reputation as an imperial power and an expression of the promise to promote the evolution of Africa while preserving the new global order. For the rest of the decade, Germany was determined to participate in this system and test all of these assumptions.

6

The French Mandates between Theory and Practice, 1921–1925

Geneva's participation in European imperialism in Africa had a different meaning for France. While Britain often came to view mandates as an opportunity to demonstrate the value and vitality of empire, France generally considered them a serious disruption to the imperial structure that required substantial changes in how France exercised colonial power in the empire. Obliged to accept both League supervision and British notions of "trusteeship," French colonial officials often saw the mandates system as a paradoxical force that they had to approach with caution. In some ways, the mandates helped to insulate the empire and deflected charges of "annexation" and "militarism" from the outside that threatened to undermine France's colonial legitimacy. At the same time, however, mandates forced a re-examination of the psychological underpinnings of French colonialism and placed new limitations on the administration of the mandated territories that directly impinged on the lives of Africans. Further, in contrast to the British, on the complex level of engagement between European and African colonial institutions, African elites more effectively used the League of Nations and the international character of the mandates to confront the authority of the colonial state and exposed France to the dangers of the League's brand of internationalism and reform. These Africans attempted to reorder their position within colonial society by appealing to the potential for international criticism that constituted the ultimate power behind the mandates system.

"Separate and Autonomous"

One African, Blaise Diagne, understood this power better than many and did not hesitate to use it in his campaign to reform French imperialism. Diagne, the deputy from Senegal and the first full-blooded African elected to the National Assembly, was dedicated to securing greater political and economic rights for Africans.[1] In particular, he wanted to reform the highly controversial "indigénat" code, the comprehensive set of violations and penalties that since 1887 had formed the basis of most French colonial law. The *indigénat* was a restrictive and often arbitrary legal regime imposed on the vast majority of Africans who French colonial officials did not consider "assimilated" into European law and customs. After the First World War, Diagne enjoyed widespread popularity in France for his success in recruiting Africans for the war effort and was serving as the chairman of the influential Committee on Colonies in the Chamber.

In November 1920, he sent a letter to Colonial Minister Albert Sarraut to protest the extension of French West Africa's judicial system to Togo. In what must have annoyed dedicated officials in the Colonial Ministry, Diagne insisted that "the intellectual, moral and social level of the natives of Togo, on the whole, is higher than those in the neighboring colonies." For this reason, he argued that these Africans, many of whom had strong ties to those living in British Togo, would reject as "totally foreign" the same legal structure in place in other French colonies and would actively resist having to accept "similar treatment." If the laws governing the courts were not significantly "modified" to fit local conditions, Diagne warned that the Togolese would "make their protests known to the League of Nations" and, "perhaps under pressure from the British," would eventually demand a plebiscite.[2] By bringing together the various potential threats of political protest on the ground, international criticism in Geneva, and British agitation for control of Togo, Diagne was hoping to chip away some of the power of the *indigénat* in French Africa by increasing the number of Africans subject to a less restrictive form. The proposal did not convince Sarraut, who in November 1920 was still attempting to avoid League supervision altogether and chose to ignore Diagne's suggestion.[3]

Once France formally accepted the mandates system, however, the new commissioner of Togo, August François Bonnecarrère, used arguments very much like Diagne's in order to press for similar reforms in the legal system.[4] In late 1922 Bonnecarrère sent Paris a draft decree concerning "the regulation of the indigénat of Togo." Like Diagne, Bonnecarrère contended that the Africans in Togo were "unquestionably more advanced than the populations of neighboring French colonies" and that it "was possible and good policy to improve [améliorer] the system of the indigénat."[5] The commissioner noted that, while it would have been much easier to apply "purely and simply" the texts in force in French West Africa, he had formed a special commission composed of administrators, magistrates, lawyers, and two local African leaders "to study or revise" a legal system that would take into account Togo as "a country placed in a special legal position, born from the war."

The result was a modified form of the *indigénat* that officially removed the arbitrary disciplinary powers of individual colonial administrators to impose any penalty they saw fit. Instead, the draft decree transferred judicial authority to formal tribunals and required colonial officials to follow a specific penal code based on "native custom" allowing for exceptions only when "contrary to French civilization." When making these exceptions, however, administrators had to follow established French law. Further, unlike the courts system in French West Africa, every African from Togo had the right to appear in Lomé and appeal any conviction of over six months imprisonment. The Colonial Ministry approved the decree and Bonnecarrère issued instructions to his administrators explaining the new law.[6] These changes were relatively modest and probably affected only a small number of Africans, but they did institute a higher degree of predictability and accountability in the way French officials used the legal system to maintain control within the colonial state.[7] As important, if not more so, Bonnecarrère must have been aware of the decree's usefulness for presenting a favorable image of his new administration to the outside world.

Diagne was not alone within the imperial structure in late 1920 in appealing to the mandates system as a means to reform French colonialism and challenge traditional assumptions about Africans. Victor Augagneur, the governor-general of French Equatorial Africa from 1920 to 1924, was convinced that the terms of the Treaty of Versailles compelled France to pursue humanitarian goals and end the use of violent force in Africa. Yet, like Diagne, Augagneur was an atypical man of empire. He had spent most of his life as a doctor, a university professor, and an active member of the center-left Socialist Republicans in the National Assembly.[8] He was appointed the first civilian governor-general of Madagascar in 1905, but in 1910 returned to ten years of active politics in the Chamber. In 1920, Augagneur once again joined the colonial service just as a number of French socialists and communists were meeting in Tours in late December to denounce "imperialism" and found the modern French Communist Party (PCF).[9] Perhaps with this political context in mind, Augagneur complained bitterly to Paris about the use of colonial troops against "incompletely subjugated populations" in northern Cameroon and the effect that employing such military force might have on public opinion of French rule in Africa:[10]

> The process used until now, in this part of the Colony, seems reprehensible to me from the humanitarian point of view [and] susceptible, if they are repeated and become known, to create an unfavorable moral position for us in the minds of the signatories of the Treaty of Versailles.

He went on to ask the Colonial Ministry if he could instruct the new commissioner of Cameroon, Jules Carde, to establish state control without the use of such "violent actions." Paris responded quickly to condemn "terror inspired by the use of colonial troops" and any possible harm this practice could have on the attitudes of the "signatories of the treaty of Versailles:"

> I give, therefore, my entire assent to the form of peaceful penetration that you recommend, that is to say, based on the respectful methods of the principles of humanity and with regard for the native populations.[11]

The rhetoric of post-war anti-imperialism and the mandates system was now creeping into the internal official language of the French colonial bureaucracy. Augagneur had used the international nature of the mandates to achieve formal authority to restrain subordinates, regulate civilian control over organized violence, and avoid political embarrassments that could damage French imperial legitimacy. This emerging shift in official language may have been largely symbolic, but significant because it symbolized some of the new tensions within France's changing colonial culture.

Just as the mandates system pressed London to frame and then impose policies on the mandated territories that differentiated them from other colonial possessions, Paris found itself compelled to do much the same after 1920. In early 1921, Sarraut was dedicated to transforming the French Empire into a source of economic recovery and strength for postwar France.[12] Prior to accepting the post of colonial minister only a few months earlier, he had served as governor-general of Indochina for six years before becoming the president of the revived *groupe colonial* in the Chamber of Deputies, a bloc of nearly two hundred loosely allied pro-colonial nationalists, many of whom were also members of the dominant *Bloc National*.[13] This group, while not always coherent or cohesive, was dedicated to the vague notion of colonial "mise en valeur," or an intensive economic "development" of the colonies for the benefit of the metropole. By late 1920 Sarraut had lost his battle to escape the mandates system and annex Togo and Cameroon into their respective neighboring French colonial federations. He also discovered that the League's decision to delay issuing official mandates until after both Britain and France completed their negotiations with the United States meant that the Colonial Ministry could not legally attach the two former German colonies to other French possessions.[14] While preparing to announce a huge development program for every part of the empire in the Chamber in April, Sarraut decided that his ambitious plans for the two mandated territories could not wait for the League.[15]

Despite years of work based on the assumption that Dahomey would eventually absorb Togo while Cameroon would form the new center of French Equatorial Africa, Sarraut gave instructions to transform the ex-German colonies into two "special territories" with "autonomous administrations" directly responsible to Paris rather than the governor-general of either of the federations. While some common services such as the military would remain organized under the control of the governor-generals, the Colonial Ministry told local French officials that the continuing talks with the Americans tied to "successive interventions by the League of Nations" made it necessary to create "separate and autonomous" colonial administrations in Togo and Cameroon.[16] Paris gave the commissioners unique and independent powers over all internal financial and political institutions, including the authority to devote all revenues to local development and to charge customs duties on goods entering from adjoining French colonies.[17]

Sarraut's decision presented a number of immediate advantages. The Colonial Ministry found that it now had an ideal opportunity to demonstrate publicly France's "firm and loyal intentions to distinguish clearly Togo and Cameroon from her other great groups of colonies in Western and Central Africa" and to "assure the League of Nations" that it would take up the task of resuscitating the "economic prosperity" of the two mandated territories.[18] In one stroke, Paris could portray itself as an ardent defender of the mandates system and proceed with economic development without further delay. The following month, Sarraut produced his massive colonial investment scheme which, among other things, called for extensive expenditures to repair the wharf and railroads in Togo as well as to construct new roads, hospitals, government buildings and railroads in Cameroon.[19] Also, at least by implication, France successfully defended itself against accusations that it hoped to annex the mandates and was able to direct such criticism to Great Britain which still planned to administer its mandates in West Africa as parts of Gold Coast and Nigeria. British colonial officials immediately grasped the significance of this turn of events and complained that it was "impossible to make our wretched little fragment of Togoland shorn of its port [and] communications an independent unit."[20]

The volte-face in Paris had direct and far-reaching implications for the colonial regimes in Togo and Cameroon. Both Bonnecarrère in Togo and Carde in Cameroon discovered that they now had a great deal of new administrative freedom and control. This may help explain why, despite a notoriously high turnover rate among French administrators in Africa, Bonnecarrère remained commissioner of Togo from 1922 to 1931 before assuming the same post in Cameroon. Carde's successor in 1923, Théodore Paul Marchand, served until 1932.[21] Both Bonnecarrère and Marchand took advantage of their unique powers as commissioners.

The Colonial Ministry's sweeping decision to segregate the two mandated territories from the rest of the French African empire had a range of unintended results. Since Togo and Cameroon were now "autonomous administrations" corresponding directly with Paris, the

Colonial Ministry had to create a special "Togo-Cameroun" sub-division of the Africa department and add to its already complex and often chaotic bureaucracy.[22] Once Paris began treating the mandates as separate units, the Union colonial française, the main colonial interest group in France, had to form its own "Section du Togo-Cameroun" in order to keep track of the two possessions.[23] It complained a number of times to the Foreign Ministry about the "special" character of the two territories, but since "the League of Nations is completely aware of our intentions" to treat the possessions as distinct entities, the Quai d'Orsay refused to try to change Sarraut's mind.[24] Paris even astonished Bonnecarrère, who, despite his delight at having such a large degree of executive independence, advocated a "gradual" union between Togo and Dahomey in order to avoid expensive duplication in administration or any unnecessary customs barriers.[25] As far as the Colonial Ministry was concerned, Sarraut's policy made any such union impossible. Paris curtly told Bonnecarrère that "no modification to the autonomous regime will be introduced."[26]

Most importantly, by calling public attention to the anomalous status of the mandated territories and putting the League on notice that France would uphold the principles of the mandates system, Paris found that it was more exposed than ever to international supervision and outside scrutiny. Albert Duchêne, now the director of the political affairs division of the Colonial Ministry, decided that the commercial equality clauses of the mandate meant that the French merchant marine could not have the same special shipping privileges in Togo and Cameroon that it had in the rest of the French Empire.[27] The threat of international criticism pressed the Colonial Ministry to issue instructions to Carde in late March demanding that he follow all of the stipulations of the draft mandate, including the restriction against allowing Africans from Cameroon to participate in military units that might serve outside of the mandated territory. Paris warned that it attached "great importance, particularly with regard to recruitment, to not permitting anyone to dispute the legality of the acts of the French Government."[28] The Colonial Ministry was fully aware that this order would have an impact on Africans living in the mandated territory since in the summer of 1920 it had allowed the commissioner to recruit 2,500 Africans from Cameroon for military service in Algeria, Morocco, and Syria.[29] Yet ultimate control of the military remained in the hands of the commandants of West and Equatorial Africa who took their orders from the War Ministry. On the urging of the Colonial Ministry, the Foreign Ministry warned the military authorities of the "very real dangers" of violating the terms of the mandate.[30]

While mandates presented limitations for French colonial officials, they also offered new opportunities. The same system that prevented France from completely absorbing Togo and Cameroon into the two French colonial federations of Africa, also had important propaganda value and could even work to serve the traditional priorities of the colonial state. Paris issued detailed instructions to Bonnecarrère and Carde to draft their reports to the League with care in order to control all public information about the French mandates.[31] In Togo, the new commissioner reported that he had to protect the "interests" of those Africans "placed under our tutelage" by instituting a passport law and other tight restrictions against African immigration in order to prevent workers from going into neighboring British territory where wages and conditions were more attractive.[32] The colonial governments in both Togo and Cameroon told the public that they were adopting the "prestation," or system of "tax labor" contained within the *indigénat* code and used throughout French Africa as a source of unpaid labor, because it was in "the interest and welfare" of Africans and conformed to "the obligations which the Treaty of Versailles imposes on us."[33] None of these policies violated the letter of the mandate, but did little to enhance the spirit of greater internationalization and genuine colonial reform.

Still, French colonial officials did not use the language of the mandates system without reflection or consequence. In describing old policies with new rhetoric, the men who were responsible for the machinery of empire had to confront embarrassing questions about their shared assumptions and perceptions of colonialism. This problem was particularly true for the French since they advocated the doctrines of "assimilation" and "association" in Africa, not the British concept of "trusteeship."[34] According to French colonial theory, the empire was indivisible and was becoming increasingly centralized. The policy of "assimilation" sought to integrate France's colonial subjects politically and culturally with the metropole. Any African who acquired the French language and customs could become a French citizen with the same rights and benefits of any Frenchman. With the swift expansion of the Empire into Africa in the late nineteenth century, the French decided that the cultural gap between Africans and Europeans was too wide. As a result, France adopted the more limited doctrine of "association" as the immediate goal. This policy rested on the assumption that a certain degree of extended collaboration between French rulers and local elites was necessary since African communities could only develop slowly toward eventual assimilation into French culture.[35]

Still, the ideal behind both doctrines was to create eventually a centralized colonial structure bound together in a common French culture. Independence or even ultimate self-administration was never the objective. In contrast, the mandates system, rooted in the anti-annexationist sentiments of the Anglo-American political left and British conceptions of "trusteeship" while preparing Africans to "stand by themselves under the strenuous conditions of the modern world," directly challenged France's ideology of imperialism and caused French officials to initiate a self-conscious reexamination of their colonial relationship with Africans.

An early example of this challenge arose in late 1921 when the PMC decided to form a special sub-committee that would visit London and Paris to investigate the question of the nationality of inhabitants of mandated territories.[36] This sub-committee, comprised of Alberto Theodoli, the chairman, W. G. A. Ormsby-Gore, the British member, William Rappard, the director of the League of Nations Mandates Section, and the Portuguese member, wanted to ensure that the Africans living in the B mandates had "a national status wholly distinct from the nationals of the mandatory Power." After a short debate, British officials agreed to the term "British-protected persons," the same one used in other British protectorates in Africa, and the PMC easily concurred.[37] In Paris, agreement was not nearly so simple and the meeting with the PMC far less congenial. Since French colonial law in Africa recognized only "sujets," those Africans subject to the *indigénat*, and "evolués," those elites who were supposedly assimilated into French culture and had rights equal to those of French citizens, the PMC objective posed a predicament. In theory, "sujets" could eventually attain the status of "evolués" and were not "wholly distinct from the nationals of the mandatory Power." To create a different status for Africans living in mandated territory thoroughly contradicted the notion of "assimilation" and the fundamental notion of "la mission civilatrice et providentielle" that lay at the root of the French culture of colonialism.

A few days before the arrival of the PMC sub-committee in Paris, representatives of the Colonial Ministry, Justice Ministry, and Foreign Ministry met at the Quai d'Orsay to try to resolve their common problem.[38] The French member of the PMC, Jean Beau, while not part of the sub-committee in any official capacity, attended as well. Under the chairmanship of Jean Gout, the head of the League of Nations section of the Foreign Ministry, the various participants quickly fell into a tangle of confusion and disagreement. Beau opened the discussion by explaining the uncertainties surrounding the question of sovereignty in the C mandates until Gout reminded him that France did not have any C mandates.

The Colonial Ministry representative, Fernand-Alexandre Tesseron, insisted that Africans belonged to diverse "tribes" and that the whole notion of "nationality" was nonsensical. Gout generally agreed, but insisted that a wide definition of "national" already included "sujets français," but did not necessarily denote "the idea of nationality." This remark sparked a long and complicated discussion over whether the term "nationality" had any meaning at all since, under Article 22 of the Treaty of Versailles, France was a "mandatory power" and not "a sovereign power." In exasperation, Gout argued that they could not use the name "sujets" for Africans in mandated territory for the simple reason that it implied French nationality and would cause protests from the League. On this point, Beau agreed and suggested that they had to find a word that kept them from being "treated as annexationists." The group considered using Britain's term of "protected person," but the Justice Ministry officials rejected it since the word "protégés" did not adequately indicate "allegiance" to French colonial authority. Further, the term "protected persons" was already the specific legal designation for the inhabitants of the French protectorates of Tunisia and Morocco, both of which were under control of the Foreign Ministry. Finally, after much convoluted negotiation and compromise, everyone decided to recommend the slightly awkward phrase of "administered persons [*administrés*] under mandate" as their first choice. If the League wanted to "unify the description given by all mandatory powers," the officials agreed to accept "protected persons under mandate" instead.[39]

French officials soon discovered that this decision did not put an end to their problems. The meeting with the PMC sub-committee did not go smoothly. Rappard complained that they were "not well received" and that the League representatives encountered "an air of resentment at the intrusion of the Mandates Commission into the question of the nationality of the inhabitants of mandated areas."[40] The following year, the League formally accepted France's first choice of "administrés" and Gout informed the Colonial Ministry in early 1923 that Togo and Cameroon would have to adopt special legislation acknowledging that the "nature of the mandate" conferred on the African inhabitants "a different quality from those inhabitants of other neighboring colonies under plain French sovereignty."[41] This change did not please the commissioners of the two mandated territories who found that adopting the term "administrés" was not mere semantics. They pressed Sarraut to tell the Foreign Ministry that the change would not just require revising every colonial law in the mandated territories, but would cast a serious shadow on their legitimate authority to apply the *indigénat* to "natives" [*indigènes*] who were "not French citizens and not subject to the French tribunals."[42] French colonial officials had accepted that the restrictions in the mandate texts combined with international supervision would sometimes require them to treat the *indigènes* of Togo and Cameroon too differently from those of neighboring French colonies. But Lomé and Yaoundé would not accept that these same Africans somehow possessed such "a different quality" from all other Africans under French rule which necessitated an entirely new set of laws founded on a nebulous legal foundation. For these reasons, the commissioners proposed the cumbersome phrase "natives of Togo (or of Cameroon), protected persons under French mandate." For both Bonnecarrère and Marchand, this title would retain the separate identity of the mandates and denote a break with French colonial doctrine, but would not undermine their right to govern.

This seemingly inconsequential controversy over how to categorize Africans under the law went on for the next six years before it was finally resolved to the satisfaction of the commissioners.[43] Yet this type of controversy was not inconsequential to the men who shaped colonial policy and devoted enormous amounts of time to legal and administrative questions. Legal definitions and official designations served as vital psychological underpinnings to the culture of colonialism and functioned to organize and rationalize the imperial structure in the minds of Europeans. By 1925 the language of the mandates system was becoming firmly entrenched in the French colonial bureaucracy and served as a constant reminder of the international status of the territories. For France, Togo and Cameroon comprised a separate category with internal correspondence conspicuously designating "Territoire du Togo placé sous le mandat de la France" or "Afrique Equatoriale et Cameroun" or "les Territoires Africans sous mandat."[44] For most of the interwar period, the two French mandates remained legally adjacent to, but not an integrated part of, the French African empire.

Military Recruitment and Africans

While French colonial policy-makers confronted a number of substantive problems because of the mandates system in the early 1920s, it was the British government's surprising surrender to the PMC on the question of military recruitment in 1924 that perhaps most shocked the French and caused some of the most sweeping reforms during this period. London's announcement put Duchêne in a particularly difficult position. As the accredited French representative before the PMC that year, he was entirely unprepared to discuss the matter and only cryptically told the Commission on the last day of the session that he accepted in the name of his government the "British formula" concerning recruitment, but gave no indication what that meant and may not have known himself.[45] To have said nothing would have left France in an unenviable position that would have only opened the way for future embarrassing questions from Geneva and accusations of exploitation and militarism from critics. After he returned to Paris, Duchêne's problem was to persuade the French military authorities that the only way to demonstrate France's acceptance of the "British formula" convincingly was to sever Togo and Cameroon completely from the military control of the neighboring French colonial federations.

Getting the French military to relinquish any of its prerogatives was a imposing task by any standard. After the experience of the trenches during the First World War as well as prime minister Raymond Poincaré's disastrous decision to use French troops to occupy the Ruhr in Germany from

1922 to 1923, few military officials were willing to consider anything that might diminish the size or latitude of the French colonial army. In 1924 both mandated territories had fiscal and administrative autonomy, but the military forces in both Togo and Cameroon remained under the command of the "Général Commandant Supérieur des Troops du Groupe" in their respective federation. Further, Paris, not the local governments, was responsible for all the costs of maintaining these troops.[46] To the military leadership, this system of tight centralization and fiscal control was crucial for the overall strength and preparedness of the French colonial army and was the essence of empire. For many military men, the colonies had helped France win in 1918 and would be indispensable in any future war with Germany. In July, the director of the military department of the Colonial Ministry instantly rejected Duchêne's request to hand over control of Cameroon's military to the commissioner and make the local government pay the costs of training and maintaining troops.[47] The director insisted that the current arrangement was in complete compliance with Article 3 of the mandates for Togo and Cameroon which gave France "in the event of general war" the right to use Africans from the mandated territories to "repel an attack or for the defense of the territory outside that subject to the mandate."[48] He considered any alteration of the military organization of French Equatorial Africa a security threat to the French Empire and even to France itself.

Duchêne did not give up. For him, his promises to the PMC and the international considerations surrounding the mandate were more important than the military considerations surrounding France's colonial army. He drafted a seven-page memorandum for the military department pleading his case. Duchêne provided a detailed history of controversies surrounding the creation of the mandates system and explained how he routinely had to answer questions from the PMC concerning the relative "autonomy" of the mandated territories. He argued that these questions pressed France to regard Cameroon as "an entity that was clearly distinct from the possessions and protectorates" under French colonial rule and required accepting "a distinctive nationality for the inhabitants of the countries under mandate." According to Duchêne, the PMC was currently "preoccupied" with the issue of military recruitment with "certain members wanting to accentuate the separation between local troops and the army of the Mandatory Power." Most importantly,

> The question of recruitment has been specially examined by the Commission: Great Britain, on the formal request of the League of Nations – motivated by a report by the Commission ratified by the Council – recently expressly declared that it will refuse to recruit any African volunteers from British Cameroons, even if they enter into an agreement in Nigeria . . . I must stress the advantages of adopting this definitive solution which

> conforms not only with the views of the League of Nations, but also, in reality, to the spirit of the mandate.[49]

He pledged that the commissioner would have control over the military only in peacetime and in the event of a general mobilization the local militia and reserves would again come under the command of the respective federations.

After consultation with the War Ministry and with much reluctance, the military department finally relented. It promised that "[n]o formation of colonial troops will any longer be stationed in the mandated territory of Cameroon." Further, the department was willing to place the entire police force, "necessary for internal security," under the control of the commissioner who would maintain it "by the special budget of the territory." The composition of the local police and militia, while commanded by officers seconded from the regular colonial army, would "be determined by the commissioner subject to the approval of the colonial minister."[50] The grateful Colonial Ministry quickly adopted the necessary legislation and immediately informed both Bonnecarrère and Marchand of their new powers and responsibilities.[51] Paris also wasted no time in notifying the League of the change and taking full credit for satisfying the wishes of the PMC.[52]

France's decision to reorganize the military had an immediate impact in the two mandated territories. Marchand agreed that the reform was the best way to deflect League criticism, but was not happy that he would have to pay for the local forces out of Cameroon's budget. As a result, he informed Paris that he was instituting substantial cuts in the military and police forces.[53] By early 1925 the administration in Cameroon claimed to have only one battalion of African troops, divided into four companies, composed of 656 soldiers under the command of fifteen French officers and thirty-six African non-commissioned officers. The police force officially numbered 894 Africans.[54] Just two years earlier, Cameroon had possessed two battalions, divided into three companies each, employing 870 African troops, seventy-eight French officers, and fifty-four African NCOs. The police force had numbered one thousand.[55] While Marchand only trimmed the police by a little more than 10 percent, he cut the military staff of French officers by 80 percent and the number of African soldiers by one fourth. These cuts helped him to keep the expenditures of the armed services under 10 percent of the total budget.

Bonnecarrère in Togo similarly shrank the military by dissolving one 185-man company and not organizing any local militia at all. Instead, he enlarged the police force from 270 Africans to approximately four hundred, eliminating 12 percent of the overall armed force available to maintain order.[56] Still, this service accounted for only 6 percent of the total expenditures of the territory. Most importantly, neither commissioner instituted the often difficult and disruptive policy of conscription in their mandated territories. While this decision made the task of preserving political stability for local colonial administrators that much easier, it also ensured that Africans from Togo and Cameroon were not forced to join the nearly ten thousand Africans conscripted each year from French West Africa or the one thousand similarly drawn from Equatorial Africa.[57]

Ending conscription in the mandates marked a complete break with traditional French imperial practice and obliterated a fundamental assumption within the French colonial culture about the nature and purpose of empire. It also stood as a conspicuous exception to the rest of the French colonial structure and was a tangible result of the internationalization and reformation of European imperialism under the League of Nations. Yet, as in the British mandates, this reform in imperial policy was not without its mix of advantages and costs for Africans. While Africans in the two mandates did not have to experience the usually severe and often perilous burden of military service, they also lost one of the few opportunities for engaging the institutions of the colonial state and exercising a form of power within it.

In general, while French reaction to the mandates system during this period was usually far less pronounced that it was over the question of military recruitment, it was becoming increasingly pervasive. In early 1923 Bonnecarrère told the Colonial Ministry that there was an Anglo-German plot to use the mandates system against French rule in Togo. He reported that British merchants, often with financial support from the German government, were working with Anglican missionaries to take advantage of League protection to conduct a covert "offensive" against Togo.[58] Further, he claimed that newspapers in the Gold Coast were publishing "German propaganda" aimed either at making Togo a British possession or at returning it to the Germans who would better serve British commercial interests than France. The Colonial Ministry took the report seriously enough to warn the Foreign Ministry.[59] This growing Anglo-French antagonism helped to kill a proposed "inter-colonial council between British and French colonies in Africa" built around the international cooperation between "the Governors of Mandated Territories."[60] In 1924 Marchand was worried that "poorly informed critics" might attack him for violating Article 3, the clause prohibiting naval bases in a mandated territory, if he greeted visiting ships in Douala harbor with a ceremonial gun salute.[61] After consulting the military authorities, the Colonial Ministry gave Marchand permission to discontinue the practice.[62]

Such examples of seemingly relatively trivial concerns, however, demonstrate how much international supervision had impinged upon the changing culture of colonialism among Europeans. The French were particularly sensitive to this constant outside pressure and took it seriously. During this period, Marchand specifically altered Cameroon's mining law to conform to the commercial equality clauses of the mandate and avoid criticism from the League, Bonnecarrère took the unusual step of permitting foreigners to participate on Togo's Chamber of Commerce, and the Colonial Ministry issued detailed instructions to both commissioners on how to produce their annual reports to the League.[63] In 1924 Bonnecarrère decided to introduce greater "liberalism" into the local "Conseils de Notables" system, the African advisory councils composed of ethnic and village notables, because, in part, "I have been guided by the strong interest shown by the League of Nations since its start in the institution of the Conseils de Notables" and forms of African political participation within the colonial government.[64]

Between 1922 and 1924, Togo had four councils whose members were selected by the commissioner and local district officers. Bonnecarrère expanded the number of councils to six and established an electoral college that allowed local chiefs to send their representatives to the councils for three-year terms. The government also extended greater responsibilities to the councils to advise local colonial administrators on questions of taxation, public works, and the local budget.[65] In Cameroon, Marchand issued orders to every district officer in late 1925 to administer the law in strict accordance with the mandatory principles and with a continuous awareness that "certain European elements" were always watching them.[66]

African Protest and the League

Africans also appropriated the power of the mandates system to attempt to control the parameters of both French and British imperialism. In early 1921 J. T. Mensah, a former clerk for a British trading company operating in Lomé who had sent petitions to the League of Nations in 1920, reemerged to criticize the mandatory administration in Togo and to use the international status of the territory to try to embarrass the French. This time Mensah found an eager ally in the Liverpool Chamber of Commerce whose agents in Togo had received his petition, signed by more than thirty other Africans, that complained about the French tax system. For Mensah the British merchants represented not only a powerful voice in London, but a potential future employer if Britain dislodged France from Togo. A number of members of the Chamber who were still angry that Britain had handed over so much of the former German colony to France, realized the usefulness of the petition for its own purposes and promptly gave a copy to the Foreign Office with the self-serving suggestion that London send it to the League of Nations.[67] Colonial officials told the Foreign Office that French tax policy was not the official concern of the British government and in fact might even serve to encourage African emigration to labor-poor Gold Coast.[68]

While British colonial officials were not willing to act on these African complaints about French rule, Ormsby-Gore was. In 1921, he was still a member of the League of Nations Union, a Conservative MP, and had just joined the PMC. The Liverpool Chamber of Commerce had sent him a copy of Mensah's petition at about the same time that Ormsby-Gore had received a bizarre report from one Martin Kpapko Abibu that French authorities had deported 425 African men and fifteen women from Lomé to perform forced labor in France. While the two issues seemed unrelated, Ormsby-Gore used them as a basis for a parliamentary question in early May.[69] The under-secretary of state for foreign affairs, Cecil Harmsworth, publicly responded that he had "no information" about the complaint, but privately told Ormsby-Gore he that wanted nothing to do with the matter and told him to raise it in Geneva instead. As the British member of the PMC, Ormsby-Gore tried to explain this whole baffling episode to Lord Robert Cecil who in turn asked the British representative on the Council of the League to call attention to the problem.[70] Without concrete proof that France had violated the mandate, however, no responsible British official wished to go to the League.

In July, Ormsby-Gore asked the Colonial Office to conduct an unofficial investigation in order to find out who Mensah and Abibu were and what was really happening in French Togo.[71] In late August, C. D. Trotter, a clerk in the Gold Coast, reported that "the Abibus are related to the Mensahs and come from Porto-Seguro, which is that part of the Togo Coast which has been administered by the French since 1914."[72] Both men belonged to the large Adjigo family, one of the most important coastal Anécho families, which had long ties to British and German commercial interests in West Africa. Many within the family spoke English, still the primary trade language on the coast, or German. The two Anglophone Africans had been using the Gold Coast postal service to correspond with the Liverpool Chamber of Commerce, the League of Nations Union, the Permanent Mandates Commission, and J. H. Harris, the secretary of the Anti-Slavery and Aborigines Protection Society, in a campaign to try to expel the French from Togo. They had also succeeded in publishing their views in *West Africa*, a Gold Coast newspaper, claiming to speak "on behalf of the native community" of Togo. Trotter described the men as members of "the band of irreconcilables" whom the French authorities had placed under tight surveillance for "indulging in correspondence similar to that in question." Further, the British authorities in Accra were sure that the group of Africans reportedly transported out of Lomé were "indubitably impressed" from the French Sudan, not Togo. Armed with this information, the Colonial Office told Ormsby-Gore that Mensah and Abibu were not only unrepresentative of the majority of Africans in Togo, but were "probably wrong" in their charges.[73] Ormsby-Gore let the matter drop. Still, even though Mensah and Abibu did not spark the end of French colonial rule in Togo, they did manage to circumvent the French authorities in Togo, exploit the gaps between British and French mandatory rule, and generate a great deal of speculation and confusion in Accra, the Colonial Office, the Foreign Office, the House of Commons, the headquarters of several special interest groups, and Geneva before British officials decided that "it seems clear that the charges made by our dusky friends are not really substantial."[74]

Still, the Adjigo family's active and public resistance to French colonialism came at a price both for them and for France. In 1922 Bonnecarrère conducted an election for the contested throne, or "stool," of Anécho and named Frédérick Body Lawson as chief instead of his rival Amoussou Bruce, a member of the Adjigo family who had been educated in Germany.[75] Lawson spoke French and belonged to another extended and prominent Anécho family with a history of confrontation with German colonial rule.[76] After the election, the commissioner expelled Bruce and his followers in the Adjigo family to Mango, over three hundred miles north, the most remote district in the territory. One deportee, Mensah Agboko Gaba, whose "father, brothers and many others" were now "refugees from Anécho," followed a familiar pattern of drafting a number of petitions angrily protesting Bonnecarrère's decision and sending them to the Foreign Office, the Colonial Office, the Anti-Slavery and Aborigines Protection Society, and the League of Nations.[77] He also sent a petition to the Colonial Ministry in Paris.[78] London insisted that it could do nothing and Geneva replied that it could not act unless the petitioners expressed their grievances through the mandatory power.[79]

Bonnecarrère, convinced that he could not let such African criticism pass without comment, decided to risk the consequences inherent in responding officially to the charges of the Adjigo. He permitted the Foreign Ministry to report to the League that the elections had been conducted fairly and had served to restore order and "calm" to Anécho.[80] The PMC cautiously accepted the public explanation and in a brief, yet diplomatically worded response, said that

> the mandatory power is responsible for public order and except for serious reasons, which do not arise in this case, we are not called upon to discuss the propriety of such measures as it thinks fit to take to ensure the maintenance of order.[81]

Since the mandatory powers had "full powers of legislation and administration," the League's only practical option was to side with the institutions of colonial control. To do otherwise would have undermined its ability to exert moral suasion in matters where its authority was more clearly defined. Still, the League had put the mandatory powers on notice that it possessed the authority to define "serious reasons" and to discuss the "propriety" of colonial policy. Further, since Bonnecarrère chose to respond formally to the criticisms, both the reputations of France and the PMC were now committed to making sure that these particular African grievances did not attract international attention again. J. T. Mensah, Martin Kpapko Abibu, and Mensah Agboko Gaba had demonstrated how Africans could make their voices heard as far away as Geneva and test both the power and sincerity of international public opinion. It would not be the last or most effective time that the Adjigo family would use this tactic to put political pressure on French colonial authorities.

In late 1925 other members of the Adjigo family found a different way to use the mandates system as a weapon against the French in Togo. Several Germanophone members of the family, led by Johan Kanyi, a fifty year-old former clerk in the German colonial government who had emigrated to the Gold Coast during the war, began a fifteen-year agitation against French mandatory rule.[82] He and his group may have had some covert financial and political support from a German merchant company, the *Deutsche Togo Gesellschaft*.[83] In December he printed a number of anonymous leaflets, written in German, announcing the existence of a "Bund der Deutsch Togoländer" dedicated to compelling Geneva to return Togo to Germany. The circular claimed that the *Bund*, founded in Accra two years earlier, intended to establish a "close link with Germany" and would perform "the important task of representing Togo before the League of Nations."

The League of Nations itself "has inscribed on its flag" the right of peoples to decide for

> themselves and if we all plainly and unanimously express our sentiments and wish, we will undoubtedly attain our goal. We have already sent petitions twice, in the name of the Togolese people, to the League of Nations in Geneva, asking for the evacuation of France from Togo and the restoration of the country to Germany.

The notice went on to call on every Togolese to support the campaign by signing the circular or by offering advice. "So, dear fellow countrymen, stand by your intention to sacrifice and help the Bund der Deutsch Togoländer, the league which fights for freedom, rights, and peace."[84] In the last days of 1925, however, the *Bund* only posed a mysterious and faintly foreboding threat to French colonial officials. The government in Lomé still did not know where the leaflets were coming from, if they were genuine or merely clever pieces of "German propaganda," or if the "Bund" was serious in its declared intention to send its grievances to the League.

International Criticism and Imperial Legitimacy

For France, establishing highly autonomous administrations with little or no military character in both Cameroon and Togo in the early 1920s eliminated any serious accusations of "annexationism" or escalating "militarism" in postwar Africa, the two strongest charges leveled against Paris at the end of the First World War. French colonial officials were acutely sensitive to international criticism and were learning better ways to prevent it from threatening either France's imperial legitimacy or its colonial priorities. Still, extending the mandates system to Togo and Cameroon required French colonial officials to reexamine their perceptions of Africans and accept a range of limitations in the way the colonial regime exerted power, particularly in the practice of drafting Africans into the military service. Further, some African were starting to exploit the implications of League-inspired internationalization and reform and would use the power behind the mandates system to even greater effect in the years after 1925. Lastly, mandates meant that all members of the League of Nations had equal rights and privileges in Togo and Cameroon while any member of the PMC could raise questions about French colonial rule in the two territories. While these aspects of the system were of little immediate worry to France, they would quickly become much more when Germany joined first the League and then the Permanent Mandates Commission.

7

Germany Joins the League: The British Mandates, 1926–1929

The League of Nations reached its height of prestige and authority after it admitted Germany as a member in 1926. Germany received a permanent seat on the Council, joining Britain, France, Italy, and Japan. Gustav Stresemann, the German foreign minister, considered membership necessary in his determination to revise the Treaty of Versailles and gradually restore his nation's great-power status.[1] French and British political leaders hoped that membership symbolized Germany's acceptance of the results of the First World War.[2] The League's many critics could no longer argue that it was merely an association of victorious powers designed to isolate Germany from the rest of the world. For many contemporaries, Germany's entry seemed to offer the imperfect international organization a fresh start and was an important reason for the general peace and prosperity that Europe enjoyed until the end of the 1920s.[3]

One of the many problems surrounding Germany's entry into the League was mandates. Before 1926, French and British officials had worried that Berlin would ask for the return of its former colonies as soon as it achieved membership.[4] The demands of the German colonial societies and a number of vocal conservatives in the Reichstag were as unrelenting as ever.[5] During the delicate Locarno Conference negotiations in 1925 that resulted in League membership for Germany, both the British Foreign Minister Austen Chamberlain and his French counterpart Aristide Briand resolutely opposed relinquishing any mandated territories.[6] The German government decided that colonial revision was not a primary concern and chose not to make it a formal issue during these discussions, but Briand remarked cryptically that it was "from the inside of the League that Germany could make her views prevail." Chamberlain observed that the Germans "would be a possible candidate for mandates like all other members of the League."[7] Stresemann was consistently and conveniently vague about mandates by insisting on "Germany's claim to colonial activity" and the intention to "participate actively in the mandates system," but never explaining exactly what he meant.[8] In 1926 the mandates system remained part of the often shifting and apprehensive relations between Geneva and the Weimar Republic.

Germany's membership in the League made a conspicuous mark on both the mandates system and the British mandated territories. Not only did Germany regain equal access to its former colonies, but a German national joined the Permanent Mandates Commission in 1927 and took part in their international supervision. For Britain, Berlin's participation in Geneva made mandates a matter of serious concern for the Foreign Office and pressed colonial officials to become more cautious and solicitous in their relations with the PMC. Protected by the terms of the mandate, a large influx of German settlers and missionaries into the Tanganyika Territory altered local economic and political conditions and added to the growing tensions between European settler communities and the colonial state. For Sir Donald Cameron, the governor of Tanganyika, the sharper political edge of the mandates system enhanced his ability to impose his own administrative order upon the African population. As the decade of the 1920s came to an end, the mandates system continued to affect every level of British rule as it further internationalized and reformed the perceptions and functions of British colonialism.

Chamberlain Confronts the PMC

Chamberlain abruptly took an active interest in mandates as a consequence of German membership in the League of Nations. Whereas Briand was willing to let the permanent officials in the Foreign and Colonial Ministries worry about Togo and Cameroon, Chamberlain personally took it upon himself to involve his office in League issues that had previously been left almost exclusively to the Colonial Office. In 1926 he was bent on holding Germany to the terms of the Treaty of Versailles and not letting Berlin use the League either to endanger the interests of the British Empire or to manipulate public opinion against the Allies and force substantive treaty revision.[9] When he realized that the mandates system was a potential threat to these preoccupations, he launched an open and determined attack on the PMC. The foreign minister's assault marked an important turning point in the relations between London and the leading members of the PMC and shaped the circumstances surrounding the eventual inclusion of a German member on the Commission in 1927.

Chamberlain began his campaign against the PMC just days before Germany formally joined the League on 10 September 1926. During a public meeting of the Council, the British foreign secretary unexpectedly and harshly castigated the PMC for attempting to usurp the authority of the mandatory powers.[10] Chamberlain pointed to a revised questionnaire for the mandatory powers that had increased the number of questions from approximately 60 to more than 200. He also did not like the implications of a request from the PMC that the Council rule on whether the Commission was competent to hear oral petitions from inhabitants of mandated territories.[11] The PMC insisted that it had no "definite proposal" for changing the petitions procedure, that the questionnaire would merely replace one that had been in use for several years, and that the Colonial Office had already approved the expanded form. But Chamberlain exploded. He called the questionnaire "inquisitorial" and declared that the Commission was trying to "extend its authority to a point where the government would no longer be vested in the mandatory Power but in the Mandates Commission." He then convinced the Council that it would be "unwise, imprudent, and even dangerous" to come to any decisions concerning the petitions procedure or the questionnaire without having the "observations of the various mandatory powers" first.

Chamberlain was worried that an overly powerful international organization immersed in so many aspects of mandatory administration, united with full and public German participation, could not only endanger London's relations with both the southern Dominions and Paris but could undermine British control within the former German colonies. In a private letter to Sir William Tyrrell, the permanent under-secretary of state for foreign affairs, Chamberlain said that he had decided to rebuke the PMC because both South Africa and New Zealand were "violently opposed" to the new questionnaire and in order to strengthen Anglo-French cooperation within the League.[12] While he was happy to report that "I need not say that I got a strong backing from Briand, who was only too delighted to see me indict the Commission," he confessed his displeasure with Leo Amery, serving as colonial and dominions secretary, for not blocking the PMC earlier. Because of this "failure," Chamberlain ordered a discussion of mandates at the coming Imperial Conference in order to prepare a common British Empire rebuff to the League.[13] Tyrrell told his chief that he was "delighted to see the line you took over mandates. You are in a very strong position as you have the backing of the Dominions."[14]

Within days, Chamberlain faced a whole range of challenges that made his condemnation of the PMC even more politically charged and a matter for international attention. German Foreign Ministry officials in Geneva informed the Allies that they wanted a German member on the Commission as soon as possible.[15] Gilbert Murray, the chairman of the League of Nations Union, told his Conservative vice-chairman, John Waller Hills, "I am afraid that Austen's snub to the Mandates Commission and his condemnation of the proposals, for which Lugard is responsible, is a bad blunder which may have serious consequences."[16] He went on to stress the importance of marshaling public opinion in Britain and suggested that the LNU pass a resolution in defense of the PMC. Hills affirmed that "we will pass some pretty stiff resolutions" to publicize the issue, but thought that contacting W. G. A. Ormsby-Gore, the under-secretary of state for the colonies, would help put pressure on the government from the inside. Hills argued that Ormsby-Gore "has a very fine idea what mandates mean: and truly if we allow Austen to rampage there will be no mandates left."[17]

John H. Harris, secretary of the Anti-Slavery and Aborigines Protection Society and unrelenting Labour critic of unreformed imperialism, was more troubled. He wrote Murray from Geneva that "[w]e are all of us greatly disturbed here at the attack made by the Council upon the Permanent Mandates Commission. The *proces verbal* is much worse than anything which has been published."[18] Harris said that he was writing pointed articles for publication in Britain, the United States, and Germany after having private conversations with members of the PMC including William Rappard, the former director of the Mandates Section and now Swiss member of the PMC, who was "of course burning with indignation."[19] Further, he reported that Labour MPs would ask questions in the houses of parliament and that he was working directly with representatives of small League member states, including Dr Fridtjof Nansen of Norway, probably the most outspoken advocate of the mandates system in the Assembly, and Eduard Beneš of Czechoslovakia to draft an official Assembly resolution expressing its "high appreciation of the admirable work" performed by the PMC as a counter to the Council's remarks.

As the defenders of the League were starting to mobilize for action, officials of the Foreign Office, Colonial Office, and Dominions Office together were drafting detailed criticisms of the PMC's proposals and discussing Germany's request for a seat on the Commission.[20] Amery shared the view of many in the Foreign Office that adding a German national to the PMC any time soon was unthinkable. He spent little time in serious debate on the issue.[21] Instead, Chamberlain and Amery concentrated on how best to check what they both agreed was the PMC's attempt to go beyond the terms of Article 22 of the Covenant. Chamberlain called the PMC's proposals "matters of first rate consequence," but was more worried by what the questionnaire represented rather than what it specifically asked.[22] He argued that the response should remind the PMC of its supervisory responsibilities:

> I think it ought to begin by an examination of the theory and purpose of mandates which I describe shortly as being not to create a superior Council of Administration but to assure the world that the abuses of King Leopold II's personal exploitation in the Congo are not being repeated elsewhere . . . the main thing is to get a proper definition of the purpose of the League's supervision of the Commission's tasks. The rest follows.

Amery disagreed. He wanted to identify every offending question so the PMC would never ask such questions in the future.[23] In October, Chamberlain, Amery, and the prime ministers of South Africa, Australia, and New Zealand met a number of times and finally agreed on a compromise draft that attached Amery's detailed list to Chamberlain's general statement of principle.[24] Almost as an afterthought, the special Mandates Committee of the Imperial Conference, which included both Chamberlain and Amery, briefly discussed the possible appointment of a German national to the PMC. The committee's conclusions exposed a manifest fear of both Germany and the changing nature of international supervision:

> The Committee recommend that the German Government be, if possible, privately dissuaded from putting forward this claim at the present time. It is hardly possible to expect that, so soon after the War, a German member of the Commission should be an impartial judge of the conditions existing in the former German Colonies or should not be influenced by a desire to criticise the Administrations which now control them.

Further, when that far distant day for deciding whether a German member should join the PMC finally did arrive, the decision "must be largely governed by the character of Germany's co-operation with the League and by the use she makes of her position" as well as "the general conditions of European peace and the relations existing between Germany and the former Allies . . . "[25]

While Chamberlain and Amery were busy with their drafts, the League's allies continued to go to great lengths to shield the PMC. Lugard attended a special meeting of the Mandates Committee of the LNU and warned ominously that restricting the Commission's power to ask questions would "be an end to the Mandatory System" and that "it might be expected that the present members of the Commission would be disinclined to continue their work under such restrictions."[26] He went on to explain what he thought was the underlying problem:

> The present controversies, however, were not essentially concerned with the questionnaire or the petitions, but were an attempt to restrict the supervision of the League to a mere formality, except in the case of outrageous maladministration.

Lord Robert Cecil (chancellor of the Duchy of Lancaster but responsible for League matters and still serving as president of the LNU) complained to Baldwin when he learned of the plans of the Imperial Conference.[27] Cecil, the most powerful advocate for the League in the cabinet, did not mask his genuine indignation:

> The action taken by the Foreign Secretary at Geneva on the Council has been the subject of considerable criticism here, criticism which, speaking as your colleague to his Prime Minister, I am bound to say was at any rate in part justified. It is quite unfair to suggest that the Mandates Commission have attempted to take over the duties of the Mandatories, and I am informed they bitterly resent the charge. If it is now repeated, coming from the Imperial Conference, I do not think it impossible that the Mandates Commission will resign in a body, a step which would be very unfortunate both for the League of Nations and for our Colonial reputation.

Baldwin responded that Cecil's protest came too late.[28] The members of the Imperial Conference were in no mood to change their minds and within days delivered their official "observations" concerning the PMC to the League's secretary-general.[29]

The final form of the British Empire note to the League, while not as curt as Chamberlain's earlier comments before the Council, presented the Foreign Office with more problems than it solved. While the foreign minister may have won some admiration from Amery and the leaders of the Dominions, he had angered the LNU, irritated the League and its supporters, and endangered the effectiveness of the PMC. During a private meeting with Hills and Cecil, Chamberlain "warmly disclaimed any intention of speaking in an acrimonious manner at the recent meeting of the Council, and spoke in very complementary terms of the work of the Mandates Commission."[30] Despite this seemingly more moderate tone, the foreign minister had to listen to a lecture from Hills about how, like the LNU itself, "the Commission must be regarded both as an ally and as a critic." To attack it was self-defeating. Sir Eric Drummond, the general-secretary of the League of Nations, gave the Foreign Office similar advice. Drummond argued that the controversy between the British Empire and the PMC was pointless:

> Not only is it having a bad effect on countries which have no mandates and which therefore are inclined to be very suspicious of the Mandatory system, but also I can imagine few things which would give greater pleasure and activity to the extreme German Colonial Party than a dispute between the Council and the Mandates Commission.[31]

The best way to repair this damage was to appoint a German to the PMC without delay.[32]

A few days later, Chamberlain got the same recommendation from inside the government. Ormsby-Gore, who was in Geneva as an accredited representative before the PMC, reported that the members of the PMC were "distinctly sore" over the recent controversy. "I personally take the view that the addition of a German to the Commission would be a help both to the Commission and to the Mandatory Powers, and as far as Great Britain is concerned we have nothing to fear."[33] In late November, Lugard told a fellow Conservative that "it would be deplorable" if the controversy with the PMC "afforded a weapon to the Opposition to attack the Government, as it seems it has already done in Australia. It would be still more deplorable if it led to an acute difference in the League itself."[34]

This warning did not stop the LNU from issuing resolutions opposing Chamberlain's decisions or Labour MPs from suggesting that the government was attempting to undermine the League.[35] While concluding that the PMC deserved some blame, Hills remained highly critical of the foreign minister.[36] In addition to writing letters to *The Times* defending the League, he told Murray in early December that "Austen has put the fat in the fire over the questionnaire. His despatch has not been well received, to put it mildly, and various other bodies besides the [League of Nations] Union are sending the torch round."[37] He was particularly angry that Chamberlain had not only made it easy for Briand to hide behind British complaints, but had unwittingly made it more difficult for the PMC to press for reform in the French mandated territories.

> Briand, who followed, clever as the devil as usual, realized that Austen had incurred all the odium and that he could be bland, which he was. Consequently, we are landed in a mess in that we are protecting French misdeeds in the French Cameroons and elsewhere, and, at the same time, giving the world the impression it is we and not France who have something to hide . . . [38]

By the end of 1926, Chamberlain had little to show for his attempt to restrain the PMC and only had succeeded in strengthening the resolve of those who wanted to protect it. Once tempers had cooled, the PMC agreed not to recommend any changes in the petition procedure.[39] Yet, since the members only wanted a clear ruling on the issue in the first place, the PMC lost nothing. The Council also decided not to recommend the PMC's new questionnaire to the mandatory powers, but did so because of form rather than content.[40] Again, since the first questionnaire had never been obligatory and the mandatory powers always had the prerogative to respond to any PMC question as it saw fit, there was no diminution in the Commission's powers of interrogation. Nothing on the new questionnaire had not been asked in some fashion before and nothing prevented the PMC from asking similar questions in the future. This probably explains why none of the members of the PMC resigned because of Chamberlain's condemnation. In this way the Commission preserved its most important assets, including its institutional memory and the international reputation of its leaders.

If anything, the dispute gave the PMC an opportunity to reaffirm its aim slowly to reform and internationalize European imperialism as well as to tighten its relations with the mandatory powers. In November 1926, soon after London's formal note, the Commission said that its duty was "one of supervision and co-operation." It would "do the utmost that lies in its power to assist the mandatory Governments in carrying out the important and difficult tasks which they are accomplishing on behalf of the League of Nations."

> Supervision and co-operation are functions which, though neither incompatible nor in conflict with one another, may yet be accompanied with genuine difficulties when they have to be carried out simultaneously. If the task of the Mandates Commission were merely to supervise the administration of the mandated territories, it would be natural that, in all difficult cases, it should propose to visit these territories itself, or should recommend the holding of inquiries on the spot. If, on the other hand, the role of the Mandates Commission were merely to facilitate the task of the Mandatory Power, it should offer lavish encouragement and abstain from passing any critical judgements which, if conveyed to the population under mandate, might create embarrassment and render the task of the Government more difficult of execution.[41]

Chamberlain, and others, who had never seriously concerned themselves with mandates before 1926, did not understand the PMC when they attacked it. They found support in Amery who had always disliked the PMC, but rarely tried to resist it actively. A third and much more diverse group, including Murray, Harris, Nansen, Cecil, Ormsby-Gore, Drummond, and Lugard, was quick to defend the PMC against the other two. Representing the interrelated pressures of the LNU, national politics, the government, and an international organization, this group demonstrated the most success by year's end.

Dr Kastl and Kenya

Chamberlain's attack on the PMC merely postponed its expansion to include a German while ensuring that one would have to join the following year. As he and his counterparts in the southern Dominions, France, and Belgium were all vehemently opposed to giving in to German demands, a growing number of voices called for compromise as a way to demonstrate the Council's complete faith in the PMC.[42] The most potent pressure came from Drummond, who in late November 1926 met Carl von Schubert, the German foreign minister, to discuss potential candidates.[43] As a bargaining tactic, the secretary-general warned that von Schubert might have formally to endorse Dr Heinrich Schnee or Friedrich von Lindequist, two of the most rabid leaders of the German colonial movement, if an early compromise failed. Schnee was particularly objectionable to London since he had recently published a book demanding that Germany regain its lost overseas empire.[44] Berlin also continued to remind the British ambassador, Sir Ronald Lindsay, that the German colonial societies were extremely restless and that the government "hoped that their wishes would be met now in Geneva."[45] A few days later he reported that Albert von Rechtenberg, a former governor of German East Africa, was currently the "candidate favoured by the German government."[46] Still, Chamberlain remained resolute and Stresemann, not wishing to cause a rupture with Britain so soon after joining the League, formally withdrew his request from the Council.[47]

The delay did not last long. Less than five months later, Stresemann renewed his agitation.[48] In the face of continued Anglo-French recalcitrance, Drummond personally negotiated with British, French, and German officials for several months to find a general agreement.[49] The PMC, while admitting that such decisions belonged to the Council, helped Drummond by insisting that there were "no technical objections" to expanding the Commission with a German.[50] In early August, Drummond submitted a new list of candidates that he and the German Foreign Ministry had composed after London had rejected all of the previous names. He promised than none of the latest possibilities were associated with "an extreme Colonial policy" and urged an immediate decision.[51] With Berlin's patience running thin, London and Paris finally indicated that Dr Ludwig Kastl, a name on Drummond's list, would make an acceptable "official candidate."[52] The Council confirmed Kastl on 8 September.[53]

In many ways, Kastl was the ideal German candidate for the PMC.[54] He had spent several years in the German colonial service and was an expert in economic policy, but his highest rank before the war had been "Financial Advisor" to the governor of German South-West Africa. When Allied troops conquered the protectorate in July 1915, Kastl became the "Commissioner of the German Government to the Occupying Government," which had required close cooperation with authorities in the Union of South Africa. In 1920, he returned to Germany to serve in the Finance Ministry as chief of the Department of Reparation Matters until he retired in 1925 to accept the post of managing director for the Reich Association of German Industry. His relative lack of interest in national politics, limited experience in high-level colonial administration, and demonstrated ability to work with the Allies put many in London and Paris at ease. That Kastl had been in the colonial service at all, however, was of some consolation to the leaders of the German colonial movement. The president of the influential *Deutsche Kolonialgesellschaft* (DKG), Theodor Seitz, had been Kastl's chief in German South-West Africa. Further, Kastl did tangentially participate in some of the less propagandistic activities of the colonial movement and maintained ties with business and government leaders.[55] While outspoken polemicists such as Schnee or Seitz may have considered Kastl too moderate, he did enjoy widespread credibility inside and outside of Germany.

Kastl's greatest strength as the German member on the PMC, however, was what he represented rather than who he was. His participation gave Germany its greatest direct influence over its former overseas empire since the war and magnified international attention on the mandates system. The German member had an immediate impact on the operation of the PMC. T. K. Lloyd, a Colonial Office official who attended Kastl's first session, told the Foreign Office that he was struck by the heightened sense of seriousness in Geneva.[56] According to Lloyd, Kastl largely restrained his nationalist sentiments and was "rather intolerant (almost more intolerant than are Accredited Representatives) of the stupid nature of many of the questions asked and of the discursiveness of certain members of the Commission."

> Taken as a whole the members of the Commission were less inclined than ever before within my experience to ask trivial questions or questions of detail. Most of them managed to find questions of principle or of some importance which they could raise.

Kastl's seriousness even seemed to diminish Lugard's prestige. Lloyd hinted that the former British governor-general was becoming less influential as attention seemed to shift to the German member. This last conclusion was particularly disturbing to Chamberlain. In a terse minute, he complained that "I wish that Sir F. Lugard would resign. I do not think that he is now equal to the task."[57] Another colonial official who served as an accredited representative for British Togoland before the PMC, H. S. Newlands, made a special trip to Berlin after the end of the PMC session and had "several opportunities of meeting Herr Kastl."[58] Newlands happily reported that Kastl thought the PMC should always defend "the man on the spot." He did not want a return of South-West Africa to Germany. But Newlands also warned that Kastl did not have a high opinion of his colleagues on the Commission and that he would oppose efforts by the British settler community in East Africa to acquire local political control over the Tanganyika Territory. Thus, Kastl held a moderate, yet markedly German, perception of the mandates system: it should not serve the interests of either the anti-imperialists or the German colonial reactionaries, but it must not symbolize either the inferiority of German colonialism or the confirmation of straightforward annexation.

Just as the members of the PMC became more deliberate in their approach to the mandate system after German membership, so did many British colonial officials. The Colonial Office became much more wary about who it chose to send as accredited representatives to Geneva. When Cameron requested in late 1926 to appear before the PMC the following June in order to defend his own administration in Tanganyika, Ormsby-Gore wrote: "[c]ertainly if there is a German on [the PMC] by then [and] any discussion about the new questionnaire likely at the June meetings both Sir Donald [and] I had better go."[59] A German did not join before summer. When it was uncertain if one would be present by the autumn session to review the reports for Togoland and the Cameroons, Ormsby-Gore again noted that "if there is no German member I need not go."[60] With Kastl on the PMC, one Colonial Office official was adamant that Cameron should represent Tanganyika in Geneva again:

> It is of special importance that Tanganyika should be well represented next June. We do not want anything that might look like an anti-climax to the great impression produced last year by Sir Donald Cameron; and this will be the first year in which a German member will be taking an active part.[61]

When Cameron replied that it was impossible for him to make the trip, only Amery was actually pleased. He complained that "I dislike the increasing practice of wasting the time of our best men by sending them to Geneva to justify ourselves before the P.M.C."[62] Amery's irritation aside, others in the Colonial Office realized that the new composition of the League made sending "our best men" to Geneva to justify British mandatory rule more important than ever.

The new composition of the League also forced the Colonial Office to scrutinize more closely the annual reports and other official documents sent to the PMC. While London had always been careful to edit the annual reports to the League in order to ensure that they did not "contain matters of a contentious nature" or embarrass the local administration, it now had to consider German sensibilities.[63] In early 1928 London edited Cameron's draft report for the League "with the object of making the Report more palatable to the Germans" by cutting out overt references to German colonial misrule and specific German military defeats in the territory during the war. It changed almost nothing else.[64] Even these alterations proved inadequate for Kastl, who complained in a private letter to the British representative that the report contained a number of "allegations" that were "wrong and misleading" and "must be regarded as an insult to Germany."[65] The letter went on to give a detailed history of colonial administration in German East Africa and urged that the next annual report reflect that "the German native policy corresponded with the wishes and interests of the natives." Lloyd advised offering no apologies, but reported that Kastl was "displaying increased activity on the P.M.C." and that

> I venture to suggest that, since such incidents serve no useful purpose and are resented by the German member who is, I think, genuinely helpful, a hint might be given to Sir Donald Cameron that any report sent to the Mandates Commission should be carefully scrutinised with a view to ensuring that criticisms likely to be distasteful to the Germans are excised.[66]

Kastl received a polite but non-committal response while both the Colonial Office and the colonial administration in Dar es Salaam were put on notice that they must draft each report with care.[67] Still, even though officials in London tended to edit more heavily after 1928, these changes were usually superficial and concerned direct comparisons between British and German colonial rule.[68] London remained hesitant to make many substantive alterations and never edited the numerous published departmental reports from the mandated territories that went to Geneva. In late 1929 one official explained why:

> If you cut a piece out of a printed document, the members of the M[andates] C[ommission] will merely have their curiosity aroused [and] will go look at the complete copy in the League Library. If, on the other hand, you suppress the document, they will notice that the supply has stopped [and] will ask why. On the whole I think that trying to keep printed [and] published documents from the P.M.C. is a dangerous policy, and it gives them an additional handle, if they can charge the Mandatory Govt. with attempted suppression as well as with the original crime.[69]

Others in the office agreed and insisted that "[t]here can, of course, be no question of 'editing' a published report or withholding published T.T. reports from the P.M.C."[70]

Not all British colonial officials reacted with such caution and solicitude to Germany's entry into the League of Nations. Sir Edward Grigg, the governor of Kenya from 1925 to 1930, was an outspoken opponent of the mandates system and feared that improved relations with Berlin might lead to a restoration of Germany's lost colonies. Grigg wrote to Baldwin early in 1926 to beg him to dissolve the mandate for the Tanganyika Territory and begin to consolidate it with Kenya and Uganda.[71] He argued that the international status of Tanganyika was a detriment not only to the future of Kenya, but to the entire British Empire:

> I therefore cannot help repeating that if Mandated Territory is still to be regarded as a water-tight, economic, political and administrative whole, there will be little advantage to the Empire, especially the East African portion of it, in having won the Mandate from Germany.

Grigg made similar complaints to Amery whom he knew shared many of his assumptions about British imperialism. The governor was especially exasperated with Cameron, who seemed to perpetuate and even to expand the differences between the mandated territory and its neighboring British colonies and protectorates:

> I think, in point of fact, that he regards Tanganyika as in some ways a peculiar and exceptional territory, responsible to other authorities outside the Empire as well as to the Imperial system with yourself as the controlling head. In talking with him I came again and again upon a sort of Chinese wall which he seems to draw around the Mandated Territory and which he appears to think essential to the administrative progress on which his whole heart is set at the present time.[72]

Grigg's bitterness went far beyond a personal dislike of Cameron:

> I also cannot help resenting from the bottom of my soul any suggestion that the League of Nations has any superior authority to the British Empire, any higher standards to assert, or any right to interfere in what we may regard as the best system of organisation and the best lines of policy for British East Africa as a whole.

Amery had a similar distrust of Geneva and was disturbed by the growing expectation within the German colonial movement in 1926 that League membership might serve as a first step toward the return of the overseas empire.[73] This same expectation worried the Tanganyika Development Company as well as the Tanganyika European Civil Servants Association, which both expressed their fears about the "political future" of the mandated territory.[74] Amery decided in early June that he would try to end this widespread speculation and uncertainty by telling an audience in London that the "foundations of the East Africa of the future were as sure and as permanent in Tanganyika as they were in any other East African territory."[75] He then gave copies of the speech to the governors of Tanganyika, Uganda, and Kenya and told them that the "situation should accordingly be regarded as definitely settled."[76] A few days later, however, Amery himself admitted that the problem was not "definitely settled" and had to modify his earlier comments by insisting that while the mandate was permanent, Britain would "fulfil in the fullest sense, in the letter as in the spirit, our obligations to the League of Nations with regard to that Mandate."[77]

Despite this last disclaimer, Amery's remarks caused an angry outburst from the German colonial movement and irritated some MPs. Schnee called the statements "in direct contradiction to the League Covenant," while Noel Buxton, a Labour MP and brother of the fervent critic of "old" imperialism, Charles Roden Buxton, implied that the government was trying to subvert both the Treaty of Versailles and the Locarno agreements.[78] In the end, Amery's speeches did not extinguish the uncertainty surrounding the mandated territories which persisted for the rest of the interwar period. Still, the loud protests and angry rhetoric of Grigg and Amery did demonstrate the powerful resistance that the mandates system continued to encounter and reveals how this same system made even the most unwavering British imperialists increasingly defensive and agitated about the impact of mandates on empire.

Cameron's Mandated Territory

Amery's public pledge that Britain would never relinquish Tanganyika did not mean that he could prevent the international status of the territory from continuing profoundly to shape Tanganyika's economic, cultural, and political complexion. Protected by the terms of the mandate, Germans were able to return to the former German possession and soon control much of the local economy, dominate the European settler community, and become part of the colonial state system. By 1930 Germans were the largest single group of European settlers in the mandate and accounted for half of the local white population. The British constituted only about one quarter.[79] During the interwar period sisal became Tanganyika's chief export crop, and by 1934 Germans owned more sisal estates than any other group of Europeans or Asians and perhaps controlled as much as one third of the total acreage under cultivation.[80]

These German estates employed a large number of Africans, many of whom migrated from outlying regions into north-east Tanganyika to work as sisal-cutters, and contributed to the fundamental shift away from peasant production to plantation enterprise as the basis of the local economy during the 1920s.[81] The terms of the mandate also protected German missionaries who recovered almost all of their former mission property in Tanganyika and quickly returned to operate dozens of schools educating thousands of African students.[82] Most of these schools received grants-in-aid from the colonial government and participated in Cameron's expanding plan to make mission schools responsible for the bulk of African education.[83] As the 1920s came to a close, Germans had managed to become an integral part of the colonial structure of Tanganyika and were a source of the relative economic prosperity as well as of the increasingly systematic permeation of European institutions and labor patterns among the indigenous African population.

This influx of Germans into Tanganyika did not distress the local colonial administration or most permanent officials in the Colonial Office. Since British emigrants found Tanganyika less attractive than other places (such as Kenya), colonial officials decided that productive German plantations were preferable to idle or impoverished British ones. Further, because local authorities alienated no new land to the Germans and did not extend any political control to settler communities, Dar es Salaam and London were satisfied that Tanganyika would remain predominately a "Black man's country." For Cameron, Tanganyika's restrictive land legislation, the territory's climate and geography, his commitment to his own brand of Indirect Rule, and Article 7 of the mandate prevented extensive white settlement anyway. He insisted in 1926 that "the land laws as they stand should be carried out in the most scrupulous manner in order to protect the interests of the natives" and that "it is not, I think, necessary for me to affirm again that the interests of the native should be paramount."[84] Charles Strachey, an assistant under-secretary of state for the colonies and one of the original drafters of the land law for Tanganyika, agreed with Cameron and reminded the Colonial Office that the "special reason for proceeding very cautiously in the Tanganyika Territory is, of course, that we can give no preference to British subjects" because of the equality clauses of the mandate.[85] Together, these arguments served to thwart every proposal for large scale or government assisted British immigration to Tanganyika designed to counter the increase in the German settler population.[86]

The interrelated issues of German immigration and the mandates system did alarm many British settlers and merchants, who accused the colonial government of impairing their interests and preventing them from participating in local administration. Some were certain that Dar es Salaam was doing nothing to prevent Berlin from subsidizing German settlers bent on undermining British mandatory rule.[87] F. S. Joelson, the editor of the newspaper *East Africa* and outspoken defender of the British settler community, complained that the land auction system in Tanganyika favored the Germans and made adopting Kenya's policy of direct government allocation to British settlers impossible.[88] In early 1928 the "Arusha Coffee Planters Association" complained about Cameron's "anti-settler" remarks before the PMC which were subsequently published in local newspapers.[89] As the British accredited representative, Cameron had told the PMC that Tanganyika was poorly suited for white settlement and that large-scale land alienation was not in the interests of Africans. The Association firmly disagreed with this interpretation and accused Cameron of subscribing to an "idealistic policy, the fulfillment of which appears to necessitate the discouragement of European Settlement in Tanganyika." In late October, the "Tanganyika Congress of Associations," a loose cluster of predominately British settler groups, met in Dodoma and passed a similar resolution denouncing the mandatory regime. They proclaimed that "the methods now adopted by Government to promote settlement in this Territory are insufficient and unsatisfactory" and demanded that Dar es Salaam allocate greater funds to help whites "develop" regions that Africans were not developing.[90]

Cameron hotly rejected the declaration:

> The Governor must lose no time in repudiating the view expressed in the Congress that the native has no moral right to the land which he occupies; that the person who has the moral right to the land is the one who makes the best economic use of it. This conception is contrary to the terms of the Mandate, and under the laws of the Territory the native has the legal as well as moral right to the land which he occupies.[91]

Cameron's relations with the European settlers, particularly the British coffee planters in the Tanga and Northern provinces who identified with their counterparts in Kenya, quickly eroded as the governor pursued his definition of mandatory administration.[92] In July 1929 Cameron met with a delegation of settlers from Moshi who wanted to discuss the possibility of "unofficials," or Europeans not in the colonial service, participating in local government.[93] Cameron and the settlers treated each other with contempt and their discussion swiftly degenerated into an exchange of threats and insults. The governor condemned the planters for intentionally misrepresenting their supposed plight while they accused him of constructing a personal dictatorship. In his report to the Colonial Office, Cameron argued it was useless to contemplate involving settlers in any plans for political devolution until London made "a definite affirmation of the principles which in their judgement should govern political development in the Territory in the spirit of Article 22 of the Covenant of the League of Nations."[94]

Cameron's appeal to the mandates system to contain European settlers was not an isolated example of the power that the international status of Tanganyika gave him to impose his personal brand of administrative order. Between 1925 and 1931, Cameron relied on his private ties with men like Lugard, the mounting admiration from the PMC, and a consistent endorsement of the tenets of Article 22 to institute his "Native Administration" structure in Tanganyika and to convince many that his colonial government was the best display of the mandatory principles in action.[95] The sharper political edge of the mandates system after Germany joined the League coincided with Cameron's rapidly expanding command over Tanganyika. By taking advantage of a combination of institutional support and international attention, Cameron constructed a network of local government divisions, or "Native Authorities," that invested a degree of financial, legislative, and executive control either in single "traditional" African rulers or in a council of rulers. This highly complex and bureaucratic system did allow indigenous leaders to arrest criminals, direct public works, and collect taxes, but it also systematically centralized the colonial state and increased its ability to intervene in the lives of

Africans.[96] Much of Cameron's achievement hinged on the influence he derived from the mandates system and his ability to harmonize his idea of imperialism with that of the PMC. He and the League developed an effective alliance that extended as well as strengthened the League's gradual internationalization and reformation of colonialism.

Throughout this period, one of Cameron's most important political allies was Lugard. In addition to Cameron's appearance before the PMC in 1927, the two men maintained regular private contacts and provided each other with information and advice. Most often, it was Sir Donald who gave his former chief details about a wide variety of future policies while hinting that "[a] little backing from the C.P.M. [PMC] would help me with the people here and with the C.O., if the latter raise any questions."[97] Lugard made suggestions about "ensuring to the native a right to the land which he is occupying" and Cameron supplemented the official material that London sent to the League "especially as the C.O. cut considerable portions out of my report."[98] On at least one occasion, the Colonial Office was aware that Lugard had private access to unpublished material from Tanganyika and suspected Cameron was the source, but did not complain since London could not prove it and because the PMC did not use the material to undermine the local administration.[99] In early 1928 Pierre Orts, the Belgian member of the PMC, visited Tanganyika and Cameron was not only quick to show him "something of the N[ative] A[dministrations] and our methods," but to report the entire matter to Lugard and thank him for warning him about the visit ahead of time.[100] The governor particularly wanted the PMC's help to resist the desire of Grigg and Amery to amalgamate Tanganyika, Kenya, and Uganda into a single administrative unit within the British Empire:

> I am very anxious about the future of this place and I must use every power at my command to frustrate Grigg's most dangerous proposals if the Sec. of State lends them any countenance. From the personal point of view I care little as I am prepared *at any moment* to resign from Tanganyika if I consider the interests of the natives are being made a pawn in any political game.[101]

By 1929 the governor was sure that most white settlers in East Africa were against him and remarked that "[i]t is natural that they are doing their best to get rid of me" and that "I want all public backing in England that I can obtain" to resist them.[102] As the decade came to a close, Lugard and Cameron, along with others in Britain such as J. H. Oldham, the secretary of the International Missionary Council, were working together to oppose large-scale European settlement in East Africa and forms of settler self-government that included the mandated territory. Cameron gratefully told Lugard: "I am glad to think that Tanganyika has Oldham and yourself at work on her behalf in the U.K."[103]

The governor of Tanganyika routinely associated himself with Lugard and the mandatory principles in order to overcome opposition, avoid criticism, and distinguish his administration from British colonies and protectorates. In April 1926 Cameron wrote Lugard to tell him that Grigg wanted a coordinated labor policy for the Masai, whose lands were divided between Kenya and Tanganyika.[104] At the next meeting of the PMC, Lugard raised the issue and strongly advocated unifying the Masai under a single administration that "does not involve any limitation of the control exercised by the League of Nations under mandate."[105] When Cameron refused to adopt Kenya's labor policy and suggested placing all Masai lands within the mandated territory, Grigg promptly decided to drop the whole matter.[106] Dar es Salaam took particular glee in reporting several months later that the Masai apparently were proving the superiority of Tanganyika's administration by emigrating from Kenya into Tanganyika in large numbers.[107]

Cameron used the PMC again in early 1927 by referring to embarrassing questions from the League as a reason for repealing a law that allowed the police to arrest Africans without a warrant and to punish convicted offenders by imprisonment without the option of a fine.[108] During a meeting of the Oversea Defence Committee of the Committee of Imperial Defence, the governors of Tanganyika, Kenya, Northern Rhodesia, Gold Coast, and several other British colonies and protectorates discussed common security issues.[109] While Cameron promised that Tanganyika was "fully aware of her defence obligations," he lost no time in reminding everyone that the international status of the territory placed limits on his ability to recruit Africans into the military. The mandate was not a colony.

> His three colleagues, who had previously spoken were all from British possessions, whereas he spoke for a Mandated territory, where special difficulties were encountered in the matter of raising local forces . . .

Dar es Salaam was also often careful to conform to the equality clauses of the mandate when drafting mining legislation, granting railroad concessions, and establishing public utilities.[110] Cameron even managed to get a substantial pay raise in 1928 because of "the special responsibilities of T.T. as a Mandated Territory."[111]

The mandates system was probably most useful to Cameron during this period in his determination to institute his Native Administrations and recast the complexion of British colonial rule in Tanganyika. In early 1927, he proposed eliminating virtually all of the British High Court's jurisdiction over his emerging "Native Courts," the local judicial component of the Native Administration system.[112] The Native Courts, much like those in Nigeria, only applied to Africans, but in theory could settle a wide variety of civil and criminal disputes in conformity with African customary law.[113] The governor wanted to place these courts under the supervision of district officers in their "executive capacity," effectively making them ex-officio magistrates with the special authority to hear "important" cases when necessary.

While the High Court would still supervise cases tried by administrative officers, the Chief Justice, Sir Alison Russell, was furious to discover that professional magistrates would not be responsible for all subordinate court work and that the High Court could not "by its own motion or on petition hear matters in which it considers that a real injustice may have been done" in the Native Courts.[114] Under this proposal, legal activity would become a systematic part of local colonial administration. The governor, not the relatively independent colonial judicial system of provincial and supreme courts, would have ultimate control over African tribunals. Cameron dismissed Russell's objections since "[o]ur system of indirect administration in Tanganyika is of paramount importance" and cited passages from the minutes of the PMC and some recent advice from Lugard to the mandatory powers to defend the reforms.[115] The governor's proposals even shocked officials in the Colonial Office, who argued that they went beyond the standard legal practice in Nigeria where Africans could appeal to "ordinary" British courts.[116] London was unwilling to disallow the proposal, but strongly urged Dar es Salaam to consider copying the Nigerian model before final adoption.[117] The local administration refused all such suggestions and amended the draft legislation to give Africans the right to appeal to district officers or the Governor.[118]

The controversy surrounding the Native Courts became a protracted one pitting Cameron and his subordinates against the judiciary and most of the unofficial members of the Legislative Council in Dar es Salaam. The quarrel proved too much for Russell, who finally chose early retirement rather than submit to Cameron.[119] As before, the governor appealed to the mandates system to overcome the objections of the leading unofficials in Tanganyika. During a Council meeting in April 1929 Cameron and his attorney-general, Edward St. John Jackson, insisted that the reforms not only would have the support of London, but would give "effect to the views of the Permanent Mandates Commission of the League of Nations" and would have the support of "those gentlemen in Geneva."[120] Jackson specifically quoted Lugard and argued that "[t]hose gentlemen who form that Commission have experience of the government of territories such as this" and their advice was that African courts should be based on "the law and the will and the understanding and the traditions" of Africans. Many of the "unofficials" complained that the Native Courts would give far too much power to Africans and asserted that the opinion of the

League of Nations was not as important as adopting traditional methods of British legal order in Tanganyika. Major Sir William Lead, the founder and president of the Tanganyika Sisal Growers Association as well as the leader of the unofficial side of the Council, cited his own selected passages from the minutes of the PMC to try to defeat the plan. An Asian member, G. H. Ghose, was certain that the African "must be taught to look to British ideals of justice, rather than his own ideas of justice." A third member, who did not trust either the administrative staff or the indigenous rulers, attacked the notion that Geneva could override imperial traditions of the British Empire:

> [s]urely this miniature League of Nations under a British Flag, comprising 450 million souls, does depend very much on one sure truth that within the Empire you can always demand the administration of justice and judgements that will be delivered with strict impartiality.

Cameron remained unmoved. Since he and his subordinates outnumbered the unofficials on the Council, the governor got his Native Courts ordinance despite the protests of his Chief Justice, the widespread displeasure of the leading unofficials in his government, and the serious apprehensions of the Colonial Office.[121]

By late 1929, Cameron's reforms meant that Africans in Tanganyika were increasingly exposed to the wider range of dangers and opportunities inherent in a courts system that depended on the "advice" of district officers and the political skills of individual African leaders to control change within local conditions.[122] By merging judicial and executive power, the colonial state was able to penetrate much deeper into African society, to reorder local communities into often artificial cultural categories, and to form static definitions of "native rule" and African "customary law." The Native Courts served further to integrate as well as complicate the relations between Europeans and Africans as both encountered a highly bureaucratic administrative structure that required each to exercise diverse forms of power. Together, these broad changes forever changed British colonial rule in Tanganyika and made the mandated territory a model of Indirect Rule for other colonial regimes in Africa. Cameron achieved this administrative transformation by overtly aligning himself with an international organization and its agenda for progressive reform and pragmatic paternalism. In the process, he staked much of both his and the League's reputation on the relative success or failure of the Tanganyika Territory to represent the changing face of European imperialism and postwar international order.

While Cameron did much to make his administration and the mandates system synonymous, he was not above forsaking Geneva when it suited him. The same influence that he derived by consistently appealing to the international status of Tanganyika also allowed him to evade the League and undermine its purpose when necessary. For example, he did not let the mandate's prohibition against "general monopolies" stop him from granting a meat-canning company "exclusive rights in a restricted area" near Mwanza that included reduced rents, a guaranteed profit, and the right to control the local cattle market for ten years.[123] Given the ambiguous meaning of "general monopoly," Cameron and several colonial officials in London were sure that there was no violation of Article 7.[124] Yet, because the company's "restricted area" encompassed the only region in Tanganyika with high-quality stock and adequate transportation facilities, at least one official argued that the arrangement made the ban on monopolies virtually meaningless.[125] After much debate, the permanent under-secretary of state for the colonies, Sir Samuel H. Wilson, and Ormsby-Gore both decided to trust Cameron and "take the risk of criticism at Geneva."[126]

The following year, the Colonial Office trusted the governor again when he insisted that one private British lighterage company should handle all the cargo entering Dar es Salaam harbor as "a public service" in conformity with Article 7.[127] Cameron claimed that the monopoly would end "the un-coordinated efforts" of the various companies already in business, but some in the Colonial Office suspected that he really intended to block German and Japanese firms from squeezing out their British competitors.[128] The governor sparked similar doubts when responding to protests from the PMC about why he had not explained to Africans that they lived in a mandated territory instead of British colony or protectorate:

> It is impossible to explain, as we attempted in the first place to explain to the chiefs and natives, that Tanganyika was regarded "as part of the framework of the British Empire and was administered as such." He would have been unable to understand it . . . [129]

In early 1928 Dar es Salaam introduced a highly controversial "collective punishment" ordinance even though one colonial official in London warned: "I am afraid that the Permanent Mandates Commission will not like this."[130] Lastly, Cameron himself authorized an unabashed circumvention of Tanganyika's land law which prohibited individual "non-natives" from possessing single plots of more than 5,000 acres. In 1929 he let a Colonel Arthur Fawcus acquire 51,200 acres of land by renting 11 adjoining plots and treating all of the leases as one.[131] The transaction astounded one London official who wondered why the governor had discarded Lugard's Nigerian rule that "co-terminus areas, or areas so contiguous to each other as to amount to an evasion of the law, will not be granted."[132] Still, reluctant to lecture Cameron on land alienation and the interests of Africans, London ultimately gave its consent.[133]

The British Empire and Article 22

German membership in the League and the sweeping administrative changes in Tanganyika were two of the most prominent features of this period, but by 1926 the mandates system was so firmly fastened to the British imperial structure that neither Berlin nor Cameron could seize or destroy Geneva's initiative in fostering a transformation of the culture of British colonialism. The trend established during the first half of the decade continued throughout the second. Government agencies outside of the Colonial Office remained convinced that the mandated territories were not juridically part of the British Empire and required separate procedures under international law.[134] The LNU was unrelenting in reminding London of the force of public opinion in shaping policy for the mandates and routinely proposed expanding the powers of the PMC.[135] Lugard maintained his connections with the LNU, colonial administrators, the Colonial Office, and the British government.[136] He became even more involved in national affairs when Baldwin offered him a peerage in late 1928 and as Baron Lugard of Abinger he joined the House of Lords.[137] The Labour Party intensified its official support for the mandates system and "Trusteeship" as the best guard against "the old Imperialism:"

> the Labour party frankly accepts, for the whole of the "backward" races in the Empire, the principle underlying the Mandate System established by the League of Nations. It proposes that all imperial powers should be invited to assume the same responsibilities.[138]

Finally, some Asians in Tanganyika continued to find the international status of the territory and the right to petition the League useful tools in pressing the local administration to protect their economic and political interests while combating racial discrimination.[139]

Perhaps most importantly, while much of the chaotic uncertainty surrounding the mandates system in the early 1920s had disappeared, the Colonial Office continued to take the work of the PMC seriously and made evaluating the "international considerations" of major colonial policy in the mandated territories a routine part of its oversight responsibilities.[140] In West Africa, Britain's mandatory obligation to provide yearly reports for Togo and Cameroon forced officials to continue to supply separate financial, administrative, and legislative information on the two territories. This constant reminder of the international status of the mandates not only tended to perpetuate the perception that they were distinct entities, but gradually exposed the larger administrations of Gold Coast and Nigeria to international scrutiny as officials tried to justify why the two possessions were treated "as integral parts" of their neighboring British colonial regimes.[141] In the process, the two territories never found a comfortable place within the British colonial lexicon and changed names each time officials discovered that they could not absorb the mandates and keep them entirely separate at the same time. In 1921 the Colonial Office apparently had no difficulty in reporting on "the British Sphere of the Cameroons" as well as "the British Mandated Sphere of Togoland."[142] By 1926 it found that the different titles were confusing and adopted "British Sphere of Togoland" and "the British Sphere of the Cameroons" instead, which only caused Amery to complain that "I don't like these expressions. They assume Cameroons and Togoland are still entities of which we are temporarily occupying part."[143] When colonial officials discovered that the Order in Council establishing Togo's constitution contained the phrase "British Sphere of Togoland" and they could not easily change it, they decided to keep the name while changing that of the other mandate to "the British Cameroons."[144] This latest revision, however, immediately raised embarrassing questions in Geneva which forced British officials finally to settle on "Togoland under British Mandate" and "the Cameroons under British Mandate."[145] While the League may have been pleased, Lagos and Accra were still grumbling about these cumbersome and inhibiting titles as late as 1938.[146]

As the decade came to an end, the mandates system had demonstrated a remarkable resiliency. A collection of government leaders, special interest groups, colonial officials, and an international organization had successfully protected the PMC from serious political attack and, after the addition of a German national, had helped the commission to remain a prominent part of the administration of the British mandates. Many inside and outside of the British Empire had concluded that the fate of the mandates system was the same as that for the empire itself. Amery and Grigg resented how both the specific language and general notion of the mandates had caused this shift within the ideology of imperialism. Yet Geneva's power was not merely symbolic nor entirely benign. The international status of Tanganyika had resulted in important political and economic changes within the territory and had enhanced Cameron's ability to place an ideologically progressive, yet highly intrusive, administrative order upon Africans. The mandates system had changed the nature of the colonial state, but ten difficult years as the world's largest overseas empire had convinced British colonial officials that British imperialism and Article 22 must remain synonymous in order to justify an imperfect past as well as to contemplate an uncertain future.

8

Germany Joins the League: The French Mandates, 1926–1929

The extension of the mandates system to include Berlin affected the French and British colonial structures differently. Germany's joining the League dramatically heightened the anxiety and defensiveness of France as a mandatory power. It added to a mounting fear of German intrigue and prompted colonial officials to institute tighter state restrictions over Europeans and Africans in the mandated territories. Despite these repressive measures, however, a number among the African elite exploited France's apprehensions and continued to use the mandates system to test and restrict French colonial rule. In addition, even though France was more careful to control public information about Togo and Cameroon, it continued to take pains to avoid international criticism by maintaining and even expanding their distinctive character. As with Britain, the mandates system persisted in having an impact on every level of French rule and exemplified an internationalization and reformation of colonialism.

French officials were horrified by the prospect of Germany's using the mandates system to exert influence in its former colonies and were willing to go to great lengths to protect French rule in Togo and Cameroon. Many were sure that the Weimar Republic was a dangerous threat to France's imperial legitimacy which wanted to undermine the empire and weaken the metropole.[1] The memories of the First World War were still vivid and bitter, particularly among those who were aware of France's persistent vulnerabilities despite "victory" and Germany's increasing strengths despite "defeat." Throughout the interwar period, local officials kept extensive dossiers on all suspected "pro-German" Africans and tried to exclude as many Germans as possible from the mandates.[2] As early as 1922, the Colonial Ministry had prepared an expensive and elaborate surveillance procedure for Togo and Cameroon that would require all European visitors, including French citizens, to provide detailed itineraries, medical reports, and financial records before obtaining the written permission of the commissioner and an official visa from the Foreign Ministry.[3] This policy was unlike that for the rest of the empire where French citizens did not need a visa for travel.[4] It was designed specifically to go into effect when Germany became a member of the League and would give the colonial state the authority to deport anyone who engaged in "anti-French propaganda" or was "considered suspect" of subversive activity.[5] Even during the Locarno Conference in 1925, the Colonial Ministry argued that the government should compel the Germans to pledge never to accept either a mandate or a seat on the PMC.[6] This deep-seated fear of Germany along with France's marked apprehension about the uncertainties of international supervision combined to influence colonial administration in Togo and Cameroon for the rest of the decade.

French Fears and Colonial Control

Once it was clear that Germany would join the League in 1926, French colonial officials dedicated themselves to insulating the mandated territories from Berlin. André Perier, the colonial minister, tried to convince the Foreign Ministry that since Germany had renounced its rights to its colonies by signing the Treaty of Versailles, it was not entitled to any privileges under the mandates system.[7] Further, he was willing to risk international litigation by prohibiting Germany from commercial equality in the mandated territories since he was convinced that "our national interests" were at stake.[8] After a number of sharp exchanges, the Foreign Ministry told Perier to instruct the commissioners of Togo and Cameroon to obey all of the stipulations of the mandate.[9] Having insisted since 1919 that Germany must obey its obligations under the Treaty, the Foreign Ministry would not risk the certain German protest that would follow any request that France be excused from the mandate clauses. Lomé and Yaoundé reluctantly agreed to conform to the mandate and vowed to monitor the activities of every German merchant company in their territories, but warned that their return would have indeterminate "political repercussions" for Africans under French control.[10]

Tight entry controls and surveillance were not enough for those who feared Germans using the mandates system to endanger French colonial rule and incite African political agitation. While under international law France was unable overtly to discriminate against Germany, colonial officials could further regulate the lives of Africans and restrict the rights of all Europeans in the mandates in an effort to guard against possible subversion. The commissioner of Togo, Auguste Bonnecarrère, introduced a much stricter passport law not only to limit emigration into neighboring Gold Coast, but to prevent Africans from accepting employment with German companies operating in the Spanish and Portuguese colonies in the Gulf of Guinea.[11] For Bonnecarrère, the probable economic and social problems that unemployment in Togo would cause were preferable to exposing Africans to potentially dangerous foreign influences or going beyond the terms of the mandate to serve the economic interests of the Weimar Republic. Bonnecarrère also demanded loyalty oaths from many of the leading chiefs while the commissioner of Cameroon, Théodore Marchand, arrested and imprisoned a number of Africans for "sedition" and "anti-European propaganda" as a means of social control.[12]

Both commissioners, however, remained careful not to directly violate international law or attract the criticism of the PMC as they tightened their colonial rule in the mandates after 1926. For example, both consulted the PMC before they adopted a harsh expulsion ordinance that gave them the power to deport without trial any "undesirable person" from their mandates.[13] Since the law applied to everyone irrespective of nationality, the PMC did not object. Instead, it was the *Ligue Française pour la Défense des Droits de l'Homme et du Citoyen*, a group in France concerned with civil liberties, that was outraged. It demanded that French citizens should have "special protections" in any territory under French colonial rule.[14] The Colonial Ministry responded that such protection was

> incompatible with the fundamental rules of administration in the territories of Togo and Cameroon under French mandate and with the terms which the mandatory power must assure to all nationals of member states of the League of Nations . . . [15]

Thus, conforming to the mandate required universal discrimination. For the administrators in Togo and Cameroon, the added costs and complications involved in this increased degree of state repression far outweighed either the priorities of Africans or the legal rights of French citizens living in the mandated territories.

Together with tighter administration within the mandates after Germany joined the League, French officials painstakingly controlled public information about Togo and Cameroon, worked to improve France's imperial reputation with the PMC, and were alert to even the seemingly most insignificant German threats to the mandates system. In 1926 Paris heavily edited Marchand's report to the League and the commissioner himself appeared as the accredited representative in an effort to circumvent criticism as well as to demonstrate how sincerely France took its mandatory responsibilities.[16] When Jean Beau, the French member of the PMC, died in February 1926, Aristide Briand's Foreign Ministry chose a successor who was less of a diplomat by training than Beau and whose colonial credentials rivaled those of Lugard.[17] Martial Henri Merlin had spent nearly forty years in the colonial service and had been governor-general of French Equatorial Africa, Madagascar, French West Africa, and Indochina.[18] With Merlin in Geneva, the Colonial Ministry could count on a reliable advocate and issued detailed new instructions for drafting annual reports which insisted that officials comply meticulously with every League request while always accenting the accomplishments of French mandatory rule.[19]

Worries about Germany's exploiting the mandates system were constant. In Cameroon, Marchand complained that a German merchant corporation, the *Neu Guinea Kompanie*, had a charter that was founded on pre-war German legislation that granted trade with Germany's overseas possessions.[20] In a lengthy and impassioned despatch, Marchand insisted that the wording of the charter was not an accident. It not only revealed a blatant disregard for the mandates system, but made a subtle claim of sovereignty over the lost overseas empire. The commissioner denied entry to the company for nearly a year until the German government finally reported that it had expressly altered the charter to authorize the company to trade in "the former German colonies and protectorates."[21] Marchand was equally wary of a second German firm in Cameroon, the once powerful *Firma C. Woermann*, which hosted a dinner for local French officials in early 1928 on one of its ships.[22] The commissioner took delight in telling Paris about how impressed the local Africans were by "the sight of Germans serving dinner to the French at the ship's table. Their administrator told them that this was a consequence of the French victory."[23] Even as late as September 1929 the Foreign Ministry, in cooperation with London, delivered a formal protest to Berlin calling attention to some official German government publications that referred to the mandated territories by their old German place names.[24] Despite four years of German membership in the League, French officials lost none of their suspicions and continued to expend a great deal of energy watching every step of their former enemies.

Since Germany was at the root of the enormous political insecurity of the colonial bureaucracy during this period, the repressive nature of the mandatory regimes resulted in a number of successes for France. By 1929, even under the protection of the mandates system, few Germans had returned to Togo and Cameroon. In contrast to the British sphere of Cameroon, the local authorities had liquidated almost all of the former German plantations before 1926, leaving only a few small properties for possible re-sale to German buyers.[25] Given the meager economic opportunities, combined with the lack of official encouragement and the inhibiting entry laws, the French continued to predominate among the European population within both mandates.[26] Also unlike the British West African mandates, but in strict conformity with the terms of the Treaty of Versailles, the French had transferred all the captured German missionary property to French or Swiss missions, making it virtually impossible for the ousted societies to return to their previous work.[27] Germany eventually did surpass both France and Britain as Togo's largest export market, but this was more than offset by the fact that France imported nearly six times as much as either Germany or Britain into the territory.[28] Thus, while the mandatory regime was happy to comply with the commercial equality clauses of the mandate by selling as much cacao and palm oil as it could to the Weimar Republic, it was not obliged to buy German goods and unfailingly avoided doing so. As a result, the metropole probably benefitted most from Germany's trade with the mandated territories. By 1929 France had successfully demonstrated that it could operate within the letter of the mandates system to insulate Togo and Cameroon from much direct German influence while escaping serious criticism from Berlin.[29]

The Return of the *Bund*

In contrast to France's relative success with Germany, French colonial officials failed to prevent Africans from exploiting the mandates system to criticize and curb French mandatory rule during this period. Bonnecarrère discovered that the members of the Adjigo family he had exiled in 1922 had hired an African lawyer from Britain's neighboring possession of the Gold Coast to submit another petition to the League in 1926.[30] This time, the PMC was far less circumspect in its conclusions and was irritated to discover that the matter remained unresolved. It admonished France by professing that Geneva had relied on the local government not to take any "severe measures" in maintaining public order in Togo, but that "the Commission's hopes were not realized."[31] The PMC went on to draft a series of embarrassing questions that pressed the French to explain why the Adjigo had been "subjected to unmerited hardships and humiliations" and to justify exile once again. Without admitting to anything, Bonnecarrère decided that the best way to respond to the League was to allow the deportees to return immediately to Anécho and establish a special court where the family could resolve their disputes with the Lawsons, the rival family that retained the local throne.[32] The Adjigo accepted the commissioner's terms and agreed to end their long legal and international agitation. Yet, in the process they had successfully demonstrated that they could use the mandates system to secure political concessions and to reorder their position within colonial society by taking full advantage of the gaps between French and British mandatory rules.

Over the next several years, Bonnecarrère discovered that other Africans were exploiting the differences between the two Togo mandates in a different way to reject French colonial rule. In late 1929 the commissioner realized that his rigid passport ordinance for Africans seeking work outside of Togo was failing to stop workers from moving permanently into the adjoining British mandated territory. When the commissioner asked the governor of the Gold Coast, Sir Alexander Ransford Slater, for a joint effort to curtail the exodus, local British district officers objected on the grounds that such measures would "appear to be inconsistent with the spirit of Article VI of the Mandate," which required the mandatory power to "respect the rights and safeguard the interests of the native population."[33] H. W. Leigh, the chief commissioner of the northern territories of Gold Coast who supervised the colonial administration of part of the mandated territory, argued that

> Article 6 of the Mandate appears to imply that freedom of movement is to be allowed to all Nationals of States, Members of the League of Nations, which applies to the Natives of French Ordinary and Mandated Territory . . .[34]

Colonial officials in London agreed. They noted that Africans were undoubtedly looking to escape "French taxation, the poll requisition and labour requirements" in Togo.[35] The international status of the territories provided a useful means for the British to welcome these much needed workers into thinly populated regions. Once Britain opted to combine its colonial interests with the ideals of the mandates system, the chance for any Anglo-French collaboration to contain African emigration in Togo vanished. As a result, Africans were able to move between the two mandatory powers in pursuit of greater political and economic autonomy while continuing to expose the divisions and incongruities of European imperialism in West Africa.

The group of Africans whose use of the mandates system probably represented the most potent political threat to French rule in Togo after Germany joined the League was the mysterious *Bund der Deutsch Togoländer*. When the *Bund* officially had announced its existence to the general public within the mandated territory in late 1925, it had already sent two petitions to Geneva demanding the return of Togo to Germany. The League of Nations Mandates Section, responsible for the day to day functions of the PMC, decided that the petitions were "too general" for review and returned them.[36] Still, they greatly alarmed French colonial officials, who in early 1926 told the Foreign Ministry that the *Bund* was part of a larger German colonial propaganda campaign.[37] For some, this dark suspicion was confirmed when public appeals allegedly from the *Bund* appeared in a German newspaper.[38] Since the group's leaders were living in Accra, it was difficult for French authorities to investigate the organization and it was impossible for them to prevent the *Bund* from meeting or using the British postal service. The fact that the group was composed of Germanophone members of the Adjigo family was an additional source of worry for the colonial government. In June and August 1926, having learned from its first attempts, the *Bund* sent much more detailed petitions to Geneva and Paris accusing the French of instituting oppressive taxation, restricting emigration, and "torturing" Africans in Togo.[39]

This time, the PMC decided that it could not ignore the petition and formally asked the French government to respond to the *Bund*'s charges. After examining the government's explanations, however, the PMC concluded that the charges were groundless.[40] As before, Geneva allied itself with the authority of the mandatory power and demonstrated a strong preference for cooperation with European colonialism rather than try to undermine it. Yet, in the process, the PMC had forced France to defend its colonial policies openly and to answer embarrassing accusations from African critics. The interests of both the League and the French were served by allowing the mandatory power to emerge unscathed, but leading members of the PMC had already privately wondered if the dangers posed by such petitions from the inhabitants of B mandates were too great. Pierre Orts, the Belgian member, told Lugard that Africans "did not understand their right to appeal" and could become the agents of unscrupulous polemicists looking to spread "racial antipathy, communism, probably Bolshevism, and every other poisonous 'ism.'"[41] While Lugard admitted that he was "very discontented with the present system of petitions which does not secure justice and is only likely to promote discontent," both men agreed that:

> We must not give a handle to the anti-Mandate and anti-League people nor must we lay ourselves open to the charge of slurring over events and withholding justice from petitioners.

Like it or not, both the PMC and the mandatory powers had to accommodate African petitioners, including those from the *Bund der Deutsch Togoländer*, while working to reform European imperialism.

Bonnecarrère revealed his growing fears about these dangers in his reports to Paris detailing the activities of the *Bund*.[42] In December 1927, he described the president, Johan Kanyi, as well as the other leading members, as merely unemployed former clerks in the German colonial government who were engaged in "pro-German propaganda" for purely selfish reasons. While the commissioner assured the Colonial Ministry that the *Bund*'s various accusations were trivial and were easy to refute, he was bothered much more by the League's willingness to entertain such petitions without certifying the signatures or investigating "the names, residences, [and] occupations" of the petitioners first. Under these circumstances, anyone using "a phoney signature and invested without the slightest accountability," inspired by "pure malevolence," could compel

Geneva to "open investigations, ask for explanations, and cast doubt on the vigilance and spirit of justice of the administration of the Mandatory Power."

This danger seemed an even more serious threat since a German member had just joined the PMC in September. By the time the Colonial Ministry asked Bonnecarrère for more information on the *Bund* in 1929, the commissioner's alarm verged on hysteria. In a nine-page report, he now insisted that the *Bund* was composed of "malcontented and corrupt natives who had been driven out of their decent country by their decent fellow countrymen."[43] The group was bent on "calling attention to its opposition to the French administration by slanderous denunciations before the High Assembly of Geneva" and was driven by "vengeance" and "profit." For the first time, Bonnecarrère also asserted that the *Bund* "probably" received financial support not only from German nationals living in Accra, but from the German government through the local German consulate. Without this patronage, the commissioner contended, the *Bund* would quickly dissolve.

For Bonnecarrère, the *Bund der Deutsch Togoländer* represented the triple threat of German subversion, international criticism, and African protest against French colonial rule. By convincing himself and the Colonial Ministry that the group was only a small and unrepresentative circle of disgruntled rogues tied to Berlin, it was easier to dismiss the *Bund*'s attacks on Togo's taxation and emigration policies. More importantly, rejecting the *Bund* meant affirming French colonial legitimacy. While those among the African coastal elite such as Kanyi resented how the end of German rule in Togo had eliminated opportunities to appropriate political and economic power within the imperial order, the mandates system provided new openings to exert influence and contest colonialism. In 1929 French colonial officials may have hoped that the *Bund* was an artificial society with little chance for long-term survival, but the group remained an active political threat for the rest of the interwar period. In 1936 French authorities in Lomé created the pro-French "Cercle des Amitiés Française" in part to counter the perceived menace of the *Bund* and in 1939 exiled or interned all of the group's suspected sympathizers.[44] Thus, France's outward contention that the group was powerless was betrayed by the preoccupations and reactions of colonial officials obsessed with maintaining control within the colonial state.

The mandatory regime in Togo was not alone in facing Africans who used the mandates system to challenge French imperialism. In Cameroon, the Duala had unsettled French colonial officials by sending a petition, written in German, to the Paris Peace Conference in 1919 asking for self-determination and the protection of certain "civil rights" including "individual freedom" and property ownership.[45] For the rest of the interwar period, the local administration faced numerous protests from the Duala, principally over the problem of land alienation around the coastal city of Douala and in the Joss plateau.[46] The Duala often relied on the international status of Cameroon to try to intimidate and embarrass the French. During a series of meetings in December 1926 between district officers and Richard Manga Bell, the paramount chief of the Duala, the French attempted to bully him into accepting an indemnity for the land that the Germans had seized in 1914 and the French refused to return.[47] Bell rejected the indemnity, but offered to lease the land directly to the government if the Duala could have complete control of the revenues. When the local administrator declared that the two sides were at a hopeless impasse, the chief threatened to take the matter to Geneva:

> In its position as Guardian [Tuteur], the French Government has the obligation to examine fairly this question which is the territory's most important. Since all of our complaints remain unanswered, we will propose to the League of Nations that they settle this old question after listening to the different parties.

The negotiations ended in failure. Marchand defended himself by reminding Paris that his policy was entirely legal and that the PMC had never criticized his land legislation. In a now familiar assessment, the commissioner also suggested that the Duala were the puppets of unnamed "local or even external elements" in search of "a personal profit" which drastically diminished the validity of the protests.[48]

Marchand's explanations did nothing to resolve the controversy. In 1928, Raymond Leslie Buell, an American scholar, called the Duala land controversy "[p]robably the most burning issue in French Cameroons today" and hinted that the PMC should investigate.[49] Over the next several years, the Duala sent several petitions to the League calling for the return of their land, harshly criticizing French colonial rule, and vaguely asserting the existence of a sovereign Cameroon Kingdom.[50] By early December 1929, the Duala chiefs were consulting a lawyer in Paris.[51] In a long and detailed petition dated 19 December and written in German, the Duala boldly proposed transforming Cameroon into a self-governing international territory under League control and administered by several powers including Germany, Norway, China, and the United States.[52] For the public record, the PMC called most of these petitions "curious." It accepted France's official explanations that every land transaction had been legal and that the petitioners were either unrepresentative or victims of self-serving outsiders.[53]

By mid-1931, after years of mutual intransigence and with the local economy in frightening decline, the Duala finally accepted a compromise with the government that provided money and free plots of land away from the city of Douala in exchange for full French control of the Joss plateau.[54]

Even though the Duala failed to regain their expropriated land, the mandates system did have significance for them. Some scholars have argued that the petitions to the League allowed the Duala to express and sharpen their brand of "radical anti-colonialism" and were a foundation for a "nationalist or proto-nationalist" movement in Cameroon that eventually contributed to the dramatic organized rebellions against French rule after 1945.[55] Further, without such sophisticated protest or the threat of outside criticism, the French might have refused to make any compromises with the group. Jonathan Derrick has suggested that the Duala's fervent and public opposition to the French mandatory regime probably "helped to restrain the French from expropriating other Duala land, which remained a good source of income."[56] This revenue, as well as that from the free plots handed over after 1931, combined with the desire of local French officials to avoid unnecessary confrontation, allowed the Duala to pay cash to commute their labor obligations under the *indigénat* code and gave the group a degree of independence that other African communities in Cameroon did not have. The Duala's awareness of the international status of the mandate and their willingness to use petitions helped to make them one of the most important groups in Cameroon during the interwar years and after.

Taxation and Labor Laws

The mandates system presented France with several baffling predicaments, not least of which was the discovery that, in order to avoid League criticism, colonial officials had to expose the mandated territories to increasing international scrutiny by overtly maintaining their distinctive character. In the process, the presence of the League continued to alter the lives of Africans within the mandated territories and have an impact on the ideology of imperialism. Since Paris did not want to risk charges of "annexation" or "militarism," it did not change the largely autonomous administrative status of the two governments or alter military recruitment policies in the mandates.[57] Equally wary of accusations of economic exploitation, officials called special attention to the large budget surpluses of Togo and Cameroon and how neither territory made contributions to the finances of French West or French Equatorial Africa as was required of French colonies.[58]

At the same time, the French government boasted that it did not advance or guarantee loans to either mandate and it prohibited the territories from directly investing in the metropole. Instead, Togo financed a public works program in Cameroon which served to strengthen their economic ties and deepen their separation from the neighboring French colonial federations.[59]

While the PMC often lavishly praised France for the relative prosperity and fiscal independence of their two mandates, it also irritated French officials by attacking the surpluses as indications of excessive taxation and an "unproductive" use of financial resources, particularly when the franc depreciated in value during the 1920s.[60] Geneva also forced the mandatory power to defend publicly the labor laws in Togo and Cameroon in the face of such economic surplus.[61] Thus, while Geneva was quick to offer its congratulations to the metropole for not enriching itself at the expense of its mandates, the League persistently pressed France to reform its demands on workers and to pass the apparent economic gains on to Africans in the form of lower taxes and lighter labor requirements. Some scholars contend that this outside public pressure resulted in a series of reforms including a rate of direct taxation in the French mandates that was only half the rate in French West Africa, four days of *prestation* labor in Togo rather than ten, tangible improvements in working conditions for Africans in Cameroon after 1927, an end to government recruitment of labor for private employers, and the gradual decline in unpaid labor in Cameroon throughout the 1930s.[62] Geneva hoped that these gradual reforms would serve not only to end some of the worst abuses of Africans, including the shockingly high mortality rates associated with railroad construction in Cameroon, but would help the local government create a much more stable labor market, avoid social and political disorder, deflect criticism from humanitarian special interest groups, and serve as a model for labor improvements in the French colonies.[63]

France's fear of criticism from the PMC and Germany widened the distinction between the mandates and French colonies in other ways. In early 1926 the inspector-general of the Health Service of the Colonial Ministry complained that the equality clauses of the mandate were permitting poorly qualified doctors from the United States to enter Togo and Cameroon.[64] Albert Duchêne, the director of the political affairs division, noted that most of these doctors were working for Presbyterian mission hospitals in African communities, so preventing their entry would "prompt questions from the Mandates Commission" and feed "German propaganda against the French mandates."[65] Paris decided not to ban the American physicians, but to require that all doctors, regardless of nationality, submit to special certification before practicing. In 1927, "because of the peculiar character of the mandate," Cameroon formed a "Consultative Chamber of Commerce" similar to the one in Togo composed of twelve French citizens, ten "nationals of States members of the League of Nations," and two Africans.[66] Since French citizens alone formed the consultative bodies in the neighboring colonies, this reform gave foreign nationals much more influence over the local colonial economy of the mandate and increased the international status of the territory.

The distinct character of the French mandates also continued to present certain difficulties for local administration. In September 1927 Bonnecarrère asked the Colonial Ministry if he could absorb the various mission schools in Togo into the state education system.[67] This practice was increasingly common in French colonies and served to strengthen and centralize the colonial state's control over Africans. Paris rejected this proposal by insisting that the mandate made Togo "special" and that the mission schools had to remain independent in order to avoid criticism from Geneva.[68] Bonnecarrère also discovered that because of France's ambiguous degree of sovereignty within the mandates, he needed specific permission from the Foreign Ministry before extending French citizenship to Africans living in mandated territory.[69] By the end of the decade, the uniquely "autonomous" colonial administrations of Togo and Cameroon remained as secure as ever and both commissioners as well as the Colonial Ministry were keenly aware that the international status of the possessions separated them from the French Empire. Even the atlas makers were aware of the separation. In 1929 Paul Pollachi produced a large and richly detailed colonial atlas that did not include Togo and Cameroon either in his history of the empire or as an integral part of it.[70]

As the 1920s came to a close, the mandates system had exposed the creeping doubts in the colonial self-confidence of France. It had also produced a number of uncomfortable contradictions in mandatory rule within Togo and Cameroon. While the threat of successful German subversion remained little more than a recurring nightmare for many French colonial officials, the effective protests of African elites were quite real. Further, even though League supervision did internationalize the two territories and resulted in reforms that eliminated such burdens on Africans as military conscription and economic contributions to the larger French colonial structure, it was because of the League that officials intervened more directly into the lives of Africans through greater state repression and surveillance. The fear of Geneva changed the relations between Europeans and Africans and altered how the state exercised power in Togo and Cameroon, but it did not always do so in unambiguous or mutually advantageous ways. An increasingly uneasy decade had taught French colonial officials that scrupulously following the letter of the mandates was often safer and required much less introspection than embracing the spirit of the system. In this way, "Togo-Cameroun" had come to represent some of the best kept promises and worst misgivings for the future of the French Empire in sub-Saharan Africa.

9

Mandate and Empire in British East Africa, 1929–1931

Throughout the 1920s, European settlers in East Africa, with influential support in the metropole, vigorously pressed for the amalgamation of Kenya, Uganda, and Tanganyika into a single, largely self-governing, imperial possession with local control over "native policy." Many hoped such "Closer Union" would ultimately create a new East African Dominion within the British Empire similar to the Union of South Africa. A loose collection of humanitarians, colonial officials, Asian settlers, members of the Labour party, and international observers opposed Closer Union unless it strengthened London's power to protect Africans or served to extend formally the principles of the mandates system to Uganda and Kenya. The League of Nations and the German government, while often pursuing different objectives, also combined to resist any threat to international sovereignty over Tanganyika. This confrontation between competing conceptions of British colonialism in Africa reached a climax between 1929 and 1931.

Closer Union had profound implications for the future of British East Africa and illuminated the central convictions and changing ideology of British imperialism. Implacable antagonisms in East Africa, partisan differences in London and threats from the German government made any political fusion that included Tanganyika difficult. But the principal reason for the failure of Closer Union was the mandate. The second Labour government saw no choice but to abandon its published plans for the future of British East Africa after it discovered that any form of political amalgamation including the mandated territory was a violation of British and international law. The failure of Closer Union demonstrates the complexity of the structure of British imperialism and is an unequivocal example of how mandates altered this structure. The debates and decisions of this period had long-term repercussions for Europeans and Africans in eastern Africa.

The "Closer Union" Debate, 1919–1929

During the decade that followed the First World War, Tanganyika was integral to the Closer Union debate and the conflict surrounding the political future of British East Africa.[1] As early as 1919, Amery, as parliamentary under-secretary of state for the colonies, had advocated fusing British East Africa and the conquered German colony into a single unit.[2] He later argued that such a consolidation was essential to preserve the security of the British Empire and was completely legal under the mandates system. According to Article 10 of the mandate for Tanganyika:

> The Mandatory shall be authorized to constitute the territory into a customs, fiscal, and administrative union or federation with the adjacent territories under his own sovereignty or control; provided always that the measures adopted to that end do not infringe the provisions of this mandate.[3]

In the same year, London granted Kenya a form of limited representative government with an elected minority on the Legislative Council. The Governor, Sir Edward Northey, insisted that "European interests must be paramount" throughout the possession.[4] After the first elections, Lord Delamere, who controlled over 150,000 acres of land near Nairobi, became the outspoken leader of the unofficials in the legislature.[5] He claimed to represent the nearly 10,000 European settlers who primarily lived in the "White Highlands," most of the best agricultural land around Mount Kenya. In 1923, Delamere and his fellow white Kenyans were undoubtedly encouraged by the British government's decision to extend responsible self-government to Southern Rhodesia, a colony with barely 30,000 Europeans and a million Africans.[6] For Delamere, a viable East African Dominion would require European-settler control of a unified African labor policy, common preferential treatment in imperial trade, and close cooperation between white settler communities. Throughout the 1920s Delamere was a prominent champion of this form of Closer Union as a step toward a "Great White State" under European-settler rule.

Powerful groups in London disagreed with these sweeping ambitions. The Duke of Devonshire, the Tory colonial secretary in 1923, issued a White Paper that directly repudiated Northey's earlier exhortations. Since Asians outnumbered whites by more than two to one and there were nearly three million Africans in Kenya, the Colonial Office had no intention of officially sanctioning white "paramountcy."[7] Devonshire insisted that "[p]rimarily, Kenya is an African territory" where the "interests of the African natives must be paramount." Echoing the language of the mandates system, he stated:

> His Majesty's Government regard themselves as exercising a trust on behalf of the African population, and they are unable to delegate or share this trust, the object of which may be defined as the protection and advancement of the native races . . . This paramount duty of trusteeship will continue, as in the past, to be carried out under the Secretary of State for the Colonies by the agents of the Imperial Government and by them alone.[8]

The colonial secretary's paper hindered any form of political union in British East Africa that did not protect Africans and Asians from the priorities of the European settlers. To the even greater irritation of white settlers, the Labour government in 1924 appointed a special commission, led by Ormsby-Gore, the former Conservative under-secretary of state for the colonies and one time British member of the PMC, to visit British East Africa and investigate options for economic development and "securing closer co-ordination" in transportation, agriculture, and health policies. The commission concluded that "the day is still far off" for "the imposition of a federal government over the whole of the territories." Since Kenya was a colony, Uganda a protectorate, and Tanganyika a mandate, Ormsby-Gore argued that the three territories were too different for amalgamation and instead recommended the creation of a simple "Governor's Conference" where the three administrations occasionally could consult on certain common questions.[9] Most importantly, the commission tried to dampen European settler agitation by appealing to a shared sense of "community." The report strongly endorsed Lugard's definition of the principle of "trusteeship."

> As Sir Frederick Lugard has pointed out in his well-known book entitled *The Dual Mandate in Tropical Africa*, we are not only trustees for the development and advance in civilization of the African, but we are also trustees for the world of very rich territories. This means that we have a duty to humanity to develop the vast economic resources of a great continent. There is no reason to suppose that these two trusteeships either should or do conflict.[10]

Adopting the ideals of Lugard's "dual mandate" would end the fruitless tendency to pit a tiny group of Europeans against a vast African population and would serve "the highest welfare of communities as a whole." The report was a conspicuous defense of the "new" imperialism and a tacit rejection of the drift toward the kind of "responsible government" existing in Southern Rhodesia and the Union of South Africa.

By the time that the commission presented its final report in April 1925, the Conservatives had returned to power and the white settlers' cause had energetic new sponsors. While Ormsby-Gore was once again under-secretary of state, Amery was now colonial secretary. He quickly appointed Sir

Edward Grigg, a former private secretary to Lloyd George and Liberal MP, as governor of Kenya. Grigg had no previous colonial administrative experience, but like Amery he had consistently pressed for quick federation and white settler control in British East Africa.[11] In July 1927 Amery produced his own White Paper entitled *Future Policy in Regard to Eastern Africa*. Appropriating the language of trusteeship, the colonial secretary insisted that Britain had "the Imperial duty of safeguarding the interests and progress of the native population as trustees for their welfare."[12] But Amery argued that the only way to prevent clashes between African and European interests was to give local white settlers "their share in the trusteeship for the progress and welfare of the natives." Cleverly bending Lugard's concept of a "dual mandate," the colonial secretary contended that Britain must pursue a "Dual Policy" in East Africa. Europeans and Africans shared a common responsibility to develop the economic resources of Africa but this "dual policy in regard to economic development should have its counterpart in the political evolution of the territories" as well.[13] Even though "it may be many years before the native can take a direct part in the central Legislatures," local whites should take part immediately in both the "trusteeship" of Africans and the "political evolution" of the three territories. The White Paper concluded with a promise to constitute another commission to visit British East Africa in order to study Closer Union and offer advice on "how [the] Dual Policy can best be progressively applied in the political as well as in the economic sphere."[14]

Future Policy in Regard to Eastern Africa was an attempt to circumvent both Devonshire's White Paper and the Ormsby-Gore report. It was drafted over the objections of a number of officials in the Colonial Office and those of Sir Donald Cameron, the governor of Tanganyika. The month before Amery had made his White Paper public, he had met Grigg, Cameron, and Ormsby-Gore, as well as Charles Strachey and William Cecil Bottomley, two senior permanent Colonial Office officials.[15] While all were agreeable to "closer federation" of some form, Cameron reminded everyone of Tanganyika's international obligations, complained that Kenya's policies toward Africans were "a menace to the dispositions which Tanganyika has made to secure the future of the native inhabitants of the Territory," and declared that he would never support Grigg's desire to make Tanganyika part of "a great White State."[16] He, Strachey, and Bottomley advised postponing federation until Indirect Rule was firmly established in both Tanganyika and Uganda and "traditional" African institutions were fully operational. Grigg disagreed and demanded that federation "should be carried out without delay." Skirting the issues of "native policy" and white self-government, he instead insisted that the mandate for Tanganyika was the cause of "general anxiety." Only federation could ensure "absolute security."

> Still thinking of the mandate, if we were to exercise it to the best advantage, it was necessary to think in terms of E. Africa as a whole, and it was inevitable that sooner or later, unless British history belied itself, some share of the responsibility for the mandate would pass to the Europeans on the spot. It was, therefore, desirable to make timely provision that any such delegation of responsibility should be on the right lines.[17]

The status and principles of the mandate thus did not obstruct political amalgamation in British East Africa, but actually made it imperative. This dexterous approach to the Closer Union controversy became the basis of Amery's "dual policy" and made the rhetoric of the mandates system a common weapon on both sides of the debate.

After Amery's White Paper and his creation of another commission to examine federation in British East Africa, a number of groups and individuals joined the conflict. In July 1927 the Labour party's Advisory Committee on Imperial Questions recommended that "the Labour Party should oppose federation at the present moment" in part because "Tanganyika is a mandated territory [and] [o]ne of the objects of those who demand federation is to get this mandated territory more within the orbit of the Kenya settlers' policy."[18] Dr J. H. Oldham, secretary of the International Missionary Council and editor of the *International Review of Missions*, recruited Lugard to oppose any form of union that gave white settlers legislative control over Africans.[19] As far as Lugard was concerned, "it is clear that no solution free from difficulty is now possible." Only "administrative separation," or creation of a tiny "British self-government Settlement" essentially confined to the areas in Kenya inhabited by most whites, would succeed in ending racial conflicts, maintaining London's responsibility for "trusteeship," and preserving the mandate.[20]

In early 1928, Dr Heinrich Schnee, the German colonial propagandist and *Reichstag* member, publicly condemned Closer Union as pure annexation and a open violation of Article 22 of the Treaty of Versailles.[21] Gustav Stresemann, the German foreign minister, warned that "the German Government are following the course of developments attentively" and that "the Reich will oppose with all emphasis any alteration in the Statutes of the League or in the Treaty of Versailles in regard to the mandate over the territory now known as Tanganyika."[22] This remark confirmed that any plans for Closer Union that included the mandated territory was a matter of international importance and could concern Anglo-German relations.

In January 1928, Amery's "Royal Commission on Closer Union in East Africa" arrived for a nearly two-month tour of Uganda, Kenya, and Tanganyika. The chairman, Sir Edward Hilton Young, was a Liberal MP and expert in international finance.[23] He was joined by Sir George

Schuster, the former financial secretary of the Anglo-Egyptian Sudan, Sir Reginald Mant, another financial advisor who had served in India, and Oldham. In its final report in early 1929, the commission failed to offer a unanimous opinion and Hilton Young was the only member to advocate amalgamation as the European settlers in Kenya wanted.[24] Oldham, Schuster, and Mant recommended creation of a powerful governor-general for British East Africa with direct control over all policies affecting Africans and rejected self-government for European settlers. They opposed Hilton Young's suggestion of giving local whites an elected majority in the Legislative Council in Kenya leaving "the obligation of trusteeship for native interests" entirely in the hands of the Imperial Government.[25] The majority opinion was a thorough rejection of Amery's "Dual Policy," but did little to resolve the problem of Closer Union.

Another issue that the majority of the commission agreed on was the mandate for Tanganyika. The report insisted that "the effect of our proposals is not, now or in the future, to change in any way the status of the mandated area." In conformity with Article 10 of the mandate, Tanganyika would remain "a separate entity in its relation to the League." The proposed governor-general would uphold the mandatory power's international obligations in terms of the annual reports, commercial equality, and defense.[26] If anything, federation would help to extend the mandatory principles to all of British East Africa and have the effect of making the entire region susceptible to indirect international scrutiny. Oldham, who wrote this particular passage, had consulted Lugard about the draft and assumed that it reflected the most authoritative interpretations of the mandate.[27] The report provoked a range of responses. White settlers in Kenya were angry and declared even Hilton Young's suggestions a betrayal of Amery's White Paper of 1927.[28] The Labour party was pleased with the majority view and called the report "much more favourable to Labour's policy than at one time seemed probable" since it "in effect accepts the principle of trusteeship, defined in the Mandate Clause of the Covenant, as applying in its full extent to British non-mandated possessions."[29] The British ambassador in Berlin, Sir Horace Rumbold, reported that Stresemann had said "he was being pressed on all sides for information as to the bearing of Hilton Young report on status of mandated territory of former German East Africa."[30] After Austen Chamberlain, the foreign secretary, discovered that the plans for federation not only seemed legal under Article 10, but also caused a great deal of irritation in Germany, he called the report "quite satisfactory" and ordered a copy sent to Geneva without delay.[31] The Mandates Committee of the League of Nations Union adopted a resolution calling on the British government to preserve the international status of Tanganyika and to promise to "ascertain the opinion of the Permanent Mandates Commission upon this view before taking any action on the Report."[32]

The Hilton Young report raised serious national, imperial, and international questions and made Closer Union a potential issue in the impending general election in Britain. Both the Tories and Labour saw Closer Union as supporting their position. While many Conservatives advocated another White Dominion, some Labourites hoped to extend the mandatory principles to the Africans of Uganda and Kenya. Supporters on both sides of the controversy adopted new tactics as the election neared. Lugard, perhaps after prompting from Oldham, wrote a letter to *The Times* on 7 February announcing that he would take advantage of his recently acquired peerage to make Closer Union the subject of his first speech in the House of Lords and open a national debate on the question.[33] An effort to raise the question of Closer Union above party politics inspired a second public letter two weeks later. This time, Lugard's name appeared first along with those of the Archbishop of Canterbury, Charles Roden Buxton, Lord Robert Cecil, the president of the LNU who had recently resigned from the Cabinet, and several others.[34] The letter called for creation of a special "Joint Committee of Both Houses of Parliament" to investigate Closer Union. Hilton Young was livid and protested to Cecil that "our scheme (with my adaptation for Kenya) can now be adopted" without further deliberation.[35]

The protest was useless. Lugard and his fellow signatories had won a major publicity victory. On 25 February an editorial in *The Times* endorsed their suggestion by insisting that the issue of Closer Union required careful consideration and national consensus.

> It touches decisively the principles that guide the administration of subject races under the Imperial Government in more than one continent and the chief task with which the present century confronts the British race. It concerns the relationship between India and the rest of the Empire, the Government's responsibility to the League, and the whole relationship of black and white throughout Africa.[36]

Amery had no intention either of adopting the majority report or advocating a Joint Committee. Within weeks of the publication of the Hilton Young report, the colonial secretary created yet another commission to go to British East Africa and offer recommendations more in line with his "Dual Policy."[37] He sent the permanent under-secretary of state for the colonies, Brigadier-General Sir Samuel Herbert Wilson, a former colonial governor. Wilson, whom Amery later called "my right-hand man," returned as expected to propose institution of a powerful high commissioner and central council for the three territories leaving the local governors in place. This high commissioner would exercise legislative and administrative control over certain common policies with the advice and consent of the council, but "native policy" would remain the responsibility of the governors and their respective legislative councils. In Kenya, the legislative council would have an elected unofficial majority. While the scheme looked like a compromise, it actually handed over Kenya and its African inhabitants to the white settlers and provided no guarantees that they would not dictate policy for the rest of British East Africa.[38]

Labour's White Papers

Wilson's report arrived too late for Amery. On 30 May the Conservatives lost 152 of their 412 seats in the House of Commons while Labour added 136 to its 151. No party achieved an overall majority, but Labour was the largest and Ramsay MacDonald returned to form his second government with Liberal support. He chose the seventy year-old Sidney Webb as colonial secretary.[39] Webb had been a dominant figure in the socialist Fabian Society, founded in Britain in 1884, and one of the principal architects of the Labour party during the war. He had been instrumental in drafting the party platform entitled *Labour and the New Social Order* in 1917. The new colonial secretary had also helped to found the London School of Economics, was the author of numerous books on local government and trade unionism, and with his wife, Beatrice Potter, was among the most important Labour political theorists of the interwar period.[40] Upon joining the Cabinet, Webb entered the House of Lords as Lord Passfield.

Despite his preoccupation with domestic reform, Passfield had some familiarity with colonial questions and probably had more interest in the empire than many of his Labour colleagues. From 1881 to 1891, he had served as a clerk in the Colonial Office responsible for supervising British administration in Natal and Zululand. He and his wife also had visited New Zealand, Australia, India, and Egypt.[41] Before the war, Passfield had argued that socialism and imperialism were not necessarily incompatible and could converge to create a more highly civilized and efficient world.[42] After the war, Passfield drifted away from this vague notion of "socialist imperialism" and generally aligned himself with the more moderate center of the Labour party, which was dedicated to the doctrine of trusteeship, social and economic development in the colonies, eventual self-government within the empire, and a positive commitment to African land and labor rights.[43]

Within weeks of the formation of the new Labour government, national and international pressures reemerged to influence plans for the future of British East Africa. Once again, the status of Tanganyika was a conspicuous feature of this growing tension. In late June, Stresemann publicly argued that Closer Union would erase the "internationality" and "non-sovereignty" of Tanganyika. In addition, "[t]he German

Government would use every means in its power to hinder an actual threat to the mandatory system in the hope of gaining the support of all those who saw the system as an essential part of the treaty which ended the war."[44] In early July, a deputation from the LNU headed by Cecil and the chairman, Gilbert Murray, met the Labour foreign secretary Arthur Henderson. Murray insisted that the government must continue to consider the mandate for Tanganyika as "sacred" and "[i]t is also desirable that the position of natives in non-mandated areas where Great Britain is responsible to herself, shall be as good as in Tanganyika." Henderson replied soothingly that "there is not very much difference between the position taken up by Professor Gilbert Murray and the position of the government."[45] Still, the LNU did not soften and, after receiving substantial advice from both Oldham and Lugard, in October announced:

> In view of the great importance of the issues involved, the League of Nations Union respectfully suggests to His Majesty's Government that the time is ripe for a fresh statement of native policy in accordance with the spirit of trusteeship, to cover all the territories which it is proposed to unite . . .

The group went on to pose a series of pointed questions to the government about the impact of any form of Closer Union on the Tanganyika mandate.[46] If white settlers in Kenya received an official majority on Kenya's Legislative Council, how would it "alter the obligations of the mandate?" Would any eventual "Central Legislative Council" within an amalgamated British East Africa constitute "a political Union" instead of the specific "fiscal and administrative union" permitted under Article 10 of the mandate?[47] The LNU was worried that white settlers might eventually win control of a central Legislative Council despite initial constitutional restrictions. Lugard had composed these questions himself and he then repeated them almost verbatim in a private letter to Passfield a few days later.[48]

Lugard returned to the political debate in other ways as well. In an earlier note to Passfield in late July, he had repeated the proposal for a Joint Committee.[49] Lugard then reported to Cameron that the colonial secretary had agreed privately that "he would do nothing without consulting me." The British member of the PMC also said that he, Oldham and Passfield had met MacDonald and that the two ministers had embraced the idea of a Joint Committee.[50] Lugard told Cameron that it was vital he not resign:

> The absolutely essential thing is that you should hold on to your Governorship until this question is finally settled. If you left before that, we should feel you had let us down badly . . . [51]

But while the British member of the PMC was anxious to keep his ally in Tanganyika, he was even more determined that his friends remain in power in the Colonial Office. Lugard had gained the confidence of the colonial secretary and Cameron, but the relative political weakness of the coalition government meant that the Conservatives could quickly return to power and bring Amery back with them. After a dinner where Passfield and Lugard discussed colonial rule in East Africa, Beatrice Webb remembered him as "the wisest and most humane governor we had known. He is a Conservative in politics, but sympathetic to the Labour Party's beneficent intentions with regard to 'natives.'" She was happy that Lugard was trying to "curb the naively barbaric capitalism of the white settlers in Kenya and elsewhere," but realized that he would probably not succeed without a Labour government.

> "You won't have a Labour government in power for long," says Sidney. "Get the most you can now, even if it is not all that you want, before the South African Dominion joins up with a reactionary British government"[52]

Passfield also faced the increasing insistence of his own party and the League of Nations to state the government's position on Closer Union and to confirm the international status of Tanganyika. Buxton, chairman of the Labour party's Advisory Committee on International and Imperial Questions, warned that he had "a list of 42 Labour MPs" who were sure that "we are at the parting of the ways in Imperial policy." He went on to insist that "it is absolutely necessary to take a firm line now" on the issue of Closer Union in order to put an end to "what may roughly be called 'South African' views of native policy."[53] A month later Buxton reminded Passfield that "[i]t sounds sensational to say so, but it is none the less true that within the next few weeks the future of the entire continent of Africa may be decided by the British Government."[54] In Geneva, the German member of the PMC, Dr Ludwig Kastl, warned that Article 10 prohibited not only the form of Closer Union that Wilson had recommended, but even the one that the majority of the Hilton Young Commission had suggested.[55] The Japanese and Dutch members raised similar objections.[56] By late November 1929 both the Advisory Committee of the Labour Party and the LNU were virtually commanding the colonial secretary to issue a White Paper on "native policy" in any future British East African federation at once.[57]

The defenders of a future "Great White State" were not idle during this period. As soon as the Wilson report became public in September, Grigg urged Passfield to adopt its recommendations.[58] The next month, the Governor of Kenya sent Passfield an ominous letter from Thomas J. O'Shea, one of the elected white settlers on the Legislative Council. O'Shea warned: "I cannot help thinking that we are at a crossroads, and that the Cabinet's decision will settle whether Kenya politically is to be another New Zealand or another Ireland."[59] Both Amery and Hilton Young wrote letters to *The Times* praising the Wilson report and arguing that further deliberations were unnecessary.[60] In early November, Field Marshal Smuts presented a "Rhodes Lecture" in Oxford on the question of Closer Union. The enthusiastic proponent of white superiority in Africa and collaborator in the creation of the mandates system proclaimed that "the native needs the white man more than the white man the native" and only by giving European settlers responsible government in East Africa would "civilization" come to the region in the tradition of the other British "White Dominions" around the world.[61] Wilson begged Robert Vansittart, assistant under-secretary of state for foreign affairs and principal private secretary to MacDonald, to "call the Prime Minister's attention" to the merits of "my Report on East Africa."[62] Still, this opposition activity actually pleased Lugard because it forced the issue to the center of national attention. Drawing on what he had learned in Geneva, he was convinced that the more open the debate, the more difficult it would be for his opponents to defend themselves. He told Cameron: "What with Amery's letter to the Times, and Smuts' Rhodes Lecture at Oxford on Saturday, we have all the cards on the table at last, and this should help us not a little."[63]

In early December, after accepting the advice of a number of officials, Passfield finally told the Cabinet that he had "no intention of abandoning or of seeking to modify in any way" the mandate for Tanganyika. "[T]he relation of His Majesty's Government to the native populations in East Africa is one of trusteeship which cannot be devolved, and from which they cannot be relieved." Passfield repudiated Amery's "Dual Policy" and returned to Devonshire's 1923 policy of insisting that "the interests of the African natives must be paramount, and that, if and when these interests of the immigrant races should conflict, the former should prevail."[64] With these principles as a guide, Passfield chaired a "Committee on Policy in East Africa" which met several times between January and April 1930 to work out the details of Labour's plan for Closer Union.[65] The committee included Lord Sankey, the Lord Chancellor, W. Wedgewood Benn, the secretary of state for India, and Lord Thomas, the Air Minister. After much debate, the group recommended a form of federation for British East Africa, immediate appointment of the Joint Committee, and a public "Statement of Native Policy."[66] The Cabinet approved the proposals at the end of April.[67] In June, Passfield at long last issued two related White Papers, one entitled *Memorandum on Native Policy in East Africa*, the other, *Statement of the Conclusions of His Majesty's Government in the United Kingdom as regards Closer Union in East Africa*.[68]

But the delay between the appearance of the Wilson report and the two White Papers had caused a great deal of frustration and had exposed serious political divisions both at home and within the empire. Wilson, who was the senior permanent official in the Colonial Office, complained privately to Grigg that "[i]t is a great pity there is such a strong section of the Labour Party who are so 'anti-Kenya' and who mistrust everything that you or anyone else in Kenya do!"[69] In Kenya, rumors began to circulate in the local *East African Standard* that Smuts soon would be the first high commissioner of a unified East African Dominion.[70] In April, King George V, through his private secretary, expressed displeasure with the government and overtly took the side of the European settlers: "His Majesty fears that the policy, or as the King ventures to think, want of policy, on the part of the Colonial Office, is really doing harm in East Africa."[71] In the same month, over 100 Labour Party and LNU members, including Buxton and Philip Noel-Baker, the principal private secretary to Henderson, signed a "Memorial on African Policy" that accused the government of "doing nothing but follow up the policy of its Tory predecessors." It demanded immediate adoption of the principle of "Trusteeship" for the entire region.[72] Dr Drummond Shiels, the under-secretary of state for the colonies, grumbled that the memorial "hardly gives justice to the Gov'ts policy on the subject." Grigg's administration was "unsympathetic and repressive" and "I do not think he understands how to manage native peoples."[73] Passfield did little to repair these poor relations with Grigg and refused to inform him of the substance of the impending White Papers before they were published.[74]

Some of this frustration on the political left evaporated, however, when the White Papers finally appeared. Those who considered themselves progressive colonial reformers dedicated to the "new" imperialism of the postwar world were the most pleased. The first White Paper firmly tied Labour to the principles of "trusteeship," the protection of Africans, and "native paramountcy." It was heavily laden with the language of Article 22 and made consistent references to the rights and interests of peoples "not yet able to stand by themselves."

> It is with the additional benefits and the exceptional safeguards called for by the special needs of the peoples "not yet able to stand by themselves under the strenuous conditions of the modern world" that the trusteeship for the native races is particularly concerned; and it is essentially to ensure the maintenance of these exceptional safeguards and the development of these additional benefits that His Majesty's Government must necessarily, as trustee, retain in their own hands the ultimate decision and the final control.[75]

Labour's policy was an undisguised recapitulation of the doctrine of Indirect Rule. It advocated "training" the African by "traditional" methods so that he "may gradually develop a political consciousness and a desire to take an increasing share of his tribal affairs" and "ultimately also in the governance of the territory in which he lives."[76] With this policy statement, London had once again confirmed that the letter and spirit of the mandates system was wholly integrated into the ideology of British imperialism and that the Lugardian administrative model was the best method for translating that ideology into practice.

The second White Paper had a similar impact. Labour's plan for Closer Union closely resembled that of the majority of the Hilton Young Commission of 1929 and confirmed that there would indeed be a "Joint Committee of two Houses of Parliament" to review the proposals. The colonial secretary advocated placing a high commissioner over the three existing governors who would be assisted by a central "Council" composed of 3 officers from the high commissioner's staff and 21 other members. The high commissioner would appoint all of the council members with each territory having 7 members, 4 of whom would be officials and 3 unofficials. The high commissioner would have administrative and legislative control over a wide range of common services including railroads, customs, ports, postal service, and extradition. He would also have complete supervisory powers over the governors, including authority to review draft legislation, examine annual budgets, and approve any changes in "native policy." This high commissioner could suspend racially discriminatory laws, investigate complaints, and offer criticisms or proposals to the governors "as he may think fit." He would be directly responsible to the secretary of state, who ultimately maintained undivided control over all policies concerning Africans. Passfield did not yield to European settlers' demands for an unofficial majority on the Legislative Council in Kenya, but did recommend granting Asians greater participation in the electoral process and establishing machinery for an eventual general franchise for all races based on education and "advancement in civilization."[77]

Labour's blueprint for Closer Union gave special attention to Tanganyika. The White Paper promised that federation would "not involve any change in the status of the mandated territory or of its inhabitants" and that "Tanganyika must preserve its individuality as a territorial unit." The mandatory power would continue to carry out all of its international obligations including the restrictions on military recruitment, the prohibition against fortifications, and the maintenance of commercial equality for members of the League of Nations. In the process, many of the mandate's provisions would apply to Uganda and Kenya since "any union or federation unifying these rights over a number of dependencies which include Tanganyika must extend over all of them many of the privileges secured by the Mandate."[78] The high commissioner and the governor of Tanganyika would together produce the annual report for the League and the PMC would maintain its supervision over the territory's budget and legislation. The government was confident that its form of amalgamation not only respected the mandates system, but expanded it by including Tanganyika within a carefully designed British East African union.

Lugard's Questions

Passfield's proposals generated a great deal of attention. Leading members of the Labour party and LNU were pleased, but the European settler community was enraged and sent Delamere to London to register this widespread anger.[79] Lugard, who somehow managed to learn the details of the White Papers before publication, told Cameron that he was happy with the government's formal acceptance of a Joint Committee, but was "strongly opposed" to a central Legislative Council which might leave open the possibility for an eventual European settler majority. He was still "doubtful" that any type of Closer Union with the settlers was possible and reiterated his "administrative separation" approach.[80] Cameron was more optimistic. In a private letter to Lugard, Cameron admitted that "I am strongly inclined to support the scheme proposed by H.M.G. as the best we shall get." He argued that London had demonstrated a great deal of "courage and wisdom" in containing the ambitions of the local Europeans and that "I am more 'Labour' than ever . . . "[81]

Nevertheless, Cameron did not publicly endorse the White Papers. In a second letter to Lugard, the governor revealed that his official response to the proposals would be that "from the point of view of the interests of Tanganyika alone," no constitutional changes were necessary. In other words, avoiding federation altogether would best safeguard Cameron's administrative system in Tanganyika. Yet, if he had to adopt Labour's plan, Cameron was sure that Closer Union would have "a chance of functioning with a measure of success, but with some impairment of administrative efficiency."[82] For Cameron, the real danger was Kenya. As long as Closer Union preserved the system of "Native Authorities" and his concept of mandatory rule, he was willing to accept federation as a step toward the day when Europeans and Africans would work "side by side" in a "model mixed State" that would "have a great influence on the shaping of affairs in East Africa."[83]

Reaction in Germany to the White Papers was immediate and far less sympathetic. Schnee launched another round of polemical attacks and once again characterized colonial federation in East Africa as blatant annexation and the destruction of the mandates system.[84] The British ambassador in Berlin reported that a variety of German publications had expressed robust opposition to the government's proposals and must "be combated with determination, not only in any German historical interests, but in the interest of the mandatory idea itself and of respect for the principles of the League of Nations."[85] This news alarmed one junior Foreign Office official who noted that "[t]he Germans are taking this question seriously now. I am afraid it may give us considerable trouble."[86] Sir William Malkin, the Foreign Office legal advisor, quickly dismissed these worries by citing Article 10 of the mandate and contending that Closer Union was entirely legal under international law.[87]

Others did not share Malkin's confidence. Kastl, who coincidentally had just resigned from the PMC, wrote a private letter to tell Lugard of his disapproval. Kastl complained bitterly that the scheme was virtually identical to those already criticized by the PMC in 1929. Any high commissioner with legislative powers, assisted by a central legislative council "in which the influence of the non-mandated territories will be predominant," would destroy the international status of Tanganyika.

> After these proposals had been carried out the mandated territory would no longer form an entity in international law – perhaps not even a separate entity any longer – but merely a part of a decentralized large British colony . . . The majority of the German population will, further, attach less importance to these questions of international law and be more under the impression that Great Britain is creating a dangerous precedent in incorporating the most important of the now international and formerly German colonies *de facto* in the British Empire . . .

He ended the letter with ominous warnings about the impact that Schnee's recent protests in the *Reichstag* had on German public opinion and asked Lugard that if he agreed "I should be sincerely grateful if you would communicate them to the authorities concerned."[88]

Lugard swiftly replied to Kastl's note. The government's proposals were in strict conformity with Article 10 of the mandate. Tanganyika's international identity would remain entirely intact within an amalgamated British East Africa. He insisted that the White Paper provided ample protection for Africans and that the mandatory power retained "absolute control" over the administration of Tanganyika. In addition,

> The British Government points out that the effect of these stipulations is rather to bring the adjoining territories in some degree under the supervision of the Mandates Commission than to relax its control over the Mandated Territory.

He did not pretend that he entirely supported London's policy since "I am myself somewhat doubtful of the desirability of Closer Union between Tanganyika and its neighbours – and especially of the advisability of the Central Legislative Council, even with its very limited powers." Thus,

Lugard was doing his best to explain, but not advocate, his government's position:

> You must regard what I have said purely as my own personal views as a Member of the Mandates Commission. I have not shown your letter to the Colonial Office or consulted them at all. I only write to you as a friend who has asked for my personal opinion.[89]

Before long, professional diplomats were concerned with the legal questions surrounding the Closer Union controversy. While it was true that Germany's relations with Britain had steadily improved since 1926, a number of moderate German political leaders still detested the Treaty of Versailles and hoped to continue to negotiate with Britain and France for substantive revisions, particularly of Germany's borders with Poland. Many Germans were frustrated with the slow progress, but the "Spirit of Locarno" remained popular. Still, German moderates were always wary of the political right since protests from men like Schnee could ignite public opinion and endanger opportunities for peaceful modification of the Treaty. For these reasons, the fragile Weimar Republic took Passfield's White Paper on Closer Union very seriously and on 4 September the German chargé d'affaires in London, Count Bernstorff, sent an aide-mémoire to the Foreign Office to complain about the plans for federation in British East Africa.

Berlin did not conceal its disagreement with the proposals. The aide-mémoire baldly announced: "In the opinion of the German Government a realization of the project in its present form would hardly be compatible with the principles of the mandate system." It reminded the British government of its public promise to give the PMC, including its new German member, Dr Julius Ruppel, a former German Colonial Ministry official and recently retired *ministerialdirektor* in the Foreign Ministry, "an opportunity to express their opinion on the question." Further, "[i]n view of the great interest which German public opinion takes in the matter the German Government could not however omit to communicate their misgivings to the British Government at once." The rest of the aide-mémoire provided a detailed critique of Labour's Closer Union scheme. In tone and substance, it was similar to Kastl's letter to Lugard a few months earlier and focused on international legal questions including those surrounding Article 10 of the mandate Article 22 of the Covenant:

> The far-reaching executive and legislative powers of the High Commissioner and his Council, which extend directly and indirectly to the most important branches of economic life and administration as well as to questions of policy regarding natives and other matters . . . would abrogate or considerably limit the independent status which is accorded to the terri-

tory by Article 22 of the League of Nations Covenant. It would not only establish an administrative union but also a political and constitutional union of the three participating territories in which the mandated territory would scarcely possess the rank of a province. Article 10 of the Tanganyika Mandate cannot, according to the German view, be applied, as a provision carrying into effect Article 22 of the League of Nations Covenant, in such a manner that the principle of the independence of the mandated territory established in the latter article would thereby be impaired.[90]

The German aide-mémoire did not cause much immediate alarm in London. One junior Foreign Office clerk thought that it was merely advance warning of the position that Ruppel would take at the next meeting of the PMC.[91] A second official, Reginald Leeper, suggested that Closer Union was largely the concern of the Colonial Office and British representatives in Geneva.[92] C. Howard Smith, the highest official to comment on the paper, noted that "[t]his is perfectly legitimate criticism of the scheme," but that it "will be for the C.O. to counter it and for the Mandates Commission to decide after hearing both sides."[93] Colonial officials simply suggested that the Foreign Office thank Berlin and inform the Chargé d'Affaires that London would give "earnest consideration" to the German note.[94]

This "earnest consideration" did not prevent Passfield from keeping his promise to submit his proposals to the "Joint Select Committee on Closer Union in East Africa" before he adopted any type of federation. Ten members from each house of Parliament agreed to serve, Lugard among them. A mix of personalities filled out the rest of the group including Passfield, Shiels, Buxton, Ormsby-Gore, Amery, Lord Parmoor and Lord Phillimore, both renowned constitutionalists and original architects of the League of Nations, and Sir John Sandeman Allen, the chairman of the Joint East Africa Board, a pressure group representing the interests of white settlers.[95] Lord Stanley of Alderley, a Conservative, accepted the chairmanship. He extended invitations to more than fifty witnesses, including Oldham, Grigg, Wilson, Hilton Young, and various representatives from the European, Asian, and African communities in East Africa.[96] Lugard took particular pains to convince Cameron to appear.[97] After adopting this ambitious agenda, the Joint Committee scheduled its first meeting for December 1930 and anticipated meeting throughout much of 1931.[98]

Meanwhile, Lugard demonstrated the greatest "earnest consideration" for Germany's protests in the months before the joint committee formally met. Because of his many years on the PMC and his private contacts with Kastl, Lugard knew that the German government considered the international legal questions surrounding Closer Union important. While he generally regarded the latest proposals for amalgamation as legal, he wanted authoritative answers to these questions not only because he knew that Germany would probably raise them in public as a member of the League, but because they struck at the heart of any future constitution of a unified British East Africa. As early as October, he began warning some of his fellow committee members of the importance of the mandate for Tanganyika, international law, and the "German argument" against federation. Lugard suggested to Sandeman Allen that Delamere's demand to "make Tanganyika part of the British Empire is playing into the hands of the Germans."[99] In a thirty-three page draft paper entitled "Memorandum on the Kenya Question," the British member of the PMC carefully detailed Berlin's contention that amalgamation would obliterate the independent status of Tanganyika in international law and cited his private letter from Kastl to illustrate the point.[100] He warned that the German government might exercise its right as a member of the League of Nations to bring the matter before the Permanent Court of International Justice at the Hague. London must resolve these international legal issues before it was too late:

> it is conceivable that [Germany] might succeed in her contention that Article 10 is not authorised by the Treaty. This would not of course affect Gt. Britain's tenure of the Mandate, but it would be inconvenient if Closer Union had already been adopted.[101]

Lugard was determined to get answers to these questions. But instead of asking the legal advisors of the Colonial Office, he appealed directly to the Foreign Office. He hoped to force officials into revealing what they would do if faced with a German legal challenge by asking how he should respond to similar attacks in Geneva:

> In these circumstances, I have the honour to enquire whether you can inform me of the reply which His Majesty's Government would make if the German representative or other members of the Commission argued that the legality of the proposed Closer Union between the Mandated Territory of Tanganyika and its neighbours . . . is not in accordance with the terms of the Covenant of the Treaty of Versailles.[102]

The Foreign Office, unconvinced that there were any serious legal or international problems involved and unwilling to let Lugard serve as London's spokesman for a proposal that "must not be regarded as forming the final policy" of the government, politely rejected the request.[103]

By late October, however, Lugard was causing international problems of his own. Sir Eric Drummond, the secretary-general of the League of Nations, complained that Lugard's participation on both the Joint Committee and the PMC constituted a serious conflict of interest.[104] A number of officials in the Foreign Office agreed, including E. L. A. Robertson-Fullarton:

> How can Lord Lugard as a member of a Parliamentary Committee to which he is to formulate the final decisions of H.M.G. with regard to the question of Closer Union in E. Africa and [sic] then go off to Geneva, as a member of the Permanent Mandates Commission[,] and criticise his own decisions?[105]

Leeper argued that "[w]hatever the right of Lord Lugard's to serve on both Committees, I am sure that it would be a bad mistake politically."[106] Lugard refused to resign from the PMC.[107] He insisted that both bodies were advisory and did not conflict, but as a compromise he promised not to attend any of the November sessions of the PMC when Tanganyika was the subject of discussion. Aware of the politically charged issues involved, however, the rest of the Commission refused to address Closer Union without the British member present.[108] In particular, Ruppel had no reason to raise the matter since there was no opportunity to learn how Britain might respond to a German legal challenge. Thus, the PMC remained officially silent on Passfield's White Paper.

While the PMC had managed to skirt an awkward situation and was entirely free to criticize the White Paper the next year, London lost a crucial opportunity to find out how many members of the PMC shared Germany's views about the legality of Labour's plans when still preliminary. Had a majority found no objection and recommended that the Council sanction union in East Africa, the British government would have been in a much stronger legal position if Germany chose to appear before the Permanent Court of International Justice. Conversely, a dissenting PMC opinion would have served as a useful guide for either revising the White Paper or preparing a defense against any possible international litigation. Lugard was probably most aware of this missed chance and how it made the joint committee's deliberations more difficult. He was so embarrassed that he apologized directly to the prime minister's son and personal secretary, Malcolm MacDonald, a Labour MP who worked closely with his father. While not accepting any of the blame himself, Lugard contended that both Drummond and the PMC were responsible for the "very stupid" and "futile" decision to let the League remain officially silent about Closer Union.[109]

On 4 December, the Joint Committee had its first preliminary meeting and Lugard did not waste any time in pressing for consideration of the international legal questions surrounding Closer Union. During a discussion on 11 December, Lugard learned of the German aide-mémoire for the first time and became greatly alarmed. After a lengthy and complicated exchange in which Lugard had "a good deal to say," he convinced his colleagues that international law was a central concern for any form of federation in British East Africa. The Joint Committee agreed to submit a list of explicit legal questions to the Foreign Office legal advisor before going any further.[110]

As Lugard drafted the Joint Committee's questions for the Foreign Office, officials in the Colonial Office started to wonder what might happen if Closer Union was indeed illegal under international law. Despite the careful construction of the portions of the White Paper concerning the mandate, A. C. C. Parkinson, as assistant under-secretary of state, assumed that if the Foreign Office returned an adverse decision, London would have to tell all of the witnesses from East Africa not to come. The Joint Committee "might decide then and there that they could not proceed with their investigation" and Passfield would have to start afresh and "will wish to save as much of [the proposals] as he can."[111] These were consequences that few wanted to contemplate. After seeing the memorandum, Passfield merely jotted "I confirm the above" and added no further instructions.[112]

On 18 December, the secretary of the Joint Committee sent Lugard's "Memorandum on the Proposals for 'Closer Union' in East Africa," containing his legal questions, to the Foreign Office and asked Malkin to present his responses at the next meeting of the Committee scheduled for 27 January 1931.[113] The paper posed four specific problems:

> (a) Is the form of closer union proposed by His Majesty's Government in accord with clause 10 of the mandate? If not, in what respects is it repugnant?
> (b) Would the appointment of a High Commissioner, with an Advisory instead of a Legislative Council, be compatible, and what limitation must be placed on the legislative and executive powers of the High Commissioner?
> (c) Has Germany legal grounds for protest in view of the terms of articles 118 and 119?
> (d) Can she claim the right to refer it to the International Court under clause 12 of the mandate?[114]

Malkin promised to draft his answers over the Christmas holiday, but because Lugard's memorandum raised a number of serious constitutional and international issues, recorded that "in view of the importance of the matter, I thought it would be necessary for the Law Officers to be consulted at some stage . . . so that the view which goes before the Committee may represent the best advice which the Government can take."[115]

The law officers, the attorney-general and the solicitor-general, represented the most authoritative source of legal counsel available to the government. The British constitution compelled the government to comply with official opinions from the law officers. Labourites were acutely aware of this obligation as a result of the "Campbell Case" during the first Labour government. In July 1924, the acting editor of the Communist *Workers' World*, J. R. Campbell, had published an appeal to soldiers not to fire on striking workers. MacDonald asked the law officers to withdraw an original decision to prosecute Campbell for sedition leading to opposition charges of Communist influence on the Labour government and political interference in the course of justice. A successful demand for an inquiry forced MacDonald's government to resign.[116] In late 1930 and early 1931, the attorney-general was William Allen Jowitt, a Liberal who had crossed the floor to join MacDonald's Cabinet. Stafford Cripps, Passfield's nephew, was serving in his first public post as the solicitor-general.[117] Henry Grattan Bushe, the Colonial Office legal advisor, noted that Cripps had agreed "to take the papers away over Christmas, to make a preliminary study of the matter, and we reckon that we should have the memorandum finally approved to circulate a good week before the Committee next meets."[118]

The Foreign Office's legal advisor finished his draft responses to Lugard's four questions on 9 January 1931 and distributed copies to officials in the Colonial Office. They were relieved to discover that Malkin maintained that even though Germany did have the right as a member of the League of Nations to present grievances before the Permanent Court of International Justice, the White Paper on Closer Union was in strict conformity with both Article 10 of the mandate and Article 22 of the Covenant.[119] As far as Malkin was concerned, the British government would have little to fear if Germany decided to initiate international litigation. After reading the opinion, Bottomley noted calmly: "We now wait for L.O. views."[120]

The Law Officers' Answers

The law officers' conclusions, however, were entirely different from Malkin's. Instead of finding the White Paper on sturdy international legal foundations, the law officers insisted that Article 10 only authorized "a customs, fiscal and administrative union," not a legislative one. A high commissioner, with or without a central council, who exercised any degree of legislative authority "is contrary to the terms of the mandate." Only a unified government that did not pass laws and that had no independent political power was possible without violating Article 10. The law officers agreed that Germany had every right to bring any matter relating to the administration of a mandated territory before the Permanent Court. Thus, not only was the proposed constitution for a future British East African federation a breach of international law, but the German government would be entitled to pursue international litigation to undo such a federation.[121]

The law officers' views caused a crisis in the Colonial Office. Passfield immediately postponed the next meeting of the joint committee and sent his subordinates scrambling to find alternatives that did not violate the mandate.[122] After a few days of this hurried work, the colonial secretary called a special meeting with the law officers, whose "opinions appeared to affect somewhat fundamentally the scheme put forward by His Majesty's Government," in order to determine what alternatives, if any, were possible. Jowitt and Cripps joined Wilson, Bushe, Bottomley, Parkinson, and several other colonial officials for a frustrating exchange. The law officers continued to reject "any form of closer union which involved any unification of legislative powers." The permanent officials argued that federation without such powers was meaningless. When Passfield suggested creating two offices of high commissioner, one for Kenya and Uganda, the other for Tanganyika, with both offices "being held normally by the same person" and sharing "a joint Advisory Council," Cripps said that "the effect would be to constitute a single legislative authority, and the same difficulties might arise." When the law officers agreed that a single high commissioner assisted by three councils, each voting separately on legislation, was legal under the mandate, Bottomley replied that this was no improvement over the present structure. He then asked if a genuine high commissioner of any kind was legal.

> The Attorney-General said that he could see no legal objection to the appointment of a High Commissioner provided he was given no legislative powers. He would then be faced with the necessity for getting identical legislation passed through the three Legislative Bodies.[123]

The prospect of one man, even if he possessed the best administrative skills and had almost unlimited patience, traveling among three different territories and required to do everything in triplicate was too absurd for even the most optimistic "Closer Union" advocate to contemplate.

Passfield now had several problems. He needed to contemplate making sweeping changes to his flawed White Paper, dissolving the Joint Committee, and presenting his government with a foreign relations fiasco. The colonial secretary told those at the meeting that "the scheme in its present form excited considerable animosity in Germany" and that "it appeared probable" that Berlin would complain to the Permanent Court if London did not dramatically alter the White Paper, but particularly if the law officers' views became public. For all of these reasons, Passfield argued that it was "undesirable that publicity should be given to the opinion of the Law Officers" and asked them not to submit a final written opinion. Instead, he and Malkin would draft a letter for the Joint Committee that would indicate the general difficulties, but not offer any specific details:

> the letter suggested might state the objections made and say that they had been referred to the Law Officers, and, without indicating their opinion in regard to the substance of these objections, say that the L.O. considered that it would be possible for Germany, as a member of the League of Nations, to have the matter referred to the Hague Court . . . the letter might conclude by asking the Committee to bear these points in mind in their future deliberations.

Meanwhile, "a revised scheme should be worked out and submitted to the Law Officers for their opinion on its legal aspects. This revised scheme could then be placed before the Joint Committee."[124] Since the Committee was supposed to meet on 5 February, colonial officials had less than a week to come up with their "revised scheme."

Passfield was now desperate to salvage what he could from his quickly unraveling White Paper in order to avoid any national or international political embarrassment.[125] If he tried to disregard the views of the law officers and the evasion became public, the Labour government could suffer a repeat of the 1924 Campbell fiasco at home while jeopardizing Britain's relations with Germany, the League, and other interested nations. To Passfield's dismay, Bushe was unable to find a form of Closer Union that was both legal and practical while the law officers were reluctant to withhold their formal written opinion to the committee.[126] In early February, with the meeting of the Joint Committee only three days away, the colonial secretary instructed both Bushe and Malkin to convince the law officers of "the extreme undesirability (in view of the German agitation [and] probably litigation) of any legal discussion of Mandates being circulated."[127] Under this mounting pressure, Jowitt and Cripps relented. They would not change their opinion, but agreed not to state it formally to the Committee; "we will adapt the form of our Opinion so far as we can to suit the circumstances."[128]

While this arrangement solved one problem, Passfield still had to persuade the Joint Committee to continue its deliberations in spite of the law officers' view that not workable form of Closer Union was legal and his own staff's view that no legal form was workable. The chairman, who admitted that he was "somewhat impressed by the case made against Closer Union for the three territories," agreed that the Committee could proceed and would probably eventually recommend an alternative to amalgamation anyway.[129] On 3 February, Passfield privately told Lugard about the law officers' views and asked him to continue supporting the Committee's efforts. Perhaps detecting an opportunity to revive his "administrative separation" idea, Lugard agreed that the law officers' conclusions were "not of a nature to prevent the Committee from considering its work." He argued that the Committee was still able to offer any final recommendations it thought fit and the Cabinet was not bound to accept them. Further, he hinted that if the government did adopt recommendations that he personally could support, he would privately defend them in Geneva since "I might be useful in this way – especially with the Germans with whom I am on good terms."[130] Thus, while both Stanley of Alderley and Lugard were willing to save the Joint Committee, they did not do so for the sake of Passfield or his White Paper. As far as the colonial secretary was concerned, abandoning the White Paper and his plans for Closer Union in British East Africa and handing the Committee over to men like Lugard was the smallest price he could pay to avoid personal and political humiliation.

During the period between the law officers' statements in January and the Joint Committee meeting in early February, one of Passfield's most serious preoccupations was Germany. His office had reports of increased hostility toward Closer Union in the German press.[131] Schnee sent a pamphlet to the colonial secretary that bluntly condemned Closer Union and insisted that German rights were "being brushed aside" by the White Paper. The pamphlet called on the German government to thwart Closer Union at the Hague since "[t]he union means practically the incorporation of German East Africa in the British Empire even if the outward appearance of the Mandate should be upheld" and was "incompatible with the definition of Article 22."[132] He later sent copies to the members of the Joint Committee, *The Times*, and a number of German newspapers.[133]

All of this came at a bad time for the colonial secretary. As the leading spokesman on colonial issues for the Labour government and one of the ideological pillars of the party, Passfield was undoubtedly infuriated by the realization that not only was Schnee more right than wrong on the question of the legality of Closer Union, but that Berlin could accuse the Labour government of old-fashioned imperialism in an international court and might well win. While conspicuously not mentioning the law officers' views, the colonial secretary begged Henderson to assure the German government that the mandate was not, and ver would be, part of the British Empire.

> Of course, H. M. Government are not proposing the 'incorporation of Tanganyika in the British Empire.' It is not British territory, and will not become so. The inhabitants are not, as such, British subjects, and will not be made so. Whether or not the powers *proposed* to be given to the suggested High Commissioner go beyond what the Mandate authorises, – and on this there may be room for doubt – we can confidently assure the

> German Government that nothing will actually be *done* that goes beyond the Mandate. The Joint Committee will certainly not propose more than the Mandate expressly allows.
>
> I am now convinced that Tanganyika must not only continue to be a distinct unit, but also that the legislation applicable to it must continue to be Tanganyika legislation, so that it will always have its own laws.[134]

In one stroke, Passfield had admitted the defeat of his White Paper as well as the impossibility of any realistic amalgamation in British East Africa that included the Tanganyika Territory. While Henderson told Passfield not to worry about German propaganda and to say nothing to Berlin until after the Committee finished its work, the foreign minister had missed the point.[135] The government's two highest legal advisors, not Schnee, the German government, national politics, or conflicting imperial interests, had killed Closer Union in British East Africa.

Even though a few members of the Joint Committee knew that the law officers had decided that the government's plans for Closer Union were illegal, most did not. Passfield must have known that the Committee still faced the threat of a rupture and that his government remained exposed to political embarrassment at home and abroad when the members gathered for their private meeting on 5 February.[136] This probably explains why, despite the promise he made on 27 January, he decided not to produce a letter laying out the legal troubles surrounding the mandate. Instead, with the chairman's help, the colonial secretary tried to avoid any discussion of specific legal opinions by insisting that since the government would never propose an illegal form of Closer Union, no formal opinions were necessary. Stanley of Alderley opened the discussion by insisting the Foreign Office had "not yet submitted a legal opinion, and if they do it will probably be highly confidential and not to be circulated." Since the law officers' answers to Lugard's questions had superseded Malkin's, the chairman's remark was technically correct, but deliberately misleading. He then went on to insist that the Committee could continue its work since an opinion might not be necessary if the members decided to exclude Tanganyika anyway.

> If so then we do not need the law officers' opinion. So we could continue our enquiry for some time without deciding whether or not Tanganyika can legally be included. If we conclude that Tanganyika should be included in Closer Union the question of the power to do this can be considered later. Therefore we can postpone hearing from the Foreign Officers, [sic] or the Law Officers; first we do not have the legal opinion, and secondly it was not essential.

Lord Cranworth, a former settler and the chairman of the East African

Dinner Club, immediately exclaimed "[b]ut if Tanganyika drops out, surely everything goes by the board." Sandeman Allen agreed and demanded to know the answers to Lugard's legal questions since the Closer Union "is so linked up with Tanganyika that we must clear that up, and *public* enquiry in regard to this will be of propaganda value to the Germans in opposing us."[137]

Passfield continued to try to hold the Committee together without admitting that the White Paper had a central legal defect or that there was anything seriously wrong at all. He repeated the chairman's dodge that "[t]he legal opinion has not yet been given," but did admit that he had discussed the matter with the legal advisers of the Colonial Office and Foreign Office. As a result,

> I am clear that full federation, or the appointment of a Governor-General, would be beyond the Mandate . . . If the Committee have in mind a Governor-General, or anything like a High Commissioner with *power* over the separate Territories (except for economic services), as was contemplated by the Hilton Young Commission, that is out of the question legally. I think we should go on and hear witnesses as to Closer Union as is prima facie permissible.

Amery exploded. He insisted that the mandate did not prevent federation, but "I should much object to wasting time on enquiry without proper foundation" and demanded an official legal opinion. Ormsby-Gore was fearful that if Closer Union was illegal under international law, Germany could drag Britain to the Permanent Court and successfully attack the decisions of the British Empire. He exclaimed:

> Lord Passfield's utterance comes to me as a bombshell . . . Any member of the League of Nations can take to the Hague Court the question whether any form of closer union is or is not consistent with the Treaty and the high question of international policy now raised by Lord Passfield must be cleared up.

Another member, Lord Mersey, made the stark observation that when the public found out about these problems, they will conclude that "we do not know how to manage our affairs."[138]

Passfield's hope that the Committee would trust his contention that a formal legal opinion was unnecessary evaporated. While Lugard and many of the Labourites were willing to proceed without formal legal advice, Amery was relentless in his demand for an official opinion. He rejected the suggestion that federation, particularly in the form that he and Grigg had always pressed for, was a violation of the mandate. He and some of the other Conservatives may have suspected that the entire legal question was a Labour Party trick to scrap Closer Union altogether. Passfield warned that "I think it most likely that a case will be taken to the Hague Court in the next two years; hence no views of Legal Advisers must become public." Phillimore reminded everyone that "[i]f we bring in legal advice we become involved in a discussion which will go to the Hague Court. We do not want to get mixed up in that." He insisted they "[w]e do not want to get involved in an examination of what is really the foreign policy of this country" and was far outside the competence of the committee. When Amery retorted that when Belgium incorporated its mandated territory into the Congo in 1924 "not a dog barked," Lugard remarked that Berlin had indeed objected, but "their objection was overruled on the ground that Germany was not then a member of the League."[139]

Given the fear of international litigation and with so many members, including Passfield, Ormsby-Gore, Sandeman Allen, Phillimore, and Lugard, all expressing a fear of possible international litigation, the Committee finally adopted an uneasy compromise. The members agreed that "the Law Officers' opinion, when obtained, should not be communicated in any form to the Committee," but Malkin would read a brief précis of the legal issues involved during a private meeting and explain "the limits within which closer union to Tanganyika with neighbouring British Dependencies would be legally permissible." Further, "no copies [of the précis] should be taken away" and "only one copy should be made as a record of what passes at the meeting." In this way, the Committee would know why legislative union in East Africa was impossible, but the law officers' opinion would not enter into the public record and the German government would not receive any free legal advice it could use against Britain.[140] This solution also prevented Berlin from some day citing the law officers at the Hague against the British government, a nightmare British officials probably hoped to avoid.

This compromise, while not entirely satisfactory to anyone, did keep the Joint Committee together and served to avert more serious problems for Passfield and his government. Over the next several days, the law officers worked with Malkin and Bushe to compose the précis.[141] The Colonial Office legal advisors, already resentful of how the Foreign Office had intervened in a matter of colonial policy, complained that nobody would know that there had ever been any divergence between the law officers and the Foreign Office while everyone would get "the distinct impression that the C.O. alone was in error" from the start.[142] Sometime in mid-February, Malkin presented the précis to the members of the Joint Committee during a private meeting.[143] He carefully explained the legal arguments for and against Closer Union, but concluded that "I think that it might not be prudent" to adopt any scheme of legislative union that included Tanganyika.[144] Once back in the Foreign Office, the legal advisor characterized the previous several weeks as a "good deal of bother of one sort and another," but left the Committee to sort out its own problems.[145]

The members of the Joint Committee met nearly fifty times over the next eight months and produced their final report in October 1931.[146] They examined dozens of witnesses, drafted numerous papers, and watched as the worsening world economic crisis helped to topple the Labour government in August. In the process, the Committee served as a platform for Grigg to make his case for a White Dominion one last time and for Cameron to defend "the paramountcy of the Native" as well as to insist that constitutional changes in British East Africa were not necessary.[147] Nevertheless, such arguments did little to alter the final results. In the end, the Committee formally rejected Closer Union and recommended no substantive changes to the status quo.

The reasons that the Committee did not simply dissolve in early February when it learned of the legal problems surrounding Tanganyika reside in the tangled motives of the twenty personalities involved. Inconsequential committees were nothing new to most modern governments, but Stanley of Alderley told Passfield that several members wanted to continue to advocate their own favorite plans that did not involve complete federation.[148] In particular, Lugard never gave up his campaign to create a high commissioner for Uganda and Kenya while making the "White Highlands" some sort of tiny, semi-autonomous white zone surrounded by a giant British colony for Africans.[149] Some of the pro-settler Conservatives were happy simply to delay while hoping that an eventual Tory government might sponsor something similar to the original Wilson report that new law officers might approve.[150] Amery still did not consider legislative union in British East Africa a violation of the mandate and was willing to risk international litigation in order to secure federation.[151] Most members simply concluded that breaking up the Committee would not serve any useful purpose and conspired to hide their predicament from the public. Exposure would only embarrass the government, worsen political division in East Africa, and imperil any "Great White State" as long as Germany wanted to challenge it. Thus, the British public and the larger world were spared the discovery not only that Labour's proposals for Closer Union were a violation of British and international law, but that the government had not bothered to ask if their plans were illegal before publishing them.

At the center of all this controversy was the international constitution of the Tanganyika Territory. In April, months before the Committee formally finished its work, the chairman began to draft the final recommendations as to why "[t]he Committee cannot recommend Political Closer Union." In a seven-page paper, Stanley of Alderley explained:

> Any close unification of economic services of the three territories involves

> a greater or less degree of political union especially if any legislation for this purpose is required. An effective economic union would necessitate legislative action. This may perhaps be effected through existing legislatures, but there are difficulties in the way which have to be faced. A Closer Union that imposes changes in Tanganyika, unless it can be shown that such changes carry corresponding direct advantages to Tanganyika, would probably be a breach of the mandate.[152]

But the final report did not contain this passage. As the months passed, direct references to either questions of international law or definitions of the terms of the mandate vanished.[153] By the time that the report appeared in public in October, it reaffirmed the notions of trusteeship and the general mandatory principles, but blamed the Depression, the resistance of some local colonial administrators, and the reluctance of the African and Asian communities for its determination that federation in British East African was impossible.[154] From the public's point of view, the committee's report was entirely compatible with the White Papers even though it repudiated Labour's plans for Closer Union. After months of private wrangling and public exertion, the subterfuge was complete. As long as there was not official record of the law officers' views, pro-settler Conservatives did not have to concede that Closer Union with Tanganyika was illegal while Labourites avoided admitting, in the words of Lord Mersey, that "we do not know how to manage our affairs."

The Failure of "Closer Union"

The collapse of Closer Union between 1929 and 1931 demonstrated the changed culture of British colonialism and had important implications for Africans in Tanganyika, Uganda, and Kenya. The national political parties, leading pressure groups, public opinion, and various local communities were never again as powerfully focused on Closer Union or its implications for the relations between colonized peoples and Europeans in East Africa. This debate had taken a decade to evolve and had found expression in, and was in many ways driven by, the language and tenets of the mandates system. While mandates became an increasingly serious issue in Anglo-German relations in the 1930s and some colonial officials explored the possibility of federation in British East Africa during the Second World War, Britain never transformed the region into the larger possession once envisioned by either Amery or Grigg.[155] Deep antagonisms made successful colonial federation in British East Africa difficult, but what the mandates system represented and was in the process of transforming made these antagonisms even more divisive. The nature of Europe's role in Africa was a pivotal consideration on both sides of the argument. Amery, Grigg, and others had come to realize that mandates threatened their vision of the British Empire and appropriated the rhetoric of the "new" imperialism in order to try to preserve what they could of the "old." For others, including Lugard, Cameron, Oldham, and the men of empire in the Labour party, the international supervision of European colonialism in Africa was more than mere rhetoric. It was a model founded on the very best British imperial intentions and served as a constant reminder of why so much of the "old" imperialism had failed. Since the mandates system was ingrained in the postwar world order and remained an inherent part of the shifting conceptions of European attitudes of Africans, it shaped much of the Closer Union controversy from its inception.

Still, the interrelated domestic and imperial pressures inherent in the Closer Union debate proved far less decisive than Tanganyika's relationship with the League of Nations. While the second Labour government thwarted the demands of white settlers, the broader international context forced the government to surrender its own plans for Closer Union. International concerns superseded colonial priorities and frustrated the creation of a unified East African Dominion dominated by white settlers, but also dashed Labour's plan for a single East African British Protectorate that would have erased nearly one thousand miles of artificial colonial partitions and consolidated the communities and resources of the vast region surrounding Lake Victoria in the north to Lake Nyasa in the south. As a result, African groups such as the Masai remained divided between Tanganyika and Kenya and white settlers in the highlands of Kenya never had to conform to the policies of a powerful high commissioner responsible for protecting African land and labor rights. Furthermore, modern Africa lost the opportunity to build a large multiethnic state that would have, as Lugard once explained, brought Uganda and Kenya "in some degree under the supervision of the Mandates Commission." Geneva's internationalization and reformation of colonialism may have saved British East Africa from the lingering impulses of late-nineteenth century European imperialism, but it had also hindered those who had hoped to bind the liberal principles of the mandates system even more closely to the practice of British colonial rule in East Africa.

Conclusions

It may be asked why Britain then consented to accept this country under a mandate. I think the answer is that she did not want to appear laden with the spoils of war. It was a gesture of renunciation of imperialistic aims and ambitions. And with that gesture I believe the grand conception of Empire was discarded. From that time onward our standing as a colonial power has declined. To-day the word Empire is taboo; we may not speak of subject races, they have become backward peoples; colonial rule had become 'trusteeship,' implying that it is to endure only until the ward comes of age. A chapter of world history has herewith been closed.

Sir Charles Dundas, former Secretary for Native Affairs for the the Tanganyika Territory, *African Crossroads* (London, 1955), pp. 144–5

I suppose fundamentally you, as a historian, are more interested in the fruits of victory and less in the hope of permanent peace!

Lord Robert Cecil to Winston Churchill, 8 January 1929

Today the sharp ideological clash between the "old" imperial order and the "new" resulting from the First World War may appear remarkably narrow and even hypocritical. It is easy to assume that the League of Nations mandates system was merely another empty promise during a seemingly brief and illusory period that ended in economic collapse and another global war. Yet for the leading politicians, pressure groups, colonial bureaucracies, and the many in Europe, America, and elsewhere during this period who were weary and afraid of war, the future of European imperialism was intimately bound together with the future of the peace and progress of the world. The men responsible for creating the new international order devoted a tremendous amount of time and energy to the questions surrounding the role of colonialism not only in preserving global stability, but in extending western economic and political institutions to non-western peoples. Most believed that European imperialism was necessary in Africa and would remain so for many decades. The debate over its future was a central preoccupation of the opening days of the Paris Peace Conference. It was important enough to Woodrow Wilson that he endangered the entire conference in order to advocate a system of "mandates" that would internationalize and reform European imperialism under the supervision of the new League of Nations. Similarly, British and French colonial officials including Henry Simon, Lord Milner, and Albert Sarraut considered traditional conceptions of empire important enough to defy the decisions of the peacemakers. Only in the face of persistent and often acute international pressures from the League, the United States, the League of Nations Union, Germany, and a diverse collection of other political parties, pressure groups, and individuals did the defenders of the old order give way.

Once in place, the mandates system represented the changing character of postwar European imperialism in Africa. The leading members of the Permanent Mandates Commission, including the British member Sir Frederick Lugard, created a network of political alliances that gave the PMC a great deal of informal power to advance what it considered was progressive change and practical administration in Africa. The League also exercised substantial formal influence by relying on the constant threat of public criticism, the importance of international law, and its reputation as a cooperative, experienced, and credible organization dedicated to what seemed to many was best about modern colonialism. In this way, the mandates system not only symbolized the internationalization and reformation of European imperialism, but gradually played a transforming role in its operation. The PMC developed close ties with various colonial officials which extended and strengthened the League's purpose. Despite flaws, mandates contributed to an evolution in the culture of colonialism that affected not only the vast diplomatic and colonial bureaucracies of both Britain and France, but Europeans and Africans within all the mandated territories as well.

Many of these changes for Africans were profound. Starting first with Tanganyika and then spreading to Togo and Cameroon, British and French colonial structures gradually, and sometimes inadvertently, adopted policies that had long-term economic, political, and cultural consequences. The PMC successfully prodded the mandatory powers to reunify modern Rwanda. The blending of mandatory principles with colonial policies produced important slavery and land legislation in Tanganyika that directly impinged on African interests and tightened the ties between the metropole and the mandated territory. Paris did much the same by making Togo and Cameroon into "autonomous administrations" instead of absorbing them into the neighboring French colonial federations. Abandoning conscription in the French mandated territories, constricting military recruitment in all mandates, maintaining commercial equality, extending Cameron's version of mandatory rule throughout Tanganyika, allowing the Germans to return to the British mandates, and obstructing the creation of an East African Dominion were some of the consequences of attaching the League of Nations to French and British colonialism in Africa. Such results demonstrated how mandates restricted imperial power and inspired more internationally-oriented colonial practices. Lastly, the international status of the French mandates gave some among the African elite, particularly the Duala and members of the Adjigo family, a powerful means for contesting and confining French colonial rule while exposing a number of the strengths and weaknesses inherent in the colonial state.

The mandates system was not only a complex and often contradictory blend of theory and practice, it brought both benefits and disadvantages to Africans and Europeans. Both French and British colonial officials learned how to use the League to extend greater state control over the lives of Africans by insisting that such policies were for their "well-being and development" in the spirit of the mandate. Competing missionary societies, exercising their "complete freedom of conscience," sometimes disrupted local African communities. Keeping mandates separate from neighboring colonial possessions curtailed direct cooperation between African groups, divided resources, impaired communications and common services, and hindered migration. Restricting military recruitment shrank employment opportunities, diminished a means for engaging the power of the colonial state, and eliminated chances for Africans to encounter a wider world. Lastly, melding the British mandates to the Lugardian dogma of Indirect Rule encouraged unimaginative colonial officials to maintain highly artificial "traditional" African institutions that in time often became stagnant and divisive.

The impact of the mandates system on the ideology of imperialism among Europeans was as penetrating and extensive. The League internationalized and institutionalized the principle of "trusteeship" and publicly held the mandatory powers to their pledge that they would comply with the stipulations of the mandate, submit to international supervision, and assume the responsibilities of the "sacred trust of civilization." In this way, mandates constituted a form of international blackmail. The League persistently pressed the two largest overseas imperial powers to translate more of their colonial rhetoric into reality. The stakes were high. While the League had its own reputation and position within the global order to maintain, the mandatory powers were determined to preserve their imperial legitimacy among the international community and Africans. Merely adopting the language of the mandates system to disguise traditional assumptions proved impossible. The psychological and legal foundations of the empires depended on words that had meaning. Gradually adopting the new vocabulary of the mandates system subtly forced colonial officials to reconsider traditional assumptions about Africans and adopt new ones. Some within the broad structure of imperialism resisted the language of the League while others embraced it, but none could ignore the changed international conditions that this language reflected.

Britain and France shared some common responses to the mandates system, but taken together, they reacted differently. British colonial officials considered mandates primarily as expressions of the very best intentions of British imperialism in Africa. While always mindful of international accountability, few feared it and many welcomed any opportunity to demonstrate what they assumed was the superiority of British rule. As the world's largest overseas empire whose survival depended on cooperating with the League in Europe and on the ideals of trusteeship in the empire, Britain could only gain by taking the spirit of the mandates system seriously. Largely dedicated to decentralization and to the political rather than economic development of the empire, the League's objective of administering a mandate until the inhabitants were able to "stand by themselves" was compatible with the theoretical goals of British imperialism. Thus, the League served to push Britain faster and further along a path that it professed it had already chosen for itself. For these reasons, Britain usually hoped for the best when engaging Geneva and often tolerated the inconveniences and failings of the system.

French colonial officials considered mandates primarily a danger to the intentions of French imperialism in Africa. Always anxious about international accountability, many feared it as an unwelcome opportunity for enemies – including Germans and subversive Africans – to assert the inferiority of French rule. As the world's second largest overseas empire whose survival depended on containing Germany in Europe and on the ideals of "assimilation" and "association" in the empire, France could only lose by taking the spirit of the mandates system seriously. Largely dedicated to centralization and to the economic rather than political development of the empire, the League's objective was incompatible with the theoretical goals of French imperialism. Thus, by tightly controlling the mandates and avoiding conspicuous violations of their stipulations, France hoped to insulate itself from harmful outside criticism. For these reasons, France usually expected the worst when engaging Geneva and often tried to suppress the inconveniences and failings of the system.

The worldwide economic crisis of the 1930s caused new and perplexing problems for Britain and France, the League of Nations, and international relations. The rise of Adolf Hitler in Germany, the failure of disarmament, and Italy's invasion of Ethiopia severely tested not only the limits of Geneva, but some of the familiar political convictions and many of the highest hopes of the 1920s as well. Further, the Great Depression placed new burdens on European imperialism and intensified a number of the fractures and unresolved dilemmas within colonial society. While for many contemporaries the League of Nations mandates system was a fixed part of the international order, an examination of the system after 1931 will necessitate comprehending a sharply different political and economic international context. Since Germany's lost colonies became part of Anglo-French appeasement policy, scholars must evaluate how the rapidly shifting international conditions altered both the supervision and administration of the mandated territories. Did the worsening world crisis serve to strengthen objections to "annexation" and "militarism" in the African mandates? How did the growing problems of the League, particularly after Italy's conquest of Ethiopia in 1935 and Lugard's resignation the following year, affect the influence and agenda of the PMC? To what degree did public opinion and the attitudes of anti-imperialists, the Labour Party, the LNU, or the United States change toward the mandates system in the 1930s? In what ways did the mandates continue to have an impact on Africans and how did they persist in using the international status of Togo and Cameroon against French colonial rule? Lastly, how did the system shape both the United Nations "Trusteeship System" (which operated during the entire Cold War period) and the conceptions of European colonialism after the Second World War?[1]

Judgments about the impact and significance of the mandates system have shifted widely since its creation. In 1919 Wilson called the system an "absolute revolution."[2] A decade later, the American international lawyer Quincy Wright concluded that mandates were "perhaps the most important innovation wrought by the peace treaties and the Covenant in the system of international law."[3] During the troubled 1930s, a few defenders of the "old" imperialism continued to denounce the system as a failure, a danger to the British Empire, and a cause for Anglo-German antagonism.[4] But Lord Hailey, in his extensive and highly influential survey of Africa in 1938, was much impressed with the League's use of public opinion to inspire reforms in the mandated territories.[5] Some French scholars took a similar view.[6] Lugard, late in life and under the darkening shadow of the Second World War, was still convinced of the merits of mandates and understood the real power of the system:

> This procedure has I think had a very good effect upon the administration of the Mandatory, not only by means of criticism and suggestion, but also because the Colonial Powers are exceedingly sensitive to public opinion.[7]

Lugard's friend and former colleague, William Rappard, offered a comparably circumspect view of the mandates system:

> To be sure, the solution adopted was far from being free from hypocrisy. But not only did it imply, as hypocrisy always does, a tribute of wrong to right, but it was in itself a step in the direction away from narrow and exclusive nationalism toward world organization.[8]

Even during the Second World War, when the failures of the League of Nations seemed manifest, the American historian Thomas A. Bailey decided that "[c]ertainly the mandate system proved to be one of the more successful and creditable enterprises of the League of Nations. It was, as someone has said, 'an angel conceived in sin'."[9] More recently, however, despite the staggering amount of public documentation and the availability of a wide variety of archival and private materials, a number of recent historians are willing to declare that the system had "very little practical effect" and the mandates were "colonies in camouflage."[10]

Such scholarly assertions not only would have surprised many of the Europeans and Africans who encountered the system between 1914 and 1931, but seriously distort an understanding of these important years. Mandates are part of the modern history of Europe, Africa, and the world. In purpose and practice, the League of Nations and the PMC undertook to resolve some of the most pressing problems of modern international society. Unwilling and unable to prevent the world revolution of westernization, the League hoped that international cooperation and accountability, the rule of law, and the principles of "trusteeship" would rectify the dilemmas resulting from an increasing global interdependence. These dilemmas proved not only immense, but enduring. During the dramatic international events of the early 1960s, Kenneth Robinson observed:

> The problems of trusteeship were the problems of power, of the responsibilities of the strong towards the weak. The unequal distribution of political and economic power in the world, which was the fundamental basis of colonialism, has not been suddenly abolished by the accession of most colonies to political independence.[11]

Such "problems of power" in the relations between "the strong and the weak" continue to challenge the major national and international institutions of the post-Cold War era. In particular, the invariably uneven, usually ambiguous, and sometimes pernicious relationships that tie Africa to the larger world have not disappeared. The current dominant "developed" states, the "new" United Nations, the array of multinational financial and commercial interests, the many religious and humanitarian groups, and the increasing number of local governmental and non-governmental organizations still contend with the myriad competing interests and cultures in Africa. These institutions can provide aid, diminish conflict, and increase opportunities. They also can exploit, demean, and undermine. Lord Robert Cecil may have assumed that historians "are more interested in the fruits of victory and less in the hope of permanent peace," but even historians admit that both of these powerful pursuits have profoundly marked the twentieth-century world and doubtless will shape the twenty-first.

Appendices

APPENDIX A
Article 22 of the League of Nations Covenant

1. To those colonies and territories which as a consequence of the late war have ceased to be under the sovereignty of the States which formerly governed them and which are inhabited by peoples not yet able to stand by themselves under the strenuous conditions of the modern world, there should be applied the principle that the well-being and development of such peoples form a sacred trust of civilization and that securities for the performance of this trust should be embodied in this Covenant.

2. The best method of giving practical effect to this principle is that the tutelage of such peoples should be entrusted to advanced nations who, by reason of their resources, their experience or their geographical position, can best undertake this responsibility, and who are willing to accept it, and that this tutelage should be exercised by them as Mandatories on behalf of the League.

3. The character of the mandate must differ according to the stage of the development of the people, the geographical situation of the territory, its economic conditions and other similar circumstances.

4. Certain communities formerly belonging to the Turkish Empire have reached a stage of development where their existence as independent nations can be provisionally recognized subject to the rendering of administrative advice and assistance by a Mandatory until such time as they are able to stand alone. The wishes of these communities must be a principle consideration in the selection of the Mandatory.

5. Other peoples, especially those of Central Africa, are at such a such a stage that the Mandatory must be responsible for the administration of the territory under conditions which will guarantee freedom of conscience and religion, subject only to the maintenance of public order and morals, the prohibition of abuses such as the slave trade, the arms traffic and the liquor traffic, and the prevention of the establishment of fortifications or military and naval bases and of military training of the natives for other than police purposes and the defense of territory, and will also secure equal opportunities for the trade and commerce of other Members of the League.

6. There are territories, such as Southwest Africa and certain of the South Pacific islands, which, owing to the sparseness of their population or their small size, or their remoteness from the centers of civilization, or their geographical contiguity to the territory of the Mandatory, and other circumstances, can be best

administered under the laws of the Mandatory as integral portions of its territory, subject to the safeguards above mentioned in the interests of the indigenous population.

7. In every case of mandate, the Mandatory shall render to the Council an annual report in reference to the territory committed to its charge.

8. The degree of authority, control or administration to be exercised by the Mandatory shall, if not previously agreed upon by the Members of the League, be explicitly defined in each case by the Council.

9. A permanent Commission shall be constituted to receive and examine the annual reports of the Mandatories, and to advise the Council on all matters relating to the observance of the mandates.

APPENDIX B
Text of the Mandate for the Tanganyika Territory

The Council of the League of Nations:

Whereas by Article 119 of the Treaty of Peace with Germany signed at Versailles on June 28th, 1919 Germany renounced in Favor of the Principal Allied and Associated Powers all her rights over her oversea possessions, including therein German East Africa; and

Whereas, in accordance with the treaty of June 11th, 1891, between Her Britannic Majesty and His Majesty the King of Portugal, the River Rovuma is recognized as forming the northern boundary of the Portuguese possessions in East Africa from its mouth up to the confluence of the River M'Sinje; and

Whereas the Principal Allied and Associated Powers agreed that, in accordance with Article 22, Part I (Covenant of the League of Nations), of the said treaty, a mandate should be conferred upon His Britannic Majesty to administer part of the former colony of German East Africa, and have proposed that the mandate should be formulated in the following terms; and

Whereas His Britannic Majesty has agreed to accept the mandate in respect of the said territory, and has undertaken to exercise it on behalf of the League of Nations in accordance with the following provisions; and

Whereas by the afore-mentioned Article 22, paragraph 8, it is provided that the degree of authority, control or administration to be exercised by the Mandatory, not having been previously agreed upon by the Members of the League, shall be explicitly defined by the Council of the League of Nations;

Confirming the said mandate, defines its terms as follows:

ARTICLE 1. The territory over which a mandate is conferred upon His Britannic Majesty (hereinafter called the Mandatory) comprises that part of the territory of the former colony of German East Africa situated to the east of the following line:

[Clauses indicating frontier lines]

ARTICLE 2. [Clauses indicating provisions for Anglo-Belgian Boundary Commission]

ARTICLE 3. The Mandatory shall be responsible for the peace, order and good government of the territory, and shall undertake to promote to the utmost the material and moral well-being and the social progress of its inhabitants. The

Mandatory shall have full powers of legislation and administration.

ARTICLE 4. The Mandatory shall not establish any military or naval bases, nor erect any fortifications, nor organize any native military force in the territory except for local police purposes and for the defence of the territory.

ARTICLE 5. The Mandatory:

(1) shall provide for the eventual emancipation of all slaves and for as speedy an elimination of domestic and other slavery as social conditions will allow;
(2) shall suppress all forms of slave trade;
(3) shall prohibit all forms of forced or compulsory labor, except for essential public works and services, and then only in return for adequate remuneration;
(4) shall protect the natives from abuse and measures of fraud and force by the careful supervision of labor contracts and the recruiting of labor;
(5) shall exercise a strict control over the traffic in arms and ammunition and the sale of spirituous liquors.

ARTICLE 6. In the framing of laws relating to the holding or transfer of land, the Mandatory shall take into consideration native laws and customs, and shall respect the rights and safeguard the interests of the native population.

No native land may be transferred, except between natives, without the previous consent of the public authorities, nd no real rights over native land in favor of non-natives may be created except with the same consent.

The Mandatory will promulgate strict regulations against usury.

ARTICLE 7. The Mandatory shall secure to all nationals of States Members of the League of Nations the same rights as are enjoyed in the territory by his own nationals in respect of entry into and residence in the territory, the protection afforded to their person and property, the acquisition of property, movable and immovable, and the exercise of their profession or trade, subject only to the requirements of public order, and on condition of compliance with the local law.

Further, the Mandatory shall ensure to all nationals of States Members of the League of Nations, on the same footing as to his own nationals, freedom of transit and navigation, and complete economic, commercial and industrial equality; provided that the Mandatory shall be free to organize essential public works and services on such terms and conditions as he thinks just.

Concessions for the development of the natural resources of the territory shall be granted by the Mandatory without distinction on the grounds of nationality between the nationals of all States Members of the League of Nations, but on such conditions as will maintain intact the authority of the local Government.

Concessions having the character of a general monopoly shall not be granted. This provision does not affect the right of the Mandatory to create monopolies of a purely fiscal character in the interest of the territory under mandate, and in order to provide the territory with fiscal resources which seem best suited to the local requirements; or, in certain cases, to carry out the development of natural resources either directly by the State or by a controlled agency, provided that there shall result therefrom no monopoly of the natural resources for the benefit of the Mandatory or his nationals, directly or indirectly, nor any preferential advantage which shall be inconsistent with the economic, commercial and industrial equality hereinbefore guaranteed.

The rights conferred by this article extend equally to companies and associations organized in accordance with the law of any of the Members of the League of Nations, subject only to the requirements of public order, and on condition of compliance with the local law.

ARTICLE 8. The Mandatory shall ensure in the territory complete freedom of conscience and the free exercise of all forms of worship which are consonant with public order and morality; missionaries who are nationals of State Members of the League of Nations shall be free to enter the territory and to travel and reside therein, to acquire and possess property, to erect religious buildings and to open schools throughout the territory; it being understood, however, that the Mandatory shall have the right to exercise such control as may be necessary for the maintenance of public order and good government, and to take all measures required for such control.

ARTICLE 9. The Mandatory shall apply to the territory any general international conventions already existing, or which may be concluded hereafter, with the approval of the League of Nations, respecting the slave trade, the traffic in arms and ammunition, the liquor traffic, and the traffic in drugs, or relating to commercial equality, freedom of transit and navigation, aerial navigation, railways, postal, telegraphic, and wireless communication, and industrial, literary and artistic property.

The Mandatory shall co-operate in the execution of any common policy adopted by the League of Nations for preventing and combating disease, including diseases of plants and animals.

ARTICLE 10. The Mandatory shall be authorized to constitute the territory into a customs fiscal and administrative union or federation with the adjacent territories under his own sovereignty or control; provided always that the measures adopted to that end do not infringe the provisions of this mandate.

ARTICLE 11. The Mandatory shall make to the Council of the League of Nations an annual report to the satisfaction of the Council, containing full information concerning the measures taken to apply the provisions of this mandate.

A copy of all laws and regulations made in the course of the year and affecting property, commerce, navigation or the moral and material well-being of the natives shall be annexed to this report.

ARTICLE 12. The consent of the Council of the League of Nations is required for any modification of the terms of this mandate.

ARTICLE 13. The Mandatory agrees that if any dispute whatever should arise between the Mandatory and another Member of the League of Nations relating to the interpretation or the application of the provisions of the mandate, such dispute, if it cannot be settled by negotiation, shall be submitted to the Permanent Court of International Justice provided for by Article 14 of the Covenant of the League of Nations.

States Members of the League of Nations may likewise bring any claims on behalf of their nationals for infractions of their rights under this mandate before the said Court for decision.

The present instrument shall be deposited in original in the archives of the League of Nations. Certified copies shall be forwarded by the Secretary-General of the League of Nations to all Members of the League.

DONE at London, the twentieth day of July one thousand nine hundred and twenty-two.

APPENDIX C
Text of the Mandates for Togo and Cameroon

The Council of the League of Nations:

Whereas by Article 119 of the Treaty of Peace with Germany signed at Versailles on June 28th, 1919, Germany renounced in favor of the Principal Allied and Associated Powers all her rights over her oversea possessions, including therein the Cameroons; and

Whereas the Principal Allied and Associated Powers agreed that the Governments of France and Great Britain should make a joint recommendation to the League of Nations as to the future of the said territory; and Whereas the Governments of France and Great Britain have made a joint recommendation to the Council of the League of Nations that a mandate to administer in accordance with Article 22 of the Covenant of the League of Nations that part of the Cameroons lying to the west of the line agreed upon in the Declaration of July 10th, 1919, referred to in Article 1, should be conferred upon his Britannic Majesty; and

Whereas the Governments of France and Great Britain have proposed that the mandate should be formulated in the following terms; and

Whereas His Britannic Majesty has agreed to accept the mandate in respect of the said territory, and has undertaken to exercise it on behalf of the League of Nations in accordance with the following provisions;

Confirming the said mandate, defines its terms as follows:

ARTICLE. [Clauses indicating frontier lines]

ARTICLE 2. The Mandatory shall be responsible for the peace, order and good government of the territory, and for the promotion to the utmost of the material and moral well-being and the social progress of its inhabitants.

ARTICLE 3. The Mandatory shall not establish in the territory any military or naval bases, nor erect any fortifications, nor organize any native military force except for local police purposes and for the defence of the territory. [The French mandates add: "It is understood, however, that the troops thus raised may, in the event of general war, be utilized to repel an attack or for the defence of the territory outside that subject to the mandate."]

ARTICLE 4. The Mandatory:

(1) shall provide for the eventual emancipation of all slaves, and for as speedy an elimination of domestic and other slavery as social conditions will allow;

(2) shall suppress all forms of slave trade;

(3) shall prohibit all forms of forced or compulsory labor, except for essential public works and services, and then only in return for adequate remuneration;

(4) shall protect the natives from abuse and measures of fraud and force by the careful supervision of labor contracts and the recruiting of labor;

(5) \shall exercise a strict control over the traffic in arms and ammunition and the sale of spirituous liquors.

ARTICLE 5. In the framing of laws relating to the holding or transfer of land, the Mandatory shall take into consideration native laws and customs, and shall respect the rights and safeguard the interests of the native population.

No land may be transferred, except between natives, without the previous consent of the public authorities, and no real rights over native land in favor of non-natives may be created except with the same consent.

The Mandatory shall promulgate strict regulations against usury.

Article 6. The Mandatory shall secure to all nationals (*ressortissants*) of States Members of the League of Nations the same rights as are enjoyed in the territory by his own nationals in respect of entry into and residence in the territory, the protection afforded to their person and property, the acquisition of property, movable and immovable, and the exercise of their profession or trade, subject only to the requirements of public order, and on condition of compliance with the local law.

Further, the Mandatory shall ensure to all nationals of States Members of the League of Nations, on the same footing as to his own nationals, freedom of transit and navigation, and complete economic, commercial and industrial equality; provided that the Mandatory shall be free to organize essential public works and services on such terms and conditions as he thinks just.

Concessions for the development of the natural resources of the territory shall be granted by the Mandatory without distinction on the grounds of nationality between the nationals of all States Members of the League of Nations, but on such conditions as will maintain intact the authority of the local Government.

Concessions having the character of a general monopoly shall not be granted. This provision does not affect the right of the Mandatory to create monopolies of a purely fiscal character in the interest of the territory under mandate, and in order to provide the territory with fiscal resources which seem best suited to the local requirements; or, in certain cases, to carry out the development of natural resources either directly by the State or by a controlled agency, provided that there shall result therefrom no monopoly of the natural resources for the benefit of the Mandatory or his nationals, directly or indirectly, nor any preferential advantage which shall be inconsistent with the economic, commercial and industrial equality hereinbefore guaranteed.

The rights conferred by this article extend equally to companies and associations organized in accordance with the law of any of the Members of the League of Nations, subject only to the requirements of public order, and on condition of compliance with the local law.

Article 7. The Mandatory shall ensure in the territory complete freedom of conscience and the free exercise of all forms of worship which are consonant with public order and morality; missionaries who are nationals of State Members of the League of Nations shall be free to enter the territory and to travel and reside therein, to acquire and possess property, to erect religious buildings and to open schools throughout the territory; it being understood, however, that the Mandatory shall have the right to exercise such control as may be necessary for the maintenance of public order and good government, and to take all measures required for such control.

Article 8. The Mandatory shall apply to the territory any general international conventions applicable to his contiguous territory.

Article 9. The Mandatory shall have full powers of administration and legislation in the area subject to the mandate. This area shall be administered in accordance with the laws of the Mandatory as an integral part of his territory and subject to the above provisions.

The Mandatory shall therefore be at liberty to apply his laws to the territory under the mandate subject to the modifications required by local conditions, and to constitute the territory into a customs, fiscal or administrative union or federation with the adjacent territories under his sovereignty or control, provided always that the measures adopted to that end do not infringe the provisions of this mandate.

ARTICLE 10. The Mandatory shall make to the Council of the League of Nations an annual report to the satisfaction of the Council, containing full information concerning the measures taken to apply the provisions of this mandate.

ARTICLE 11. The consent of the Council of the League of Nations is required for any modification of the terms of this mandate.

ARTICLE 12. The Mandatory agrees that if any dispute whatever should arise between the Mandatory and another Member of the League of Nations relating to the interpretation or the application of the provisions of the mandate, such dispute, if it cannot be settled by negotiation, shall be submitted to the

Permanent Court of International Justice provided for by Article 14 of the Covenant of the League of Nations.

The present instrument shall be deposited in original in the archives of the League of Nations. Certified copies shall be forwarded by the Secretary-General of the League of Nations to all Members of the League.

DONE at London, the twentieth day of July one thousand nine hundred and twenty-two.

APPENDIX D
Constitution of the Permanent Mandates Commission

Approved by the Council on November 29, 1920

The Council of the League of Nations, in accordance with paragraphs 7 and 9 of Article 22 of the Covenant, namely:

In every case of Mandate, the Mandatory shall render to the Council an Annual Report in reference to the Territory committed to its charge.

A Permanent Commission shall be constituted to receive and examine the Annual Reports of the Mandatories, and to advise the Council on all matters relating to the observance of the Mandates.

has decided as follows:

(a) The Permanent Mandates Commission provided for in Paragraph 9 of Article 22 of the Covenant, shall consist of nine Members. The majority of the Commission shall be nationals of non-Mandatory Powers.

All the Members of the Commission shall be appointed by the Council and selected for their personal merits and competence. They shall not hold any office which puts them in a position of direct dependence on their Governments while members of the Commission.

The International Labor Organization shall have the privilege of appointing to the Permanent Commission an expert chosen by itself. This expert shall have the right of attending in an advisory capacity all meetings of the Permanent Commission at which questions relating to labor are discussed.

(b) The Mandatory Powers should send their annual report provided for in Paragraph 7 of Article 22 of the Covenant to the Commission through duly authorized representatives who would be prepared to offer any supplementary explanations or supplementary information which the Commissions may request.

(c) The Commission shall examine each individual report in the presence of the duly authorized representative of the Mandatory Power from which it comes. This representative shall participate with absolute freedom in the discussion of this report.

(d) At the end of this discussion, and after the representative of the Mandatory Power has withdrawn, the Commission shall decide on the wording of the observations which are to be submitted to the Council of the League.

(e) The observations made by the Commission upon each report shall be communicated to the duly authorized representative of the Mandatory Power from which the report comes. This representative shall be entitled to accompany it with any comments which he desires to make.

(f) The Commission shall forward the reports of Mandatory Powers to the Council. It shall annex to each report its own observations as well as the observations of the duly authorized representative of the Power which issued the report, if the representative so desires.

(g) When the Council publishes the reports of the Mandatory Powers and the observations of the Permanent Commission, it shall also publish the observations of the duly authorized representatives of those Mandatory Powers which have expressed such a desire.

(h) The Commission, acting in concert with all the duly authorized representatives of the Mandatory Powers, shall hold a Plenary Meeting to consider all the reports as a whole and any general conclusions to be drawn from them. The Commission may also utilize such a Meeting of the representatives of the Mandatory Powers to lay before them any other matters connected with Mandates which in their opinion should be submitted by the Council to the Mandatory Powers and to the other States Members of the League. This Plenary Meeting shall take place either before or after the presentation of the annual reports, as the Commission may think fit.

(i) The Commission shall regulate its own procedure subject to the approval of the Council.

(j) The Commission shall sit at Geneva. It may summon technical experts to act in an advisory capacity for all questions relating to the application of the system of Mandates.

(k) The Members of the Commission shall receive an allowance of 100 gold francs per day during their Meetings. Their travelling expenses shall be paid. Expenses of the Commission shall be borne by the League of Nations.

Notes

Introduction

1 For more, see Marc Michel, *L'Appel à l'Afrique: contributions et réactions à l'effort de guerre en A.O.F., 1914–18* (Paris, 1982); Melvin E. Page, ed., *Africa and the First World War* (New York, 1987) and A. Adu Boahen, *African Perspectives on Colonialism* (Baltimore, 1987).

2 For studies of European perceptions of Africa during this period, see Penelope Hetherington, *British Paternalism and Africa 1920–1940* (London, 1978); Andrew Roberts, ed., *The Cambridge History of Africa*, vol. 7 (Cambridge, 1986), pp. 24–76; Denise Bouche, *Histoire de la colonisation française* II (Paris, 1991), pp. 207–73 and P. J. Cain and A. G. Hopkins, *British Imperialism: Crisis and Deconstruction, 1914–1990* (London, 1993), pp. 201–34.

3 Imperial War Cabinet, Report of Committee on Terms of Peace, 28 April 1917, CAB 21/77.

4 Minutes of the "Commission d'étude des questions coloniales posées par la guerre," 24 June 1918, Archives Nationales, Section Outre-Mer, Aix-en-Provence (ANSOM), Affaires Politiques (AP) 96. Also see report of the Commission, "Les ambitions coloniales de l'Allemagne," 6 November 1918, ANSOM, AP, 95 and Ministère des Colonies (MC) to Ministère des Affaires Etrangères (MAE), 17 December 1918, ANSOM, AP, 1044.

5 The standard works on the background and functions of the League of Nations mandates system are H. Duncan Hall, *Mandates, Dependencies and Trusteeship* (Washington, D.C., 1948) and Quincy Wright, *Mandates under the League of Nations* (Chicago, 1930) (hereafter cited as *Mandates*).

6 For a general description of the various mandates, see Article 22 of the Treaty of Versailles in *Papers Relating to the Foreign Relations of the United States* (hereafter cited as *FRUS*), *The Paris Peace Conference, 1919*, vol. 13 (Washington, D.C., 1942–47), pp. 93–104.

7 For the final texts of the various B mandates, see Appendix B and C and Wright, *Mandates*, pp. 611–18.

8 For bibliographies, see Wm. Roger Louis, "Great Britain and International Trusteeship: The Mandate System" in Robin W. Winks, ed., *The Historiography of the British Empire-Commonwealth: Trends, Interpretations, and Resources* (Durham, North Carolina, 1966), pp. 298–311 and George W. Baer, ed., *International Organizations 1918–1945: A Guide to Research and Research Materials*, revised edition (Wilmington, Delaware, 1991), pp. 135–43.

9 The best example is Wm. Roger Louis, *Great Britain and Germany's Lost Colonies* (Oxford, 1967) (hereafter cited as *Germany's Lost Colonies*). Also see Gaddis Smith, "The British Government and the Disposition of the

German Colonies in Africa, 1914–1918," in Prosser Gifford and Wm. Roger Louis, eds., *Britain and Germany in Africa* (New Haven, 1967), pp. 275–99; H. Duncan Hall, "The British Commonwealth and the Founding of the League Mandate System," in K. Bourne and D. C. Watt, eds., *Studies in International History* (Hamden, Conn., 1967), pp. 345–67; Andrew J. Crozier, "The Establishment of the Mandates System 1919–1925: Some Problems Created by the Paris Peace Conference," *Journal of Contemporary History* 14 (1979): 483–513; and Peter J. Yearwood, "Great Britain and the Repartition of Africa, 1914–1919," *Journal of Imperial and Commonwealth History* 18 (1990): 314–41 (hereafter cited as "Great Britain and the Repartition of Africa, 1914–1919").

10 The best example is Christopher M. Andrew and A. S. Kanya-Forstner, *France Overseas: The Great War and the Climax of French Imperial Expansion* (London, 1981) (hereafter cited as *France Overseas*). Also see, André Kaspi, "French War Aims in Africa, 1914–1919," in Prosser Gifford and Wm. Roger Louis, eds., *France and Britain in Africa: Imperial Rivalry and Colonial Rule* (New Haven, 1971), pp. 369–96 and Christopher M. Andrew and A. S. Kanya-Forstner, "The French Colonial Party and French War Aims, 1914–1918," *The Historical Journal* 17 (1974): 79–106.

11 An example of the former is Brian Digre, *Imperialism's New Clothes: The Repartition of Tropical Africa 1914–1919* (New York, 1990) (hereafter cited as *Imperialism's New Clothes*) which examines British, French, and Belgian colonial war aims in Africa, yet adds little to the work of Louis, Andrew, and Kanya-Forstner. An example of the latter is Andrew J. Crozier, *Appeasement and Germany's Last Bid for Colonies* (New York, 1988) (hereafter cited as *Appeasement*). Also see Wolfe W. Schmokel, "The Hard Death of Imperialism: British and German Colonial Attitudes, 1919–1939," in Gifford and Louis, eds., *Britain and Germany in Africa*, pp. 301–35 and A. Edho Ekoko, "The British Attitude Towards Germany's Colonial Irredentism in Africa in the Inter-War Years," *Journal of Contemporary History* 14 (1979): 287–307.

12 Louis, *Germany's Lost Colonies*, p. 7. Andrew and Kanya-Forstner argue that "[t]he colonial dispossession of Germany at the Peace Conference caused the French few problems" and that the mandates were "treated virtually as colonies." *France Overseas*, p. 184 and 235. Crozier agrees with Robert Lansing, American secretary of state from 1915 to 1920, who asserted that the mandates system was of "little if any, real value." *Appeasement*, p. 10.

13 For examples see John Illife, *A Modern History of Tanganyika* (Cambridge, 1979) and Ralph A. Austen, *Northwest Tanzania under German and British Rule* (New Haven and London, 1968). Also see, Martin H. Y. Kaniki, *Tanzania Under Colonial Rule* (London, 1980); D. M. P. McCarthy, *Colonial Bureaucracy and Creating Underdevelopment: Tanganyika, 1919–1940* (Ames, Iowa, 1982) and Isria N. Kimambo, *Penetration and Protest in Tanzania: The Impact of the World Economy on the Page, 1860–1960* (London, 1991). For the mandates in West Africa, see Engelbert Mveng, *Histoire du Cameroun* (Paris, 1963); Victor LeVine, *The Cameroons from Mandate to Independence* (Berkeley, 1964); Tambi Eyonetah, *A History of the Cameroon* (London, 1987 edition); Philippe Gaillard, *Le Cameroun* 2 vols. (Paris, 1989); Mark W. DeLancey, *Cameroon: Dependence and Independence* (Boulder, Colorado, 1989); Emmanuel Chiabi, *The Making of Modern Cameroon: A History of Substate Nationalism and Disparate Union, 1914–1961* vol. I (Lanham, Maryland,

1997); Robert Cornevin, *Le Togo: Des origines à nos jours* (Paris, 1987) and N. L. Gayibor, ed., *Les Togolais face à la colonisation* (Lomé, 1994).

14 A few works of this type are Campbell L. Upthegrove, *Empire by Mandate: A History of the Relations of Great Britain with the Permanent Mandates Commission of the League of Nations* (New York, 1954); B. T. G. Chidzero, *Tanganyika and International Trusteeship* (London, 1961); and David E. Gardinier, "The British in the Cameroons, 1919–1939," in Gifford and Louis, eds., *Britain and Germany in Africa*, pp. 513–55. Also see, Laurent Péchoux, *Le Mandat français sur le Togo* (Paris, 1939) and Rayford W. Logan, *The African Mandates in World Politics* (Washington, D.C., 1948).

15 "Varieties of Trusteeship: African Territories under British and French Mandate, 1919–1939," in Gifford and Louis, eds., *France and Britain in Africa*, pp. 515–41.

16 *Colonie ou Mandat international? La politique française au Cameroun de 1919 à 1946* (Paris, 1992).

17 *Tanganyika under International Mandate, 1919–1946* (Lanham, Maryland, 1995) (hereafter cited as *Tanganyika*).

18 For example, see Emmanuel Chiabi, "British Administration and Nationalism in the Southern Cameroons, 1914–1954" in Martin Njeuma, ed., *Introduction to the History of Cameroon: Nineteenth and Twentieth Centuries* (New York, 1989), p. 180.

19 E. A. Brett, *Colonialism and Underdevelopment in East Africa: The Politics of Economic Change 1919–1939* (London, 1973), p. 106 and footnote 145.

20 Stephen Constantine, *The Making of British Colonial Development Policy 1914–1940* (London, 1984), p. 231.

21 The best examples of studies of this kind, particularly concerning the workings of the British Foreign Office, include D. C. Watt, *Personalities and Politics: Studies in the Formulation of British Foreign Policy in the Twentieth Century* (South Bend, 1965); Zara S. Steiner, *The Foreign Office and Foreign Policy, 1898–1914* (Cambridge, 1969); Ephraim Maisel, *The Foreign Office and Foreign Policy, 1919–1926* (Brighton, 1994) and Lorna Lloyd, *Peace Through Law: Britain and the International Court in the 1920s* (Suffolk, 1997). Also see Edward Hallett Carr, *The Twenty Years' Crisis: An Introduction to the Study of International Relations*, 2nd edn. (New York, 1946); Lamar Cecil, *The German Diplomatic Service, 1871–1914* (Princeton, 1976); William Wallace, *The Foreign Policy Process in Britain* (London, 1977); Paul Kennedy, *The Realities Behind Diplomacy* (London, 1981); R. Bullen, ed., *The Foreign Office, 1782–1982* (Frederick, Maryland, 1984) and R. Warman, *The Foreign Office, 1916–1918: A Study of its Role and Functions* (New York, 1986).

22 For some recent discussions of colonialism and culture, a good starting point is Dane Kennedy, "Imperial History and Post-Colonial Theory," *Journal of Imperial and Commonwealth History* 24 (1996): 345–63 and Phillip Darby, "Taking Fieldhouse Further: Post-Colonializing Imperial History," *Journal of Imperial and Commonwealth History* 26 (1998): 233–50. Also see John M. MacKenzie, *Imperialism and Popular Culture* (London, 1986); J. A. Mangan, ed., *Making Imperial Mentalities: Socialisation and British Imperialism* (New York, 1990); Akira Iriye, "Culture and International History" in Michael J. Hogan and Thomas G. Paterson, eds., *Explaining the History of American Foreign Relations* (Cambridge, 1991); Frederick Cooper, "Conflict and Connection: Rethinking Colonial African History," *The American Historical Review* 99 (1994): 1516–45 and Alice L. Conklin,

A Mission to Civilize: The Republican Idea of Empire in France and West Africa, 1895–1930 (Stanford, Calif., 1997). For a concise critique of Edward W. Said's, *Culture and Imperialism* (New York, 1993), see John M. MacKenzie, "Occidentalism: Counterpoint and Counter-polemic," *Journal of Historical Geography* 19 (1993): 339–44.

23 For a useful survey of some of these global forces, see Theodore H. Von Laue, *The World Revolution of Westernization: The Twentieth Century in Global Perspective* (New York, 1987).

24 The best essays on the notion of "trusteeship" in British imperial history remain Kenneth Robinson, *The Dilemmas of Trusteeship: Aspects of British Colonial Policy between the Wars* (London, 1965) (hereafter cited as *The Dilemmas of Trusteship*).

25 Quotations from Louis, *Germany's Lost Colonies*, p. 160; Dumbuya, *Tanganyika*, p. xv and Digre, *Imperialism's New Clothes*, p. 196.

Chapter 1 The Great War and Imperial Expansion

1 For a discussion of Germany's war aims in Africa, see Fritz Fischer, *Germany's Aims in the First World War* (New York, 1967), p. 104 and pp. 586–91.

2 For descriptions of the military campaigns, see F. J. Moberly, *Official History of the War: Military Operations, Togoland and the Cameroons, 1914–1916* (London, 1931); Joseph-Gaudéric Aymerich, *La Conquête du Cameroun* (Paris, 1933) and Lt. Col. Charles Hordern, *History of the Great War: Military Operations, East Africa* (London, 1941).

3 See Lewis Feuer, *Imperialism and the Anti-Imperialist Mind* (Buffalo, New York, 1986) and Stephen Howe, *Anticolonialism in British Politics: The Left and the End of Empire 1918–1964* (Oxford, 1993).

4 For basic studies of the German colonial empire, see John Iliffe, *Tanganyika Under German Rule* (Cambridge, 1969; L. H. Gann and Peter Duignan, *The Rulers of German Africa 1884–1914* (Stanford, 1977); Woodruff D. Smith, *The German Colonial Empire* (Chapel Hill, North Carolina, 1978) and Arthur J. Knoll, *Togo Under Imperial Germany 1884–1914* (Stanford, 1978).

5 Japan, Australia, New Zealand, South Africa, and Belgium conquered the rest of the German overseas empire. The statistical information here was drawn from the "Peace Handbooks" issued by the British Foreign Office and published as *German African Possessions (Late)* (London, 1920).

6 As a result of the Moroccan crisis in 1911, Cameroon gained another 100,000 square miles of territory from French Equatorial Africa. This region was returned to France at the Peace Conference and was not included in the French mandated territory.

7 In 1907 the total amount of trade that Germany did with Togo was only 7.5 million marks. See Woodruff D. Smith, "Julius Graf Zech auf Neuhofen (1868–1914)" in L. H. Gann and Peter Duignan, eds., *African Proconsuls: European Governors in Africa* (Stanford, 1978), pp.473–91.

8 Using German official publications, the British Foreign Office concluded that the total amount of public debt in Cameroon for 1914 stood at 49,209,000 marks while German East Africa received over 3,000,000 marks a year in subsidies from Berlin. In Cameroon, rubber was the most important commodity before 1914 and accounted for about half of the total value of all exports. In German East Africa, rubber and sisal were the chief exports and

together comprised just under half of the total value of all exports. Still, according to Louis, Germany's entire trade with the colonies was never more than 1 per cent of its total imports or exports and the overseas empire "never ran at a profit; in 1913 the deficit amounted to over £6,000,000." Louis, *Germany's Lost Colonies*, p. 10.

9 MC to Merlin, 4 August 1914, ANSOM, Séries Géographiques: Togo-Cameroun (SG: Togo-Cam), 11/91.

10 MC to MAE, 8 August 1914, ANSOM, SG: Togo-Cam, 7/67 and copy of Pierre de Margerie (director of political and commercial affairs in the Foreign Ministry) to Paul Cambon (French ambassador in London), 10 August 1914, Archives du Ministère des Affaires Etrangères, Paris (AE), Série Guerre: 1914–1918, 1545.

11 Minutes of the "Offensive Sub-Committee of the Committee of Imperial Defence," 5 August 1914, Harcourt Papers, Bodleian Library, Oxford University (BLO) 508/6.

12 For the influence that colonial interest groups had on French colonial policy, see Charles-Robert Ageron, *France coloniale ou parti coloniale?* (Paris, 1978) and Stuart Michael Persell, *The French Colonial Lobby 1889–1938* (Stanford, 1983).

13 Union coloniale française to Doumergue and MC to Union coloniale française, 19 Dec. 1914, ANSOM, SG: Togo-Cam, 7/73.

14 Banque Française de l'Afrique Equatoriale to MC, 22 Jan. 1915, ANSOM, SG: Togo-Cam, 1/2.

15 For example, 5 March 1915, 13 March 1915, and 17 March 1915, ANSOM, SG: Togo-Cam, 7/73.

16 FO to CO, 4 Jan. 1915, CO 649/3 and minute by Alfred John Harding (clerk in the Nigeria Department) to Sir Charles Strachey (principal clerk), 16 Jan. 1915, FO to CO dated 14 Jan. 1915, CO 649/3. On this occasion, the FO dissuaded the CO from publishing the reports since the Home Office was already preparing a report on all German atrocities committed during the war. Eventually the government did produce a report entitled *Papers Relating to German Atrocities, and Breaches of the Rules of War, in Africa* in 1916.

17 Minute by Harding, 30 June 1915, on FO to CO, 23 June 1915, CO 649/3. Also see FO to CO, 2 Aug. 1915, CO 649/3; FO to CO, 2 Oct. 1915, CO 649/4 and FO to CO, 24 Dec. 1915, CO 649/2.

18 Harcourt memorandum entitled "The Spoils," 25 March 1915, CAB 37/126/27.

19 Colonial Ministry report entitled "Operations contre les colonies allemandes d'Afrique," October 1914, ANSOM, SG: Togo-Cam, 7/73 For examples of Anglo-Belgian relations in German East Africa, see FO to CO, 18 Sept. 1916, CO 691/1; FO to CO, 2 Oct. 1916, CO 691/1 and CO copy of Sir Francis H. Villiers (British ambassador to Belgium) to FO, 11 Oct. 1916, in FO to CO 14 Oct. 1916, CO 691/1. Also see Wm. Roger Louis, *Ruanda-Urundi 1884–1919* (Oxford, 1963).

20 For detailed discussions of some of these problems, see Lovett Elango, "The Anglo-French 'Condominium' in Cameroon, 1914–1916: The Myth and the Reality," *International Journal of African Historical Studies* 18 (1985): 657–73 and Peter J. Yearwood, "'In a Casual Way with a Blue Pencil': British Policy and the Partition of Kamerun, 1914–1919," *Canadian Journal of African Studies* 27 (1993): 218–44.

21 For an explanation of this agreement, concluded after the quick conquest of the colony, see William Merlaud Ponty (governor-general of French West

Africa) to MC, 1 Sept. 1914, ANSOM, SG: Togo-Cam, 6/66.

22 Marie François Joseph Clozel (governor-general of French West Africa) to MC, 1? Feb. 1916, ANSOM, SG: Togo-Cam, 6/66; Clozel to MC, 10 May 1916, ANSOM, SG: Togo-Cam, 6/63; and Acting governor-general of French West Africa to MC, 26 Oct. 1916, ANSOM, SG: Togo-Cam, 6/57.

23 Copy of telegram from Marie Casimir Joseph Guyon (lieutenant governor of Gabon) to Merlin, 9 Oct. 1914, ANSOM, SG: Togo-Cam, 9/78.

24 "Rapport sur le fonctionnement de la Trésorerie au Cameroun," dated 14 Sept. 1915, ANSOM, SG: Togo-Cam, 1/1.

25 Dobell to CO, 25 March 1915, CO 649/1.

26 FO to CO, 27 Oct. 1915, CO 649/4.

27 Merlin to MC, 6 Oct. 1915, AE, Série Guerre: 1914–1918, 1544. Merlin repeated this argument in Merlin to MC, 20 Jan. 1916, ANSOM, SG: Togo-Cam, 11/91.

28 The larger southern portion, however, did include some large ex-German cocoa plantations and Mount Cameroon. For some of the correspondence concerning these negotiations, see Merlin to MC, 20 Jan. 1916, ANSOM, SG: Togo-Cam, 11/9; MC to MAE, 26 Jan. 1916, AE, Série Guerre: 1914–1918, 1544; George Vanderleur Fiddes (permanent under-secretary of state for the colonies) to Bonar Law, 28 Jan. 1916, Bonar Law Papers, House of Lords Record Office (HLRO) 50/1/29; FO to CO, 15 Feb. 1916, CO 649/9; CO copy of FO memorandum on conversations between French and British representatives in FO to CO, 24 Feb. 1916, CO 649/9; MAE to FO, 3 March 1916 and FO to MAE, 4 March 1916, AE, Série Guerre: 1914–1918, 1544/218 and Dobell to CO, 29 March 1916, CO 649/7.

29 MC to Clozel, 6 April 1916, ANSOM, SG: Togo-Cam, 6/63.

30 Since 1914, the French zone of Togo had been administered by the lieutenant governor of Dahomey, Charles Noufflard. According to Clozel, this system had caused "grave inconveniences" and too much duplication of procedure. Clozel to MC, 10 May 1916, ANSOM, SG: Togo-Cam, 6/63.

31 MC to MAE, 22 Aug. 1916; MAE to MC, 26 Aug. 1916 and MC to Fourn, 13 Sept. 1916, ANSOM, SG: Togo-Cam, 6/63.

32 See "Notice sur le Togo" dated 8 Oct. 1915, ANSOM, SG: Togo-Cam, 7/72 and Doumergue to Braibant (deputy to the National Assembly), 24 May 1916, ANSOM, SG: Togo-Cam, 6/60.

33 CO to CO, ? March 1916, CO 649/11. Lugard's administration of this sphere became effective 1 April 1916. Lugard to CO, 18 May 1916, CO 649/7.

34 Minute by Sir John Risley (principal legal advisor in the Colonial Office), 9 March 1916 on CO to CO, ? March 1916, CO 649/11.

35 For the French budgets, see General Pineau (commander of French forces in French Equatorial Africa) to MC, 10 April 1915, ANSOM, SG: Togo-Cam, 1/1; MC to Ponty, 24 June 1915, ANSOM, SG: Togo-Cam, 6/66 and Note by Albert Duchêne (head of the African department of Colonial Ministry), 18 Aug. 1915, ANSOM, SG: Togo-Cam, 1/1. For British policy toward Swiss missions, see FO to CO, 17 April 1915, CO 649/3; Dobell to CO, 21 July 1915, CO 649/2; FO to CO, 20 Sept. 1915, CO 649/4 and Dobell to CO, 21 Feb. 1916, CO 649/7.

36 For examples of these reports, see Clozel to MC, 15 May 1916, 4 July 1916, 6 Sept. 1916, and 3 May 1917, SG: Togo-Cam, 6/58. For Togo's budget for 1918, see Alfred Louis Woelffel (commissioner of Togo) to MC, 2 Dec. 1917, ANSOM, SG: Togo-Cam, 6/66. Woelffel requested a total of 425,000 Francs for his administration.

37 See "Etude Politique, Géographique, Economique, & Administrative de la Colonie Allemande du Cameroun au Debut de 1914," 15 April 1916, ANSOM, SG: Togo-Cam, 4/51 and Report by L. Béroult, 28 Dec. 1916, ANSOM, SG: Togo-Cam, 4/44.

38 Clozel to MC, 1 Feb. 1916, ANSOM, SG: Togo-Cam, 6/66; Gabriel Louis Angoulvant (acting governor-general of French Equatorial Africa) 21 Aug. 1916, ANSOM, SG: Togo-Cam, 6/61 and decree dated 6 May 1916 in *Journal Officiel du Cameroun* no. 9.

39 Lugard to CO, 18 May 1916, CO 649/7.

40 Lugard to CO, 31 May 1916, CO 649/7.

41 Lugard to CO, 23 Feb. 1917, CO 649/12 and Lugard to CO, 2 Nov. 1917, CO 649/12.

42 In March 1917, the colonial secretary, Walter Long, was asked in the House of Commons about Africans and the division of Cameroon. Harding advised that the colonial secretary should admit that the "existing administrative division is not altogether satisfactory" since it separated indigenous groups. Instead, Long said "[m]y information does not enable me to say whether tribes have been divided by this arrangement." Strachey noted that the response was "not quite accurate as we had plenty of info[rmatio]n from Sir [F.] Lugard on the point." See minute by Harding 28 Feb. 1917 and minute by Fiddes, 1 March 1917 on House of Commons to CO, parliamentary question by Charles Allen for Long, 27 Feb. 1917, CO 649/14.

43 Report entitled "Réorganisation de l'Ouest African Empire après la cessation des hostilities," 22 Sept. 1917, ANSOM, AP, 1044. For more on Van Vollenhoven's career and impact on the French colonial service, see William B. Cohen, *Rulers of Empire: The French Colonial Service in Africa* (Stanford, 1971).

44 The decree was issued by Lucien Louis Fourneau (commissioner of Cameroon) on 30 June 1917. It prohibited Africans from leaving French Cameroon without permission and a "security" payment of 500 francs. Violations of the decree were punishable by fines of up to 1,000 francs, imprisonment of up to 3 months, or both. The punishment was double for repeat offenders. See FO to CO, 30 Aug. 1917, CO 649/13.

45 Ministry of Supply to MC, 6 June 1918, ANSOM, SG: Togo-Cam, 6/65.

46 In addition to the above cited sources on the war, see Paul von Lettow-Vorbeck, *My Reminiscences of East Africa* (London, 1920?); Richard Meinertzhagen, *Army Diary, 1899–1926* (Edinburgh, 1960) and Brian Gardner, *German East: The Story of the First World War in East Africa* (London, 1963).

47 Draft telegram signed by Andrew Bonar Law (secretary of state for the colonies) to Byatt, 12 Sept. 1916, CO 691/3 and Proclamation issued from the Area of Occupied German Territory, 22 Dec. 1919, CO 691/4.

48 A. H. M. Kirk-Greene, *A Biographical Dictionary of the British Colonial Governor*, vol. 1 (Stanford, 1980), p. 88.

49 Hollis Papers, unpublished autobiography, Rhodes House Library, Oxford University (RH) Mss. Brit. Emp. s. 297, vol. 5, p. 1. Hollis, who was one year older than Byatt, called the offer to serve under the new administrator "an Irishman's promotion" and described Byatt as often suffering from bad health as well as "selfish and unsympathetic."

50 For the internal workings of the Colonial Office, see Sir Charles Jeffries, *The Colonial Office* (London, 1956) and the memoirs of Sir Arthur Charles Cosmo Parkinson, *The Colonial Office from Within: 1909–1945* (London, 1947).

51 Board of Trade to CO, 18 Sept. 1916, CO 691/3 and War Trade Dept of Colonial Office to East Africa Dept, 20 Dec. 1916, CO 691/3.
52 CO to Byatt, 17 Oct. 1916, CO 691/3; Byatt Report, 19 Dec. 1916, CO 691/1; Byatt to CO, 27 Feb. 1917, CO 691/4; Byatt to CO, 10 March 1917, CO 691/4 and Byatt to CO, 14 Aug. 1917, CO 691/5.
53 For Byatt's prickly relations with local military authorities, see Byatt to CO, 17 Dec. 1917, CO 691/6 and War Office to CO, 25 Sept. 1918, CO 691/19.
54 War Cabinet discussion of "The Captured German Colonies," 8 Feb. 1917, CAB 23/1/57.
55 *Congressional Record*, Special Session and 65th Congress, 1st Session, vol. 55 (1917), pt. 1, pp. 102–4.
56 War Cabinet Minutes, 9 May 1917, CAB 23/13/135a.
57 *Journal Officiel. Chambre des Députés. Debats parlementaires.* (*JOC*) Minutes of "Comité secret du 1er juin 1917," published in 16 May 1925, *JOC*, pp. 495–544.
58 Ibid. and *JOC*, 5 June 1917. Sir Francis Bertie, the British ambassador to France, explained to Arthur James Balfour, the British foreign secretary, that France did not "consider that the restitution to France of Provinces torn from her by force can be regarded as an annexation" and that "the word 'indemnity' is susceptible of various interpretations." Bertie to Balfour, 29 July 1917, PRO, FO 800/201.
59 For discussions of the Stockholm conference, the British League of Nations Society, and the political left in general during this period, see David Whol, *French Communism in the Making, 1914–1924* (Stanford, 1966); Peter Stansky, ed., *The Left and War: The British Labour Party and World War I* (New York, 1969); Jacob Moneta, *La Politique du parti communiste français et la question coloniale (1920–1963)* (Paris, 1971) and Donald S. Birn, *The League of Nations Union 1918–1945* (Oxford, 1981).
60 "Conference on German Colonies," 7 July 1917, Papers of the Anti-Slavery and Aborigines Protection Society, RH, Mss. Brit. Emp. s. 22 G 437. John H. Harris, the secretary of the society, did not favor international administration in Africa, yet he did advocate international control. See copy of Harris to Sir Harry Johnson, 17 Sept. 1917, ibid.
61 For example, see various correspondence including G. Lowes Dickenson (publicist and a leader of the League of Nations Society) to Morel, ? May 1915, and Philip Kerr (editor of *The Round Table*) to Morel, 29 July 1915, Morel Papers, London School of Economics and Political Science (LSEPS), F6/4. For a detailed examination of the UDC, see Marvin Swartz, *The Union of Democratic Control in British Politics During the First World War* (Oxford, 1971).
62 E. D. Morel, *Africa and the Peace of Europe* (London, 1917), p. 115.
63 Inter-allied Labour and Socialist Conference, *Memorandum on War Aims*, 28 December 1917, p. 13.
64 Final agreement, "Prime Minister's forthcoming speeches in Scotland," 27 June 1917, CAB 23/3/171.
65 "Address of Prime Minister Lloyd George at Glasgow on Peace Terms," 29 June 1917, in James Brown Scott, *Official Statements of War Aims and Peace Proposals: December 1916 to November 1918* (Washington, D.C., 1921), pp. 107–14 (hereafter cited as *Official Statements*).
66 See "Instructions Issued by the Central Executive Committee of Soviets to their Representative for the Paris Peace Conference of the Allies on War Aims," 20 Oct. 1917, *Official Statements*, pp. 167–8.

67 *The Daily Telegraph*, 29 Nov. 1917.
68 Long to Balfour, 4 Oct. 1917, Balfour Papers, PRO, FO 800/201.
69 "East Africa," 21 Nov. 1917, CAB 23/4/279.
70 Ibid.
71 War Cabinet agreement, "East Africa," 22 Nov. 1917, CAB 23/4/280.
72 Memorandum by Curzon for the War Cabinet, "German and Turkish Territories Captured in the War," 5 Dec. 1917, Curzon Papers, India Office Library (IOL), Mss. Eur. F 112/18.
73 Copy of Kerr to Smuts, 14 Dec. 1917, Lothian Papers, Scottish Record Office (SRO), GD 40 17/219.
74 Memorandum by Sir H. Llewellyn Smith for the prime minister, "The Future of Equatorial Africa (From a Commercial [and] Industrial Point of View)," 7 Jan. 1918, Lothian Papers, SRO, GD 40 17/49.
75 *JOC*, 20 Nov. 1917.
76 Marc Michel, "La genèse du recrutement de 1918 en Afrique noire française," *Revue Française d'Histoire d'Outre-Mer* 58 (1971).
77 See copy of "secret" report by Bertie for Balfour entitled "Note on Socialist Pacifist Revolutionary Propaganda in France," 15 March 1918, Bertie Papers, BM, 63049 and D. Stevenson, *French War Aims against Germany, 1914–1919* (Oxford, 1982).
78 For example, see Vollenhoven to MC, 8 Oct. 1917, Report entitled "L'Afrique Equatoriale et le Cameroun (Pourquoi nous devons conserver le Cameroun)," ANSOM, SG: Togo-Cam, 22/195 and MC to MAE, 30 Nov. 1917, 8 Jan. 1918, and 25 Jan. 1918, AE, Série Afrique: 1918–1940, 93/79–85.
79 For the texts of these speeches, see Scott, *Official Statements*, pp. 225–33 and *Congressional Record*, 65th Congress, 2nd Session, vol. 56, pp. 680–1.
80 Ibid. Clemenceau sent a telegram to Lloyd George on 6 January 1918 endorsing his speech of 5 January. See Scott, *Official Statements*, p. 225.
81 Undated copy of letter from Morel to Wilson, ? 1918, Morel Papers, LSEPS, F6/6 and copy of note on conversation with Henderson in Bertie to Balfour, 18 Feb. 1918, Bertie Papers, BM, 63049.
82 MC to MAE, 22 Jan. 1918, AE, Série A Paix, 78.
83 Minutes of the "Commission d'étude des questions coloniales posées par la guerre," 11 Feb. 1918, ANSOM, AP, 97. Also see *La Dépêche Coloniale*, 12 Feb. 1918.
84 Minutes of the Commission, 11 Feb. 1918, ANSOM, AP, 97.
85 For biographical information on Doumergue, see Persell, *The French Colonial Lobby*, pp. 24, 47, 112 and 161 and David S. Bell, Douglas Johnson, and peter Morris, eds., *Biographical Dictionary of French Political Leaders since 1870* (New York, 1990), p. 123.
86 Minutes of the Commission, 25 Feb. 1918, ANSOM, AP, 97.
87 Minutes of the Commission, 18 March, 15 April, and 16 May 1918, ANSOM, AP, 97.
88 Report by Philippe Millet (member of the Commission) entitled "Les Intérêts Coloniaux de l'Angleterre," 29 May 1918, ANSOM, AP, 96. For the Foreign Ministry copy, see Série Afrique: 1918–1940, 92/75–119. The French had extremely detailed information about the internal debates and decisions of the British War Cabinet, FO, and CO on the issue of the German colonies. A copy of this report also exists in the papers of Lord Milner, member of the War Cabinet and later colonial secretary. See Milner Papers, BLO, 388.
89 Minutes of the Commission, 24 June, 1 July, 4 Nov. 1918, ANSOM, AP, 97 and 96.

90 See report by Duchêne entitled "La Politique Indigène de la France," 31 May 1918 and report by August Terrier entitled "Les Ambitions Coloniales de l'Allemagne," 6 Nov. 1918, ANSOM, AP, 96 and 95.
91 Cambon to Pichon, 23 Oct. 1918, AE, Série A Paix, 78/7–8. Also see Clemenceau Papers, Service Historique de l'Armée de Terre (SHAT), 6 N 79.
92 "Note relative au programme général de politique indigène que la Conférence de la Paix peut-être appellée à envisager," Nov. 1918, AE, Série Afrique: 1918–1940, 92/227–236.
93 Copy of "secret" telegram from Long to the administrators of all captured German colonies in Africa and the Pacific, 8 Jan. 1918, CO 691/20 and CO 649/15.
94 Ibid.
95 Lugard to CO, 26 Jan. 1918; Lugard to CO, 11 Feb. 1918; and Lugard to CO, 4 April 1918, CO 649/15.
96 Lugard to CO, 15 March 1918, CO 649/15.
97 CO report entitled "German Colonies. Attitude of natives towards remaining under British Rule," 15 Oct. 1918, CAB 24/66. Also see Curzon Papers, IOL, Mss. Eur. F 112/183. For examples of Lugard's "evidence," see Lugard to CO, 3 July 1918, CO 649/15 and Lugard to CO, 10 Oct. 1918, CO 649/15.
98 On Wilson's views of "self-determination" and the non-western world, see John W. Coogan, "Wilsonian Diplomacy in War and Peace," in Gordon Martel, ed., *American Foreign Relations Reconsidered, 1890–1993* (London, 1994), pp. 71–89.
99 Copy of letter signed by Peter Gozo "for the Foreigners of Togoland" to General Dobell in Dobell to CO, 16 Oct. 1915, CO 649/2.
100 For examples, see Woelffel to MC, 14 Jan. 1919, ANSOM, SG: Togo-Cam, 83/1 and Fourneau to MC, 14 Jan. 1919, ANSOM, SG: Togo-Cam, 83/2.
101 Copy of the Bishop of Nyasaland to CO in CO to FO, 31 Dec. 1918, PRO, FO 371/3774 and copy of John Holt and Co. (Liverpool), Ltd. to FO in FO to CO, 31 Jan. 1919, CO 649/18
102 Edward C. Holder (British consulate official in Duala) to FO, 22 Dec. 1918, PRO, FO 371/3774; Admiralty to CO, 3 Jan. 1919, CO 694/18 and CO to FO, 24 Jan. 1919, PRO, FO 371/3774.
103 Fourneau to MC, 19 Jan. 1919, ANSOM, SG: Togo-Cam, 30/268.
104 Copy of letter from Archdeacon G. H. Morrison of St. Cyprian's at Kumasi (Gold Coast) to Bishop George H. Frodsham, 16 Aug. 1918, Lloyd George Papers, HLRO, F/23/3/14.
105 Copy of Bishop Frodsham to Balfour, 28 Sept. 1918, and Eric Drummond (Balfour's private secretary) to Hankey, 2 Oct. 1918, Lloyd George Papers, HLRO, F/23/3/14.
106 For example, see Long to Lord Robert Cecil (minister of blockade and parliamentary under-secretary of state for foreign affairs), 1 March 1918, sent by Cecil to Balfour, Balfour Papers, PRO, FO 800/201.
107 Balfour memorandum "Thoughts on German Colonies," 2 May 1918, Balfour Papers, BM, 49704. For Long's response, see memorandum dated 11 June 1918, CAB 24/54.
108 Memorandum by Smuts entitled "The German Colonies at the Peace Conference," 11 July 1918, PRO, CAB 29/1/3. Smuts was careful to define "Tropical Africa" as excluding both South Africa and German South-West Africa.
109 For example, see memorandum by Winston Churchill (minister of munitions)

to the War Cabinet, 7 July 1918, PRO, CAB, 1/27/2. Churchill argued that "[w]e could never allow any question connected with the disposal of the German Colonies to be *the sole obstacle* to the conclusion of peace" and "[w]e must not press British territorial claims to such a point as to alienate the sympathies of the United States." Leo Amery (assistant secretary to Imperial War Council and Supreme War Council) told Smuts that his proposal would "do a lot to steady Cabinet opinion," but did not like the suggestion of an international board "interfering with administration." Amery to Smuts, 16 July 1918, Smuts Papers, CU, reel 684/10.

110 Imperial War Cabinet minutes, 15 Aug. 1918, CAB 23/43.

111 Amery to Smuts, 16 Aug. 1918, Smuts Papers, CU, reel 684/11.

112 Memorandum by Curzon for the War Cabinet, "Bases of Policy Concerning German Colonies and Turkish Possessions," 16 Oct. 1918, Curzon Papers, IOL, Mss. Eur. F 112/183. Curzon drafted this paper "under tremendous pressure" with the help of Smuts and Maurice Hankey (secretary of War Cabinet). According to Hankey, Curzon wanted "to prove his contention that the War Cabinet were in reality in agreement on the question of the disposal of the captured German Colonies and Turkish possessions." See Hankey diary entry, 17 Oct. 1918, Hankey Papers, Churchill College (CC), 1/5.

113 "Note" concerning Togo's budget for 1919, ANSOM, SG: Togo-Cam, 6/66.

114 "Note" concerning Cameroon's budget for 1919, ANSOM, SG: Togo-Cam, 1/1.

115 Copy of Clifford to CO in CO to FO, 31 Dec. 1918, PRO FO 371/3774.

116 Resolutions of the "Commission d'étude des questions coloniales posées par la guerre," 13 Nov. 1918, AE, Série Afrique: 1918–1940, 92/137–158 and Simon to MAE, 5 Dec. 1918, AE, Série Afrique: 1918–1940, 92/182–191. Also see "Note sur le Cameroun: Arguments en faveur de son attribution à la France" and "Note relative à l'attribution éventuelle du Togo à France," copy of MC to MAE, 17 Dec. 1918, ANSOM, AP, 1044.

117 Byatt to CO, 8 Jan. 1919, CO 691/21.

118 Memorandum by Long to the Imperial War Cabinet, 8 Jan. 1919, PRO, CAB 29/2 and "Return of Enemy Subjects to the Colonies and Protectorates," 15 Jan. 1919, CAB 23/9/516.

119 Memorandum by Byatt entitled "New Name for German East Africa," 21 Jan. 1919, CO 691/29.

120 Hollis to CO, "Estimates, 1919–1920," dated 8 March 1919, CO 691/21.

121 The precise origins of the "mandates system" remains ambiguous and controversial. Many historians give most credit for the idea to George Louis Beer, the chief American expert on Africa and member of the American Commission to Negotiate Peace. In addition to those sources cited in the introduction above, see *George Louis Beer: A Tribute to His Life and Work in the Making of History and the Moulding of Public Opinion* (New York, 1924); Lawrence E. Gelfand, *The Inquiry: American Preparations for Peace, 1917–1919* (New Haven, 1963); Wm. R. Louis, "The United States and the African Peace Settlement of 1919: the Pilgrimage of George Louis Beer," *Journal of African History* 4 (1963) and Arthur Walworth, *Wilson and His Peacemakers: American Diplomacy at the Paris Peace Conference, 1919* (New York, 1986).

122 Memorandum by Sir William Wiseman , 16 Oct. 1918, Arthur Link, ed., *The Papers of Woodrow Wilson* (Princeton, 1966–93), vols. 1–69 (hereafter cited as *Papers of Woodrow Wilson*), vol. 51, p. 350.

123 For a copy of the complete text of the commentary, see Charles Seymour, ed.,

The Intimate Papers of Colonel House (New York, 1928), vol. IV, pp. 193–200.

124 Copy of MC to MAE, 8 Nov. 1918, ANSOM, AP, 1044.

125 See the diary of William C. Bullitt (member of American delegation to the Paris Peace Conference), 10 Dec. 1918, *Papers of Woodrow Wilson*, vol. 53, p. 351.

126 Derby to Balfour, 22 Dec. 1918, Balfour Papers, BM, AM 49744.

127 Copy of Lloyd George to Hughes, 11 Nov. 1918, Lloyd George Papers, HLRO, F/28/2/10.

128 Minutes taken by Aimé Joseph de Fleuriau of a meeting between Cambon and Lloyd George in London, 12 Nov. 1918, Cambon Papers, AE, Série Papiers d'Agents, 42/68/93–95.

129 Cambon to his son, 11 Dec. 1918, Paul Cambon, *Correspondance 1870–1924* (Paris, 1940–6), III, p. 292 and Balfour to Lloyd George, 29 Nov. 1918, Lloyd George Papers, HLRO, F/3/3/45.

130 For more on conceptions of Anglo-American cooperation, see Michael G. Fry, *Illusions of Security: North Atlantic Diplomacy 1918–1922* (Toronto, 1972).

131 Long memorandum for War Cabinet entitled "Internationalism and Equatorial Africa," 16 Nov. 1918, Curzon Papers, IOL, Mss. Eur. F 112/183.

132 Amery to Smuts, 1 November 1918, Smuts Papers, CU, reel 684/16. Amery later drafted a memorandum for Lloyd George entitled "United States and the Occupied Enemy Territories" making his case against giving German East Africa to the Americans. See Amery to Smuts, 21 Dec. 1918, Smuts Papers, CU, reel 19/19 and Hankey to Lloyd George, 21 Dec. 1918, Lloyd George Papers, HLRO, F/23/3/32.

133 Memorandum by Smuts entitled "The German Colonies at the Peace Conference," 7 Nov. 1918, PRO, CAB 29/1.

134 Smuts to Long, 28 Nov. 1918, Smuts Papers, CU, reel 766/49.

135 Balfour to Smuts, 17 Dec. 1918, Smuts Papers, CU, reel 766/61.

136 Jan C. Smuts, *The League of Nations: A Practical Suggestion* (London, 1918), p. 19.

137 Ibid., p. 15.

138 For a detailed examination of the close similarities between the pamphlet and Wilson's drafts, see Pitman B. Potter, "Origin of the System of mandates under the League of Nations," *American Political Science Review* 16 (1922): 563–83.

139 Minutes of the Imperial War Cabinet, 20 Dec. 1918, CAB 23/42. Also see, Hankey to Lloyd George, draft "resolutions" of the Imperial War Cabinet, 21 Dec. 1918, Lloyd George Papers, HLRO, F/23/3/31.

140 Minutes of Imperial War Cabinet, 30 Dec. 1918, *Papers of Woodrow Wilson*, vol. 53, pp. 562–3.

141 See "French Proposals for Peace with Germany" communicated by the French Ambassador to the FO on 26 Nov. 1918 and then circulated to the War Cabinet, 1 Dec. 1918, PRO, CAB 1/27/25.

142 "Peace Conference. Memorandum respecting German Colonies," ? Jan. 1919, PRO CAB 29/1. The French Foreign Ministry had a copy of this "secret" memorandum as well. See ? Jan. 1919, AE, Série A Paix, 78/62–74.

143 Minutes of the Imperial War Cabinet, 20 Dec. 1918, CAB 23/42. Curzon suggested making the United States a mandatory power for Armenia or Constantinople while Smuts argued for Palestine.

144 Ibid.

145 David Lloyd George, *The Truth about the Peace Treaties* (London, 1938), I, p. 115.
146 Ibid., p. 122.
147 Minutes of the Imperial War Cabinet, 20 Dec. 1918, CAB 23/42 and Lloyd George, *The Truth about the Peace Treaties*, I, p. 118.
148 Diary entry, 23 Dec. 1918, Hankey Papers, CC, 1/5.

Chapter 2 Reforming European Imperialism, 1919

1 Andrew and Kanya-Forstner, *France Overseas*, p. 182.
2 Resolutions of the "Commission d'étude des questions coloniales posées par la guerre," 13 Nov. 1918, AE, Série Afrique: 1918–1940, 92/137–158; Raymond Poincaré (president of the Republic), diary entry, 10 Jan. 1919, Bibliothèque Nationale, n. a. fr. 16033/19; Woelffel to MC, 14 Jan. 1919, ANSOM, SG: Togo-Cam, 83/1; Fourneau to MC, 14 Jan. 1919, ANSOM, SG: Togo-Cam, 83/2.
3 Among the members of this inter-departmental committee were Sir Charles Strachey and Sir Herbert J. Read from the Colonial Office, Cecil J. B. Hurst, Gerald S. Spicer, and Hughe Montgomery Knatchbull-Hugesson of the Foreign Office, and Sir H. Llewellyn Smith of the Board of Trade. For an early reference to this committee, see diary entry, 1 Dec. 1918, Knatchbull-Hugesson Papers, CC, 1/3.
4 These instructions were originally drafted in December and issued in January. See "Peace Conference. Memorandum respecting German Colonies," ? Dec. 1918, Curzon Papers, IOL, Mss. Eur. F 112/183 and ? Jan. 1919, PRO, CAB 29/1.
5 Copy of Smuts to Lloyd George, 14 Jan. 1919, Smuts Papers, CU, reel 766/64.
6 Minutes of meeting, 20 Jan. 1919, Cecil Papers, BM, 51105.
7 For examples of this fear of "Black armies," see memorandum by Curzon entitled "German and Turkish Territories Captured in the War," 5 Dec. 1917, CAB 24/4 and Imperial War Cabinet memorandum entitled "Our Desiderata in Regard to the Disposal of Territory taken from the Enemy," ? Oct. 1918, PRO, CAB 29/2.
8 Minutes of meeting, 20 Jan. 1919, Cecil Papers, BM, 51105.
9 Diary entry, 20 Jan. 1919, Cecil Papers, BM, 51131.
10 Minutes of the Council of Ten, 24 Jan. 1919, *Papers of Woodrow Wilson*, vol. 54, p. 249–54.
11 Minutes of the Council of Ten, 27 Jan. 1919, *Papers of Woodrow Wilson*, vol. 54, pp. 291–5.
12 Ibid., p. 294.
13 Ibid., p. 295.
14 Ibid., pp. 295–6.
15 Minutes of the British Empire Delegation, 27 Jan. 1919, PRO, CAB 29/28/1.
16 Diary entry, 27 Jan. 1919, Cecil Papers, BM, 51131.
17 Minutes of the Council of Ten, 28 Jan. 1919, *Papers of Woodrow Wilson*, vol. 54, pp. 310–14 and 318–29.
18 Ibid., p. 330.
19 Minutes of the British Empire Delegation, 28 Jan. 1919 and 29 Jan. 1919, PRO, CAB, 29/28/1 and "General Memorandum No. 6," 1 Feb. 1919, Borden Papers, National Archives of Canada, C-4364, pp. 81582–81586. Also see, W. M. Hughes, *Policies and Potentates* (Sydney, 1950).
20 For the full text of the proposal entitled "Draft Resolutions in Reference to

Mandates," see the minutes of the Council of Ten, 30 Jan. 1919, *Papers of Woodrow Wilson*, vol. 54, pp. 359–61.

21 "Draft resolutions in Reference to mandates," see the minutes of the Council of Ten, 30 Jan. 1919, *Papers of Woodrow Wilson,* vol. 54, pp. 359–61.

22 House diary entry, 29 Jan. 1919, *Papers of Woodrow Wilson,* vol. 54, p. 347.

23 Minutes of the Council of Ten, 30 Jan. 1919, *Papers of Woodrow Wilson,* vol. 54, p. 350–71.

24 Ibid., p. 351.

25 Ibid., p. 352.

26 Ibid., pp. 366–8.

27 For example, see diary entry of George Riddell (British press representative at the Paris Peace Conference and personal friend of Lloyd George), 30 Jan. 1919, Riddell Papers, BM, 62983; Copy of Long to Lloyd George, 1 Feb. 1919, Long Papers, BM, 62424 and Sir Charles Hardinge (permanent under-secretary of foreign affairs and delegate to the Paris Peace Conference) to Sir Valentine Chirol, 8 Feb. 1919, Hardinge Papers, CU, 40.

28 House diary entry, 30 Jan. 1919, *Papers of Woodrow Wilson*, vol. 54, pp. 386–7.

29 Kerr to Milner (now colonial secretary), 31 Jan. 1919, Milner Papers, BLO, Ms. Eng. Hist. c. 700.

30 *The Times*, London, 4 Feb. 1919, p. 10 and 5 Feb. 1919, p. 8 respectively.

31 Smuts to Margaret Clark Gillett, 1 Feb. 1919, Smuts Papers, CU, reel 687/204.

32 *The Times*, London, 6 Feb. 1919, p. 10.

33 The French Foreign Ministry kept a close eye on the German government's public statements and informed the Colonial Ministry of any statements concerning the former German overseas empire. In this case, the German foreign minister spoke to the *Chicago Daily News* in early February. See Foreign Ministry report entitled "La question des Colonies dans l'opinion allemande" in MAE to MC, 13 Feb. 1919, ANSOM, AP, 1038.

34 Commission to MC, 7 Feb. 1919, ANSOM, AP, 96 and minutes of the Commission 17 Feb. 1919, ANSOM, AP, 97. Some of the French colonial societies cited by the Commission included the Société des Etudes Coloniale et maritime, the Ligue Coloniale Française, the Comité Bordeaux-Moroc, the Société de propagande coloniale, and the Société anti-esclavagist de France.

35 According to Milner's diary, Lloyd George agreed to Amery's appointment "with some reluctance." Diary entry, 8 Jan. 1919, Milner Papers, BLO, Ms. Milner dep. 90. For Milner's career and imperialist views, see his *Questions of the Hour* (London, 1925) and Terence H. O'Brien, *Milner: Viscount Milner of St. James's and Cape Town 1854–1925* (London, 1979).

36 Minutes of the Imperial War Cabinet, 20 Dec. 1918, PRO, CAB 23/42 and Lloyd George, *The Truth about the Peace Treaties*, I, pp. 118–22.

37 Amery to Smuts, 20 March 1919, Smuts Papers, CU reel 685/5. Also see Amery to Smuts, 16 July 1918, Smuts Papers, CU, reel 684/10.

38 Ibid. and diary entry, 3 Feb. 1919, Milner Papers, BLO, Ms. Milner dep. 90.

39 Minutes of the British Empire Delegation, 20 Feb. 1919, Milner Papers, BLO, Ms. Milner dep. 389.

40 David Hunter Miller (legal expert of the American delegation) to Wilson, 3 Feb. 1919, *Papers of Woodrow Wilson*, vol. 54, pp. 456–7.

41 Minutes of the Commission on the League of Nations, 8 Feb. 1919, *Papers of Woodrow Wilson*, vol. 55, pp. 4–7.

42 Proposed amendment by M. Leon Bourgeois, 8 Feb. 1919, attached to memorandum by Miller dated 11 Feb. 1919, *Papers of Woodrow Wilson*, vol. 55, pp. 68–70.
43 Address to the Third Plenary Session of the Peace Conference, 14 Feb. 1919, *Papers of Woodrow Wilson*, vol. 55, pp. 170–1.
44 Draft of the Covenant of the League of Nations, 28 April 1919, *Papers of Woodrow Wilson*, vol. 58, pp. 196–7.
45 *FRUS: The Paris Peace Conference, 1919*, vol. 13, pp. 93–104.
46 Colville Barclay (British embassy official) to FO, 1 Feb. 1919, PRO, FO 371/3774.
47 In March 1919, Vance McCormick, an American technical adviser on economic and blockade issues at the Paris Peace Conference, recorded that Wilson had asked him to go to Syria in order "to report to him upon the preference of the people there as to mandatory." According to McCormick, the "President told me he had promised the Allies to try to get our country to agree to act as mandatory for Armenia and Constantinople." Diary entry, 22 March 1919, Vance McCormick Papers, Michigan State University microfilm collection, no. 23028. For the Lloyd George quotation, see Lloyd George, *The Truth about the Peace Treaties*, I, p. 551.
48 Diary entry, 22 Feb. 1919, Riddell Papers, BM, 62983. According to a "secret" memorandum by Hankey entitled "British Empire Interests," dated 23 March 1919, German East Africa was now included with Palestine, Mesopotamia, South-West Africa, and the South Pacific islands as British "interests." There was no mention of either Togo or Cameroon. See Hankey Papers, CC, 8/11.
49 See memorandum by Strachey entitled "Mandate for German East Africa," 21 Feb. 1919, Milner Papers, BLO, Ms. Milner dep. 389; Diary entries, 24 Feb. 1919, 25 Feb. 1919, and 26 Feb. 1919, Knatchbull-Hugesson Papers, CC, 1/3. Knatchbull-Hugesson noted that during the meetings there was "[m]uch amusement between idealism of [Philip Noel] Baker of the League of Nations Section and practical point of view of Strachey of Colonial Office . . . "
50 Memorandum by Strachey entitled "Cameroons and Togoland," 7 March 1919, Milner Papers, BLO, Ms. Milner dep. 389.
51 It is of no surprise that British trading firms in Cameroon and that Sir Hugh Clifford, the governor of Gold Coast, were not pleased with these proposed partitions. See copy of Irvine and Dundas, Ltd. to FO in FO to CO, 9 May 1919, CO 649/18 and copy of despatch from Clifford to CO in CO to FO, 13 May 1919, PRO, FO 371/3774.
52 Diary entries, 6 March 1919 and 7 March 1919, Milner Papers, BLO, Ms. Milner dep. 90.
53 See memorandum by Milner entitled "Mandates," 8 March 1919, PRO, CAB 29/9/1 and copy in Milner Papers, BLO, Ms. Milner dep. 389. Despite Milner's poor understanding of the supervisory powers of the League, his tendency to dismiss the unfamiliar, and his heavy work load, Wm. Roger Louis generally accepts this memorandum as an accurate and coherent explanation of the nature of the B mandates. See Louis, *Germany's Lost Colonies*, pp. 144–5.
54 Ibid.
55 For first hand accounts of these problems, see Robert Lansing, *The Big Four and Others at the Paris Peace Conference* (Boston, 1921); Georges Clemenceau, *Grandeur and Misery of Victory* (New York, 1930); Lord

Hardinge of Penshurst, *Old Diplomacy* (London, 1947); Lord Hankey, *The Supreme Control at the Paris Peace Conference 1919: A Commentary* (London, 1963); and Harold Nicolson, *Peacemaking 1919* (New York, 1965).

56 Minutes of the Council of Four, 6 and 7 May 1919, *Papers of Woodrow Wilson*, vol. 58, pp. 484–6, 507 and 510; *FRUS*, vol. 5, Appendix II, pp. 508–9 and Paul Mantoux, *The Deliberations of the Council of Four (March 24–June 28, 1919: Notes of the Official Interpreter* (Princeton, 1992), translated and edited by Arthur S. Link, vols. I and II (hereafter cited as *Deliberations*), vol. I, pp. 496–9, 502, and 507–9. In addition to the official minutes kept by Sir Maurice Hankey, the source for *FRUS* and *Papers of Woodrow Wilson*, Paul Mantoux, the official French translator, maintained a set of notes that sometimes provides different versions of these discussions.

57 *Deliberations*, vol. I, p. 498.

58 Ibid., p. 499.

59 Ibid., p. 502.

60 Ibid., p. 508.

61 Ibid.

62 Copy of Lloyd George to Milner, 14 May 1919, Lloyd George Papers, HLRO, F/39/1/18 and Milner to Lloyd George, 15 May 1919, Lloyd George Papers, HLRO, F/39/1/19.

63 Raymond Poincaré, *Au service de la France: Neuf années de souvernirs* (Paris, 1928–1974), vol. 11, *A la recherche de la paix 1919* (Paris, 1974), diary entry for 16 May 1919, p. 431.

64 Milner memorandum to CO entitled "Cameroons and Togoland," 29 May 1919, CO 649/18.

65 Copy of Milner to Simon, 29 May 1919, and Simon's undated response attached, Milner Papers, Ms. Milner dep. 389. The Colonial Office was further convinced that the mandates system would not apply to West Africa when on the following day the Foreign Office reported that a "semi-official communiqué" issued by the French government announced to the public that "Cameroon and Togoland will not be under the control of the League of Nations but that these two colonies will form the subject of negotiations between England and France which will be simply communicated to the League . . . " See FO to CO, 30 May 1919, CO 649/18.

66 See memorandum by Strachey entitled "French Proposal for Partition of Togoland," 23 May 1919, PRO, FO 608/216/70142; Memorandum by Strachey entitled "French Proposals for Partition of the Cameroons," 27 May 1919, PRO, FO 608/215/70142; Strachey to Harding, 19 July 1919 and 27 July 1919 in Alexander George Boyle (lieutenant-governor of Nigeria, southern provinces) to CO, 18 June 1919, CO 649/17; Harding to Strachey, 16 June 1919 in Boyle to CO, 10 June 1919, CO 649/17; Diary entry, 27 June 1919, Milner Papers, Ms. Milner dep. 90 and CO file marked "Mandates. Memos, Minutes, and Copies Correspondence," June–Aug. 1919, CO 691/28.

67 The British model B mandate, first drafted by British officials on 20 January and then revised in early February, was largely adopted by Milner on 8 March and was subsequently altered slightly at various times by Lord Robert Cecil and those working with him, including Philip Noel Baker. On 24 May, Cecil unofficially gave his own drafts of the A, B, and C mandates to House who in turn gave them to George Louis Beer, the American expert on colonial matters. The differences between Milner's version and that of Cecil were

slight. Beer, using Cecil's drafts as a guide, produced his own drafts of the various mandates on 10 June and submitted them to Wilson on 27 June. In a memorandum to Wilson, Beer said that neither the Cecil nor the Milner draft was "altogether satisfactory, especially in that they do not give adequate protection to the native populations; nor do they provide fully for the open door." On 26 June, the British delegation formally gave Milner's draft mandates to the Conference. See Cecil to House, 24 May 1919, and Wilson to House, 27 June 1919, *Papers of Woodrow Wilson*, vol. 59, pp. 475–6 and vol. 61, pp. 259–70, respectively.

68 Copy of British draft B mandate in Wilson to House, 27 June 1919, *Papers of Woodrow Wilson*, vol. 61, p. 262.

69 Unidentified minute to Bottomley, 12 March 1919, Byatt to CO dated 18 Jan. 1919, CO 691/21.

70 Copy of Cecil to Milner dated ? May 1919 in Bottomley to Read, 15 May 1919, Milner Papers, BLO, Ms. Milner dep. 389.

71 For biographical information on Bottomley, see Parkinson, *The Colonial Office from Within*, p. 27; Sir Ralph Furse, *Aucuparius: Recollections of a Recruiting Officer* (London, 1962), p. 27; and *Who Was Who* (London, 1961), vol. 5.

72 Copy of minute by Bottomley to A. J. Harding, 13 May 1919, ibid.

73 Copy of minute by Grindle to Fiddes, 14 May 1919, ibid.

74 Minute by Bottomley to Grindle, 13 May 1919, Hollis to CO dated 28 April 1919, CO 691/22.

75 See FO to CO, 15 July 1919, CO 691/38; Conference of Missionary Societies to CO, 23 Sept. 1920, CO 691/40; CO to FO, 9 Oct. 1920, PRO, FO 371/4800; FO to CO, 13 Nov. 1920, CO 691/38 and Byatt to CO, 5 March 1921, CO 691/43. For the final wording of the stipulation of the mandate concerning missionaries, see Article 8 of the mandate for the Tanganyika Territory in Appendix B and Wright, *Mandates*, p. 614.

76 Copy of British draft B mandate in Wilson to House, 27 June 1919, *Papers of Woodrow Wilson*, vol. 61, p. 262.

77 Minute by Grindle to Fiddes, 10 March 1919, Byatt to CO dated 18 Jan. 1919, CO 691/21.

78 General Department of the Treasury to CO, 19 May 1919, included in Byatt to CO dated 2 May 1919, CO 691/29.

79 Minute by Risley to Bottomley, 29 May 1919, Byatt to CO dated 15 May 1919, CO 691/29.

80 Minute by Bottomley to Grindle, 17 May 1919, Byatt to CO dated 21 Jan. 1919, CO 691/29. For more, see Michael D. Callahan, "NOMANSLAND: The British Colonial Office and the League of Nations Mandate for German East Africa, 1916–1920," *Albion* 25 (1993): 443–64.

81 Minute by Eric Gustav Mächtig (clerk in the East Africa Department) to Bottomley, 6 June 1919, and minute by Bottomley, 30 June 1919, Hollis to CO dated 8 March 1919, CO 691/21.

82 Minute by Bottomley to Grindle, 17 June 1919, Hollis to CO dated 27 May 1919, CO 691/22.

83 Copy of British draft B mandate included in Wilson to House, 27 June 1919, *Papers of Woodrow Wilson*, vol. 61, p. 262.

84 Byatt to CO, 8 February 1919 and minute by Fiddes, 10 June 1919, CO 691/29.

85 Minute by Amery, 11 June 1919 and minute by Bottomley, 18 June 1919, Byatt to CO dated 8 Feb. 1919, CO 691/29.

86 Grindle to Fiddes, 18 June 1919 and minute by Fiddes, 23 June 1919, Byatt to CO dated 8 Feb. 1919, CO 691/29.
87 Meeting of the Council of Four, 27 June 1919, *Papers of Woodrow Wilson*, vol. 61, pp. 275–7.
88 Ibid., diary entry, 27 June 1919, Milner Papers, BLO, Ms. Milner dep. 90, and Hankey to Milner, 27 June 1919, Ms. Milner dep. 390. Also see diary of Colonel House, 27 June 1919, *Papers of Woodrow Wilson*, vol. 61, p. 283. Silvo Benigno Crespi, an economic and financial advisor in the Italian delegation was appointed to represent Italy and Viscount Sutemi Chinda, the Japanese ambassador at London, was chosen to represent Japan.
89 Minutes of the first meeting of the "Special Commission on Mandates," 28 June 1919, Milner Papers, BLO, Ms. Milner dep. 390.
90 Diary entry, 28 June 1919, Milner Papers, BLO, Ms. Milner dep. 90.
91 *FRUS: The Paris Peace Conference 1919*, vol. 13, p. 276.
92 Undated memorandum entitled "Concessions in a Ceded Territory" with cover letter by C. J. B. Hurst dated 17 Jan. 1919 in FO to CO, ? Jan. 1919, CO 691/25.
93 Minute by Risley to Read, 31 July 1919, FO to CO, ? Jan. 1919, CO 691/25.
94 House to Wilson, 9 July 1919, *Papers of Woodrow Wilson*, vol. 61, pp. 408–9.
95 As discussed above, the Council of Ten never did arrive at a clear definition of this principle during their meeting of 30 January. Article 22 of the Treaty of Versailles, based on the conclusions of this meeting, prohibited the mandatory powers from recruiting Africans except for local police purposes and "the defense of territory." Milner's original draft of the B mandate avoided the exact wording of Article 22 and simply forbade recruitment except for the "preservation of order" and stipulated that "[n]o military or naval works or bases shall be erected or maintained except for the defense of the territory." Beer's original draft B mandate used this same wording. During the negotiations of the Commission, however, House insisted that the clause prohibit recruiting Africans except for local police purposes and "the defense of *the* territory" [emphasis added] and translated it into French to read "la défense du territoire." Simon rejected this construction and demanded the expression "la défense de son territoire tant colonial que métropolitan" instead. This form would have made the entire clause meaningless. The Commission eventually adopted House's version perhaps without realizing that it was far more specific than the wording of Article 22. See copy of Milner to P. Dutasta (secretary-general of the Peace Conference), 15 July 1919, included in file marked "Mandates. Memos, Minutes, and copies correspondence," CO 691/28 and the long and detailed minute by A. J. Harding to Ellis and Read, 5 Jan. 1920, FO to CO, 29 Dec. 1919, CO 649/18.
96 Ibid., pp. 408–9. House told Wilson that Simon had "positive instructions to insist upon the exact words of the French proposal."
97 House to Wilson, 11 July 1919, *Papers of Woodrow Wilson*, vol. 61, pp. 451–5. Also see Wilson to House, 27 June 1919, *Papers of Woodrow Wilson*, vol. 61, pp. 259–70. For the final text of the entire B mandate, see Wright, *Mandates*, pp. 611–16.
98 Simon to Milner, 1 Aug. 1919; copy of Milner to Simon, 2 Aug. 1919 and Simon to Milner, 4 Aug. 1919, Milner Papers, BLO, Ms. Milner dep. 390. Simon had also informed the Foreign Ministry of his decision not to attend the Commission meetings. See MC to MAE, 1 Aug. 1919, AE, Série Afrique: 1918–1940, 94/1–3. Copies of all this correspondence can also be found in ANSOM, AP, 1944.

99 Wilson to House, 18 July 1919, *Papers of Woodrow Wilson*, vol. 61, p. 520 and Sir Eric Drummond (secretary-general of the League of Nations) to Beer, 3 Oct. 1919, FO 800/400.

100 Minute by Milner, 22 Aug. 1919, CO to CO, ? Aug. 1919, CO 649/18. C. J. B. Hurst, who met with Simon on 1 September to overcome the impasse, came to the same conclusion as Milner and told Balfour and the Foreign Office that "the French attitude had hardened within the last month" and that "[i]t is clear that the French intend to press vigorously for the principle that Togoland and the Cameroons were not to be subject to a mandate at all, and that the language of the decision by the Supreme Council of 7 May in which they allotted the mandates is meaningless except upon this hypothesis." See Hurst to Balfour, 5 Sept. 1919, PRO, FO 371/3774.

101 MC to Gabriel Louis Angoulvant (governor-general of both French West Africa and French Equatorial Africa), 2 Aug. 1919 and 8 Aug. 1919, ANSOM, SG: Togo-Cam, 6/64.

102 Ibid. The Colonial Ministry repeated this policy in September. See, telegram from MC to Angoulvant, 4 Sept. 1919, ANSOM, SG: Togo-Cam, 6/64.

103 Foreign Ministry memorandum entitled "Note sur le Reglement de l'affaire Togo-Cameroun," 13 Aug. 1919, AE, Série Afrique: 1918–1940, 94 and British Embassy in Paris translation of Simon's speech in copy of Sir G. Grahame to FO, 18 Sept. 1919 in FO to CO, 2 Oct. 1919, CO 649/18. After Simon's speech, the Colonial Ministry demanded that the Foreign Ministry conclude the joint Anglo-French agreement on Togo and Cameroon that Simon wanted. See copies of MC to MAE, 11 Oct. 1919 and 22 Oct. 1919, ANSOM, SG: Togo-Cam, 6/64 and Cambon to MAE, 4 Nov. 1919, AE, Série Société des Nations, 620/2.

104 Arrêté signed by Simon establishing a "Commission chargée d'étudier l'organisation du Cameroun et de l'Afrique Equatoriale Française," 6 Sept. 1919, ANSOM, AP, 649/16. The Commission met at least eleven times and as late as 31 May 1920.

105 See Angoulvant to MC, 24 June 1919, ANSOM, SG: Togo-Cam, 33/301; Angoulvant to "Mon cher ami," 7 Sept. 1919, ANSOM, SG: Togo-Cam, 1/1 and "Note pour la Direction du Contrôle" concerning the "Mission au Togo et au Cameroun," 23 Oct. 1919, ANSOM, AP, 3139.

106 Digre cites a few examples of Africans belonging to the educated elite in British West Africa who used local newspapers to express their "painful displeasure" with the fact that their definition of Wilsonian self-determination did not seem to apply to Germany's former colonies in Africa. See Digre, *Imperialism's New Clothes*, pp. 176–80.

107 For studies of this group, see Jonathan Derrick, "The 'Germanophone' Elite of Doula under the French Mandate," *Journal of African History* 21 (1980): 255–67; Jonathan Derrick, "Colonial élitism in Cameroon: the case of the Duala in the 1930s," in Martin Njeuma, ed., *Introduction to the History of Cameroon: Nineteenth and Twentieth Centuries* (New York, 1989), pp. 106–33 and Andreas Eckert, "Cocoa Farming in Cameroon, *c.* 1914– *c.* 1960: Land and Labour," in William Gervase Clarence-Smith, ed., *Cocoa Pioneer Fronts since 1800: The Role of Smallholers, Planters and Merchants* (London, 1996).

108 Fourneau to Merlin, 4 Feb. 1919, ANSOM, SG: Togo-Cam, 30/268.

109 For France's copy of this petition, see Duala to High Conference, 18 Aug. 1919, ANSOM, AP, 3138. For Britain's copy, see Duala to Lloyd George, 21 Aug. 1919, PRO, FO 371/3774.

110 Report by M. Méray (inspector-general of the colonies and head of the 1919–1920 mission to Togo and Cameroon), 10 Jan. 1920, ANSOM, AP, 3138.

111 Ibid. For more on pan-Africanism and the pan-African congresses held after the First World War, see R. D. Ralston, "Africa and the New World" in A. Adu Boahen, ed., *Africa under Colonial Domination 1880–1935*. Also see, Elliot P. Skinner, *African Americans and U.S. policy toward Africa 1850–1934: In Defense of Black Nationality* (Washington, D.C., 1992).

112 Ibid. A few months later, in a "confidential" report, Méray provided even more detail on the "political situation" in Cameroon. See report by Méray, 20 April 1920, ANSOM, AP, 3138.

113 Minute by Strachey, 14 Oct. 1919, FO to CO dated 30 Sept. 1919, CO 691/25.

114 Solicitor's Department memorandum included in Board of Trade to CO, 25 Nov. 1919, CO 691/26.

115 Minute by Parkinson, 27 Nov. 1919, Board of Trade to CO dated 25 Nov. 1919, CO 691/26.

116 Milner memorandum entitled "Memorandum by the Secretary of State for the Colonies," dated 19 Nov. 1919 and appendix to "Conference held in the Leader of the House's Room, House of Commons," 20 Nov. 1919, CAB 23/18/10/19.

117 Final agreement of the Conference, 20 Nov. 1919, appendix 3 to Cabinet minutes of 3 Dec. 1919, CAB 23/18/10/19. Also see "Conclusion of a Conference Held in the Leader of the House's Room, House of Commons, on Thursday, Nov. 20th, 1919" CO copy, 1 Dec. 1919, CO 691/28.

118 Minute by Risley, 4 Dec. 1919 and draft Order in Council dated 28 Jan. 1920, Board of Trade to CO dated 25 Nov. 1919, CO 691/26.

119 Minute by Harding to Walter Devonshire Ellis (a principal clerk in the West Africa Department) and Read, 18 Nov. 1919, on FO to CO, 10 Nov. 1919, CO 649/18.

120 Minute by Milner, 26 Nov. 1919, FO to CO, 10 Nov. 1919, CO 649/18. In fact, Milner had already asked Lloyd George, Bonar Law and Curzon the previous week "[w]hat is to be done if, as now seems probable, *we never get formal Mandates at all*!" See copy of Milner to Lloyd George, Bonar Law, and Curzon, 18 Nov. 1919, Milner Papers, BLO, Ms. Milner dep. 46/25.

121 CO to FO, 26 Nov. 1919 and 28 Nov. 1919, PRO, FO 371/3775.

122 Diary entry, 29 Nov. 1919, Milner Papers, BLO, Ms. Milner dep. 90. For a general discussion of British policy in Egypt during this period, see John Darwin, *Britain, Egypt and the Middle East: Imperial Policy in the Aftermath of War, 1918–1922* (London, 1981) and M. W. Daly, *Empire on the Nile* (Cambridge, 1986).

123 Cecil to Milner, 27 Oct. 1919, Milner Papers, BLO, Ms. Milner dep. 699. Also see Cecil to Kerr, 27 Oct. 1919, Lothian Papers, SRO, GD 40 17/75.

124 Milner to Cecil, 2 Nov. 1919, Milner Papers, BLO, Ms. Milner dep. 699.

125 In late September, Drummond had pleaded with Milner to settle the question of mandates before leaving, but Milner had responded that "I very much regret, as you know that B. and C. Mandates have not been finally disposed of. But I am afraid I can do nothing more to clear up the points you refer to before I go to Egypt." See copies of Drummond to Milner, 23 Sept. 1919 and Milner to Drummond, 29 Sept. 1919, in CO file of general correspondence dated June 1920, CO 649/21 and CO 691/39.

Chapter 3 Accommodating the League of Nations, 1920

1 Louis, *Germany's Lost Colonies*, pp. 155–60; Digre, *Imperialism's New Clothes*, pp. 196–9 and Peter J. Yearwood, "Great Britain and the Repartition of Africa, 1914–1919."

2 Minute by Eric Mächtig, 9 Jan., FO to CO dated 3 Jan. 1920, CO 649/21.

3 For examples, see Ligue coloniale française to MAE, 13 March 1920, AE, Série Afrique: 1918–1940, 96/77–78 and copy of Union coloniale française to MC, 9 July 1920, AE, Série Afrique: 1918–1940, 95/232–233. The Ligue, founded in 1907 by Eugène Etienne, was an umbrella organization for the colonial lobby and contained many of the same members as the Union coloniale française.

4 Copy of Sarraut speech included in Aimé Joseph de Fleuriau (chargé d'affaires) to FO, 28 April 1920, PRO, FO 371/3775 and FO to CO, 17 July 1920, CO 649/21.

5 For some of the correspondence concerning this period, see copies of Harold Nicolson (Foreign Office official) to Drummond, 9 Dec. 1919; Drummond to Nicolson, 15 Dec. and 31 Dec. 1919; and Philip J. Noel Baker (official in the League of Nations secretariat) to Drummond, 3 Jan. 1920, Noel Baker Papers, CC 4X/37; CO to FO, 22 Dec. 1919, PRO, FO 371/3775; Copy of telegram by Crowe to FO in FO to CO, 29 Dec. 1919, CO 649/18; FO to CO, 29 Dec. 1919, CO 649/18; W. H. Malkin (assistant legal advisor in the Foreign Office) to Sir Lancelot Oliphant (assistant secretary in the Foreign Office), 23 Jan. 1920, PRO, FO 371/3775; Copy of MC to MAE, 4 March 1920, ANSOM, SG: Togo-Cam, 6/64; MAE to Cambon, 5 March 1920 and MC to MAE, 12 May, 1920, AE, Série Afrique: 1918–1940, 95/73 and 144–5; Ralph Follet Wigram (third secretary, British Embassy in Paris) to FO, 24 March 1920, PRO, FO 371/4775 and copy of the procés-verbal marked "secret," MAE to MC, 21 July 1920, AE, Série Afrique: 1918–1940, 97/1–5.

6 India Office to FO, 12 Feb. 1920, PRO, FO 371/3775.

7 Minute by H. W. Malkin, 18 Feb. 1920, India Office to FO, 12 Feb. 1920, PRO, FO 371/3775.

8 See large FO file concerning parliamentary questions dated 1920 in PRO, FO 371/4766 as well as House of Commons to FO, 11 March 1920, PRO, FO 371/3775; Wigram to FO, 24 March 1920, PRO, FO 371/4775 and House of Commons to CO, 7 May 1920, CO 691/21.

9 "Mandates. A Duty of the League of Nations," *The Times* (London), 25 June 1920.

10 Britain developed an elaborate system for exercising jurisdiction outside of its national domain. The Foreign Jurisdiction Act of 1890, and other similar acts governing the empire, distinguished between "protectorates" and "colonies" in a number of ways. The term "colony" was more narrowly defined as being British soil and the inhabitants as British subjects. In "protectorates," British authority usually rested upon institutions of treaty rather than customary law. Britain was far less reluctant to assume continuous power of internal control in their colonies. For more, see William Edward Hall, *A Treatise of the Foreign Powers and Jurisdiction of the British Crown* (Oxford, 1894) and Sir C. P. Lucas, "The Meaning of Protectorate," *History* (January 1918): 241–3.

11 Bottomley to Read, 5 Jan. 1920, CO to CO, 5 Jan. 1920, CO 691/39.

12 Minute by Read, 5 Jan. 1920, CO to CO, 5 Jan. 1920, CO 691/39.

13 Copy of telegram from CO to Byatt, 17 Jan. 1920, CO to CO, 5 Jan. 1920, CO 691/39 and Byatt to CO, 19 Jan. 1920, CO 691/30. Also see, Church Missionary Society to CO, 13 April 1920, CO 691/40.
14 Minutes by Harry Fagg Batterby (clerk in the East Africa Department) and Bushe, 14 Jan. and 17 Jan. 1920, Byatt to CO dated 17 Nov. 1919, CO 691/24.
15 Byatt memorandum in Byatt to CO, 15 June 1920, CO 691/32.
16 Minute by Risely, 22 June 1920, Byatt to CO dated 15 June 1920, CO 691/32 and CO to FO, 8 July 1920, PRO, FO 371/4800.
17 Copy of telegram from the Dar es Salaam Chamber of Commerce to Byatt in Stewart Spencer Davis (deputy to the administrator) to CO, 6 April 1920, CO 691/31 and FO to CO, 29 April 1920, CO 691/37.
18 Minute by Strachey to Fiddes, 17 April 1920, CO to CO, CO 691/39.
19 Final draft of Order in Council submitted for the approval of the King in Council, 16 July 1920, Byatt to CO dated 26 April 1920, CO 691/31. On at least one occasion, Byatt did ask if the word "mandate" should appear in the preamble of the Order. See Byatt to CO, 29 April 1920, CO 691/31.
20 Minute by Strachey, 2 June 1920, CO to CO dated 31 May 1920, CO 691/31.
21 Minute by Risely, 2 June 1920, CO to CO dated 31 May 1920, CO 691/39.
22 Minute by Risley, ? July 1920, Byatt to CO dated 26 April 1920, CO 691/31.
23 Copy of Milner to Byatt, 5 Aug. 1920, included in Byatt to CO dated 26 April 1920, CO 691/31.
24 Minute by Fiddes to Amery, 22 July 1920, Byatt to CO dated 26 April 1920, CO 691/31.
25 Amery to Milner, 23 July 1920, Byatt to CO dated 26 April 1920, CO 691/31.
26 Minute by Milner, 27 July 1920, Byatt to CO dated 26 April 1920, CO 691/31.
27 Minute by Mächtig, 18 May 1920, Byatt to CO dated 13 may 1920, CO 691/13.
28 Ibid. and Crown Agents to CO, 12 July 1920, CO 691/37.
29 Minute by A. Ehrhardt (clerk in the East Africa Department), 30 Aug. 1920 and minute by Bushe, 8 Sept. 1920, Byatt to CO dated 6 July 1920, CO 691/33.
30 Strachey called this "one-sided" imperial preference. See minute by Strachey, 24 Aug. 1920, Customs to CO dated 19 Aug. 1920, CO 691/40. The question of imperial preference in mandated territories was often complicated and was of great interest to the French government, British merchants, the League of Nations Union, and the League of Nations. It was not until after Britain received its official mandates from the League and drafted special Orders in Council concerning the issue that the Colonial Office confirmed to the League that mandated territories were not bound by the same obligations of imperial preference that all other British colonies and protectorates were bound by. See MC to MAE, 28 July 1919, AE, Série Afrique: 1918–1940, 93/293; Rucker and Bencraft, Ltd. to CO, 17 April 1920, CO 691/41; Minutes of the Mandates Committee of the League of Nations Union, 19 July 1920, League of Nations Union Papers, London School of Economics and Political Science (LSEPS), vol. 38 and League of Nations to CO, 18 Dec. 1922, CO 649/25.
31 Strachey (1862–1942), was a graduate of Cambridge and was a clerk in the Foreign Office from 1885 to 1898 before entering the Colonial Office. He participated in the Anglo-German and the Anglo-French boundary conferences of 1906 and another such Anglo-German conference in 1909. He was

also the British plenipotentiary at the Brussels International Liquor Conference in 1912 and was British representative in negotiating the St. Germain conventions of 1919. For biographical information on Strachey, see *Who Was Who*, 4: 1941–1950 (London, 1951) and A. H. M. Kirk-Greene, *A Biographical Dictionary of the British Colonial Service, 1939–1966* (London, 1991).

32 John Illife suggests that Strachey's interest in defending African land rights and upholding the principles of the mandate, particularly during the first Labour government in 1924, is an example of "left-wing affinities" and cites P. S. Gupta's study of imperialism and the British labour movement for support. Yet, Strachey's long foreign and international experience, tied with his genuine desire to protect the interests of Africans, may better explain his strong regard for the specific stipulations of the mandate as well as for the international implications of the mandates system. See Illife, *A Modern History of Tanganyika*, p. 262, ft. 2 and Partha Sarathi Gupta, *Imperialism and the British Labour Movement 1914–1964* (London, 1975), pp. 74–5.

33 Minute by Strachey, 19 Sept. 1920, Byatt to CO dated 15 July 1920, CO 691/33.

34 Copy of CO to Byatt, 20 Sept. 1920, Byatt to CO dated 15 July 1920, CO 691/33.

35 The petition was dated 18 May 1920 and Mensah sent copies addressed to both Milner and Lloyd George. As the petition concerned Togo, it was directed to the West Africa Department of the Colonial Office. Later petitions from Mensah, and from other members of his family, prompted the Colonial Office to make unofficial enquiries into his background in 1921. For this first petition, see Mensah to CO, 24 July 1920, CO 724/1. For the "unofficial" report on Mensah by C. D. Trotter (Gold Coast record officer) dated 24 Aug. 1921, see R. H. W. Wilkinson (clerk in the Gold Coast secretariat) to J. E. W. Flood (clerk in the West Africa Department), 1 Sept. 1921, CO 724/2.

36 Mensah to CO, 24 July 1920, CO 724/1.

37 Minute by Flood, 18 Aug. 1920, Mensah to CO dated 24 July 1920, CO 724/1.

38 Committee minutes, 18 June, 28 June, 19 July 1920, League of Nations Union Papers, LSEPS, vols. 38 and 44.

39 For example, in early July, the French Ambassador in Berlin, Charles Laurent, warned Paris that the German colonial societies had protested to the chancellor that France intended to annex Togo and Cameroon. See Laurent to MAE, 7 June 1920, AE, Série Afrique: 1918–1940, 95/208.

40 The standard study of the activities of the German colonial movement after the war remains Wolfe W. Schmokel, *Dream of Empire: German Colonialism, 1919–1945* (New Haven, 1964).

41 For studies of Germany and the Treaty of Versailles, see Christoph M. Kimmich, *Germany and the League of Nations* (Chicago, 1976), pp. 1–48 and E. Kolb, *The Weimar Republic* (London, trans. edn., 1988).

42 The League specifically cited clause 8 of Article 22 which gave the Council this power to produce mandate texts "if not previously agreed upon" by the Allies. See League to FO, 12 July 1920, PRO, FO 371/4766. The President of the League of Nations, Leon Bourgeois, himself warned the French prime minister, Etienne Millerand, of this threat at least twice. See Bourgeois to Millerand, 23 July 1920 and 7 Oct. 1920, AE, Série A Paix, 78/125 and 130.

43 Curzon to Balfour, 24 July 1920, Balfour Papers, BM, 49734.

44 FO to CO, 11 Aug. 1920, CO 649/21.
45 MC to MAE, 12 and 16 Oct. 1920, AE, Série Afrique: 1918–1940, 97/100–103 and 128–9. Also see Hurst to FO, 28 Oct. 1920, PRO, FO 371/4767.
46 MAE to Fleuriau, 4 Nov. 1920, AE, Série Afrique: 1918–1940, 97/174. Crowe, who met with Fleuriau on 4 November to negotiate a modified B mandate exempting France from the recruitment restrictions, reported on the French position to the Foreign Office. See Crowe to FO, 4 Nov. 1920, PRO, FO 371/4767.
47 Minute by Curzon, 6 November 1920, Crowe to FO dated 4 Nov. 1920, PRO, FO 371/4767.
48 Fleuriau to MAE, 4 Nov. 1920, AE, Série Afrique: 1918–1940, 97/172.
49 MC to MAE, 12 Nov. 1920, AE, Série Afrique: 1918–1940, 97/202–209.
50 MAE to Cambon, 14 Nov. 1920, AE, Série Afrique: 1918–1940, 97/214–222.
51 MAE to Jean Gout (Foreign Ministry official in Geneva), 20 Nov. 1920, AE, Série Afrique: 1918–1940, 98/42 and Cambon to FO, 20 Nov. 1920, PRO, FO 371/4768.
52 Minute by Malkin, 23 Nov. 1920, Cambon to FO dated 20 Nov. 1920, PRO, FO 371/4768.
53 Debate surrounding the composition of the PMC was complicated as officials argued about the size of the commission, its ratio of members from mandatory and non-mandatory powers, and whether the commission should have a woman member. See CO to FO, 26 Oct. 1920, PRO, FO 371/5477; Diary entries of Henry C. M. Lambert (an assistant under-secretary of state and Colonial Office representative in Geneva) 14, 24, 26, 28, 29 Nov. and 1, 5 Dec. 1920, Lambert Papers, CO 867/2 A; Diary entry 14 Nov. 1920, Cecil Papers, BM, 51131; MAE to Cambon, 4 Dec. 1920, AE, Série Afrique: 1918–1940, 98/83; Fleuriau to FO, 4 Dec. 1920, PRO, FO 371/4768 and copy of the International Women Suffrage Alliance to League in League to FO, 14 Dec. 1920, PRO, FO 371/5483.
54 Balfour to Hankey, 25 Nov. 1920, PRO, FO 371/4768.
55 League of Nations Union to MAE, 4 Nov. 1920, AE, Série Afrique: 1918–1940, 97/186–190; Foreign Ministry "Note" for Philippe Berthelot (secretary-general of the Foreign Ministry), 18 Nov. 1920, AE, Série Société des Nations, 620/23–30; League to MAE, 1 Dec. 1920, AE, Série Afrique: 1918–1940, 98/75–76; League to FO, 1 Dec. 1920, PRO. FO 371/4768 and League to FO, 7 Dec. 1920, PRO, FO 317/5477.
56 Memorandum by the German government entitled "The Responsibility of the League Under Article 22 of the Covenant" dated 20 Nov. 1920 in League to FO, 22 Nov. 1920, PRO, FO 371/4768.
57 The Council of the League of Nations originally had four permanent members (Great Britain, France, Japan, and Italy) and, later, nine non-permanent members, chosen by the General Assembly. In 1926 Germany became a permanent member and when it left the League in 1933 its seat fell to the Soviet Union.
58 Diary entry, 19 Nov. 1920, Lambert Papers, CO 967/2 A.
59 Minute by Waterlow, 2 Dec. 1920, League to FO dated 22 Nov. 1920, PRO, FO 371/4768.
60 Minute by Crowe, 2 Dec. 1920, League to FO dated 22 Nov. 1920, PRO, FO 371/4768.
61 Diary entries, 29 Nov, 1 and 9 Dec. 1920, Lambert Papers, CO 967/2 A.

62 In addition to France's unwillingness to accept a modified B mandate, negotiations between Hurst and Henri Auguste Fromageot (Foreign Ministry legal advisor) were slow because French officials had to confer with Paris before making a decision. By 7 December, the two men had drafted a modified B mandate and a draft joint recommendation that contained a long preamble written by the French. The preamble declared that Britain and France were not bound to accept mandates, but would anyway. See diary entry, 7 Dec. 1920, Lambert Papers, CO 967/2 A.

63 Cambon to MAE, 3 Dec. 1920, AE, Série Afrique: 1918–1940, 98/79–80.

64 Hurst to FO, 10 Dec. 1920, PRO, FO 371/4767.

65 Balfour and Hurst conducted these secret conversations with Japanese officials at the Hotel Beau Rivage on 8 December. In order to soothe Japan's animosity toward Australia and New Zealand, no Colonial Office representatives were invited. Ultimately, Japan abandoned its objections to the exclusion of commercial equality in the C mandates on the condition that they attach an "understanding" to the text that Japan would not condone any "discriminatory and disadvantageous treatment in the Mandated Territories." See minutes of "secret" conversations dated 8 Dec. 1920, Cabinet to FO, 24 Dec. 1920, PRO, FO 371/4769 and diary entry, 11 Dec. 1920, Lambert Papers, CO 967/2 A.

66 Diary entry, 17 Dec. 1920, Lambert Papers, CO 967/2 A.

67 MC to MAE, 13 Dec. 1920, AE, Série Société des Nations, 620/33–43.

68 Balfour made this decision even before Paris had accepted their modified B mandates. See diary entry, 12 Dec. 1920, Lambert Papers, CO 967/2 A.

69 The mandate for the Tanganyika Territory did not contain this clause. For the final draft of the B mandates for Togo and Cameroon, see CO to CO, 17 Dec. 1920, CO 691/40, Appendix C and Wright, *Mandates*, pp. 616–18.

70 Diary entry 17 Dec. 1920, Lambert papers, CO 967/2 A and Balfour to Hankey, 17 Dec. 1920, PRO, FO 371/4768. After complaints from the Belgian government in 1919, Britain had agreed to slice Ruanda-Urundi away from German East Africa as a B mandate for Belgium. See "Proposition by the Belgian Delegation for the settlement of the respective positions of Great Britain and Belgium in the Former German Colony of East Africa," Appendix A, 19 May 1919, Milner Papers, BLO, Ms. Milner dep. 389 and Digre, *Imperialism's New Clothes*, pp. 168–72 and 186–92.

71 Diary entry, 19 Dec. 1920, Lambert Papers CO 967/2 A.

72 "Memento" entitled "Mandats pour le Togo et le Cameroun" dated 22 Dec. 1920, AE, Série Afrique: 1918–1940, 98/213.

73 Minute by Strachey, 31 Dec. 1920, CO to CO dated 17 Dec. 1920, CO 691/40.

74 Minute by Harding, 28 Dec. 1920, CO to CO date 17 Dec. 1920, CO 649/21.

75 Ibid. For two years, the colonial governments in Lagos and Accra had been kept almost entirely in the dark. The governors were finally given this information on 5 January 1921.

76 Robert Lansing, after resigning as American secretary of state in 1920, made this charge himself. See Robert Lansing, *The Peace Negotiations, A Personal Narrative* (Boston, 1921), pp. 149–61.

77 For the text of the constitution of the PMC, approved by the Council of the League of Nations on 1 December 1920, see Appendix D and Wright, *Mandates*, pp. 622–3.

78 Noel Baker to Colban, 23 March 1920, Noel Baker Papers, CC, 4X/37.

79 Wilson's address to the Columbus Chamber of Commerce, 4 Sept. 1919, *Papers of Woodrow Wilson*, vol. 63, p. 15.

80 Wilson's address to the Coliseum in Sioux Falls, South Dakota, 8 Sept. 1919, *Papers of Woodrow Wilson*, vol. 63, pp. 111–12.

Chapter 4 The United States, Germany, and the Permanent Mandates Commission, 1921–1925

1 Minute by Amery, 19 Feb. 1921, FO to CO dated 9 Feb. 1921, CO 691/49.
2 *FRUS: The Paris Peace Conference 1919*, vol. 13, p. 276.
3 For example, see Bainbridge Colby (American secretary of state) to Curzon, 20 Nov. 1920, PRO, FO 371/7049 and copy of Colby to Gastao da Cunha (president of the Council of the League of Nations) 1 March 1921, AE, Série Société des Nations, 544/1.
4 For a brief survey of the American foreign policy during these early postwar years, see Warren I. Cohen, *Empire Without Tears: America's Foreign Relations 1921–1933* (New York, 1987).
5 After learning of this request, the British under-secretary of state for foreign affairs, Sir Eyre Crowe, minuted that the League "was unreasonable in calling for an annual report on the Mandated Territories from the respective Mandatory Powers, before the Mandates were even considered, not to speak of being granted. But one cannot expect the League to be reasonable." 16 Feb. 1921, Count August de Saint-Aulaire (French ambassador to London) to FO dated 11 Feb. 1921, PRO, FO 371/5058. Also see series of correspondence from League to MAE, 1921, AE, Série Société des Nations, 544 and Wright, *Mandates*, p. 160.
6 Saint-Aulaire to FO, 11 Feb. 1921, PRO, FO 371/5058; Saint-Aulaire to FO, 12 March 1921, PRO, FO 371/5851 and Saint-Aulaire to FO, 25 May 1921, PRO, FO 371/5852.
7 Saint-Aulaire to Curzon, 25 May 1921, PRO, FO 371/5852; Herbert Albert Laurens Fisher (British member of the League of Nations Council) to Curzon, 30 May 1921, Curzon Papers, IOL, Mss. Eur. F 112/219(b); Saint-Aulaire to Balfour, 30 May 1921, PRO, FO 371/7050 and Saint-Aulaire to MAE, 6 June 1921, AE, Série Société des Nations, 544/41.
8 Copy of Churchill to Lloyd George, 9 June 1921, Curzon Papers, IOL, Mss. Eur. F 112/219(a).
9 Copy of Lloyd George to Churchill, 11 June 1921, Lloyd George Papers, HLRO, F/9/3/54.
10 Copy of letter from Drummond to Balfour, 2 June 1921, Balfour to Curzon dated 3 June 1921, PRO, FO 371/7050.
11 Cabinet minutes, 14 June 1921, CAB 23/49 and Hankey to Lloyd George, copy of cabinet minutes, 14 June 1921, Lloyd George Papers, HLRO, F/25/1/39.
12 Britain, France, and Belgium informed the Council of the League of Nations of this decision on 21 June 1921. See Wright, *Mandates*, pp. 119 and 160.
13 The Franco-American convention concerning France's B mandates for Togo and Cameroon was concluded on 13 February 1923 and the Anglo-American agreement dealing with Britain's B mandates for Togo, Cameroon, and Tanganyika wwas signed on 10 February 1925. For a copy of the Franco-American convention, see the papers of Jean Beau (former governor-general of Indochina and French member of the PMC from 1921 to 1926), 13 Feb. 1923, Beau Papers, AE, 31/20–65. For a copy of the Anglo-American treaty, see CO to CO, 17 Feb. 1925, CO 691/82.
14 Copy of note from Italian ambassador to FO in FO to CO, 17 July 1922, CO 691/59.

15 For some of the Anglo-American correspondence concerning these negotiations, see FO to CO, 2 Feb. 1921, CO 691/50; FO to CO, 8 Oct. 1921, CO 691/50; FO to CO, 30 Oct. 1921, CO 649/23; FO to CO, 8 April 1922, CO 649/25; FO to CO, 12 June 1922, CO 649/25; FO to CO, 17 July 1922, CO 691/59 and FO to CO, 5 July 1924, CO 649/28.

16 Statement prepared for Balfour, 16 July 1922, PRO, FO 371/8324.

17 Hankey to Lloyd George, "Position of the Government of the United States Concerning Mandates," 31 Aug. 1921, Lloyd George Papers, HLRO, F/25/2/10; CO to CO, 2 June 1923, CO 649/27 and various minutes on Sir Hugh Clifford (now governor of Nigeria) to CO, 9 April 1925, CO 569/30.

18 For example, Harding called the requirement to supply the United States with a "duplicate" of the annual report a "snag" that might require "a specially printed cover for the copies for the U.S.A., another cover for the L[eague of] N[ations], and a third for the issue as a non-Parliamentary Publication in this country." Minute by Harding to Strachey, 7 Nov. 1925, Major Upton Fitzherbert Ruxton (lt.-governor, southern provinces, Nigeria) to CO dated 6 Nov. 1925, CO 649/30.

19 Saint-Aulaire to MAE, 24 June 1921, AE, Série Société des Nations, 544/58.

20 Cabinet Office to CO, 21 July 1922, CO 649/25; Saint-Aulaire to MAE, 21 July 1922, AE, Série Société des Nations, 600/168; League to MC, 1 Aug. 1922, ANSOM, SG: Togo-Cam, 25/221 and Cabinet Office to CO, 9 Oct. 1922, CO 691/60.

21 See *FRUS: The Paris Peace Conference 1919, Proposals of the German Government for the Establishment of a League of Nations*, 9 May 1919, vol. 6, pp. 772–3 and memorandum by the German government entitled "The Responsibility of the League Under Article 22 of the Covenant" dated 20 Nov. 1920 in League to FO, 22 Nov. 1920, PRO, FO 371/4768.

22 For a general discussion of German foreign policy during this period, see John Hiden, *Germany and Europe 1919–1939*, second edition (London, 1993).

23 Articles 120 and 121, in conjunction with Article 297b, of the Treaty of Versailles gave the mandatory powers the legal right to liquidate German property in the mandates. See copy of German note to FO in FO to CO, 27 Jan. 1921, and minute by Fiddes, 28 Jan. 1921, CO 691/49.

24 Copy of German note in Ministère des Pensions to MC, 8 July 1921, ANSOM, AP, 611/1. The German government was still asking for these monuments as late as 1930. See copy of German "Note Verbal" to MAE, 4 March 1930, ANSOM, AP, 611/1.

25 Report of a conversation between the German Ambassador and S. P. Waterlow in the Foreign Office, 20 Aug. 1921, and minute by Waterlow, 24 Aug. 1921, PRO, FO 371/5999. It appears, however, that privately the Foreign Office did try to find out if the German protest had any foundation. According to a report by Arnold Roberts, an official attached to the Inter-Allied Rhineland High Commission in Coblenz, the French military authorities had assured their British counterparts that no Africans of any former German colony were serving anywhere in the occupied territory of Germany. See Roberts to FO, 3 Sept. 1921, PRO, FO 371/5999.

26 Copy of note from British Embassy in Paris in MAE to MC, 18 Feb. 1921, SG: Togo-Cam, 28/246.

27 Copy of MC to MAE, 14 March 1921, ANSOM, SG: Togo-Cam, 28/246.

28 Article 122 of the Treaty of Versailles gave the Allies the power to prohibit Germans "to reside, hold property, trade or exercise a profession" in the mandated territories. For examples of Germany's request for copies of the

annual reports, see German Ambassador to MAE, 25 Oct. 1922, Série Afrique, 1918–1940, 102/254–255 and MC to MAE, 3 Oct. 1925, Série Société des Nations, 621/128.

29 The Tanganyika government allowed a few individuals who were not deemed "undesirables" to return who, because of the boundary changes resulting from the Treaty of Versailles, claimed to be nationals of Poland, Denmark, France, Czechoslovakia, or Danzig. For example, see FO to CO, 13 Jan. 1920, CO 691/37; Byatt to CO, 10 June 1920, CO 691/32; Polish Minister to FO, 8 Oct. 1921, PRO, FO 371/6055 and Byatt to CO, 5 Dec. 1922, CO 691/58.

30 For example, see copy of MAE to MC, 29 Sept. 1921, SG: Togo-Cam, 24/217; Thédore Paul Marchand (commissioner of Cameroon) to MC, 3 July 1925, and MC to Marchand, 10 July 1925, ANSOM, AP, 613/1.

31 For a detailed study of the German colonial movement during the interwar period, see Wolfe W. Schmokel, *Dream of Empire: German Colonialism, 1919–1945* (New Haven, 1964).

32 Schnee wrote a number of books and pamphlets concerning the former German colonies. The most important during this period were *Braucht Deutschland Kolonien?* (Leipzig, 1921) and *Die Deutschen Kolonien unter fremder Mandatherrschaft* (Leipzig, 1922).

33 For example, see MAE to MC, 16 Sept. 1921, ANSOM, AP, 95/6; MAE to MC, 31 May 1922, ANSOM, AP, 95/7; Allizé (French ambassador in Berne) to MAE, 14 June 1922, AE, Série Internationales, 600/128–130; MAE to MC, 18 June 1925, ANSOM, AP, 95; Foreign Ministry file of correspondence, 1923–1925, AE, Série Société des Nations, 545 including Pierre de Margerie (French ambassador to Berlin) to MAE, 2 March 1925; MAE to MC, 26 Dec. 1924, ANSOM, AP, 900; MAE to MC, 18 June 1925, ANSOM, AP, 95; MAE to MC, 13 Oct. 1925, ANSOM, AP, 900/1 and report entitled "Note sur les Revendications Coloniales Allemandes. Etat actuel de la question," Oct. 1925, AE, Série Société des Nations, 545/79–125.

34 Copy of MC to MAE, 5 Oct. 1921, ANSOM, AP, 95/6; MC to MAE, 31 March 1922, AE, Série Afrique, 1918–1940, 101/125; Copy of MC to MAE, 31 May 1922, ANSOM, AP, 95/7; "Note pour le Ministère," 12 Jan. 1925, ANSOM, AP, 95/9 and MC to MAE, 24 Dec. 1925, AE, Série Société des Nations, 546/3. In 1924 Paris received a 17-page bound report from Bonnecarrère and a similar 20-page report from Marchand in response to a ministry request for information systematically to refute a series of German press articles. See Bonnecarrère to MC, 19 March 1924 and Marchand to MC, 21 April 1924, ANSOM, AP, 1038.

35 MC to MAE, 18 Sept. 1920, ANSOM, SG: Togo-Cam, 25/218; Carde to MC, 23 Nov. 1920, ANSOM, SG: Togo-Cam, 25/218; Copy of MAE to Saint-Aulaire, 24 Feb. 1923, ANSOM, SG: Togo-Cam, 24/213; MC to the commissioners of Togo and Cameroon, 4 July 1923, ANSOM, AP, 79; Marchand to MC, 2 Dec. 1924, ANSOM, AP, 1038 and Bonnecarrère to MC, 21 Aug. 1925, ANSOM, AP, 1038.

36 Copies of MC to Carde and Bonnecarrère, 29 Dec. 1922, ANSOM, AP, 95.

37 Copy of MC to Carde, 7 Oct. 1922, ANSOM, Agence F.O.M., 867/2365.

38 CO to FO, 7 March 1923 and copy of FO to Sir A. Geddes, 9 March 1923, PRO, FO 371/9440.

39 Minute by Mächtig, 24 Aug. 1921, Byatt to CO dated 16 Aug. 1921, CO 691/46.

40 Copies of CO to Byatt, 31 Aug. 1921 and 8 Sept. 1921, Byatt to CO dated 16 Aug. 1921, CO 691/46.

41 Copy of note from German government in FO to CO, 19 April 1922, CO 691/19.
42 Strachey minuted that "I have consulted Sir H. Byatt. He says that the amount due by the German Govt. to these Askaris [sic] is very large. He thought over a million (!). He considers it very desirable that the men should be paid, [and] as the Germans want to pay them, the only question is how this should be done." Minute by Strachey, 28 April 1922, FO to CO dated 19 April 1922, CO 691/59.
43 While British colonial officials agreed to the general principle of Germany's paying the former Askari as early as 1922, the details of the plan were not concluded until 1927. See FO to CO, 20 Feb. 1925, CO 691/81; Sir Donald Cameron (governor of the Tanganyika Territory) to CO, 26 March 1927, CO 691/90 and John Scott (chief secretary of the Tanganyika Territory) to CO, 14 April 1927, CO 691/93.
44 The Anglo-German commercial treaty emerged from the efforts of the new Conservative government, formed in October 1924, under the leadership of Stanley Baldwin. See Article XXXII of the "Draft Commercial Treaty between United Kingdom and Germany," 28 Nov. 1924, Baldwin Papers, CU, 112/15.
45 Memorandum by Strachey, 3 March 1925, and FO note to CO dated 20 April 1925 in Scott to CO dated 20 Dec. 1924, CO 691/73 and FO to CO, 25 April 1925, CO 691/81.
46 Cameron to CO, 10 July 1925, CO 691/78.
47 Bonnecarrère to MC, 13 July 1923, ANSOM, AP, 609/2.
48 For discussions of Anglo-French relations during this period, see the classic study by Arnold Wolfers, *Britain and France between Two Wars: Conflicting Strategies of Peace from Versailles to World War II* (New York, 1966 edition) and Martin Kitchen, *Europe between the Wars: A Political History* (London, 1988).
49 Copy of FO to MAE, 14 Jan. 1924, included in MAE to MC, dated 26 Jan. 1924, ANSOM, AP, 609/2.
50 For some of the problems surrounding the sale of the German plantations, see Harry Moorhouse (deputy governor of Nigeria) to CO, 23 Jan. 1920, CO 649/20; the various files dated 27 Jan. 1922 through 6 Dec. 1922, CO 649/26 and *The New York Times*, 23 Nov. 1924, section II, p. 5. For greater detail, see LeVine, *The Cameroon from Mandate to Independence*, p. 121–3; David E. Gardinier, "The British in the Cameroons, 1919–1939" in Prosser Gifford and Wm. R. Louis, eds., *Britain and Germany in Africa: Imperial Rivalry and Colonial Rule* (New Haven, 1967), pp. 513–55 and DeLancey, *Cameroon*, pp. 18–22.
51 *Report by His Britannic Majesty's Government to the Council of the League of Nations on the Administration of the British Cameroons for the Year 1926* (London, H.M.S.O., Colonial No. 30, 1927), p. 97.
52 Ibid., Gardinier, "The British in the Cameroons, 1919–1939," p. 549, and DeLancey, *Cameroon*, p. 19.
53 D'Abernon to FO, 20 June 1924, FO 371/9845. This view, however, was not shared by the permanent officials in the Foreign Office. In minutes dated 27 June and 30 September, Crowe described d'Abernon's suggestions as "altogether absurd" and "[i]ncorrigibly foolish."
54 Britain, France and Russia formally made these promises to Italy in the Treaty of London, signed on 26 April 1915. For Italy's wartime imperial interests and postwar diplomacy, see C. Seton-Watson, *Italy from Liberalism to*

Fascism, 1870–1923 (London, 1967) and M. Clark, *Modern Italy 1871–1982* (London, 1984).

55 For example, in 1921 Rome scolded Britain for local legislation in Tanganyika that referred to foreign nationals as "non-British subjects" instead of nationals of states belonging to the League of Nations. In 1923 Rome complained that, in certain cases, the Tanganyika government granted a form of tax relief to Asians, but not to all members of the League of Nations. Copy of Italian Ambassador to FO dated 18 June 1921 in FO to CO, 19 June 1921, CO 691/49 and copy of Italian Ambassador to FO in FO to CO, 19 July 1923, CO 691/66.

56 René Besnard (French ambassador in Rome) to MAE, 17 Nov. 1925, AE, Série Internationale, 601/32–35.

57 On 10 February 1921, the Anti-Slavery and Aborigines Protection Society held a conference on mandates. See conference papers and memorandum by John H. Harris entitled "The Colonial Mandates," 10 Feb. 1921, Anti-Slavery and Aborigines Protection Society Papers, RH, Mss. Brit. Emp. s. 22 G 440. On the same day, the League sent the Foreign Office a list of groups, including the Native Races and the Liquor Traffic United Committee, the United Kingdom Alliance, and the Women's International League for Peace and Freedom, who had all expressed views about the mandates. See League to FO, 10 Feb. 1921, PRO, FO 371/5851. Also see the Commission of the General Assembly of the United Free Church of Scotland to FO, 4 March 1921, PRO, FO 371/7049; the Consul Général de France à Genève to MAE, 19 Dec. 1921, Série Afrique 1918–1940, 125/1–3; File containing various correspondence from the Bureau Internationale pour la Défence des Indigènes to MAE, 1921–1927, AE, Série Afrique 1918–1940, 125; and copy of Native Races and the Liquor Traffic United Committee to FO in FO to CO, 24 March 1922, CO 649/25.

58 *The Times*, London, 4 March 1921, *Headway: The Journal of the League of Nations Union*, May 1921 issue; League to FO, 10 May 1921, PRO, FO 371/7050; Cabinet to CO, 18 May 1921, CO 691/52; MC to MAE, 20 May 1921, AE, Série Afrique, 1918–1940, 100/31–32; Minutes of the Mandates Committee of the LNU, 8 July 1921, League of Nations Union Papers, LSEPS, vol. 44; LNU to CO, 28 July 1921, CO 649/23 and Cabinet to CO, 22 Aug. 1921, CO 649/23.

59 Copy of note from Italian ambassador to FO in FO to CO, 19 June 1921, CO 691/49.

60 Copy of Liverpool Chamber of Commerce to League dated 31 May 1921 in League to FO, 15 Aug. 1921, PRO, FO 371/7052.

61 Noel-Baker later became a Labour MP, served in the second and third Labour governments, and was the recipient of the Nobel Peace Prize in 1959 for his dedication to international organization and world disarmament. See Partha Sarathi Gupta, *Imperialism and the British Labour Movement, 1914–1964* (New York, 1975), pp. 100–1, 277, 357, and 407.

62 Noel-Baker to Cecil, 22 Aug. 1921, Noel-Baker Papers, CC, 4/463.

63 Undated response written on original note from Noel-Baker to Cecil, 22 Aug. 1921, Noel-Baker Papers, CC, 4/463.

64 For more on Cecil's participation in the early work of the Assembly, see Viscount Cecil, *A Great Experiment* (New York, 1941), pp. 101–218. For his role in this specific incident, see pp. 116 and 130.

65 Noel-Baker to William G. A. Ormsby-Gore (British member of the PMC), 24 Sept. 1921, Noel-Baker Papers, CC, 4/440.

66 Report of the Sixth Committee of the Second Assembly, LN Documents A. 105. 1921; A. 148. 1921; Copy of League to Lloyd George dated 3 Oct. 1921 in CO to CO, 6 Oct. 1921, CO 691/52 and Cabinet to FO, 19 Oct. 1921, PRO, FO 371/7052.
67 Noel-Baker to Ormsby-Gore, 24 Sept. 1921, Noel-Baker Papers, CC, 4/440.
68 League of Nations Mandates Commission, Minutes of First Session, 4 to 8 Oct. 1921, LN Document C.416.M.296.1921.IV; League of Nations, Permanent Mandates Commission, Report, LN Document C.395.M.294.1921.VI and Rules of Procedure, LN Document C.404(2).M.294.1921.VI.
69 For copies of the questionnaire, see CO to CO, Nov. 1921 and copy of CO to Clifford, 20 April 1922, CO 649/23. Also see Minutes of the League of Nations "B" Mandates Questionnaire, LN Document C.396.M.289.1921.VI.
70 In 1925, one Colonial Office clerk in the West Africa Department still had not grasped the significance of this tactic. He complained that "The reports are being made full [and] detailed as desired. The stupidity of having a huge report for a small piece of territory does not seem to have occurred to the P.M.C." Minute by J. E. W. Flood, 7 July 1925, CO to CO dated ? Jan. 1925, CO 649/30.
71 Copy of Noel-Baker to J. H. Harris, 11 Oct. 1921, Noel-Baker Papers, CC, 4/440.
72 Minutes of the Mandates Committee, 9 Dec. 1921, League of Nations Union Papers, LSEPS, vol. 44.
73 In addition to the numerous works already cited, see P. T. Furukaki, *Les mandats internationaux de la Société des Nations* (Lyon, 1923); Moritz Bileski, *Kolonialpolitik unter internationaler Kontrolle: Die Arbeit der Mandatkommission des Völkerbundes* (Berlin, 1924); J. Stoyanovski, *La théorie générale des mandats internationaux* (Paris, 1925); Freda White, *Mandates* (London, 1926); Elizabeth Van Maanen-Helmer, *The Mandates System in Relation to Africa and the Pacific Islands* (London, 1929); Norman Bentwich, *The Mandate System* (London, 1930) and Aaron M. Margalith, *The International Mandates: A Historical, Descriptive, and Analytical Study of the Theory and Principles of the Mandates System* (Baltimore, 1930).
74 For biographical information on the various members of the PMC, see Wright, *Mandates*, pp. 626–7; Hall, *Mandates, Dependencies, and Trusteeship*, pp. 178 84 and Margery Perham, *Lugard: The Years of Authority 1898–1945* (London, 1960), pp. 647–8.
75 CO to FO, 26 Oct. 1920, PRO, FO 371/5477.
76 In accepting the chairmanship at the first meeting of the PMC, Theodoli thanked his colleagues for "the honor which they bestowed upon him, an honor which reflected on his country, the only non-Mandatory Power among those permanently represented on the Council." League of Nations Mandates Commission, Minutes of First Session, 4 to 8 Oct. 1921, LN Document C.416.M. 296.1921.IV., p. 3.
77 For Rappard's general views on mandates and colonial reform, see William E. Rappard, *The Quest for Peace since the World War* (Cambridge, Mass., 1940), pp. 86–99.
78 Hall, *Mandates, Dependencies, and Trusteeship*, pp. 249–55.
79 Drummond to Beau, 28 Feb. 1921, Beau Papers, AE, 31/3–4.
80 At least one recent scholar contends that Beau was a poor colonial administrator. See Denise Bouche, *Histoire de la colonisation française II* (Paris, 1991), p. 266.

81 See minutes for "Reunion interministerielle," 22 Nov. 1921, AE, Série Société des Nations, 619/71–76; copy of "Rapport de M. Beau sur la première séance de la Commission permanente des Mandats" in Bertrand Clauzel (head of the political section of League of Nations division of the Foreign Ministry and secretary-general of the French delegation in Geneva) to MAE, 5 Oct. 1921, AE, Série Afrique, 1918–1940, 100/224–226 and Beau to MAE, 17 Aug. 1922, AE, Série Société des Nations, 555/27–32.

82 Gout to MC, 12 Nov. 1921, and Note by Gout, 24 Dec. 1921, AE, Série Société des Nations, 619/69 and 78; Copy of Gout to Beau, 2 May 1923, AE, Série Société des Nations, 619/101–103; Beau to Doulcet (clerk in the legal section of the League of Nations division of the Foreign Ministry), 24 Nov. 1925, AE, Série Société des Nations, 552/8 and Jean Gout (head of the League of Nations division of the Foreign Ministry) to Beau, 2 May 1923, AE, Série Société des Nations, 555/27–32.

83 Flora Lugard to Major E. J. Lugard, 20 July 1923, Lugard Papers, RH, 119/4.

84 FO draft memorandum dated 14 Feb. 1921 included in Hankey to Crowe, 14 Jan. 1921, PRO, FO 371/7047.

85 The standard biography of Lugard is Margery Perham, vol. 1: *Lugard: The Years of Adventure, 1858–1898* (London, 1956); vol. 2: *Lugard: Years of Authority, 1895–1945* (London, 1960). For more recent, but less comprehensive accounts, see I. N. Nicholson, *The Administration of Nigeria, 1900–1960: Men, Methods, and Myths* (Oxford, 1969); John E. Flint, "Frederick Lugard: The Making of an Autocrat (1858–1945)" in L. H. Gann and Peter Duignan, eds., *African Proconsuls: European Governors in Africa* (New York, 1978); Harry A. Gailey, *Lugard and the Abôeokuta Uprising: The demise of ôEgba independence* (London, 1982) and Peter K. Tibenderana, "The Role of the British Administration in the Appointment of the Emirs of Northern Nigeria, 1901–1931: The Case of Sokoto Province," *Journal of African History* 28 (1987): 231–57.

86 F. D. Lugard, *Revision of Instructions to Political Officers on Subjects Chiefly Political and Administrative* (London, 1919). This document was printed privately for official use, but large portions are contained in A. H. M. Kirk-Greene, *The Principles of Native Administration in Nigeria: Selected Documents, 1900–1947* (London, 1965).

87 Lugard to Milner, 10 Jan. 1919, Milner Papers, BLO, Ms. Eng. hist. c. 705.

88 Crowe and Hurst represented the Foreign Office during this interdepartmental conference. See unidentified minute, 11 Feb. 1921, Hankey to Crowe dated 14 Feb. 1921, PRO, FO 371/7047.

89 For a discussion of the problems faced by the Coalition and Lloyd George's cabinet after the failure of "fusion" between Liberals and Conservatives, see Martin Pugh, *Lloyd George* (London, 1988), pp. 129–51.

90 Birn, *The League of Nations Union 1918–1945*, pp. 28–50.

91 Churchill became colonial secretary on 14 February. On 21 February, the Cabinet Office instructed the FO to transmit a telegram from Hankey to Balfour in Geneva that read "Cannot give answer tonight about British representative on Mandates Commission as Prime Minister wishes first to discuss question with Secretary of State for Colonies." Three days later, the Cabinet Office instructed the FO to send Balfour a telegram marked "very urgent" telling him that "Mr. Ormsby-Gore, M.P. officially appointed British Representative on the Permanent Mandates Commission." See copies of FO to Balfour, 21 Feb. 1921 and 24 Feb. 1921 in Cabinet to FO, 24 Feb. 1921, PRO, FO 371/7049.

92 Ormsby-Gore had made public his sympathies for the mandates system in a chapter entitled "Indirect International Supervision" included in *The League of Nations Starts: An Outline by its Organizers* (London, 1920).

93 Undated thirty-six page lecture by Ormsby-Gore entitled "The Mandatory System," Lugard Papers, RH, 119/1.

94 Ormsby-Gore was elected chairman of the Mandates Committee of the League of Nations Union on 18 June 1920, but after July 1921, perhaps because of his membership on the PMC, he was a very infrequent participant in the committee's activities. See Mandates Committee minutes, 18 June 1920; 28 June 1920; 19 July 1920; 8 July 1921 and 18 Oct. 1929, League of Nations Union Papers, LSEPS, vols 38 and 44. In February 1921, Ormsby-Gore attended the conference on mandates held by the Anti-Slavery and Aborigines Protection Society. See conference papers, 10 Feb. 1921, Anti-Slavery and Aborigines Protection Society Papers, RH, Mss. Brit. Emp. s. 22 G 440. For an example of Ormsby-Gore's ties to the Liverpool Chamber of Commerce, see Chapter 6 below.

95 Lugard was never a formal member of the LNU, but did agree to offer his expertise. See "Draft Report on Liquor Traffic," July 1921, League of Nations Union Papers, LSEPS, vol. 38.

96 Grey to Cecil, 16 Sept. 1922 and Cecil to Grey, 25 Sept. 1922, Cecil Papers, BLO, 51073.

97 The first edition appeared in 1922 and was revised in 1923, 1925, 1929 and reprinted with a new introduction by Margery Perham in 1965. F. D. Lugard, *The Dual Mandate in Tropical Africa* (London, 1965).

98 Ibid., p. 617.

99 Ibid., p. 619.

100 Lugard kept two undated versions of notes concerning this meeting. The first is written in Lugard's hand and was probably made either before or during the meeting. The second was probably composed later and is typed with additions. See notes of interview with Ormsby-Gore, ? 1922, Lugard Papers, RH, 119/2.

101 Ibid. According to Perham, Lugard's pension from the colonial service was not enough to pay for his wife's expensive habits including a costly "adventure in agriculture." See Perham, *Lugard II*, pp. 646 and 666–8.

102 Article entitled "Empire Problems. Sir Frederick Lugard and the Mandates," *The Times*, London, 15 Nov. 1922.

103 CO to Lugard, 19 Jan. 1923, Lugard Papers, RH, 119/2.

104 Rappard to Lugard, 12 Feb. 1923, Lugard Papers, RH, 119/2.

105 Ormsby-Gore to Lugard, 16 Feb. 1923, Lugard Papers, RH, 119/2.

106 For example, Lugard was a member of the Colonial Office advisory committee on education in Africa, the International Labour Organization, and the International Slavery Committee. He accepted directorships with the Colonial Bank (which became Barkleys Bank in 1925 and was the most important banking institution of the empire), the Empire Cotton Growing Corporation and the Huileries du Congo belge, the Belgian subsidiary of Lever Brothers. By the end of 1925, Lugard had also published nearly twenty articles on a wide range of issues concerning Africa and the Empire.

107 For examples, see minutes of the Mandates Committee, 13 June 1923, Lugard Papers, RH, 143/1 and 16 Nov. 1925, League of Nations Union Papers, LSEPS, vol. 44; Cecil to Lugard, 3 Sept. 1923, Lugard Papers, RH, 122/4; Lugard to Cecil, 15 May 1925, Cecil Papers, BLO, 51097; League to FO, 17 March 1924, PRO, FO 371/9531 and Lugard to FO, 6 Aug. 1924, PRO, FO 371/9985.

108 James Deemind (agent of the John Holt and Company (Liverpool) Limited) to Lugard, 20 Feb. and 28 May 1924, Lugard Papers, RH, 133/2.
109 Foreword by F. D. Lugard to Freda White, *Mandates* (London, 1926), pp. 8–9.

Chapter 5 The British Mandates between Theory and Practice, 1921–1925

1 For a copy of the draft oath, standard throughout the rest of the British Africa, see Byatt to CO, 6 Dec. 1920, CO 691/36.
2 Minute by Strachey, 27 Jan. 1921 and copy of CO to Byatt, 28 Jan. 1921 in Byatt to CO dated 6 Dec. 1920, CO 691/36.
3 Minute by Bottomley, 21 Jan. 1921, Byatt to CO dated 21 Jan. 1921, CO 691/36.
4 Draft note to the Petroleum Department, 1 March 1921 in Byatt to CO dated 24 Dec. 1920, CO 691/36.
5 Draft note from CO to Treasury, 28 Jan. 1921 in Byatt to CO dated 12 Nov. 1920, CO 691/35. The Colonial Office made an even more determined effort later in the year to press the colonial secretary to speak directly with Treasury officials in order to convince them of Tanganyika's special "political considerations" and why it deserved "exceptional treatment." See various minutes and correspondence attached to Byatt to CO, 2 Nov. 1921, CO 691/47. After several years of using this tactic, the Colonial Office finally had some modest success in 1925 when the Treasury reversed a decision to cut the medical budget in order to avoid "adverse" comment from the PMC. Treasury to CO, 12 March 1925, CO 691/81.
6 Minute by Bushe, 25 Jan. 1921, Guggisberg to CO dated 28 Dec. 1920, CO 742/1.
7 Clifford to CO, 13 Jan. 1921, CO 649/22.
8 Minute by Harding, 15 Jan. 1921 and draft CO telegram to Clifford, 15 Jan. 1921 in Clifford to CO dated 13 Jan. 1921, CO 649/22.
9 Copy of General Staff memorandum marked "secret" entitled "External Employment of Troops Raised in Mandated Territory" dated 22 Dec. 1920 and circulated to the Cabinet in Hankey to Hurst, 19 Dec. 1920, PRO, FO 371/5850.
10 Copy of Chetwood to Hankey dated 25 Jan. 1921 and results of an inter-departmental meeting presided over by Balfour on 3 Feb. 1921 in Cabinet to FO, 3 Feb. 1921, PRO, FO 371/5850. Also see Cabinet to FO, 4 July 1921, PRO, FO 371/7050.
11 Board of Trade to FO, 18 Aug. 1921, PRO, FO 371/7050.
12 Board of Trade to CO, 8 Aug. 1921, CO 649/23 and CO to FO, 13 Sept. 1921, PRO, FO 371/7052. Hurst agreed with the CO and remarked "let us wait till the case arises and then make a great fuss about the violation of the spirit of the Covenant etc." Minute by Hurst, 26 Oct. 1921, ibid.
13 Hankey to Curzon, 18 Aug. 1921, Curzon Papers, IOL, Mss. Eur. F 112/220(a).
14 Clifford to CO, 19 Jan. 1921, CO 649/22.
15 Minute by Harding, 5 May 1921, Clifford to CO dated 19 Jan. 1921, CO 649/22.
16 Minute by Fiddes, 6 June 1921, Clifford to CO dated 19 Jan. 1921, CIO 649/22.
17 Minute by Harding, 29 July 1921, Clifford to CO dated 19 Jan. 1921, CO 649/22.

18 Wood, along with a few fellow Conservatives and several religious leaders as well as members of the Labour Party, had signed a public memorandum entitled "Labour in Africa and the Principle of Trusteeship" in June 1920. It defended the mandatory principles and severely attacked the labor practices in Kenya and called for greater protection for Africans. See Robert G. Gregory, "Sidney Webb and East Africa: Labour's Experiment with the Doctrine of Native Paramouncy," *University of California Publications in History* (Berkeley, Calif., 1962), vol. LXXII, p. 30.

19 Draft note from CO to Clifford, 4 Aug. 1921, Clifford to CO dated 19 Jan. 1921, CO 649/22.

20 Ibid. Establishing a functioning system of Indirect Rule in Nigeria was often expensive and time consuming since, at least in theory, Native Authorities had to be trained to undertake responsibility for law and order, sanitation, and local development. Each one had its own tribunal and was required to carry out tax collection. Many N.A.s retained 50 percent of the court revenues and taxes and the funds were kept in a central Native Treasury which was under the supervision of a British district officer. For more, see Margery Perham, *Native Administration in Nigeria* (London, 1937).

21 For a discussion of Clifford's many difficulties with Lugard's legacy in Nigeria and Cameroon, see Harry A. Gailey, *Clifford: Imperial Proconsul* (London, 1982), pp. 113–52. Clifford's superiors in London were well aware of these difficulties and in 1921 Amery privately told Churchill that while Clifford was "the biggest man you have got," he was "inclined to root up everything his predecessor had done." Amery to Churchill, 2 June 1921, Churchill Papers, CC, 17/6.

22 For secondary studies of these problems, see Elizabeth M. Chilver, "Native Administration in the West Central Cameroons, 1902–1945" in Kenneth Robinson and Frederick Madden, eds., *Essays in Imperial Government presented to Margery Perham* (Oxford, 1963); David E. Gardinier, "The British in the Cameroons, 1919–1939" in Prosser Gifford and Wm. R. Louis, eds., *Britain and Germany in Africa: Imperial Rivalry and Colonial Rule* (1967) and Emmanuel Chiabi, "British Administration and Nationalism in the Southern Cameroons, 1914–1954" in Martin Njeuma, ed., *Introduction to the History of Cameroon: Nineteenth and Twentieth Centuries* (New York, 1989). For a useful memoir, see Sir Bryan Sharwood Smith, *Recollections of British Administration in the Cameroons and Northern Nigeria 1921–1957: 'But Always Friends'* (Durham, N.C., 1969).

23 The passage that Harding deleted from Clifford's draft report said that "it will not for many years be possible for my Government to secure to it [Cameroons Province] many of the material advantages which it enjoyed when it was a specially favoured portion [of] one of the principle German tropical possessions." See draft "Reports on British Spheres of the Cameroons" and minute by Harding, 10 April 1922 on Clifford to CO, 649/24.

24 This is not to say, however, that his views about the mandates system were always heeded. On one occasion, Hollis reported that he intended as acting-governor to produce a circular for all British officials in Tanganyika "encouraging" them to purchase British instead of American cars. Strachey, returning to "my old objection," insisted that the policy was in violation of the commercial equality clauses of the mandate. To complicate matters, Byatt strongly agreed with Strachey, but was on leave. The Colonial Office apparently wanted to dodge the entire issue and the papers with Strachey's

complaints were mysteriously "lost" for a year and a half. They somehow resurfaced long after Hollis had distributed his circular. See minutes by Strachey, 4 Jan. 1923 and 21 June 1924, Hollis to CO dated 14 July 1922, CO 691/56 and Byatt to CO, 19 Nov. 1923, CO 691/65.

25 See various minutes and correspondence in Byatt to CO, 8 Feb. 1919, CO 691/29.

26 Memorandum by Strachey originally entitled "Slavery in Tanganyika Territory" dated 19 Feb. 1921 in CO to CO, 19 Feb. 1921, CO 691/51 and memorandum entitled "Slavery in Tanganyika Territory. Memorandum 2" dated 28 Feb. 1921, CO to CO, 28 Feb. 1921, CO 691/52.

27 Ibid. For the text of Article 5, see Wright, *Mandates*, p. 613.

28 Strachey included this quotation in the text of his second memorandum, ibid.

29 Copy of CO to Byatt, 7 May 1921 in CO to CO, 28 Feb. 1921, CO 691/52.

30 Byatt to CO, 19 July 1921, CO 691/45.

31 Hollis to CO, 1 March 1922, CO 691/54.

32 Minute by Strachey, 25 April 1922, Hollis to CO dated 1 March 1921, CO 691/54.

33 Copy of CO to Hollis, 10 May 1922 in Hollis to CO, 1 March 1922, CO 691/54.

34 Hollis to CO, 12 July 1922, CO 691/56.

35 Minutes by Strachey, 16 Aug. 1922 and 30 Oct. 1922, Hollis to CO dated 12 July 1922, CO 691/56.

36 For the text of the mandate, see Wright, *Mandates*, p. 613. For Strachey's memo, see "Land Policy in Tanganyika" dated 3 Aug. 1921 in CO to CO, 3 Aug. 1921, CO 691/52.

37 Minute by Strachey, 5 Aug. 1921, CO 691/52.

38 Minute by Fiddes, 7 Aug. 1921, CO to CO dated 3 Aug. 1921, CO 691/52.

39 Byatt to CO, 15 March 1921, CO 691/43. Byatt made a very similar purchase the following year. See Byatt to CO, 28 Jan. 1921, CO 691/54.

40 Byatt to CO, 17 March 1921, CO 691/43.

41 Minute by Jeffries, 29 April 1921, Byatt to CO dated 17 March 1921, CO 691/43.

42 Minute by Read, 3 May 1921, Byatt to CO dated 17 March 1921, CO 691/43.

43 Byatt to CO, 16 June 1921, CO 691/45.

44 Minute by Fiddes, 29 July 1921, Byatt to CO dated 16 June 1921, CO 691/45.

45 For a discussion of Churchill and the East Africa debate during this period, see Gregory, "Sidney Webb and East Africa," pp. 13–33.

46 Wood to Churchill, 19 Aug. 1921, CO to CO dated 3 Aug. 1921, CO 691/52.

47 Churchill initial dated 25 Aug. 1921 and minute by Strachey, 29 Aug. 1921, CO to CO dated 3 Aug. 1921, CO 691/52.

48 Minute by Wood to Sir James E. Masterton-Smith (who replaced Fiddes as permanent under-secretary of state for the colonies), 6 July 1922 and copy of CO to Byatt, 18 Aug. 1922, CO to CO dated 1 July 1922, CO 691/60.

49 For autobiographical information on Colonel Wedgewood and his views on Africa, see Gupta, *Imperialism and the British Labour Movement*, pp. 34–5, 54–5, and 411.

50 CO "explanatory memo" dated 1 July 1922 included in CO to CO, 1 July 1922, CO 691/60.

51 Ibid. and minute by Read to Wood, 5 July 1922, CO to CO dated 1 July 1922, CO 691/60.

52 Minute by Risley, 5 July 1922; Minute by Masterton-Smith, 6 July 1922 and initial by Churchill, 9 July 1922, CO to CO dated 1 July 1922, CO 691/60.
53 The most important alteration to the draft was the inclusion of a clause that gave the governor the power, in "exceptional cases," to grant a right of occupancy of over 5,000 acres to a non-African. Strachey called the change "just a shadow of an indication of a 'dangerous door.'" In practice, the Tanganyika government never exercised this power. Minute by Strachey, 30 April 1923, Byatt to CO dated 5 March 1923, CO 691/62.
54 Memorandum by C. M. Clark dated 5 Jan. 1925 in Scott to CO, 31 Jan. 1925, CO 691/76.
55 The role of slaves in the history of German East Africa under German and British rule has yet to be thoroughly examined. For a brief discussion of the decline of slavery during this period, see Illife, *A Modern History of Tanganyika*, pp. 131–2, 247 and 263. For the ealier period, see Jonathon Glassman, *Feasts and Riot: Revelry, Rebellion, and Popular Consciousness on the Swahili Coast, 1850–1888* (London, 1995).
56 For a more detailed discussion of slavery in the territory, see Thaddeus Sunseri, "Slave Ransoming in German East Africa, 1885–1922," *International Journal of African Historical Studies* 26 (1993): 481–511. On the topic of slavery in Africa in general, see Suzanne Miers and Richard Roberts, eds., *The End of Slavery in Africa* (Madison, 1988); Frederick Cooper, *From Slaves to Squatters: Plantation Labor and Agriculture in Zanzibar and Coastal Kenya 1890–1925* (Nairobi, 1981) and Paul E. Lovejoy and Jan. S. Hogendorn, *Slow Death for Slavery: The Course of Abolition in Northern Nigeria, 1897–1936* (Cambridge, 1993).
57 Sunseri, "Slave Ransoming in German East Africa, 1885–1922," p. 507.
58 Minute by Strachey, 5 Aug. 1921, CO to CO dated 3 Aug. 1921, CO 691/52. Also see, Byatt to CO, 10 Jan. 1923, CO 691/62.
59 Illife, *A Modern History of Tanganyika*, p. 303.
60 Stamfordham to Ormsby-Gore in CO to CO dated 4 Aug. 1925, CO 691/82.
61 Minute by Strachey, 27 July 1925, CO to CO dated 4 Aug. 1925, CO 691/82.
62 Copy of Ormsby-Gore to Stamfordham, 4 Aug. 1925, CO to CO dated 4 Aug. 1925, CO 691/82.
63 Copy of Byatt to Bishop of Mombasa dated 10 Oct. 1921 in Byatt to CO, 10 Oct. 1921, CO 691/47.
64 Copy of report by Rivers-Smith dated 12 Sept. 1921 in Byatt to CO, 4 Nov. 1921, CO 691/47. Also see Byatt to CO, 22 Nov. 1922, CO 691/58; Byatt to CO, 7 Nov. 1923, CO 691/64 and Cameron to CO, 21 Aug. 1925, CO 691/78.
65 Memorandum by Byatt dated 10 May 1922; Memorandum by Strachey dated 6 May 1922 and minute by Sir James Stevenson (Colonial Office business advisor) concerning meeting with Lord Hindlip of the British East Africa Corporation, 23 May 1922, Hindlip to CO dated 22 May 1922, CO 691/61.
66 For example, Guggisberg to CO, 11 April 1922, CO 724/2; Hollis to CO, 10 June 1922, CO 691/55; Byatt to CO, 10 May 1923, CO 691/63; Cameron to CO, 4 April 1924, CO 649/28 and J. C. Maxwell (acting governor of Gold Coast) to CO, 5 April 1924, CO 724/3. After leaving the PMC, Ormsby-Gore himself often reviewed and changed the draft reports. See minute by Ormsby-Gore, 18 Dec. 1922, Clifford to CO dated 5 Aug. 1922, CO 649/24.
67 CO memorandum entitled "Tanganyika Territory – Proposed Declaration of a Protectorate" dated 31 July 1922 in CO to CO, 31 July 1922, CO 691/60.
68 Minute by Strachey, 31 July 1922, CO to CO dated 31 July 1922, CO 691/60.

69 See above, chapter 3, footnote 70. Also see Jean Rumuia, *Le Rwanda sous le régime du mandat Belge, 1916–1931* (Paris, 1992).
70 For the official minutes and report of the second session of the Permanent Mandates Commission, LN Document C.548.M.330.1922.VI, pp. 69–72, annex 9, and LN Document C.550.M.332.1922.VI, pp. 5–6. For a copy, see CO to CO, 19 Aug. and 9 Sept. 1922, CO 691/60 and FO to CO, 12 Sept. 1922, CO 691/59.
71 Minute by Downie, 14 Sept. 1922, FO to CO dated 12 Sept. 1922, CO 691/59.
72 Copy of Rapport sur l'administration Belge du Ruanda et du l'Urundi pendant l'année 1921; Minute by Mächtig, 7 Nov. 1922 and minute by Strachey, 8 Nov. 1922, FO to CO dated 6 Nov. 1922, CO 691/59.
73 Copy of Pol de Tellier to FO in FO to CO, 6 Feb. 1923, CO 691/66.
74 Minute by Strachey, 15 Feb. 1923, FO to CO dated 6 Feb. 1923, CO 691/66.
75 Minutes by Read and Masterton-Smith (permanent under-secretary of state for the colonies), 17 Feb. 1923, FO to CO dated 6 Feb. 1923, CO 691/66.
76 Minute by Ormsby-Gore to the Duke of Devonshire, 19 Feb. 1923, FO to CO dated 6 Feb. 1923, CO 691/66.
77 Minute by the Duke of Devonshire, 20 Feb. 1923, FO to CO dated 6 Feb. 1923, CO 691/66.
78 For a record of an early conversation between the Belgian ambassador and Ormsby-Gore, see CO to CO, 11 April 1923, CO 691/67.
79 Lugard to CO, 15 April 1923, CO 691/68.
80 Minute by Strachey, 19 April 1923 and minute by Ormsby-Gore, 23 April 1923, Lugard to CO dated 15 April 1923, CO 691/68.
81 Minute by Strachey, 11 May 1923, Lugard to CO dated 14 April 1923, CO 691/68.
82 Copy of Belgian ambassador to FO in FO to CO, 2 May 1923, CO 691/66.
83 For copies of the various drafts of the request to the Council, delivered to the League on 3 Aug. 1923, see copy of FO to Belgian ambassador in FO to CO, 30 June and 11 July 1923, CO 691/66; Copy of FO to League in FO to CO, 28 July 1923, CO 691/66 and copy of League to FO dated 16 Aug. 1923 in FO to CO, 27 Aug. 1923, CO 691/66.
84 Rappard to Ormsby-Gore, 20 July 1923, CO 691/68.
85 Lugard to Ormsby-Gore, 22 July 1923 attached to Rappard to Ormsby-Gore dated 20 July 1923, CO 691/68.
86 Minutes of the Third Session of the Permanent Mandates Commission, LN Document A.19.1923.VI, p. 138 and LN Document A.19.(annexes).1923.VI, number 12. Also see Wright, *Mandates*, p. 120.
87 Copy of George Grahame (British ambassador in Brussels) to FO in FO to CO, 8 Sept. 1923, CO 691/66.
88 Copy of *Correspondence regarding the modification of the Boundary between British Mandated Territory and Belgian Mandated Territory in East Africa*, Cmd. 1974 included in FO to CO, 23 Oct. 1923, CO 691/66.
89 Extract from the minutes of the 26th Session of the Council of the League of Nations included in FO to CO, 10 Sept. 1923, CO 691/66.
90 Byatt to CO, 22 Feb. 1924, CO 691/69 and John Scott (acting governor of Tanganyika), 14 Aug. 1924, CO 691/71. For the estimated population and geography figures, see Wright, *Mandates*, pp. 628–30; Hall, *Mandates, Dependencies and Trusteeship*, annex II and George Louis Beer, *African Questions at the Paris Peace Conference* (New York, 1923), p. 66. Also see, Rumuia, *Le Rwanda sous le régime du mandat Belge*, pp. 87–129.

91 Belgian colonial officials established an administrative union between the Belgian Congo and the mandated territory in 1925. The German government angrily protested against the move, but as Germany was not yet a member of the League of Nations, "had no right to intervene in the question." See copy of Belgian ambassador to FO in FO to CO, 22 April 1925, CO 691/81.

92 Rumuia, *Le Rwanda sous le régime du mandat Belge*, pp. 145–57. For an older general survey of Belgian colonialism, see L. H. Gann, "Belgian Administration in the Congo: An Overview" in L. H. Gann and Peter Duignan, ed., *African Proconsuls*, pp. 367–73. Also see A. A. J. Van Bilsen, *Vers l'indépendence du Congo et du Ruanda-Urundi* (Brussels, 1958); George Martelli, *Leopold to Lumumba: A History of the Belgian Congo, 1877–1960* (London, 1962) and Robert Harms, "The End of Red Rubber: A Reassessment," *Journal of African History* 16 (1975): 73–88.

93 For examples, see Rappard to E. J. Harding, 8 Dec. 1922, CO 691/61; Rappard to Ormsby-Gore, 18 Dec. 1922, CO 649/25; Copy of Ormsby-Gore to Rappard, 5 Jan. 1923, Lugard Papers, RH, 122/2; Lugard to CO dated 27 Dec. 1923 included in Phillericle to CO, 27 Sept. 1923, CO 724/2.

94 Minute by Strachey, 14 Jan. 1924, Byatt to CO dated 27 Nov. 1923, CO 691/65 and minute by Williams, 31 July 1924, FO to CO dated 28 July 1924, CO 691/74.

95 CO to Lugard, 12 March 1923, Lugard Papers, RH, 140/1. Lugard kept a large file on German colonial propaganda, some of it supplied by the Colonial Office. See Lugard Papers, RH, 140/2.

96 Copy of "Record of an Interview with Dr. Julius Ruppel" dated 18 Sept. 1923 and copies of Lugard to FO, 12 April and 6 May 1924, Lugard Papers, RH, 140/2.

97 Perham, *Lugard*, II, pp. 657–62. Other members of the advisory commission included Major Hans Vischer (director of education in Nigeria during Lugard's governor-generalship), Dr J. H. Oldham (secretary of the World Missionary Conference), and Strachey. See extracts from the minutes of the commission, 17 Dec. 1925, Cameron to CO dated 21 Aug. 1925, CO 691/78.

98 Copy of Lugard to CO dated 15 Sept. 1923 in CO to CO, 11 Oct. 1923, CO 649/27 and Lugard to CO, 20 April 1924, CO 649/29.

99 Minute by Holmes (clerk in West Africa Department), 29 May 1924, CO to CO dated ? May 1924, CO 649/29.

100 Minutes by Flood, Ellis, and Reed, 29–31 May 1924, CO to CO dated ? May 1924, CO 649/29.

101 Lugard to Chamberlain, 29 Nov. 1924, Chamberlain Papers, PRO, FO 800/256, p. 263.

102 Chamberlain to Lugard marked "strictly confidential," 1 Dec. 1924, Lugard Papers, RH, 119/2.

103 Byatt to CO, 26 March 1923, CO 691/62.

104 Minute by Ormsby-Gore, 7 May 1923, Byatt to CO dated 26 March 1923, CO 691/62.

105 Byatt to CO, 27 April 1923, CO 691/62 and Byatt to CO, 10 May 1923, CO 691/63.

106 Minute by Mächtig, 2 June 1923, Byatt to CO dated 10 May 1923, CO 691/63.

107 Minutes by Strachey and Read, 4 June 1923, Byatt to CO dated 10 May 1923, CO 619/63.

108 Conference of Missionary Societies to CO, 22 Oct. 1923, and draft CO to Conference of Missionary Societies, 1 Nov. 1923, CO 691/68.

109 Minutes of the Third Session of the Permanent Mandates Commission, LN Document, A.19.1923.VI, pp. 141–2.

110 Report of the Third Session of the Permanent Mandates Commission, LN Document, A.46.1923.VI, p. 4 and 10.

111 Copy CO to Byatt dated 16 Jan. 1924 included in Byatt to CO, 15 Nov. 1923, CO 691/65 and CO to CO, 21 Jan. 1924, CO 691/75.

112 For the growth of missions during this period, see Illife, *A Modern History of Tanganyika*, pp. 358–70 and Marica Wright, *German Missions in Tanganyika 1890–1941* (Oxford, 1971), pp. 137–58. Also see, Carl J. Hellberg, *Missions on a Colonial Frontier West of Lake Victoria: Evangelical Missions in North-West Tanganyika to 1932* (Lund, 1965); Gordon Hewett, *The Problems of Success: A History of the Church Missionary Society 1910–1942* (London, 1971) and T. O. Ranger, *The African Churches of Tanzania* (Nairobi, n.d.). In the annual report to the League for 1925, the government of Tanganyika claimed that the "rivalry between societies of different denominations" was decreasing, but "in one district interdenominational hostility and mutual recrimination have sorely tried the tact and patience of the Administrative Officers." *Report to the Council of the League of Nations on the Administration of the Tanganyika Territory*, 1925, p. 28.

113 Cameron to CO, 21 Aug. 1924, CO 691/78; Cameron to CO, 22 Sept. 1925, CO 691/79; Cameron to CO, 9 Nov. 1925, CO 691/80 and minute by J. E. W. Flood (clerk in Colonial Office), 15 April 1935, Sir Harold MacMichael (governor of Tanganyika) to CO dated 22 Nov. 1934, CO 691/138.

114 For examples, see minute by Ellis, 13 Feb. 1923, Clifford to CO dated 14 Sept. 1922, CO 649/24; Draft "Order of the King in Council providing for the administration of the British Cameroons" included in Clifford to CO, 28 Jan. 1923, CO 649/27; Risley's "Notes on Revised Order in Council for Togoland" dated 23 June 1923 in Maxwell to CO, 14 May 1923, CO 724/2; Privy Council Office to CO, 15 Oct. 1923, CO 724/2 and Guggisberg to CO, 20 Feb. 1924, CO 724/3. Also see *Report on the Administration under Mandate of British Cameroons*, 1924, p. 3.

115 The PMC widened this latitude during its third session by insisting that, despite the wording of Article 9 of the mandate texts for Togo and Cameroon that allowed the mandatory power to administer the mandate "as an integral part of his territory," this did not mean that the mandates could "become an integral part" of the neighboring colonial possession. Further, the PMC insisted that Britain produce the estimated expenditures of the two mandates even though they did not have separate budgets. See minute by Lloyd, 12 Feb. 1924, CO to CO dated ? Jan. 1924, CO 649/29 and Report of the Third Session of the Permanent Mandates Commission, LN Document A.46.1923.VI, pp. 11–13.

116 Minute by Ormsby-Gore, 12 June 1923, Cameron to CO dated 8 May 1923, CO 649/27.

117 Minute by Ormsby-Gore, 12 June 1923, Byatt to CO dated 8 June 1923, CO 691/63.

118 Byatt to CO, 26 June 1923, CO 691/63. Also see Illife, *A Modern History of Tanganyika*, pp. 301–11.

119 Minute by Ellis, 11 Sept. 1923, Maxwell to CO dated 17 April 1923, CO 724/2.

120 Minute by Ormsby-Gore, 27 Sept. 1923 and minute by Strachey, 9 Oct. 1923, Maxwell to CO dated 17 April 1923, CO 724/2. Also see various minutes contained in FO to CO, ? Jan. 1924, CO 649/28.

121 Copies of CO to Clifford and Guggisberg, 22 Jan. 1924, FO to CO dated ?

Jan. 1924, CO 649/28 and copy of CO to Byatt, 8 Feb. 1924, CO to CO dated 21 Jan. 1924, CO 691/75.

122 Report of the Third Session of the Permanent Mandates Commission, LN Document A.46.1923.VI, p. 4.

123 Before the PMC submitted their final reports to the Council, the mandatory powers had the right to respond by attaching specific "observations" to PMC conclusions. See Ormsby-Gore's draft "special observation no. 5" entitled "Regarding military recruitment of natives in mandated territory" contained in CO to CO, ? Sept. 1923, CO 649/27. Also see FO to CO, 6 Sept. 1923, CO 649/27.

124 Copy of minute by Mächtig, 4 Sept. 1923, CO to CO dated 11 Sept. 1923, CO 691/67.

125 Copy of CO to FO, 7 Sept. 1923 in FO to CO dated 6 Sept. 1923, CO 649/27.

126 Copy of Mächtig to M.E. Antrobus, 21 Sept. 1923 contained in FO to CO, 13 Sept. 1923, CO 649/27.

127 M. E. Antrobus to Mächtig, 25 Sept. 1923 included in FO to CO dated 27 Sept. 1923, CO 649/27.

128 Minute by Lloyd, 12 Feb. 1924, CO to CO dated ? Jan. 1924, CO 649/29.

129 For more on the general imperial perceptions of the Labour Party during this period, see Gupta, *Imperialism and the British Labour Movement, 1914–1964*, pp. 24–92, 397, 410 and Lowe, *Anticolonialism in British Politics*, pp. 1–50. Also see Feuer, *Imperialism and the Anti-Imperialist Mind*, *passim* and Paul B. Rich, *Race and Empire in British Politics* (Cambridge, 1986).

130 "Note on Tanganyika Territory" dated 30 Jan. 1924, CO to CO, 30 Jan. 1924, CO 691/75. In a postscript, Strachey noted that an "interesting and very readable article on the administration of tropical African countries, by E. D. Morel, appeared in the 'Contemporary Review' of last September, entitled 'Two African Policies.' The library of this office can produce it if required."

131 Minute by Strachey, 5 April 1924, Byatt to CO dated 26 Feb. 1924, CO 691/69.

132 Minute by Harding, 26 April 1924, CO to CO dated ? Jan. 1924, CO 649/29.

133 Minute by Flood, 12 May 1924, CO to CO dated ? Jan. 1924, CO 649/29.

134 CO to Lugard, 20 May 1924, Lugard Papers, RH, 122/4.

135 Minute by Mampbell, 29 May 1924, CO to FO dated 14 May 1924, PRO, FO 371/10566.

136 Ibid.

137 Minute by Crowe, 29 May 1924, CO to FO dated 14 May 1924, PRO, FO 371/10566.

138 Minute by MacDonald, 30 May 1924, CO to FO dated 14 may 1924, PRO, FO 371/10566.

139 Minute by Butler, 2 June 1924, CO to FO dated 14 May 1924, PRO, FO 371/10566.

140 Minute by Crowe to Ponsonby, 3 June 1924, CO to FO dated 14 May 1924, PRO, FO 371/10566.

141 Minute by Ponsonby, 4 June 1924, CO to FO dated 14 May 1924, PRO, FO 371/10566.

142 Copy of FO to League, 4 June 1924 and Rappard to FO, 6 June 1924 included in CO to FO dated 14 May 1924, PRO, FO 371/10566.

143 Minutes of the Fourth Session of the Permanent Mandates Commission, held from 24 June to 8 July, LN Document A.13.1924.VI, p. 13 and Annexes to

the Fourth Session, LN Document A.13.1924.VI.II, p. 179 and 182–3.

144 Minute by Harding, 6 June 1924, FO to CO dated 5 June 1924, CO 649/28.

145 Minute by Strachey, 10 July 1924, FO to CO dated 5 June 1924, CO 649/28.

146 Copy of Admiralty to FO, 25 Oct. 1924 and draft response from FO to Admiralty in FO to CO, 1 Nov. 1924, CO 649/28.

147 Admiralty to FO, 8 Jan. 1925, PRO, FO 371/11062.

148 Much of the scholarly literature concerning the history of the King's African Rifles and the West African Frontier Force is either dated or incomplete. Little systematic work has been done on recruitment policy, the rank and file, and the impact of the colonial army on colonial society. The best recent study, while concentrating largely on the post-1945 period, is Anthony Clayton and David Killingray, *Khaki and Blue: Military and Police in British Colonial Africa* (Athens, Ohio, 1989). Also see Hubert Moyse-Bartlett, *The King's African Rifles: A Study in the Military History of East and Central Africa, 1890–1945* (Aldershot, 1956); A. H. W. Haywood, *The History of the Royal West African Frontier Force* (Aldershot, 1964) and A. H. M. Kirk-Greene, "A Preliminary Note on New Sources for Nigerian Military History," *Journal of the Historical Society of Nigeria* 3 (1964).

149 *Report on the Administration Under Mandate of the Tanganyika Territory*, 1924, pp. 31–2.

150 In 1933, the CID debated the 1924 policy and decided that it did not prevent Tanganyika from contributing to military actions outside the possession if they were clearly in the ultimate defense of the mandated territory's security. Committee of Imperial Defense, Oversea Defense Committee, 2 March 1933, CAB 7/12.

151 Cited in Clayton and Killingray, *Khaki and Blue*, p. 250.

152 Ibid., p. 226.

153 In the annual report for 1924 to the League, the British government stated that "it has been decided that gun porters and stretcher bearers for the 2nd Battalion King's African Rifles, which is recruited in Nyasaland and is liable for service outside the Territory, should be obtained from Nyasaland and not locally as has been hitherto the practice." *Report on the Administration Under Mandate of the Tanganyika Territory*, 1924, pp. 31–2. Also see Buell, *The Native Problem in Africa*, pp. 519–20. Clayton and Killingray accept the claim that the 2nd K.A.R. recruited only in Nyasaland while serving in Tanganyika. *Khaki and Blue*, p. 200.

154 For more on German recruitment before and during the war, see Paul von Letow-Vorbeck, *My Reminiscences of East Africa*, English translation, 2nd edition (London, n.d.); Richard Meinertzhagen, *Army Diary, 1899–1926* (Edinburgh, 1960); Farwell, *The Great War in Africa*, pp. 284–92 and Illife, *A Modern History of Tanganyika*, pp. 240–7.

155 Cited in Clayton and Killingray, *Khaki and Blue*, pp. 223–4, 226, and 250.

156 The British army figure includes both the Second and Sixth battalions of the KAR, as every battalion was comprised of approximately nine hundred men. See note by Strachey entitled "Note on Tanganyika Territory" dated 30 Jan. 1924, CO to CO, 30 Jan. 1924, CO 691/75. Also see, Geographical Section of Naval Intelligence, *Handbook of German East Africa* (London, 1921), pp. 197–211 and Farwell, *The Great War in Africa*, p. 109.

157 In 1914, the Germans maintained a police force of approximately 2,140, bringing the total number of Africans in the armed service of the colonial state to more than 4,600. This figure does not include the 600 or so support personnel, the 2,000 reserves, and the roughly 4,000 irregulars. As late as

1938, the total number of Africans in the British army and police never had surpassed 3,000. Ibid.; *Report to the Council of the League of Nations on the Administration of the Tanganyika Territory*, 1938, pp. 179–87 and B. T. G. Chidzero, *Tanganyika and International Trusteeship* (London, 1961), p. 129.

158 Gilchrist Alexander, *Tanganyika Memories: A Judge in the Red Kanzu* (London, 1936), pp. 43–4 and *passim.*

159 The Nigerian government reported to the League that it had transferred one double company of the Nigerian Regiment out of Bamenda back into Nigeria in late 1924. *Report on the Administration under Mandate of the British Cameroons*, 1924, p. 31.

160 Sir Bryan Sharwood Smith, *Recollections of British Administration in the Cameroons and Northern Nigeria 1921–1957: 'But Always Friends'* (Durham, N.C., 1969), p. 27.

161 Ibid., p. 34.

162 The best sources on Cameron's life and career remain Sir Donald Cameron, *My Tanganyika Service and Some Nigeria* (London, 1939) and Harry A. Gailey, *Sir Donald Cameron: Colonial Governor* (Stanford, Calif., 1974).

163 For examples, see Cameron to CO, 8 May 1923, CO 649/27; Cameron to CO, 24 March 1924, CO 649/28 and Cameron to CO, 5 April 1924, CO 649/28.

164 Gailey, *Sir Donald Cameron*, p. 31.

165 Byatt to CO, 27 March 1924, CO 691/69 as well as Cameron memorandum entitled "Native Administration" and dated 16 July 1925 included in Cameron to CO, 1 Aug. 1925, CO 691/82 and Cameron to CO, 29 Sept. 1925, CO 691/79.

166 Cameron, *My Tanganyika Service*, p. 86.

167 Grigg, who had served as Lloyd George's private secretary from 1920 to 1922 and then as Liberal MP from 1922 to 1925, shared many of Amery's strong imperialist sentiments. He served as governor of Kenya from 1925 to 1930. For some of Grigg's views during this period, see E. W. M. Grigg, *The Greatest Experiment in History* (New Haven, 1924).

168 Emphasis in original. Cameron to Lugard, 4 June 1925, Lugard Papers, RH, 9/1.

169 Cameron to Lugard, 22 Oct. 1924, Lugard Papers, RH, 9/1.

170 Cameron to Lugard, 8 Nov. 1924, Lugard Papers, RH, 9/1. There was nothing sinister in the Colonial Office's policy of sending only a few copies of League papers to the mandated territories. Geneva had complained in 1923 that it was already printing over one hundred copies of each annual report at its own expense, but "it will evidently be hardly possible to apply for further copies free of charge." In order to control costs, London decided to create a special Office print of relevant extracts and then ask the individual governors to make copies available "to the officers principally concerned with the preparation of the Annual Report in order that they may gain an insight into the scope [and] working of the Permanent Mandates Commission." See minute by Harding, 26 April 1923, FO to CO dated 19 March 1923, CO 649/27 and copy of CO to Graeme Thomson (governor of Nigeria), 30 Nov. 1925, CO to CO dated ? Sept. 1925, CO 649/30.

171 Ibid.

172 Cameron won this fight despite active resistance in the Colonial Office. Mächtig, Strachey, and others thought adopting a postage stamp bearing the King's head would draw criticism from the PMC, but relented. See minute by

Mächtig, 9 Dec. 1925; Minute by Strachey, 11 Dec. 1925; Minute by Amery, 21 Dec. 1925 and copy of CO to Cameron, 23 Jan. 1926 in Cameron to CO dated 27 Oct. 1925, CO 691/80.

173 For general studies of Anglo-Indian relations, the imperial economy, and Asians in East Africa, see Robert G. Gregory, *India and East Africa 1890–1939* (Oxford, 1971); M. E. Chamberlain, *Britain and India: The Interaction of Two Peoples* (Hamden, Conn., 1974); G. Martin, "The Influence of Racial Attitudes on British Policy towards India during the First World War," *Journal of Imperial and Commonwealth History* 14 (1986): 91–113 and B. R. Tomlinson, *The Economy of Modern India, 1860–1970* (Cambridge, 1993).

174 Indians Overseas Association to CO, 2 Dec. 1921, CO 691/52.

175 Indians Overseas Association to CO, 31 Jan. 1922 and copy of CO to Byatt, 2 Feb. 1922, CO 691/61. The Colonial Office was furious when it discovered this overt racism in Tanganyika. It sent a curt telegram to Byatt stating that it had "received complaints as to differential treatment of Indians on railways. These should not exist in view of mandate."

176 For more on this incident, see Illife, *A Modern History of Tanganyika*, pp. 264–5.

177 Strachey memorandum entitled "Petitions to League of Nations from Inhabitants of Mandated Territories" dated 18 April 1924; Minutes by Davis and Read, 23 April 1924, CO to CO dated 18 April 1923, CO 691/67.

178 Minute by Ormsby-Gore, 24 April 1923, CO to CO dated 18 April 1923, CO 691/67.

179 India Office to CO, 20 Feb. and 1 Aug. 1925, CO 691/81 and minute by Strachey, 20 July 1927, John Scott (chief secretary and acting governor of Tanganyika) to CO dated 20 July 1927, CO 691/92.

180 CO copy of Arusha Conservative Association to Baldwin, 11 Nov. 1924, CO 691/75.

181 Minute by Strachey, 2 Jan. 1925, CO copy of Arusha Conservative Association to Baldwin dated 11 Nov. 1924, CO 691/75.

182 Minute by Downie, 2 Jan. 1924, CO copy of Arusha Conservative Association to Baldwin dated 11 Nov. 1924, CO 691/75.

183 Amery made the speech at the East Africa dinner on 25 June 1925 and it was reported in *The Times* the following day. See various minutes and correspondence in CO to CO, 22 July 1925, CO 691/82.

184 Clifford to Gowers, 30 Nov. 1924, Gowers Papers, RH, Mss. Afr. s. 1149.

Chapter 6 The French Mandates between Theory and Practice, 1921–1925

1 For a discussion of Diagne's life, see G. Wesley Johnson, "The Impact of the Senegalese Elite upon the French, 1900–1940" in Johnson, ed., *Double Impact*, pp. 159–66.

2 Diagne to Sarraut, 9 Nov. 1920, ANSOM, AP, 608/1.

3 Sarraut to MAE, 12 Nov. 1920, AE, Série K. Afrique: 1918–1940, 97/202–209.

4 For a generally sympathetic biography of Bonnecarrère, see Silvi K. d'Almeida and Seti Y. G. Gbedemah, *Le Gouverneur Bonnecarrère au Togo* (Lomé, 1982).

5 Bonnecarrère to MC, 20 Nov. 1922, ANSOM, AP, 608/1.

6 Decree dated 22 Nov. 1922 and Instructions to all "commandates de cercle" dated 13 March 1923 reproduced in *Rapport Annuel du Gouvernment*

Français sur l'administration sous mandat des territoires du Cameroun pour l'année 1923.

7 At least one sympathetic scholar called these reforms "a definite advancement." See Cornevin, *Le Togo*, pp. 253–6.

8 For biographical information, see Académie des sciences d'outre-mer, *Hommes et destins: dictionnaire biographique d'outre-mer* (Paris, 1975–), vol. III.

9 For more on this meeting at Tours and its implications for French colonialism, see Bouche, *Histoire de la colonisation française*, II, pp. 296–8 and Jacob Moneta, *La Politique du parti communiste français et la question coloniale (1920–1963)* (Paris, 1971).

10 Augagneur to MC, 14 Dec. 1920, ANSOM, SG: Togo-Cam, 30/258.

11 Copy of MC to Augagneur, 26 Jan. 1921, ANSOM, SG: Togo-Cam, 30/258.

12 Sarraut eventually produced his sweeping plans in book form in 1923, one year after Lugard's *Dual Mandate*. See Albert Sarraut, *La mise en valeur des colonies françaises* (Paris, 1923).

13 For the political activities of the groups after the war, see Persell, *The French Colonial Lobby*, pp. 140–4.

14 French officials understood before 1921 that, according to the Hague conventions and recognized international law, they had to maintain provisional administrations in the former German colonies until Germany formally renounced its sovereignty and the League ratified France's legal right to administer them. For examples, see Clozel to MC, 10 May 1916, ANSOM, SG: Togo-Cam, 6/63; Angoulvant to MC, 23 May 1919, ANSOM, SG: Togo-Cam, 1/1; MC to Angoulvant, 2 Aug. 1919, ANSOM, SG: Togo-Cam, 6/64; Copy of MC to MAE, 4 May 1920, ANSOM, SG: Togo-Cam, 6/64 and note entitled "Note au sujet des Mandats B" dated 31 Jan. 1921, AE, Série Internationale, 600/42–46.

15 Sarraut, *Mise en valeur*, pp. 340 and 579–96.

16 Copies of telegrams from MC to Augagneur, 5 March 1921 and MC to Carde, 7 March 1921, ANSOM, SG: Togo-Cam, 33/300.

17 "Décret déterminant les attributions et pouvoirs du commissaire de la République au Cameroun," 23 March 1921, ANSOM, SG: Togo-Cam, 33/300. Paris also issued an identical decree for Togo at the same time. See *Journal Officiel de la République Française*, 25 Aug. 1921, pp. 156–7.

18 *Le Temps*, 25 March 1921.

19 Sarraut, *Mise en valeur*, pp. 408–13 and 441–61. The "Sarraut Bill" did not include an estimate of the total cost, but was generally assumed to be between 3.5 and 4 billion francs. France's serious economic and political troubles during this period, however, prevented the bill from ever being seriously debated before the government fell and both Sarraut and the Bloc National were replaced in the elections of 11 May 1924 by an alliance of radicals and socialists. For more, see Andrew and Kanya-Forstner, *France Overseas*, pp. 210–12 and 226–7.

20 Minute by Walter Devonshire Ellis (assistant-secretary), 13 April 1921, FO to CO dated 1 April 1921, CO 649/23.

21 For a discussion of the French colonial service and the high turnover rates during this period, see William B. Cohen, *Rulers of Empire: The French Colonial Service in Africa* (Stanford, 1971).

22 There is no modern comprehensive history of the organization of the Colonial Ministry, but for general descriptions see Jean Favier, *Les archives nationales, section outre-mer: état général des fonds* (Paris, 1980), pp. 14 and 438–9;

Jean Martin, *Lexique de la colonisation française* (Paris, 1988), pp. 259–60; Persell, *The French Colonial Lobby*, pp. 75–83; Andrew and Kanya-Forstner, *France Overseas*, pp. 19–22 and Cohen, *Rulers of Empire*, pp. 21, 58–9, 134–7 and 160–1.

23 Union coloniale française to MC, 13 Sept. 1921, ANSOM, AP, 1051.

24 Union coloniale to MAE, 18 Dec. 1922, AE, Série Société des Nations, 620/245–244; MAE to Union coloniale, 14 Jan. 1923, AE, Série Société des Nations, 621/1–3; Union coloniale to MAE, 13 Feb. 1923, AE, Série Société des Nations, 621/23 and MAE to Union coloniale, 17 March 1923, AE, Série Société des Nations, 621/24–25.

25 Bonnecarrère to MC, 17 Oct. 1922, ANSOM, AP, 605/1.

26 Copy of telegram from MC to Bonnecarrère, 15 Nov. 1922, ANSOM, AP, 605/1.

27 Marine Marchand to MC, 18 April 1921 and draft response by Duchêne, 28 May 1921, ANSOM, SG: Togo-Cam, 29/249.

28 MC to Carde, 28 March 1921, ANSOM, SG: Togo-Cam, 29/248.

29 MC to MAE, 25 July 1921, AE, Série Société des Nations, 620/145 and MC to MAE, 5 July 1921, AE, Série Afrique: 1918–1940, 100/128–129.

30 AE to le Ministre de la Guerre, 16 June 1921, AE, Société des Nations, 620/146.

31 Copies of MC to Bonnecarrère and Carde, 26 Jan. 1921, ANSOM, SG: Togo-Cam, 25/226.

32 Draft decree, 2 Dec. 1922, ANSOM, AP, 610/2; *Journal Officiel du Territoire du Togo placé sous le mandat de la France*, 1 Jan. 1923; Bonnecarrère to MC, 7 Dec. 1925 and report by Bonnecarrère, 9 Dec. 1925, ANSOM, AP, 610/2.

33 Order dated 3 July 1922 and circular dated 4 July 1922, *Rapport Annuel du Gouvernment Français sur l'administration sous mandat des territoire du Togo pour l'année 1922*, pp. 85 and 176. Order dated 1 July 1921, *Rapport Annuel du Gouvernment Français sur l'administration sous mandat du territoire du Cameroun pour l'année 1921*, p. 84 and order dated 7 Sept. 1925, *Rapport Annuel du Gouvernment Français sur l'administration sous mandat du territoire du Cameroun pour l'année 1925*, p. 141.

34 For the standard discussions of these doctrines, see Henri Brunschwig, *Mythes et réalités de l'impérialisme colonial français 1870–1914* (Paris, 1960) and Raymond F. Betts, *Assimilation and Association in French Colonial Theory, 1890–1914* (New York, 1961).

35 For a contemporary study of assimilating African children through the doctrine of "association," see W. Bryant Mumford, *Africans Learn to Be French* (London, 1936).

36 For the various official papers concerning this sub-committee, see *National Status of the Inhabitants of the Territories Under B and C Mandates*, LN Document C.546.1922.VI. Also see copy of Gout to MC, 12 Nov. 1921, AE, Série Société des Nations, 619/69.

37 In late October, representatives from the Colonial Office and Foreign Office met to prepare for the arrival of the sub-committee which took place in late November. See FO memorandum, 8 Nov. 1921, PRO, FO 371/7053 and minute by Hurst, 23 Nov. 1921, Cabinet to FO dated 10 Nov. 1921, PRO, FO 371/7053.

38 Minutes of "Reunion Interministerielle pour l'Etude de la Nationality des Habitants des Territoires sous Mandat," 22 Nov. 1921, AE, Série Société des Nations, 619/71–76.

39 Note by Gout, 24 Dec. 1921, AE, Société des Nations, 619/78.

40 Minute by Hurst, 23 Nov. 1921, Cabinet to FO dated 10 Nov. 1921, PRO, FO 371/7053.

41 Note by Gout, 5 May 1922, AE, Série Société des Nations, 555/5; MAE to MC, 20 May 1922, AE, Série Société des Nations 555/5; Copy of League to Cabinet in Cabinet to CO, 5 Sept. 1922, CO 691/60; and copy of MAE to MC, 2 May 1923, AE, Série Société des Nations, 619/101–103.

42 MC to MAE, 23 May 1923, AE, Série Société des Nations, 619/115.

43 After several communications with the PMC, the Foreign Ministry finally told the Colonial Ministry to use "natives of Togo (or of Cameroon), protected persons under French mandate." Copy of MAE to MC, 22 Feb. 1929, AE, Série Société des Nations, 619/115.

44 These designations remained in use throughout the interwar period and even into the period of the Vichy regime during the Second World War. See various correspondence from 1940 to 1944, ANSOM, AP, 2705.

45 Minutes of the Fourth Session of the Permanent Mandates Commission, LN Document A.13.1924.IV., p. 136.

46 For some general studies of the French colonial army in Africa, Charles Mangin, *La Force noire* (Paris, 1910); A. S. Kanya-Forstner, *The Conquest of the Western Sudan: A Study in French Military Imperialism* (London, 1969); Général Robert Huré, *L'Armée d'Afrique: 1830–1962* (Paris, 1977); Charles J. Balesi, *From Adversary to Comrades-in-arms: West Africans and the French Military 1885–1918* (Waltham, Mass., 1979); Myron J. Echenberg, *Colonial Conscripts: The Tirailleurs Sénégalais in French West Africa, 1857–1960* (London, 1991) and Nancy Ellen Lawler, *Soldiers of Misfortune: Ivoirien Tirailleurs of World War II* (Athens, Ohio, 1992).

47 Duchêne to le Général Directeur des Services Militaire, 24 July 1924 and "Note pour la Direction des Affaires Politiques" entitled "Au sujet de l'organisation militaire au Cameroun" dated 29 July 1924, ANSOM, SG: Togo-Cam, 29/248.

48 Ibid., and Wright, *Mandates*, pp. 616–18.

49 "Note pour la Direction des Services Militaires" signed by Duchêne and dated 5 Aug. 1924, ANSOM, SG: Togo-Cam, 29/248.

50 "Note pour la Direction des Affaires Politiques" by the le Direction des Services Militaires stamped 12 Sept. 1924, ANSOM, SG: Togo-Cam, 29/248.

51 *Rapport Annuel du Government Français sur l'administration sous mandat des territoires du Cameroun pour l'année 1925*, and Rapport *Annuel du Government Français sous mandat des territoires du Togo pour l'année 1925*. Also see Buell, *The Native Problem in Africa*, II, pp. 281–3 and Cornevin, *Le Togo*, p. 247.

52 Vito Catastini (director of the Mandates Section) to Duchêne, 5 Feb. 1925, ANSOM, SG: Togo-Cam, 29/248.

53 Marchand to MC, 8 Oct. 1924, ANSOM, SG: Togo-Cam, 29/248.

54 *Rapport Annuel du Gouvernment Français sur l'administration sous mandat du territoire du Cameroun pour l'année 1925*, chapter II, p. 13. Also see Buell, *The Native Problem in Africa*, II, p. 282.

55 *Rapport Annuel du Gouvernment Français sur l'administration sous mandat du territoire du Cameroun pour l'année 1923*, chapter II, pp. 38–9.

56 *Rapport Annuel du Government Français sur l'administration sous mandat du territoire du Cameroun pour l'année 1925*, chapter II, p. 29. Also see Buell, *The Native Problem in Africa*, II, p. 283.

57 Dahomey, a French colony similar in size to Togo, was required to conscript

eight hundred Africans a year into the French colonial army. In addition to those works already cited, see Buell, *The Native Problem in Africa*, II, pp. 3–22.

58 Bonnecarrère to MC, 29 Jan. 1923, ANSOM, SG: Togo-Cam, 24/211.

59 Copy of MC to MAE, 20 March 1923, ANSOM, SG: Togo-Cam, 24/211.

60 Minute by Charles Dodd (clerk in the Foreign Office), 5 June 1923, Consul-General of Dakar to FO, 11 April 1922, PRO, FO 371/7157.

61 Marchand to MC, 8 May 1924, ANSOM, SG; Togo-Cam, 29/257.

62 Copy of MC to Marchand, 5 July 1924, ANSOM, SG: Togo-Cam, 29/257.

63 Marchand to MC, 22 April 1924 and copy MC to Marchand, 7 June 1924, ANSOM, AP, 1051; Bonnecarrère to MC, 4 Nov. 1924, ANSOM, AP, 606/4 and copy of MC to Marchand and Bonnecarrère, 2 Oct. 1925, ANSOM, Agence F.O.M., 867/2365.

64 Bonnecarrère to MC, 4 Nov. 1924 and draft arrêté dated 4 Nov. 1924, ANSOM, AP, 606/4. Also see *Rapport Annuel du Gouvernment Français sur l'administration sous mandat du territoire du Togo pour l'année 1924*, pp. 195–6.

65 For more, see d'Almeida and Gbedemah, *Le Gouverneur Bonnecarrère au Togo*, pp. 44–64 and Cornevin, *Le Togo*, pp. 241–3.

66 Copy of "Circulaire à Messieurs les Chefs de Circonscription" concerning "la justice indigène" dated 9 Sept. 1925, ANSOM, SG: Togo-Cam, 30/274.

67 Copy of J. Pickering Jones (former chairman of the African section of the Liverpool Chamber of Commerce) to FO in FO to CO, 29 April 1921, CO 724/2.

68 Minute by Flood, 2 May 1921 and minute by Ellis, 3 May 1921, FO to CO dated 29 April 1921, CO 724/2.

69 Ormsby-Gore sent his copy of Mensah's petition (along with the private report originating from Abibu dated 22 April 1921) to the Foreign Office after he had asked his question in the House of Commons. See Parliamentary Question, 4 May 1921, PRO, FO 371/6993.

70 Ormsby-Gore to Cecil, 1 June 1921 and Cecil to H.A.L. Fisher, 9 June 1921, Cecil Papers, BM, 51095.

71 Ormsby-Gore to CO, 15 July 1921, CO 724/2.

72 Report by C. D. Trotter dated 24 Aug. 1921 in R. H. W. Wilkinson (clerk in the Gold Coast Secretariat) to Flood, 1 Sept. 1921, CO 724/2.

73 Minute by Flood, 6 Sept. 1921 and copy of CO to Ormsby-Gore, 21 Oct. 1921 in Wilkinson to Flood dated 1 Sept. 1921, CO 724/2.

74 Copy of Flood to Wilkinson, 26 Oct. 1921, Wilkinson to Flood dated 1 Sept. 1921, CO 724/2.

75 Cornevin, *Le Togo*, pp. 251–2.

76 The Lawson family went on to occupy many of central positions of government in Togo after independence. See Samuel Decalo, *Historical Dictionary of Togo* (Metuchen, N.J., 1976), p. 108.

77 Adjigo to FO, 20 May 1922, PRO, FO 371/8273; CO to FO, 24 July 1922, PRO, FO 371/2881 and Cabinet Office to FO, 23 Aug. 1922, PRO, FO 371/8273.

78 Copy of Adjigo to MC, 12 May 1922 included in League of Nations to FO, 19 Feb. 1923, PRO, FO 371/9394.

79 CO to FO, 24 July 1922, PRO, FO 371/2881 and copy of League to Adjigo, 23 Aug. 1922 included in Cabinet to FO, 23 Aug. 1922, PRO, FO 371/8273.

80 Copy of Gout to League, 4 Jan. 1923 in League to FO, 19 Feb. 1923, PRO, FO 371/9394.

81 Minutes of the Fourth Session of the Permanent Mandates Commission, LN Document, A.13.1924.VI., p. 140.
82 For the intelligence report on Kanyi, as well as many of other Africans who worked with him, see Bonnecarrère to MC, 10 Dec. 1927, ANSOM, AP, 1038.
83 Cornevin makes this claim, but offers no evidence. He also wrongly contends that this organized agitation did not begin until after 1929. Cornevin, *Le Togo*, pp. 251–2.
84 French translation of "Lettre circulaire" produced by the Bund der Deutsch Togoländer, 19 Dec. 1925, ANSOM, AP, 1038.

Chapter 7 Germany Joins the League: The British Mandates, 1926–1929

1 For studies of Stresemann's policy during this period, see Henry Ashby Turner, Jr., *Stresemann and the Politics of the Weimar Republic* (Princeton, 1963); Jon Jacobson, *Locarno Diplomacy: Germany and the West 1925–1929* (Princeton, 1972); Christoph M. Kimmich, *Germany and the League of Nations* (Chicago, 1976) and M. Lee and W. Michalka, *German Foreign Policy 1917–1933: Continuity or Break* (Lemington Spa, 1987).
2 For general surveys of British and French policy toward Germany, see Michael Howard, *The Continental Commitment: The Dilemma of British Defence Policy in the Era of the Two World Wars* (London, 1974); J. Néré, *The Foreign Policy of France 1914 to 1945* (London, 1975); Jacques Bariéty, *Les relations franco-allemandes après la première guerre mondiale* (Paris, 1972); F. L. Carsten, *Britain and the Weimar Republic* (London, 1984) and Jacques Bariéty, *La France et l'Allemagne entre les deux guerres mondiales* (Nancy, 1987).
3 For a discussion of public perceptions of the League during the late 1920s, see F. P. Walters, *A History of the League of Nations* (London, 1960) and David Armstrong, *The Rise of the International Organization: A Short History* (New York, 1982).
4 For example, see Edouard Herriot (French foreign minister) to Edouard Daladier (French colonial minister), 29 Sept. 1924, AE, Série Société des Nations, 545/28; French Embassy to FO, 4 Oct. 1924, PRO, FO 371/9821; Foreign Ministry memorandum for Jules Laroche (French ambassador to Poland), 24 Sept. 1925, AE, Série Société des Nations, 545/62 and minute by Hurst dated 2 Dec. 1925, FO to FO, 2 Dec. 1925, PRO, FO 371/10755.
5 For more, see A. Edho Ekoko, "The British Attitude Towards Germany's Irredentism in Africa in the Inter-War Years," *Journal of Contemporary History* 14 (1979): 287–307.
6 For studies of the colonial question during these negotiations, see Andrew J. Crozier, "Imperial Decline and the Colonial Question in Anglo-German Relations 1919–1939," *European Studies Review* 2 (1981): 207–42 and Andrew J. Crozier, "The Colonial Question in Stresemann's Locarno Policy," *The International History Review* 4 (1982): 37–54.
7 Minutes of the Fourth Meeting of the Locarno Conference, 8 Oct. 1925, PRO, FO 371/10742 and Chamberlain to D'Abernon, 28 Nov. 1925, PRO, FO 371/10746.
8 E. Sutton, ed., *Gustav Stresemann: His Diaries, Letters and Papers* (London, 1935), II, pp. 157–9, 265–7, and 277–8. Also see English translation of interview with Stresemann in the *Gazetta del Popolo* dated 2 Sept. 1926 in Rome Chancery to FO, 2 Sept. 1926, PRO, FO 317/11281.

9 For a recent study of Chamberlain and his foreign policies during this period, see David Dutton, *Austen Chamberlain: Gentleman in Politics* (Bolton, U.K, 1985), pp. 230–99.

10 Minutes of the Fortieth Session of the Council of the League of Nations, *Official Journal*, 1926, pp. 1233–1235. Also see Foreign Ministry note entitled "La question des mandats devant le Conseil," 4 Sept. 1926, AE, Série Société des Nations, 551.

11 The PMC asked for this ruling primarily with the A mandates in mind. Syrians protesting against French mandatory rule had met informally and separately with members of the PMC in early 1926 and many thought it would have been better to have met as a formal body. See CO to CO, ? Aug. 1926, CO 649/31 and Lugard to Lady Lugard, 19 Feb. 1926, Lugard Papers, RH, 119/4. Lugard himself was adamantly opposed to oral petitions "as a general rule," but thought that the PMC should have the power to recommend that the League hear petitioners in person in special circumstances. During a meeting of the Mandates Committee of the League of Nations Union in October, Lugard said that "in certain cases the Commission could not judge the facts by hearing the Mandatory representative only . . . In such cases it ought to report to the Council that it considered that *prima facie* certain petitions deserved further investigation." Minutes of the Mandates Committee of the League of Nations Union, 19 Oct. 1926, League of Nations Union Papers, LSEPS, vol. 44.

12 Chamberlain to Tyrrell, 6 Sept. 1926, Chamberlain Papers, PRO, FO 800/259A.

13 Chamberlain to Tyrrell, 7 Sept. 1926, PRO, FO 371/11876.

14 Tyrrell to Chamberlain, 9 Sept. 1926, Chamberlain Papers, PRO, FO 800/259A.

15 Clauzel to MAE, 21 Sept. 1926, and Philippe Berthelot (secretary-general of the Foreign Ministry) to Clauzel, 22 Sept. 1926, AE, Série Internationale: 1918–1940, 601/136 and copy of Amery to Cecil, 24 Sept. 1926, PRO, FO 371/11876.

16 Murray to Hills, 17 Sept. 1926, Murray Papers, BLO, Mss. Gilbert Murray. 199/48.

17 Hills to Murray, 19 Sept. 1926, Murray Papers, BLO, Mss. Gilbert Murray. 199/49–50.

18 Harris to Murray, 17 Sept. 1926, Murray Papers, BLO, Mss. Gilbert Murray. 199/44–45.

19 Ibid. Harris wrote articles or provided information for *Foreign Affairs*, the *Christian Science Monitor*, and the *Frankfurter Zeitung*. He contacted the last, however, with some reservation. "I am not too anxious to press matters in Germany, for in conversation with the Germans I find them so utterly impossible on Colonial questions." Also see *The Times*, London, 23 Oct. 1926.

20 See memoranda entitled "Detailed Criticisms of List of Questions proposed by the Permanent Mandates Commission" and "Questions Connected with the Work of the Permanent Mandates Commission of the League of Nations" dated October 1926, CAB 32/52.

21 Copy of Amery to Cecil, 24 Sept. 1926, PRO, FO 371/11876 and minutes by Alexander Cadogan (clerk in the Foreign Office) and Chamberlain, 19 Oct. 1926, DO to FO dated 18 Oct. 1926, PRO, FO 371/11877.

22 Minute by Chamberlain, 19 Oct. 1926, DO to CO dated 18 Oct. 1926, PRO, FO 371/11877.

23 Undated minute by Amery included in FO memorandum by Cadogan, 21 Oct. 1926, PRO, FO 371/11877.
24 The first meeting of the Imperial Conference was on 21 October. The members formed a special Mandates Committee which met several times until the end of the month. Minute by Cadogan dated 28 Oct. 1926 attached to FO memorandum by Cadogan, 21 Oct. 1926, PRO, FO 371/11877 and Imperial Conference Conclusions, 29 Oct. 1926, CAB 32/52.
25 Report marked "secret" by the Mandates Committee of the Imperial Conference, 29 Oct. 1926, CAB 32/52.
26 Minutes of the Mandates Committee of the League of Nations Union, 19 Oct. 1926, League of Nations Union Papers, LSEPS, vol. 44.
27 Copy of Cecil to Baldwin, 22 Oct. 1926, Cecil Papers, BM, 51080.
28 Baldwin to Cecil, 26 Oct. 1926, Cecil Papers, BM, 51080.
29 Conclusions of the Committee on Mandates of the Imperial Conference, 17, 19 and 29 Oct. 1926 and draft FO to League, 8 Nov. 1926, CAB 32/52.
30 Minutes of the Mandates Committee of the League of Nations Union, 5 Nov. 1926, League of Nations Union Papers, LSEPS, vol. 44.
31 Drummond to Cadogan, 9 Nov. 1926, PRO, FO 371/11877.
32 Ibid. Drummond made this case again in a private letter to Tyrrell. See Drummond to Tyrrell, 28 Nov. 1926, PRO, FO 371/11877.
33 Ormsby-Gore asked Amery to give Chamberlain a copy of a letter that Ormsby-Gore had addressed to Amery. See Amery to Chamberlain, 16 Nov. 1926, PRO, FO 371/11877.
34 Copy of Lugard to Hills, 26 Nov. 1926, Lugard Papers, RH, 122/5.
35 Minutes of the Mandates Committee of the League of Nations Union, 17 and 30 Nov. 1926, League of Nations Union Papers, LSEPS, vol. 44; LNU to FO, 9 Dec. 1926, PRO, FO 371/11877; *House of Commons Debates*, Fifth Series, 22 Nov. 1926, vol. 200, col. 45; 24 Nov. 1926, vol. 200, col. 381; 7 Dec. 1926, vol. 200, col. 1934 and 14 Dec. 1926, vol. 200. cols. 2876–2899 and *House of Lords Debates*, Fifth Series, 17 Nov. 1926, vol. 65, cols. 651–652 and 661–663; 8 Dec. 1926, vol. 65, cols. 1325–1326 and 23 Feb. 1927, vol. 66, cols. 210–220.
36 Hills to Murray, 15 Oct. 1926, Murray Papers, BLO, Mss. Gilbert Murray. 199/67–68.
37 Hills to Murray, 2 Dec. 1926, Murray Papers, BLO, Mss. Gilbert Murray. 199/126–127. Also see *The Times*, London, 22 Nov. 1926.
38 Ibid. The official French reply to the League, sent soon after that of the Imperial Conference, was much more circumspect. See "Note au sujet des mandats," 20 Jan. 1927, AE, Série Société des Nations, 551/45–48.
39 CO to Graeme Thompson (governor of Nigeria), 5 May 1927, CO 583/128/161. Also see Wright, *Mandates*, p. 149.
40 Copy of MC to Marchand, 19 Feb. 1927, ANSOM, SG: Togo-Cams, 25/226. Also see Wright, *Mandates*, pp. 187–9.
41 Minutes of the Eighth Session of the Permanent Mandates Commission, 1926, p. 200.
42 For examples of the French position, see Berthelot to Clauzel, 22 Sept. 1926, AE, Série Internationale, 610/138–139 and Foreign Ministry note, 26 Nov. 1926, AE, Série Société des Nations, 555/38–39. For the Belgian view, see Herbette to MAE, 16 Aug. 1927, AE, Série Société des Nations, 546/105–106.
43 Record of conversation between Drummond and von Schubert included in Sir Walford Selby (private secretary to Chamberlain) to Tyrrell, 3 Dec. 1926, PRO, FO 371/1187.

44 Dr Heinrich Schnee, *German Colonization Past and Future: The Truth About the German Colonies* (London, 1926).
45 Lindsay to FO, 2 Dec. 1926, PRO, FO 371/11877.
46 Lindsay to FO, 7 Dec. 1926, PRO, FO 371/11877.
47 Clauzel to MAE, 11 Dec. 1926, AE, Série Internationale, 601/148.
48 Lord Crewe (British ambassador at Paris) to FO, 4 May 1926, PRO, FO 371/12680.
49 Fleuriau (now French ambassador at London) to MAE, 11 May 1927 and Clauzel to Berthelot, 30 May 1927, AE, Série Société des Nations, 555/45–47 and 87; Copy of FO to MAE in Fleuriau to MAE, 2 June 1927 and "Note Confidentielle" dated 20 July 1927, AE, Série Internationale, 601/172. The Union coloniale française violently opposed the idea of a German on the PMC. See Clauzel to Berthelot, 7 July 1927, AE, Série Société des Nations, 555/107–108.
50 Clauzel to MAE, 30 June 1927, AE, Série Société des Nations, 555/102–103. Also see Wright, *Mandates*, p. 141.
51 Drummond to FO, 12 Aug. 1927, PRO, FO 371/12681. Also to FO to CO, 13 Aug. 1927, CO 691/93.
52 Minute by Cadogan, 15 Aug. 1927, Drummond to FO dated 12 Aug. 1927 and German Ambassador to FO, 19 Aug. 1927, PRO, FO 371/12681 and Fleuriau to MAE, 25 Aug. 1927, AE, Série Société des Nations, 555/128–129.
53 League to FO, 8 Sept. 1927, PRO, FO 371/12681.
54 For biographical information on Kastl, see Drummond to FO, 12 Aug. 1927, PRO, FO 371/12681 and copy of CO to Cameron, 17 Nov. 1927, CO 691/89.
55 For example, Kastl participated in a colonial conference organized by Schnee in 1930 and kept his position with the Reich Association of Germany Industry throughout his tenure on the PMC. See Schmokel, *Dream of Empire*, pp. 7–8.
56 Report by Lloyd dated 19 Nov. 1927 included in Lloyd to FO, 12 Dec. 1927, PRO, FO 371/12681.
57 Minute by Chamberlain, 12 Dec. 1927, Lloyd to FO dated 12 Dec. 1927, PRO, FO 371/12681.
58 Report by Newlands dated 1 Dec. 1927 included in Lloyd to FO, 12 Dec. 1927, PRO, FO 371/12681.
59 Minute by Ormsby-Gore, 10 Jan. 1927, CO to CO dated 16 Dec. 1926, CO 691/89.
60 Minute by Ormsby-Gore, 8 July 1927, Maxwell to CO dated 1 June 1927, CO 96/672/4233.
61 Minute by J. F. N. Green (clerk in the Tanganyika Territory Department of the Colonial Office), 16 March 1928, Cameron to CO dated 8 March 1928, CO 691/96.
62 Minute by Amery, 24 March 1928, Cameron to CO dated 22 March 1928, CO 691/96.
63 For example, the Colonial Office heavily edited the annual report drafted by Cameron for the Tanganyika Territory for 1925 because the governor had used the opportunity overtly to attack his predecessor, the governor of Kenya, and the Colonial Office itself. Cameron's pleas for no revisions were ignored. See minute by Strachey, 24 April 1926, Cameron to CO dated 3 May 1926, CO 691/83. Also see, Cameron to CO, 19 Aug. 1927, CO 691/90. Another document, a report sent to the League concerning labor policy in Tanganyika, was edited because Cameron inserted criticism of policy in Kenya. See Cameron to CO, 24 Feb. 1926, CO 691/83. Similarly, Ormsby-Gore ordered

changes in the annual reports for Togoland and the Cameroons. See minute by Ormsby-Gore, 31 May 1926, Baddeley to CO dated 26 March 1926, CO 649/31.

64 Minute by Green, 27 March 1928, Cameron to CO dated 1 March 1928, CO 691/97.

65 Copy of Kastl to John Scott (chief secretary of the Tanganyika Territory), 10 Aug. 1928 included in Cameron to CO, 21 Oct. 1928, CO 691/100.

66 Undated report by Lloyd and minute by Lloyd, 7 Dec. 1928, Cameron to CO dated 21 Oct. 1928, CO 691/100.

67 Copy of CO to Cameron, 14 Dec. 1928 and copy of Scott to Kastl, 22 Dec. 1928, Cameron to CO dated 21 Oct. 1928, CO 691/100. Also see Scott to CO, 22 Dec. 1928, CO 691/100.

68 For example, see Douglas Jardine (who replaced Scott as chief secretary and acting governor of the Tanganyika Territory), 9 March 1929, CO 691/103; Baddeley to CO, 26 May 1929, CO 583/166/584 and Slater (now governor of Gold Coast), 12 June 1929, CO 96/689/6446.

69 Minute by Gerard Leslie Makins Clauson (clerk in the Tanganyika Territory Department of the Colonial Office), 12 Dec. 1929, CO 691/106.

70 Mächtig added: "So far as I am concerned, neither of these possibilities has ever entered my mind." Minute by Mächtig, 20 Dec. 1929, ibid.

71 Grigg to Baldwin, 29 March 1926, Baldwin Papers, CU, 96.

72 Copy of Grigg to Amery, 11 June 1926 included in Cameron to CO, 22 July 1926, CO 691/84.

73 There was a dramatic increase in German colonial propaganda in 1926, much of it calling for a return of the colonies as soon as Germany joined the League. See memorandum by John Monro Troutbeck (clerk in the Foreign Office), 11 Feb. 1926, FO to FO dated 20 Feb. 1926 and Sir A. C. Grant Duff to FO, 22 Feb. 1926 PRO, FO 371/11303; Pierre de Margerie (French ambassador to Berlin) to MAE, 25 March 1926, AE, Série Société des Nations, 546/39–45; Copy of official instructions from Chamberlain to D'Abernon, 24 April 1926, Ingram to FO dated 14 April 1926; British Library of Information to FO, 22 May 1926 and memorandum by Troutbeck entitled "The Case for a German Mandate," 22 June 1926, PRO, FO 371/11303. Also see Schmokel, *Dream of Empire*, p. 42.

74 Tanganyika Development Company to FO, 30 March 1926, PRO, FO 371/11303 and copy of Tanganyika European Civil Servants Association to Cameron, 30 March 1926 included in Cameron to CO, 14 May 1926, CO 691/84.

75 Amery spoke at an East Africa Dinner on 11 June and the speech was reported in *The Times* the next day. See FO to FO, 12 June 1926, PRO, FO 371/11303.

76 Copy of Amery to Cameron, 15 June 1926 included in CO to FO dated 5 July 1926, PRO, FO 371/11303 and Amery to Officers Administering East African Dependencies, 15 June 1926 included in CO to FO, 24 Aug. 1926, PRO, FO, 371/11610.

77 Amery made this speech to the Corona Club Dinner on 23 June. See CO to FO, 5 July 1926, PRO, FO 371/11303.

78 Fleuriau to MAE, 28 June 1926, AE, Série Société des Nations, 546/61–65; FO to FO, 28 June 1926, PRO, FO 371/11303; House of Commons to CO, 1 July 1926, CO 691/84; House of Commons Debates, Fifth Series, 6 July 1926, vol. 197, cols. 1874–1875 and memorandum by Troutbeck, 20 Aug. 1926, PRO, FO 371/11394.

79 European population figures remain sketchy since the local government

sometimes considered white Afrikaans-speaking South Africans as "British" and occasionally blurred the distinction between "officials" and "unofficials." See Cameron to CO, 15 March 1930, CO 691/107. By 1939 German settlers still seemed to outnumber the British by 2,729 to 2,100. See Sir Mark Aitchison Young (governor of Tanganyika) to CO, 10 June 1939, CO 691/171.

80 Germans owned 40 of the 131 estates in the territory while Greeks had 29, Britons 24, "British Indians" 22, and the rest were distributed among Swiss, French, Italian, and American owners. Again, these figures must be viewed with caution since estates were not of equal size and some, particularly those recorded as being owned by British and Swiss landlords, were actually owned by foreign investors, many of whom were German. See Department of Overseas Trade of the Colonial Office to CO, 13 Feb. 1934 and Philip Mitchell (chief secretary and acting governor of Tanganyika) to CO, 25 April 1934, CO 691/135.

81 For more, see E. A. Brett, *Colonialism and Underdevelopment in East Africa* (London, 1973), p. 222 and Iliffe, *A Modern History of Tanganyika*, pp. 301–11.

82 Cameron to CO, 5 Jan. 1928, CO 691/95; CO to FO, 13 Feb. 1928, PRO, FO 371/2471; Cameron to CO, 13 Oct. 1928, CO 691/95 and CO to CO, 10 May 1929, CO 691/103. Also see Marcia Wright, *German Missions in Tanganyika: Lutherans and Moravians in the Southern Highlands* (Oxford, 1971), pp. 159–82 and Appendix A.

83 Jardine to CO, 25 Oct. 1929, CO 691/106. In addition to Wright, see Judith Listowel, *The Making of Tanganyika* (New York, 1965), p. 112; Gailey, *Sir Donald Cameron*, pp. 81–3 and Iliffe, *A Modern History of Tanganyika*, pp. 338–41. Cameron increased the percent of total revenue that Tanganyika spent on education from 1.18 in 1924–1925 to 8.06 in 1931–1932.

84 Cameron to CO, 25 Feb. 1926, CO 691/83.

85 Minute by Strachey, 3 May 1926, Cameron to CO dated 25 Feb. 1926, CO 691/83.

86 For example, see Overseas Settlement Department of the Colonial Office to CO, 18 July 1927, CO 691/92; Cameron to CO, 6 July 1928, CO 691/96; Captain A. Evans (British MP) to CO, 28 Oct. 1928, CO 691/91 and Cameron to CO, 15 March 1930, CO 691/107.

87 East Africa Trade and Information Office to CO, 22 Dec. 1927, CO 691/95. Also see Douglas J. Jardine (chief secretary of Tanganyika and acting governor) to CO, 23 July 1928, CO 691/95.

88 Copy of East Africa dated 5 April 1928 attached to Cameron to CO, 14 Feb. 1928, CO 691/96. Also see Baron de Ropp to CO, 19 April 1928, CO 691/99.

89 Copy of Arusha Coffee Planters Association to Cameron dated 23 Jan. 1928 included in Cameron to CO, 28 May 1928, CO 691/96.

90 Copy of resolution passed at a meeting of the Tanganyika Congress of Associations, 24–26 Oct. 1928 included in Cameron to CO, 15 may 1928, CO 691/104.

91 Copy of Cameron's response to the Congress dated 8 May 1929 included in Cameron to CO, 15 May 1929, CO 691/104.

92 For more on the many problems surrounding European coffee growers in Tanganyika during this period, see Scott to CO, 31 Jan. 1925, CO 691/76 and Scott to CO, 8 Jan. 1929, CO 691/102.

93 Copy of minutes of meeting held in Moshi dated 22 July 1929 included in Cameron to CO, 16 Aug. 1929, CO 691/106.

94 Cameron to CO, 16 Aug. 1929, CO 691/106.

95 For some contemporary assessments that generally give Cameron high marks in carrying out the terms of the mandate, see Buell, *The Native Problem in Africa*, I, pp. 425–558; Sir Philip Mitchell, *African Afterthoughts* (London, 1954), pp. 64–7, 103–6, and 132; Sir Charles Dundas, *African Crossroads* (London, 1955), pp. 106–45 and Margery Perham, *East African Journey: Kenya and Tanganyika 1929–1930* (London, 1976). Also see the Minutes of the Eleventh Session of the Permanent Mandates Commission held on 24 June 1927; CO to CO, 27 June 1927, CO 691/89; Memorandum by the Advisory Committee on Imperial Questions, International Department of the Labour Party dated June 1928, Webb Papers, LSEPS, Coll. Misc. 156, vol. 1; Charles Roden Buxton to Lugard, 8 Jan. 1932, and Lugard to Perham, 22 Feb. 1932, Lugard Papers, RH, 79/2 and Lugard to Perham, 9 Jan. 1938, Perham Papers, RH, 22/3.

96 In addition to those scholarly works already cited concerning Cameron's legacy, see also Kenneth Ingham, "Tanganyika: The Mandate and Cameron," in Vincent Harlow and E. M. Chilver, eds., *History of East Africa* II (Oxford, 1965); Ralph A. Austen, "The Official Mind of Indirect Rule: British Policy in Tanganyika, 1916–1939," in Prosser Gifford and Wm. Roger Louis, eds., *Britain and Germany in Africa: Imperial Rivalry and Colonial Rule* (New Haven, 1967); Marilyn Little, "Imperialism, Colonialism and the New Science of Nutrition: The Tanganyika Experience," *Social Science and Medicine* 32 (1991); Marilyn Little, "Colonial Policy and Subsistence in Tanganyika 1925–1945," *The Geographical Review* 81 (1991) and Justin Willis, "The Administration of Bonde, 1920–1960: A Study of the Implementation of Indirect Rule in Tanganyika," *African Affairs* 92 (1993).

97 Cameron to Lugard, 6 April 1926, Lugard Papers, RH, 9/1.

98 Cameron to Lugard, 29 July and 25 Dec. 1926, Lugard Papers, RH, 79/2.

99 Minute by Mächtig, 23 July 1929, Cameron to CO dated 11 June 1929, CO 691/104.

100 Cameron to Lugard, 15 March 1928, Lugard Papers, RH, 9/1.

101 Cameron to Lugard, 31 Jan. 1927, Lugard Papers, RH, 9/1 (emphasis in original).

102 Cameron to Lugard, 23 May 1929, Lugard Papers, RH, 9/1.

103 Cameron to Lugard, 27 Aug. 1929, Lugard Papers, RH, 9/1.

104 Cameron to Lugard, 6 April 1926, Lugard Papers, RH, 9/1.

105 Minutes of the Sixth Session of the Permanent Mandates Commission, 1926, pp. 121–2 and 176.

106 Copy of Cameron to Grigg, 29 June 1926 included in Charles Dundas (secretary for native affairs and acting chief secretary) to CO, 1 July 1926, CO 691/86 and Cameron to CO, 19 Jan. 1927, CO 691/89. After reading the first set of correspondence, Mächtig minuted on 14 August that "Sir Donald seems to have followed the precept that offence is the best form of defence."

107 Report by Philip Mitchell (acting provincial commissioner of the Northern Province and secretary of native affairs) included in Cameron to CO, 27 Sept. 1928, CO 691/100.

108 Cameron to CO, 31 March 1927, CO 691/88.

109 Minutes of the Oversea Defence Committee, 23 May 1927, CAB 7/9.

110 For examples, see Scott to CO, 4 June 1927, CO 691/92; Cameron to CO, 28 Aug. and 13 Sept. 1927, CO 691/93; Power Securities Corporation to CO, 21 May 1928, CO 691/98 and Cameron to CO, 30 Nov. 1928, CO 691/101.

111 Minute by Grindle, 3 April 1928, Cameron to CO dated 3 Feb. 1928, CO 691/96.
112 Cameron to CO, 17 Feb. 1927, CO 691/88.
113 Native Courts fell into various categories each with different powers. Some of the minor courts exercised jurisdiction over small areas and were limited to specific questions concerning domestic relations, petty debts, and assaults while the major courts could settle disputes involving more serious crimes and had appellate jurisdiction over minor courts. See Lugard, *The Dual Mandate in British Tropical Africa*, pp. 536–69.
114 Copy of memorandum by Russell, 4 Feb. 1926 [probably misdated by one year], Cameron to CO dated 17 Feb. 1927, CO 691/88.
115 For Lugard's comments, see Minutes of the Sixth Session of the Permanent Mandates Commission, 7 July 1925.
116 Minutes by Green, Strachey, Wilson, and Ormsby-Gore, 5–30 April 1927, Cameron to CO dated 17 Feb. 1927, CO 691/88.
117 Draft CO to Cameron, 30 April 1927 attached to Cameron to CO dated 17 Feb. 1927, CO 691/88.
118 Scott to CO, 13 July 1927, CO 691/88. After much debate, the Colonial Office gave it approval of this "compromise" on 6 September.
119 Russell retired in 1929 at age 54, but returned to the colonial service in 1934 as the legal advisor to the government of Malta before becoming the assistant legal advisor in the Colonial Office in 1943. See minute by Mächtig, 18 Dec. 1928 and correspondence attached to Cameron to CO dated 17 Feb. 1927, CO 691/88 and *Who Was Who*, 4: 1941–1950 (London, 1951).
120 Minutes of the Legislative Council of 12 April 1929 included in Cameron to CO, 24 Aug. 1929, CO 691/104.
121 The legislative Council, designed by Cameron in 1925, had 23 members, 10 of whom were "unofficials." It contained no Africans and many of the "unofficials" had been selected by Cameron himself. See Cameron to CO, 29 July 1925, CO 691/78.
122 For examples the legal system in practice, see Alexander, *Tanganyika Memories*, pp. 22–8 and *passim*; E. K. Lumley, *Forgotten Mandate: A British District Officer in Tanganyika* (London, 1976), pp. 16, 20, 39, 57–8, 60–1, and *passim* and Iliffe, *A Modern History of Tanganyika*, pp. 325–41. Also see A. N. Allot, *Essays in African Law* (London, 1960); H. F. Morris and J. S. Reed, *Indirect Rule and the Search for Justice: Essays in East African Legal History* (Oxford, 1972) and M. L. Chanock, *Law, Custom and Social Order: The Colonial Experience in Malawi and Zambia* (Cambridge, 1985).
123 Cameron to CO dated 26 Oct. 1927, CO 691/93 and Cameron to CO, 14 Feb. 1928, CO 691/96.
124 Minute by Mächtig, 27 October 1927; Minute by Green, 29 Oct. 1927 and minute by Risely, 2 Nov. 1927, Cameron to CO, 26 Oct. 1927, CO 691/93.
125 Minute by Ehrhardt, 28 Oct. 1927, Cameron to CO dated 26 Oct. 1927, CO 691/93.
126 Minutes by Wilson and Ormsby-Gore, 9 Nov. 1927, Cameron to CO dated 26 Oct. 1927, CO 691/93.
127 Cameron to CO, 14 March 1928, CO 691/97.
128 Minute by Green, 12 June 1928, Sir Halford Mackinder to CO dated 28 April 1928, CO 691/97. Also see minute by Green, 26 Sept. 1931, London Chamber of Commerce to CO dated 24 Sept. 1931, CO 691/117.
129 Minutes of the Eleventh Session of the Permanent Mandates Commission, 29 June 1926 and CO to CO, 13 Dec. 1927, CO 691/89.

130 The ordinance was based on a Nigerian practice that gave the government the authority to penalize an entire African community if it failed to surrender suspected criminals or engaged in widespread tax evasion. Minute by Green, 19 March 1927, Cameron to CO dated 7 Feb. 1928, CO 691/96.
131 Cameron to CO, 14 April 1929, CO 691/102.
132 Minute by Downie, 3 Aug. 1929, Cameron to CO dated 15 April 1929, CO 691/102.
133 Copy of CO to Cameron, 14 Aug. 1929, Cameron to CO dated 15 April 1929, CO 691/102.
134 For example, in early 1926 both the Board of Trade and the Registrar of Shipping insisted that ships belonging to a mandated territory "could not be regarded as [a] *British* Government ship" while the Admiralty refused to take responsibility since the ships were not military vessels. A few months later, the Crown Agents agreed to produce new stamps for Tanganyika bearing the King's head, but had to cram the phrase "Mandated Territory of Tanganyika" into the composition. When the stamps became public, the King's private secretary was worried by an article in the *Daily Mail* that had speculated that the League would protest and that the stamps would become collectors' items. In 1928 the Law Officers of the East African Dependencies concluded that mandated territories had to adopt special patents and design ordinances that did not discriminate against League members while the Committee of Imperial Defence asked the FO if the League members would defend Togo if it were attacked by the French. The FO response to this, and to other such impossible questions, was to draft letters whose "terms would have to be carefully considered and we could not possibly go as far as we are asked." See Registrar of Shipping to CO, 2 March 1926 and Board of Trade to CO, 28 April 1926, CO 691/84; Admiralty to FO, 1 Nov. 1926, PRO, FO 371/11304; Crown Agents to CO, 10 March 1926, CO 691/85; WO to FO, 27 July 1926, PRO, FO 371/11303; *The Daily Express*, 17 Jan. 1927; Captain A. H. L. Hardinge (private secretary to King George V) to CO, 20 Jan. 1927, CO 691/85; CO to CO, 15 Aug. 1928, CO 691/96; Committee of Imperial Defence to FO, 25 Sept. 1928, PRO, FO 371/13402 and minute by Kirkpatrick, 15 Oct. 1929, Joint East Africa Board to FO, 12 Oct. 1929, PRO, FO 371/14110.
135 Among other proposals, the LNU suggested that the members of the PMC should have the authority to visit the mandated territories and that the mandatory powers inform the League before they resorted to armed force in maintaining local order. See LNU to Lugard, 16 April 1926, Lugard Papers, RH, 119/2; Minutes of the Mandates Committee of the League of Nations Union, 13 July and 17 Nov. 1926; 10 Dec. 1928 and copy of Murray to League, 13 June 1929, League of Nations Union Papers, LSEPS, vol. 44; Copy of Lugard to Freda White, 15 Oct. 1927, Murray Papers, BLO, Mss. Gilbert Murray. 202/62–63; CO to FO, 12 Oct. and 11 Dec. 1929, PRO, FO 371/14110.
136 For a few examples, see White to Murray, 14 Aug. 1926 Lugard to Murray, 1 June 1928, Murray Papers, BLO, Mss. Gilbert Murray. 199/8 and 53/161; Copy of Cecil to Lugard, 1 Dec. 1926, Cecil Papers, BM, 51089; Graeme Thompson (governor of Nigeria) to Lugard, 1 March 1926; Lugard to Amery, 15 May 1927 and Lugard to Oldham, 3 June 1927 and CO to Lugard, 9 Oct. 1928, Lugard Papers, RH, 9/1; 64/1 and 122/2 and Lugard to Flood, 28 Aug. 1928, CO 583/157/92.
137 Perham, *Lugard*, II, pp. 668–9.

138 Memorandum by the International Department of the Advisory Committee on Imperial Questions entitled "Points which should be made clear, in speeches by the Prime Minister or otherwise, on behalf of the Labour party, in the event of its forming a government," June 1928, Webb Papers, LSEPS, Coll. Misc. 156. vol. 1.

139 Copy of petition by Rajabali Esmail Bhallo Thayer (president of the Indian Merchants Claims Committee) to League, 17 Feb. 1927 included in League to FO, 12 Aug. 1927, PRO, FO 371/12681; Scott to CO, 16 Sept. 1927, CO 691/90 and CO to CO, 19 Nov. 1927, CO 691/93.

140 Bottomley used this phrase when considering land policy in Tanganyika. See minute by Bottomley, 2 April 1928, Cameron to CO dated 14 Feb. 1928, CO 691/96.

141 In addition to the minutes of the PMC during this period, see Moore to CO, 16 July 1926, CO 649/31; FO to CO, 12 Jan. 1927, CO 583/148/161; J. C. Maxwell (acting governor of Gold Coast) to CO, 1 June 1927, CO 96/672/4233; Slater to CO, 12 June and 13 Sept. 1929, CO 96/689/6446 and report by Flood to Newlands, 19 Nov. 1929, CO 96/698/6446.

142 *West Africa: Reports on the British Sphere of the Cameroons* (London, 1921) and *West Africa: Reports on the British Mandated Sphere of Togoland for 1920–1921* (London, 1922).

143 Undated minute by Amery, CO to CO date ? June 1926, CO 649/31.

144 Minute by J. A. Smith (clerk in West Africa Department), 24 June 1926 and minute by Fiddian, 6 July 1926, CO to CO dated ? June 1926, CO 649/31.

145 It is a matter of speculation what the chief printer at His Majesty's Stationery Office thought of the request to print copies of the *Report by His Majesty's Government in the United Kingdom of Great Britain and Northern Ireland to the Council of the League of Nations on the Administration of Togoland under British Mandate for the Year 1928* (London, 1929) and *Report by His Majesty's Government in the United Kingdom of Great Britain and Northern Ireland to the Council of the League of Nations on the Administration of the Cameroons under British Mandate for the Year 1928* (London, 1929).

146 See Sir Bernard Bourdillon (governor of Nigeria) to CO, 30 March 1938, CO 583/229/30153 and London (acting governor of Gold Coast) to CO, 13 July 1938, CO 96/747/31110/3.

Chapter 8 Germany Joins the League: The French Mandates, 1926–1929

1 The Colonial Ministry, Foreign Ministry, and other governmental agencies continued to maintain extensive files on German activity in Africa and shared information concerning the German colonial movement. See Foreign Ministry file concerning 1926–1929 period, AE, Série Société des Nations, 546; War Ministry to MC, 28 Jan. 1926 and copy of MC to MAE, 27 Feb. 1926, ANSOM, AP, 95/11; MAE to MC, 26 Aug. 1926, ANSOM, AP, 1038; MAE to MC, 9 April 1927, and German press clippings dated 13 Oct. 1927, ANSOM, AP, 900; Agence Economique des Territoires Africans sous Mandat to MC, 17 Oct. 1927, AP, 1039; MAE to MC, 28 Feb. 1928, ANSOM, AP, 95/5 and Margerie to MAE, 25 June 1929, AE, Série Société des Nations, 546/142–143.

2 For example, see Bonnecarrère to MC, 23 Nov. 1920, ANSOM, SG: Togo-Cam, 25/210; MAE to MC, 22 Sep 1922, ANSOM, SG: Togo-Cam, 25/218; Marchand to MC, 2 Dec. 1924, ANSOM, AP 1038; Bonnecarrère to MC, 21 Aug. 1925, ANSOM, AP, 1038 and Marchand to MC, 2 Jan. 1928, ANSOM,

SG: Togo-Cam, 31/294. For more extensive collections of such dossiers, see ANSOM, Service de liaison avec les originaires des territoires français d'outre-mer (SLOTFOM), "Sûreté intérieure de la France et de ses colonies," série III, 91–92 and "Faits, divers, agissements ou manifestations n'affectant pas la sécurité du régime: Traffic d'armes et propagande anti-française au Cameroun, 1920–1935," série IV, 5.

3 Copy of MC to Carde, 7 Oct. 1922, ANSOM, Agence FOM, 867/2365.

4 A number of French prefectures had to be reminded of this difference after they had mistakenly told French applicants that a visa was unnecessary for Togo and Cameroon. In 1929, the Colonial Ministry told the Interior Ministry that while it was true that French citizens did not need visas in any of "our colonial possessions, this is not so for Togo and Cameroon which are not French colonies, but are territories conferred to the administration of France and where all nationals of member states of the League of Nations must be treated on the same level of equality. Therefore a visa is required of French citizens as well as foreigners." See copy of MC to Interior Ministry, 16 Sept. 1929, ANSOM, AP, 614/2.

5 Ibid. The policy was enacted into law one month after Germany joined to League. In 1927, the Colonial Ministry decided to abandon the requirement to secure the written permission of the commissioner before entry since it took too much time and paper work. See MC to Bonnecarrère, 7 Nov. 1927, ANSOM, AP, 614/2. Also see official Foreign Ministry instructions, 26 Oct. 1928, ANSOM, SG: Togo-Cam, 27/238 and Marchand to MC, 12 Aug. 1929, ANSOM, AP, 614/2.

6 Foreign Ministry memorandum, 24 Sept. 1925, AE, Série Société des Nations, 545/62 and MC to MAE, 26 Sept. 1925, AE, Série Société des Nations, 545/65–69.

7 Copy MC to MAE, 19 May 1926, ANSOM, SG: Togo-Cam, 24/207.

8 MC to MAE, 30 July 1926, SG: Togo-Cam, 24/207. For more on this struggle between the Colonial Ministry and the Foreign Ministry over the commercial clauses of the mandates and the Franco German Commercial Treaty of 1926, see MAE to MC, 9 April 1926, ANSOM, SG: Togo-Cam, 24/207; "Note pour M. Clauzel," 15 April 1926, AE, Série Société des Nations, 546/59–60 and MAE to MC, 11 May 1926 and copy of MC to MAE, 19 May 1926, ANSOM, SG: Togo-Cam, 24/207. For reaction in London, see Eric Phipps (minister plenipotentiary in Paris) to FO, 14 June 1926, PRO, FO 371/11261.

9 Copy of MC to Bonnecarrère and Marchand, 1 Sept. 1926 and MC to Marchand, 19 Sept. 1926, ANSOM, SG: Togo-Cam, 24/207.

10 Bonnecarrère to MC, 21 Sept. 1926 and Bleu (head of general secretariat and acting commissioner) to MC, 23 Sept. 1926, ANSOM, SG: Togo-Cam, 24/207.

11 Previously, only Africans leaving Togo for more than ten days needed a passport. The new law required every worker to have one regardless of the amount of time he or she spent outside the territory. Note entitled "Projet de décret portant réglementation de l'émigration des indigènes au Togo," 7 Jan. 1926, ANSOM, AP, 610/2 and copy of final arrêté, 1 March 1927, ANSOM, AP, 610/2 and Journal Officiel de la République Française, 5 March 1927.

12 Copy of MC to MAE, 13 March 1926, ANSOM, AP, 95/11 and Marchand to MC, 7 April 1928, ANSOM, SG: Togo-Cam, 22/203.

13 Foreign Ministry memorandum, 14 April 1927, AE, Série Société des Nations, 621/239. Also see *Journal Officiel de la République Française*, 21 June 1927, p. 6311.

14 Ligue Française pour la Défense des Droits de l'Homme et du Citoyen to MC, 7 July 1927, ANSOM, AP, 614/4.
15 Copy of MC to Ligue Française pour la Défense des Droits de l'Homme et du Citoyen, 1 Aug. 1927, ANSOM, AP, 614/4.
16 Marchand to MC, 29 Jan. 1926, ANSOM, Agence FOM, 867/2365.
17 Reau (French ambassador to Geneva) to MAE, 8 March 1926 and Clauzel to Reau, 15 March 1926, AE, Série Internationale, 601/104–105.
18 For a review Merlin's colonial career upon retirement, see copy of MC to Merlin, 28 July 1925, ANSOM, Direction du Personnel, EE II, 1699.
19 Copy of MC to Marchand, 19 Feb. 1927, ANSOM, SG: Togo-Cam, 25/226 and memorandum entitled "Note sur la forme à adopter pour le présentation des Rapports annuels à la Société des Nations," 17 Oct. 1928, SG: Togo-Cam, 25/226.
20 Marchand to MC, 21 Sept. 1927, ANSOM, SG: Togo-Cam, 28/246.
21 MAE to MC, 20 Dec. 1927; MAE to MC, 21 Feb. 1928; Copy of MC to MAE, 29 March 1928; MAE to MC, 20 June 1928; MC to Marchand, 3 July 1928 and Marchand to MC, 18 Aug. 1928, ANSOM, SG: Togo-Cam, 28/246.
22 The Woermann Company, the influential Hamburg firm founded in 1837 by Adolf Woermann, began trading in West Africa in 1849. It opened its first trading station in Cameroon in 1868 and helped to establish the German protectorate over the territory in 1884. By 1905 the company controlled over thirty trading stations and was the economic and political foundation of the local German colonial government.
23 Marchand to MC, 3 Feb. 1928, ANSOM, AP, 94/5.
24 MAE to MC, 5 Sept. 1929, ANSOM, AP, 900.
25 The vast majority of the properties were sold to Frenchmen. The rest went to British and African buyers. For more, see René Costedot, *L'Effort français au Cameroun: Le Mandat français et la Réorganisation des Territoires du Cameroun* (Paris, 1930), pp. 162–221 and LeVine, *The Cameroons from Mandate to Independence*, p. 120.
26 In 1930 the European population of Togo included 435 French men and women and only 9 Germans. In Cameroon, there were approximately 1,500 French nationals and 250 foreigners, most of whom were Swiss, Greek, American, and British. See Victor Chazelas, *Territoires Africans sous Mandat de la France* (Cameroun et Togo) (Paris, 1931), pp. 178–9 and 233.
27 See Jaap van Slageren, *Les origins de l'Eglise évangélique du Cameroun* (Leiden, Netherlands, 1972) and Charles W. Weber, *International Influences and Baptist Mission in West Cameroon: German-American Missionary Endeavor under International Mandate and British Colonialism* (New York, 1993), pp. 23–7.
28 Cornevin, *Le Togo*, pp. 267–70.
29 At one point, Berlin did complain of discrimination in awarding railroad construction contracts in Cameroon. Paris insisted that, according to the wording of Article 7, such equality did not extend to "essential public works and services." The PMC concurred with the French interpretation and the German government was forced to retract its complaint. See copy of MC to MAE, 5 July 1927; "Note" by Duchêne, 7 July 1927; Copy of German Ambassador to MAE, 11 July 1927, and "Note" by Gaston Joseph (director of political affairs division), 19 July 1929, ANSOM, SG: Togo-Cam, 28/245.
30 For a copy of the petition, drafted by Casely Hayford and dated 9 June 1926, see Foreign Ministry file of petitions to the League of Nations, 1923–1938, AE, Série Société des Nations, 622.

31 Minutes of the Ninth Session of the Permanent Mandates Commission, LN Document, C.425.M.159.1926.VI, p. 91, 230 and Report of the Permanent Mandates Commission, LN Document, C.426.M.159.1926.VI.

32 Copy of arrêté dated 24 Sept. 1926, *Journal Officiel du Territoire du Togo*, 1 Nov. 1926, p. 382.

33 Copy of Bonnecarrère to Slater, 25 July 1929; Note by F. W. F. Jackson (acting commissioner, eastern province), 9 Aug. 1929 and copy of Slater to Bonnecarrère, 26 Oct. 1929 in Slater to CO, 26 Oct. 1929, CO 96/691/6541.

34 Copy of note by Leigh, 10 Aug. 1929, Slater to CO dated 26 Oct. 1929, CO 96/691/6541.

35 Minute by W. A. Harmon (clerk in the West Africa department), 27 Nov. 1929; Minutes by Calder and Flood, 6 Dec. 1929 and copy of CO to FO, 13 Dec. 1929, Slater to CO dated 26 Oct. 1929, CO 96/691/6541.

36 The petitions, dated 27 June and 26 Sept. 1925, may have been sent to coincide with the annual meetings of the PMC. The Director of the League of Nations Mandates Section merely informed the members that the petitions did not address any specific violations of the mandate and had been returned to the petitioners with the reasons for non-acceptance. See Report by Mme. Wicksell included in the minutes of the Eleventh Session of the Permanent Mandates Commission, 1927, pp. 215–17 and report by Bonnecarrère to MC, 10 Dec. 1927, ANSOM, AP, 1038.

37 MC to MAE, 13 March 1926, AE, Série Société des Nations, 546/25–27.

38 Copy of *Stuttgarter Tageblatt* dated 17 March 1926 included in MAE to MC, 2 Sept. 1926, ANSOM, AP, 1038.

39 For copies of the petitions, dated 27 June and 9 Aug. 1926, see Foreign Ministry file of petitions to the League of Nations, 1923–1938, AE, Série Société des Nations, 622.

40 Report by Mme. Wicksell included in the minutes of the Eleventh Session of the Permanent Mandates Commission, 1927, pp. 215–17 and report by Bonnecarrère to MC, 10 Dec. 1927, ANSOM, AP, 1038.

41 Extract of Lugard to Lady Lugard dated 20 Jan. 1926 included in Lady Lugard to Amery, 8 March 1926, Lugard Papers, RH, 119/4.

42 The report detailed the activities of the Bund from 1925 to 1927 and reviewed the responses of the PMC to the various petitions. Report by Bonnecarrère to MC, 10 Dec. 1927, ANSOM, AP, 1038.

43 Bonnecarrère to MC, 7 Nov. 1929, ANSOM, AP, 1038.

44 After the war, the Cercle emerged as the "Comité de l'Unité Togolaise," the militant nationalist pan-Ewe party. See Cornevin, *Le Togo*, p. 252 and Decalo, *Historical Dictionary of Togo*, p. 43.

45 For France's copy of this petition, see Duala to "High Conference," 18 Aug. 1919, ANSOM, AP 3138. For Britain's copy, see Duala to Lloyd George, 21 Aug. 1919, PRO, FO 371/3774.

46 For a recent study of land alienation and the Duala, see Andreas Eckert, *Die Duala und die Kolonialmächte: Eine Untersuchung zu Widerstand, Protest und Protonationalismus in Kamerun vor dem Zweiten Weltkrieg* (Münster, 1991).

47 Copy of "proces-verbal" of meetings held in Douala, 4–6 Dec. 1926, included in Inspection Mission report on Cameroon dated 1926–1927, ANSOM, SG: Togo-Cam, 2/6.

48 Observations by Marchand dated 27 Dec. 1926 included in Inspection Mission report of Cameroon dated 1926–1927, ANSOM, SG: Togo-Cam, 2/6. Also see report by the Inspector-General of the Colonies to MC, 6 March 1927, SG: Togo-Cam, 31/288.

49 Buell, *The Native Problem in Africa*, II, pp. 341–3. The "Bureau international pour la Défense des Indigène," a special interest group, used many of Buell's conclusions in 1928 as the basis for a series of petitions to the League concerning the administration of many of the mandated territories. See League to FO, 30 June 1928, PRO, FO 371/13388; League to MAE, 8 Oct. 1928, AE, Série Société des Nations, 621/285–297 and CO to FO, 17 Nov. 1928, PRO, FO 371/13389. Also see Minutes of the Fifteenth Session of the Permanent Mandates Commission, 1929, pp. 20–2, 143, 147, 241–9.

50 For example, see petitions dated 16 Sept. 1926; 11 Aug. 1929; 19 Dec. 1929; 5 Sept. 1930; and 18 March, 19 June, 14 Aug. and 21 Aug. 1931 in Foreign Ministry file of petitions to the League of Nations dated, 1923–1938, AE, Série Société des Nations, 622; Copy of MC to MAE, 21 May 1931 and copy of MC to Bonnecarrère, 30 Oct. 1932, ANSOM, AP, 615/1; Minutes of the Sixteenth Session of the Permanent Mandates Commission, 1929, p. 183–4; Minutes of the Nineteenth Session of the Permanent Mandates Commission, 1930, p. 195; Minutes of the Twenty-First Session of the Permanent Mandates Commission, 1932, pp. 142, 172, and 217; Minutes of the Twenty-Second Session of the Permanent Mandates Commission, 1932, p. 214 and Minutes of the Twenty-Third Session of the Permanent Mandates Commission, 1933, p. 178. Also see LeVine, *The Cameroons from Mandate to Independence*, pp. 111–17.

51 See copy of Jean Louis (former magistrate with the court of appeal in Brazzaville) to Duala Chiefs dated 1 Dec. 1929 in Marchand to MC, 17 March 1930 and copy of MC to Marchand, 23 June 1930, ANSOM, SG: Togo-Cam, 31/288.

52 Copy of Duala petition to League, 19 Dec. 1929, ANSOM, AP, 615/1 and minutes of the Nineteenth Session of the Permanent Mandates Commission, 1930, p. 195.

53 This last contention was taken seriously after 1931 when the Duala were represented by the shadowy Vincent Ganty, a non-Cameroonian African (probably from Guinea) living in Paris who sometimes called himself the future "president" of an independent "Cameroons Republic." He reportedly raised more that 100,000 francs in annual subscriptions for his campaign and was probably responsible for drafting the later petitions to the League from the Duala in the early 1930s. For more, see Adalbert Owona, "A l'aube du nationalisme camerounais: la curieuse figure de Vincent Ganty," *Revue Française d'Histoire d'Outre-Mer* 56 (1969): 199–235.

54 For more, see Richard A. Joseph, *Radical Nationalism in Cameroun: Social Origins of the U.P.C. Rebellion* (Oxford, 1977), pp. 7–38.

55 Joseph, *Radical Nationalism in Cameroun*, pp. 15–18; Derrick, "Colonial élitism in Cameroon" in Njeuma, ed., *Introduction to the History of Cameroon*, pp. 132–3 and Eckert, *Die Duala und die Kolonialmächte*, pp. 257–66.

56 Derrick, "The 'Germanophone' Elite of Douala Under the French Mandate," p. 260.

57 Report of Inspection Mission of Togo and Cameroon, 1926–1927, ANSOM, SG: Togo-Cam, 2/6.

58 For example, see *Rapport Annuel du Gouvernment Français sur l'administration sous mandat des territoires du Cameroun pour l'année* 1929, chapter XI, pp. 106–31 and *Rapport Annuel Gouvernment du Français sur l'administration sur l'administration sous mandat des territoires du Togo pour l'année* 1929, chapter XI, pp. 121–38 and 184–91. Also see Minutes of the

Ninth Session of the Permanent Mandates Commission, 1926, pp. 79–82 and 90.

59 Minutes of the Ninth Session of the Permanent Mandates Commission, 1926, pp. 60, 79–82, and 90; Marchand to MC, 20 March 1929, ANSOM, SG: Togo-Cam, 33/309 and Note entitled "Territoires sous mandat français. Examen de la question des emprunts du point de vue de légalité économique," 20 June 1929, ANSOM, SG: Togo-Cam, 2/21. Also see Buell, *The Native Problem in Africa*, II, pp. 284–7 and Austen, "Varieties of Trusteeship," pp. 525–6.

60 Ibid. Also see Minutes of the Third Permanent Mandates Commission, 1923, pp. 34–8 and MC to Marchand, 15 June 1925, ANSOM, SG: Togo-Cam, 28/240.

61 For example, see Marchand to MC, 21 Aug. 1926, ANSOM, AP, 2689/1; MC to Marchand, 19 Feb. 1927, ANSOM, SG: Togo-Cam, 25/226; Léon Pêtre (acting commissioner of Togo) to MC, 6 April 1928, ANSOM, AP, 2705/2 and Marchand to MC, 18 June 1928, ANSOM, AP, 2698/5.

62 Buell presented almost all of these examples in his massive 1928 study and based his conclusions on his travels in the mandates, official French sources, and League papers. In particular, see his summaries in *The Native Problem in Africa*, I, p. 944 and II, pp. 284–7 and 370–731. A second contemporary, Laurent Pechoux, made similar claims about Togo based on public sources in *Le mandate français sur le Togo* (Paris 1939), pp. 57–399. Modern scholars have added little new information on these subjects. LeVine relies heavily on Buell and Cornevin is similarly dependent on Pechoux. Other historians usually either refer to LeVine and Cornevin or cite Buell and his sources. Without better modern studies of these specific questions, particularly in the case of French administration in Togo during the interwar years, Buell's work must be viewed with caution. See LeVine, *The Cameroons from Mandate to Independence*, pp. 104–11 and *passim* and Cornevin, *Le Togo*, pp. 233–78.

63 For example, see Minutes of the Sixth Session of the Permanent Mandates Commission, 1926, p. 70 and Minutes of the Eleventh Session of the Permanent Mandates Commission, 1929, p. 131. Also see LeVine, *The Cameroons from Mandate to Independence*, p. 109 and Barbacar Fall, *Le travail forcé en Afrique-Occidentale française* (1900–1946) (Paris, 1993), pp. 253–68 who both credit the League for helping to put international pressure on France that resulted in reforms in unpaid labor practices in French Africa after 1930.

64 Note by the "Le Médicin Inspecteur Général," 16 March 1926, ANSOM, SG: Togo-Cam, 29/252.

65 Note by Duchêne, 19 March 1926, ANSOM, SG: Togo-Cam, 29/252.

66 Report of Inspection Mission of Cameroon, 14 Feb. 1927, ANSOM, AP, 3139.

67 Bonnecarrère to MC, 2 Sept. 1927, ANSOM, AP, 28/246.

68 Copy of MC to Bonnecarrère, 18 Feb. 1928, ANSOM, AP, 610/8.

69 MC to MAE, 17 Oct. 1927, AE, Série Société des Nations, 619/123.

70 Paul Pollachi, *Atlas colonial français: colonies, protectorates et pays sous mandat* (Paris, 1929), pp. 22–23, 135–8 and 165–9.

Chapter 9 Mandate and Empire in British East Africa, 1929–1931

1 For general discussions of many of the historical issues surrounding Closer

Union, see B. T. G. Chidzero, *Tanganyika and International Trusteeship* (London, 1961), pp. 61–88 and Robert G. Gregory, "Sidney Webb and East Africa: Labour's Experiment with the Doctrine of Native Paramountcy, *University of California Publications in History* vol. 71, 1962. Also see, Perham, *Lugard*, II, pp. 645–93; Gailey, *Sir Donald Cameron*, pp. 45–66; Gupta, *Imperialism and the British Labour Movement*, pp. 179–96; T. O. Lloyd, *The British Empire 1558–1983* (Oxford, 1984), pp. 305–7 and A. D. Roberts, *The Cambridge History of Africa*, vol. 7 (Cambridge, 1986), pp. 686–7.

2 Minute by Amery, 30 June 1919, Byatt to CO dated 21 Jan. 1919, CO 691/29.

3 Wright, *Mandates*, p. 615.

4 After 1919 the Legislative Assembly contained 11 ex-officio members, 9 nominated members (all government officials), 11 elected Europeans, and one nominated unofficial member to represent the African community (usually a missionary). After protests from the Asian community, the Council was expanded to include 6 allotted seats for Indians and Arabs elected under a communal system. Many of these seats, however, remained vacant in the 1920s as a sign of protest against the communal system. For useful recent studies of Kenya under colonial rule, see Bruce Berman, *Control and Crisis in Colonial Kenya: The Dialectic of Domination* (London, 1990) and Angelique Haugerud, *The Culture of Politics in Modern Kenya* (London, 1995).

5 For biographical information, see Elspeth Huxley, *White Man's Country: Lord Delamere and the Making of Kenya* (New York, 1965 edn.).

6 For more, see L. H. Gann, *A History of Southern Rhodesia: Early Days to 1934* (London, 1956) and Robert Blake, *A History of Rhodesia* (London, 1977).

7 By 1923, there had already been a number of publications in Britain protesting white supremacy in Kenya. For example, see Leonard Woolf, *Empire and Commerce in Africa* (London, 1920); H. D. Hooper, *Leading Strings: Native Development and Missionary Education in Kenya Colony* (London, 1921); "Kenya," *Round Table* XIII (1922–1923): 507–29; Norman Leys, "The Problem of Kenya," *Socialist Review*, XXI, 116 (1923): 205–12 and Sir H. H. Johnston, "Race Problems in the New Africa," *Foreign Affairs* 2 (1923–1924): 598–612.

8 *Indians in Kenya*, Cmd. 1922 (London, July 1923), pp. 9–10.

9 *Report of the East Africa Commission*, Cmd. 2387 (London, April, 1925).

10 Ibid., p. 21.

11 For more examples of the ardent imperialist views of these two men, see Leo Amery, "Economic Development of the Empire," *United Empire*, New Series, XVI (1925): 143–4 and Sir Edward Grigg, *The Greatest Experiment in History* (London, 1924) and "British Policy in Kenya," *Journal of the African Society*, XXVI (1926–1927): 193–208.

12 *Future Policy in Regard to Eastern Africa*, Cmd. 2904 (London, July, 1927), p. 5.

13 Ibid., p. 7.

14 Ibid. Also see minutes of the "Committee on Policy in Eastern Africa," 4 July 1927, CAB 27/349.

15 Minutes of meeting to discuss Federation in East and Central Africa, 9 June 1927, CAB 27/234.

16 Memorandum by Cameron entitled "Federation of the East African

Dependencies," 22 May 1927 attached to minutes dated 9 June 1927, CAB 27/349.

17 Minutes of a meeting on Federation in Easy and Central Africa, 9 June 1927, CAB 27/349.

18 Advisory Committee on Imperial Questions, "Federation of East Africa," July 1927, Webb Papers, LSEPS, Coll. Misc. 156. vol. 1.

19 Oldham to Lugard, 3 June 1927 and large file of correspondence with Oldham throughout 1928, Lugard Papers, RH, 64/4. Also see J. H. Harris to Lugard, 28 Jan. 1927, Lugard Papers, RH, 64/2.

20 Lugard, *The Dual Mandate*, pp. 317–24. Lugard remained convinced of this solution for most of this period. See Lugard to Smuts, 24 Jan. 1930, Smuts Papers, CC, Reel 710/59.

21 Sir Ronald Lindsay (British ambassador to Berlin) to FO, 15 Feb. 1928, PRO, FO 371/12907.

22 Ibid. Also see copies of Lindsay to FO dated 6 and 15 Feb. 1928 in FO to CO, 16 Feb. 1928 and FO to CO, 6 March 1928, CO 691/96.

23 For biographical information, see Perham, *Lugard*, II, p. 681 and Gregory, "Sidney Webb and East Africa," p. 69.

24 *Report of the Commission on Closer Union of the Dependencies in Eastern and Central Africa*, Cmd. 3234 (London, 1929), pp. 244–249A. For a copy, see January 1929, Baldwin Papers, CU, 91.

25 Ibid., pp. 250–251A.

26 Ibid., pp. 223–7.

27 Oldham to Lugard, 6 Oct. 1928, Lugard Papers, RH, 64/4.

28 Gregory, "Sidney Webb and East Africa," pp. 74–5.

29 Advisory Committee on Imperial Questions of the Labour Party, "Memorandum on the Report of the East African Commission in so far as it deals with Kenya, Uganda, and Tanganyika," Feb. 1929, Webb Papers, LSEPS, Coll. Misc. 156, vol. 1.

30 Rumbold to FO, 4 Feb. 1929, PRO, FO 371/13615.

31 Minute by Chamberlain, 1 Feb. 1929, CO to FO dated 24 Jan. 1929, PRO, FO 371/14108.

32 Minutes of the Mandates Committee of the League of Nations Union, 15 Feb. 1929, League of Nations Union Papers, LSEPS, vol. 44 and copy of J. W. Hills to CO, 19 March 1929, Lugard Papers, RH, 140/2.

33 *The Times*, London, 7 Feb. 1929, p. 15. For Oldham's influence in this decision, see Perham, *Lugard*, II, pp. 682–3.

34 The other signatories included Lords Oliver, Reading, and Southborough. *The Times*, London, 25 Feb. 1929, p. 13.

35 Hilton Young to Cecil, 26 Feb. 1929, Cecil Papers, BLO, 51166. Also see Cecil to Hilton Young, 27 Feb. 1929, and Hilton Young to Cecil, 28 Feb. 1929, Cecil Papers, BLO, 51166.

36 *The Times*, London, 25 Feb. 1929, p. 13.

37 Minutes of the Committee on Policy in East Africa, 12 and 25 March 1929, CAB 27/384. Also see Leo Amery, *My Political Life: War and Peace 1914–1929* (London, 1953), pp. 361–3.

38 For quotation, see Amery, *My Political Life*, II, p. 362. For Wilson's recommendations, see Chidzero, *Tanganyika and International Trusteeship*, p. 65.

39 MacDonald had originally wanted to return J. H. Thomas to the Colonial Office, but because of the constitutional requirement that a government have at least two secretaries of state from the House of Lords as well as King George's unwillingness to increase the number of hereditary peers, the prime

minister selected Webb, who was childless instead of Thomas, who had several children. When Webb agreed to join the government, he also accepted a peerage. See Amery, *My Political Life*, II, p. 502 and Gregory, "Sydney Webb and East Africa," p. 77.

40 For more, see Beatrice Webb, *Diaries 1924–32* (London, 1956); Jeanne MacKenzie, *A Victorian Courtship: The Story of Beatrice Potter and Sidney Webb* (London, 1979) and Radice Lisanne, *Beatrice and Sidney Webb: Fabian Socialists* (New York, 1984).

41 For more, see Beatrice Potter Webb, *The Webb's Australian Diary, 1898* (Melbourne, 1965 edn.) and Sidney Webb, *Indian Diary* (Delhi, 1988 edn.).

42 Pamphlet by Webb and George Bernard Shaw, *Fabianism and the Empire* (London, 1901).

43 Lowe, *Anticolonialism in British Politics*, pp. 45–52. Also see the Labour party publications, *A Labour Policy for the British Commonwealth of Nations* (London, 1925); *Labour and the Empire: Africa* (London, 1926) and "Labour and the Nation" included in the *Report of the 28th Annual Conference* (London, 1929), Appendix 10.

44 For excerpts of Stresemann's speech, see *The Times* (London), 26 June 1929. Also see CO memorandum, 26 June 1929, CO 822/13/3.

45 Minutes of meeting between LNU and Henderson, 12 July 1929, A. Henderson Papers, PRO, FO 800/280.

46 Copy of Oldham to Lugard, 18 and 23 Oct. 1929, Oldham Papers, RH, 3/1; Draft Statement on Closer Union and attached note entitled "Questions as Redrafted by Lord Lugard," 21 Oct. 1929, League of Nations Union Papers, LSEPS, vol. 44; and Freda White (member of Mandates Section of LNU) to Oldham, 1 Nov. 1929, Oldham Papers, RH, 4/3. Also see "Memo of Interview with Lord Passfield," by the Executive Committee of the LNU, 29 Nov. 1929, League of Nations Union Papers, vol. 44.

47 Draft Statement on Closer Union, 21 Oct. 1929, League of Nations Union Papers, LSEPS, vol. 44.

48 Lugard to Passfield, 25 Oct. 1929, Webb Papers, LSEPS, Coll. Misc. 156, vol. 1.

49 Lugard to Passfield, 29 July 1929 (returned original), Lugard Papers, RH, 64/8.

50 Copy of Lugard to Cameron, 4 Oct. 1929, Lugard Papers, RH, 9/1. Passfield recorded the results of this meeting differently. In a letter to his wife he wrote that "I had a whole hour's friendly talk with the P.M. yesterday, when he received Lugard and Oldham, with me present (which was, I think, not what Oldham had intended!). We spoke them fair, but non-committal [sic]." Norman MacKenzie, ed., *The Letters of Sidney and Beatrice Webb*, vol. III, *Pilgrimage 1912–1947* (Cambridge, 1978), p. 320.

51 Copy of Lugard to Cameron, 4 Oct. 1929, Lugard Papers, RH, 9/1.

52 Margaret Cole, ed., *Beatrice Webb's Diaries 1924–1932* (London, 1956), diary entry for 13 Aug. 1929, p. 214 and Norman and Jeanne MacKenzie, eds., *The Diary of Beatrice Webb*, vol. IV, *1924–1943: 'The Wheel of Life'* (Cambridge, 1985), p. 187.

53 Buxton to Passfield, 8 Oct. 1929, Webb Papers, LSEPS, Coll. Misc. 156, vol. 1.

54 Buxton to Passfield with extract from article by Raymond Buell in *The Nation*, 6 Nov. 1929, Webb Papers, LSEPS, Coll. Misc. 156, vol. 1.

55 Minutes of the Sixteenth Session of the Permanent Mandates Commission, 1929, p. 202.

56 Ibid., pp. 201 and 104, respectively.
57 Memorandum by the Labour Party Advisory Committee on International and Imperial Questions entitled "Final Memorandum on the Situation in East Africa and the Wilson Report," 29 Nov. 1929, Webb Papers, Coll. Misc. 156, vol. 1 and "Memo of Interview with Lord Passfield" by the Executive Committee of the LNU, 29 Nov. 1929, League of Nations Union Papers, vol. 44.
58 Grigg to Passfield, 11 Sept. 1929, Webb Papers, LSEPS, Coll. Misc. 156, vol. 1.
59 Copy of O'Shea to Grigg in Grigg to Passfield, 22 Oct. 1929, Webb Papers, LSEPS, Coll. Misc. 156, vol. 1.
60 *The Times*, London, 2 Nov. 1929, p. 33 and 6 Nov. 1929, p. 6.
61 See copy of lecture in *The Times*, London, 4 Nov. 1929 and in CO to Passfield, 8 Nov. 1929, Webb Papers, LSEPS, Coll. Misc. 156, vol. 1.
62 Note marked "Strictly Private" from Wilson to Vansittart, 12 Nov. 1929, MacDonald Papers, PRO/30/69/349.
63 Copy of Lugard to Cameron, 4 Nov. 1929, Lugard Papers, RH, 9/1.
64 Memorandum by Passfield entitled "Closer Union in East Africa," 9 Dec. 1929, CAB 27/410. For those in the Colonial Office who had help to draft the memorandum, see Gregory, "Sidney Webb and East Africa," pp.103–4.
65 The Committee met seven times between 16 January and 15 April. See minutes of the Committee on Policy in East Africa, 16 Jan. 1930, CAB 27/410.
66 Report of the Committee on Policy in East Africa, 15 April 1930, CAB 27/410.
67 CO to Passfield, 26 April 1930, Webb Papers, Coll. Misc. 156 vol. 1 and MacKenzie, *The Letters of Sidney and Beatrice Webb*, III, Sidney to Beatrice, 30 April 1930, p. 325.
68 *Memorandum on native Policy in East Africa*, Cmd. 3573 (London, June, 1930) and *Statement of the Conclusions of H.M.G. in the United Kingdom as regards Closer Union in East Africa*, Cmd. 3574 (London, June, 1930). For copies, see June 1930, Webb Papers, LSEPS, Coll. Misc. 156, vol. 2.
69 Wilson to Grigg, 14 Feb. 1930, Grigg Papers, BLO, Ms. Film 1011. Also see Wilson to Grigg, 10 April 1930, Grigg papers, BLO, Ms. Film 1011.
70 Extracts of the *East African Standard*, 28 Feb. 1930, Smuts Papers, CC, Reel 711/238.
71 Stamfordham to C. P. Duff (private secretary to MacDonald), 12 April 1930, MacDonald Papers, PRO 30/69/349.
72 Copy of "Memorial on African Policy by the Consultative Committee of the Labour Party" 15 April 1930, Noel-Baker Papers, CC, 4/7.
73 Minute by Shiels, 16 April 1930, Labour Party to CO dated 16 April 1930, CO 822/27/13.
74 Passfield to Grigg, 1 May 1930, Grigg Papers, BLO, Ms. Film. 1011.
75 *Memorandum on Native Policy in East Africa*, pp. 4–5.
76 Ibid., pp. 6–7.
77 In addition to the *Statement as regard Closer Union in East Africa*, see Chidzero, *Tanganyika and International Trusteeship*, pp. 66–7.
78 Ibid., section "D" entitled "The Tanganyika Mandate," p. 16.
79 Minutes of meeting held in the secretary of state's room, 7 Oct. 1930, Webb Papers, LSEPS, Coll. Misc. 156, vol. 1.
80 Copy of Lugard to Cameron, 31 May 1930, Lugard Papers, RH, 9/1.
81 Cameron to Lugard, 22 June 1930, Lugard Papers, RH, 9/1.

82 Cameron to Lugard, 30 June 1930, Lugard Papers, RH, 65/1.
83 Draft memorandum by Cameron entitled "The Political Future of Tanganyika Territory" dated 3 June 1930 attached to Cameron to Lugard, 30 June 1930, Lugard Papers, RH, 65/1. Also see Cameron to Lugard, 14 Aug. 1930, Lugard Papers, RH, 9/1.
84 See file containing German newspaper clippings of Schnee's articles including 14 June 1930, Lugard Papers, RH, 141/1.
85 Rumbold to FO, 26 June 1930, PRO, FO 371/14948.
86 Minute by E. L. A. Robertson-Fullarton, 4 July 1930, Rumbold to FO dated 26 June 1930, PRO, FO 371/14948.
87 Minute by Malkin, 10 July 1930, Rumbold to FO dated 26 June 1930, PRO, FO 371/14948.
88 Signed translation of Kastl to Lugard, 30 June 1930, Lugard Papers, RH, 141/1.
89 Copy of Lugard to Kastl, 4 July 1930, Lugard Papers, RH, 141/1.
90 German Chargé d'Affaires to FO, 4 Sept. 1930, PRO, FO 371/14948. For a copy, see Webb Papers, Coll. Misc. 156, vol. 2.
91 Minute by E. L. A. Robertson-Fullarton, 4 Sept. 1930, German Chargé d'Affaires to FO dated 4 Sept. 1930, PRO, FO 371/14948.
92 Minute by Leeper, 9 Sept. 1930, German Chargé d'Affaires to FO dated 4 Sept. 1930, PRO, FO 371/14948.
93 Minute by C. Howard Smith, 13 Sept. 1930, German Chargé d'Affaires to FO dated 4 Sept. 1930, PRO, FO 371/14948.
94 Minutes by Green and Bottomley, 17 Sept. 1930, FO to CO dated 11 Sept. 1930, CO 822/28/4.
95 The remaining members from the House of Lords were the Earl of Onslow, Viscount Mersey, Lord Lamington, Lord Cranworth, Lord Dickinson and Lord Ponsonby of Shulbrede. From the House of Commons were Sir Robert Hamilton, J. H. Hudson, J. Allen Parkinson, Lord Stanley, and W. Wellock.
96 Tanganyika was ultimately represented by three Africans: Hugh Martin Kayamba, the chief clerk of the district office at Tanga who later became an assistant secretary in the secretariat in Dar es Salaam; Chief Makwaia of Shinyanga from the central part of the territory; and Mwami Francis H. Lwamugira, the secretary of the "Chiefs' Council" at Bukoba. All three were personal friends of Philip Mitchell, the Secretary of Native Affairs, who made sure that the witnesses conformed to Cameron's tactic of rejecting any form of Closer Union. For more, see copy of Joint Committee minutes, 5 and 6 June 1931, CO 691/118. Also see H. M. T. Kayamba, *African Problems* (London, 1948); "The Story of Martin Kayamba" in Margery Perham, ed., *Ten Africans* (London, 1963), 2nd edition; "The Spokesman: Martin Kayamba" in John Iliffe, ed., *Modern Tanzanians* (Nairobi, 1973) and Richard Frost, *Enigmatic Proconsul: Sir Philip Mitchell and the Twilight of Empire* (London, 1992), pp. 27–39.
97 Copy of Lugard to Cameron, 22 Oct. 1930, Lugard Papers, RH, 9/1.
98 Perham, *Lugard*, II, pp. 687–90.
99 Copy of Lugard to Sandeman Allen, 20 Oct. 1930, Lugard Papers, RH, 67/2. Also see reply dated 25 October.
100 Both Buxton and Lord Stanley saw several portions of this draft memorandum while Oldham saw all of it.
101 "Memorandum on the Kenya Question," section 20, "Closer Union to Ensure Retention of Tanganyika," Oct. 1930, Lugard Papers, RH, 68/1.
102 Lugard to FO, 20 Oct. 1930, PRO, FO 371/14949. When the Colonial Office

learned of Lugard's letter, Bottomley approved of the FO rebuff and minuted that "[i]t is especially desirable not to put Lord Lugard in the position of a mouthpiece of views which he may not altogether agree in reply to representations which have not been precisely formulated." Minute by Bottomley, 5 Nov. 1930, FO to CO dated 31 Oct. 1930, CO 822/28/4.

103 FO to Lugard, 15 Nov. 1930, Lugard Papers, RH, 67/1.

104 Drummond to Cadogan, 31 Oct. 1930, PRO, FO 371/14949 and Drummond to Lugard, 31 Oct. 1930, Lugard Papers, RH, 119/2.

105 Minute by E. L. A. Robertson-Fullarton, 5 Nov. 1930, Drummond to Cadogan, 4 Nov. 1930, PRO, FO 371/14949.

106 Minute by Leeper, 6 Nov. 1930, Drummond to Cadogan, 4 Nov. 1930, PRO, FO 371/14949.

107 Copy of Lugard to Drummond, 1 Nov. 1930, Lugard Papers, RH, 119/2.

108 Avoiding overtly political questions, particularly those concerning a mandatory power's possible future actions, was typical of the PMC throughout almost its entire history. Offering recommendations on such issues would have made the League directly responsible for colonial administration and would have undermined the PMC's supervisory powers. See Wright, *Mandates*, pp. 190–218 and Hall, *Mandates, Dependencies and Trusteeship*, pp. 205–7.

109 Copy of Lugard to M. MacDonald, 24 Nov. 1930, Lugard Papers, RH, 67/1.

110 "Confidential" memorandum by Parkinson for Passfield, 11 Dec. 1930, CO 822/28/4. Parkinson made a record of this meeting, but seems not to have attended all of it or did not understand much of the substance. At one point he admitted that "I was otherwise occupied while most of the discussion was going on and I do not pretend to be familiar with the Mandate, but this I think represents the position." After learning of the decision to approach the FO, the CO legal advisor protested bitterly about being ignored. See minute by Bushe, 23 Dec. 1930, Joint Committee to CO dated 19 Dec. 1930, CO 822/28/4.

111 Memorandum by Parkinson, 17 Dec. 1930, CO 822/28/4.

112 Minute by Passfield, 18 Dec. 1930, memorandum by Parkinson dated 17 Dec. 1930, CO 822/28/4.

113 C. Davidson (secretary of the Joint Committee) to FO, 18 Dec. 1930, PRO, FO 371/14949.

114 For a copy, also see "Memorandum on the Proposals for 'Closer Union' in East Africa," 13 Dec. 1930, Lugard Papers, RH, 142/1.

115 Minute by Malkin, 22 Dec. 1930, Davidson to FO dated 18 Dec. 1930, PRO, FO 371/14949. Malkin's minute is misleading. He could not on his own refer a matter to the Law Officers without ministerial authority. The Joint Committee, however, had only asked for the Foreign Office legal advisor's opinion. It appears that it was the Committee's secretary, C. Davidson, who authorized going to the law officers even though he did not have the proper sanction to do so in the first place. See postscript by Parkinson on minutes of the Joint Committee marked "Very Secret," 5 Feb. 1931, Webb Papers, Coll. Misc. 156, vol. 2.

116 For more, see R. W. Lyman, *The First Labour Government, 1924* (London, 1957) and Martin Kitchen, *Europe between the Wars: A Political History* (London, 1988), p. 193.

117 Cripps was appointed solicitor-general in October 1930 and elected Labour MP for East Bristol in January 1931. See files for Oct. 1930–Jan. 1931, Cripps Papers, Nuffield College, Oxford (NCO), 688, 689, 600, and 603.

118 Minute by Bushe, 23 Dec. 1930, Joint Committee to CO dated 19 Dec. 1930, CO 822/28/4.
119 Copy of "The Mandate for Tanganyika and the Proposals of His Majesty's Government in the United Kingdom as regard Closer Union in East Africa" by Malkin dated 9 Jan. 1931 included in FO to CO, 9 Jan. 1931, CO 822/31/2. Also see Malkin to Passfield, 9 Jan. 1931, Webb Papers, LSEPS, Coll. Misc. 156, vol. 2.
120 Minute by Bottomley, 9 Jan. 1931, FO to CO dated 9 Jan. 1931, CO 822/31/2.
121 Law Officers' response to Lugard's memorandum, 10? Jan. 1931, Webb Papers, LSEPS, Coll. Misc. 156, vol. 2.
122 Undated file containing various draft proposals for alternative forms of Closer Union, Jan. 1931 and "Agenda for Joint Committee on East Africa," 23 Jan. 1931, Webb Papers, Coll. Misc. 156, vol. 2.
123 Minutes of meeting with Law Officers in the Colonial Office, 27 Jan. 1931, Webb Papers, LSEPS, Coll. Misc. 156, vol. 2.
124 Ibid.
125 For one brief moment, however, Passfield thought that he single-handedly had solved the entire crisis. He had read a copy of the mandate text for British Cameroon which gave the mandatory power the right to administer the territory "as an integral part" of the adjoining possession. He gleefully told Bushe that "This may relieve the Office from anxiety!" The Colonial Office legal advisor had the sad task to point out to his chief that the mandate text for Tanganyika was different from all of the other B mandates. See Passfield to Bushe, 4 Feb. 1931 and Bushe to Passfield, 4 Feb. 1931, Webb Papers, Misc. Coll. 156, vol. 2.
126 Bushe actually did manage to produce a plan within three days, but it was so sketchy that it only served to cause more problems than it solved. See copy of Bushe to Jowitt, 30 Jan. 1931, Webb Papers, LSEPS, Coll. Misc. 156, vol. 2.
127 Passfield to Bushe, 2 Feb. 1931, Webb Papers, LSEPS, Coll. Misc. 156, vol. 2.
128 Jowitt to Passfield, 3 Feb. 1931, Webb Papers, LSEPS, Coll. Misc. 156, vol. 2. Also see Bushe to Passfield, 2 Feb. 1931, in the same file.
129 Stanley of Alderley to Passfield, 1 Feb. and 4 Feb. 1931, Webb Papers, LSEPS, Coll. Misc. 156, vol. 2. Stanley admitted that he had always favored a roving "Inspector-General" of British Africa, similar to the one found in the French colonial system, instead of political union.
130 Lugard to Passfield, 3 Feb. 1931, Webb Papers, LSEPS, Coll. Misc. 156, vol. 2.
131 Copies of report by J. E. M. Carvell (acting consul-general at Munich), 18 Nov. 1930 in FO to CO, 18 Dec. 1930, CO 822/28/4.
132 Schnee to Passfield, 24 Jan. 1931, Webb Papers, Coll. Misc. 156, vol. 2.
133 See *The Times*, London, 2 Feb. 1931.
134 Passfield to Henderson, 2 Feb. 1931, PRO, FO 371/15225. For a copy, see Webb Papers, LSEPS, Coll. Misc. 156, vol. 2.
135 Henderson to Passfield, 4 Feb. 1931, Webb Papers, LSEPS, Coll. Misc. 156, vol. 2. Also see Passfield to Schnee, 11 Feb. 1931, in the same file.
136 The following is based on two sets of notes taken by Parkinson, both bearing the same date. The first is a rough summary of the meeting's conclusions while the second is a formal recording of the minutes. See "Closer Union Proposal in relation to the Mandate for Tanganyika," 5 Feb. 1931 and

minutes of the Joint Committee meeting marked "Very Secret," 5 Feb. 1931, Webb Papers, LSEPS, Coll. Misc. 156, vol. 2.

137 Ibid.

138 Ibid.

139 Ibid.

140 Ibid.

141 Copy of Passfield to Jowitt, 6 Feb. 1931; Minutes by Bottomley and Bushe, 6 Feb. 1931; Minute by Risley, 7 Feb. 1931; Minute by Passfield, 10 Feb. 1931 and CO draft statement, 11 Feb. 1931 all contained in Webb Papers, LSEPS, Coll. Misc. 156, vol. 2. Also see CO memoranda and correspondence concerning Closer Union, 1 March 1931, CO 822/31/3.

142 Minute by Bushe, 6 Feb. 1931 and minute by Risley, 7 Feb. 1931, CO to Passfield, 6 Feb. 1931, Webb Papers, LSEPS, Coll. Misc., 156, vol. 2.

143 There is no record of this meeting in either the Webb Papers or the CO and FO files, but it took place sometime between 11 and 17 February.

144 A copy of the undated précis was attached to Davidson to FO, 17 Feb. 1931, PRO, FO 371/15690. Another copy of the précis surfaced when the issue of Closer Union was discussed again in 1936. See CO to FO, 6 May 1936, PRO, FO 371/20468.

145 Minute by Malkin, 17 Feb. 1931, Davidson to FO dated 17 Feb. 1931, PRO, FO 371/15690.

146 *Joint Committee on Closer Union in East Africa* (London, 1932), Volume I: *Report with Proceedings of the Committee*; Volume II: *Minutes of the Evidence and Index*; Volume III, *Appendices*. Also see, *Correspondence (1931–2) arising from the Report of the Joint Select Committee on Closer Union in East Africa*, Cmd. 4141 (London, 1932).

147 Ibid. In particular, see *Minutes of the Evidence and Index*, 3 March 1932, 74. After leaving Kenya, Grigg was elected a National Conservative MP in 1933. As late as 1939 Cameron continued to argue that no federation in British East Africa was best, but could support the form of Closer Union suggested by the majority of the Royal Commission of 1929 and adopted in Passfield's White Paper. See Cameron, *My Tanganyika Service*, pp. 232–4.

148 Stanley of Alderley, 14 Feb. 1931, Webb Papers, LSEPS, Coll. Misc. 156, vol. 2.

149 See Lugard memorandum entitled "Joint Committee on East Africa," April 1931, Lugard Papers, RH, 68/1; Lugard memorandum, June 1931, Webb Papers, LSEPS, 156, vol. 5 and Lugard memorandum entitled "Closer Union in East Africa: Lord Lugard's Scheme (Embracing Kenya and Uganda Only)," June 1931, CO 822/33/6. Also see copy of Ormsby-Gore to Julian Huxley, 17 June 1931, Lugard Papers, RH, 66/1.

150 There is some indication that this was the intent of some Conservatives long before the Joint Committee ever met. See Sandeman Allen to Lugard, 25 Oct. 1930, Lugard Papers, RH, 67/2 and Grigg to Moore, 19 Dec. 1930, Grigg Papers, BLO, Ms. Film, 1011.

151 Amery to Passfield, 6 Feb. 1931 and Stanley of Alderley to Passfield, 14 Feb. 1931, Webb Papers, LSEPS, Coll. Misc. 156, 2. As late as 1953 when he was 80 years old, Amery continued to insist that Closer Union would have been perfectly legal under the mandates system and that the entire scheme had been destroyed by the Labour party. See Amery, *My Political Life*, II, pp. 360–2.

152 Memorandum by Stanley of Alderley, 28 April 1931, Webb Papers, LSEPS, Coll. Misc. 156, vol. 4. Also see memorandum by Passfield, 24 April 1931, Webb Papers, LSEPS, Coll. Misc. 156, vol. 3.

153 Draft Report of the Joint Committee on East Africa, 30 June 1931, Webb Papers, LSEPS, Coll. Misc. 156, vol. 5.

154 *Joint Select Committee: Report*, pp. 14–15, 28 and paragraphs 39–50.

155 For subsequent developments, see Andrew J. Crozier, *Appeasement and Germany's Last Bid for Colonies* (New York, 1988) and N. J. Westcott, "'Closer Union' and the Future of East Africa, 1939–1948: A Case Study on the 'Official Mind of Imperialism,'" *Journal of Imperial and Commonwealth History* 10, 1 (1981): 67–88.

Conclusions

1 In November 1994, the Security Council of the United Nations terminated the Trusteeship Agreement for Palau, the last of the original eleven Trust Territories. The Trusteeship Council, however, continues to exist and elect officers. See Charter Committee No. 6, 226th Meeting (PM), Press Release, 6 Feb. 1998, L/2852 and U.N. Press Release, "Trusteeship Council Elects Officers," 26 Oct. 1998, TR/2425.

2 Wilson's address to the Coliseum in Sioux Falls, South Dakota, 8 Sept. 1919, *Papers of Woodrow Wilson*, vol. 63, pp. 111–12.

3 Wright, *Mandates*, p. vii.

4 For example, see Leo Amery, *The Forward View* (London, 1935); Neil Macaulay, *Mandates: Reasons, Results, Remedies* (London, 1937) and F. S. Joleson, *Germany's Claim to Colonies* (London, 1939).

5 Lord Hailey, *An Africa Survey: A Study of Problems Arising in Africa South of the Sahara* (London, 1938), p. 219.

6 René Costedot, *L'Effort français au Cameroun* (Paris, 1930) and L. Pechoux, *Le Mandat Français sur le Togo* (Paris, 1939).

7 Lugard to Crofton, 11 March 1940, Lugard Papers, RH, 119/2.

8 William E. Rappard, *The Quest for Peace since the World War* (Cambridge, Mass., 1940), p. 99.

9 Thomas A. Bailey, *Woodrow Wilson and the Lost Peace* (Chicago, 1944), p. 172.

10 Quotations from Bill Freund, *The Making of Contemporary Africa: The Development of African Society since 1800* (Bloomington, IN 1984), pp. 128–9 and P. J. Cain and A. G. Hopkins, *British Imperialism: Crisis and Deconstruction 1914–1990* (London, 1993), p. 212. In addition to those sources cited in the introduction, see Raymond F. Betts, *France and Decolonisation 1900–1960* (New York, 1991), p. 24 and Denis Judd, *Empire: The British Imperial Experience from 1765 to the Present* (London, 1996), p. 255.

11 Robinson, *The Dilemmas of Trusteeship*, p. 93.

Bibliography

Manuscript Sources

Canada

Private Papers

Borden, Robert (National Archives of Canada, Ottawa).

France

Public Papers

Archives du Ministère des Affaires Etrangères, Quai d'Orsay.
- Série A Paix.
- Série Afrique: 1918–1940.
- Série Europe: 1918–1940.
- Série Guerre: 1914–1918.
- Série Internationale.
- Série Société des Nations.

Archives Nationales, Section Outre-Mer, Aix-en-Provence.
- Agence FOM.
- Direction des Affaires Economiques.
- Direction des Affaires Politiques.
- Direction du Personnel.
- Inspection Général des Travaux Publics.
- Séries Géographiques: Togo-Cameroun.
- Service de Liaison avec les Originaires des Territoires Français d'Outre-Mer (SLOTFOM).

Private Papers

Avenol, Joseph (Archives du Ministère des Affaires Etrangères).
Beau, Jean (Archives du Ministère des Affaires Etrangères).
Boisson, Pierre François (Archives Nationales, Section Outre-Mer).
Bourgois, Leon (Archives du Ministère des Affaires Etrangères).
Cambon, Paul (Archives du Ministère des Affaires Etrangères).
Clemenceau, Georges (Service Historique de l'Armée de Terre).
Doumerque, Gaston (Archives du Ministère des Affaires Etrangères).
Fleuriau, Aimé de (Archives du Ministère des Affaires Etrangères).
Goût, Jean (Archives du Ministère des Affaires Etrangères).
Herriot, Edouard (Archives du Ministère des Affaires Etrangères).
Jouvenel, Henry de (Archives du Ministère des Affaires Etrangères).
Lebrun, Albert (Archives du Ministère des Affaires Etrangères et Archives Nationales, Section Outre-Mer).

Mandel, George (Archives Nationales, Section Outre-Mer).
Moutet, Marius (Archives Nationales, Section Outre-Mer).
Pinchon, Stéphen (Archives du Ministère des Affaires Etrangères).
Poincaré, Raymond (Bibliothèque Nationale).
Tardieu, André (Archives du Ministère des Affaires Etrangères).
Sarraut, Albert (Archives Nationales, Section Outre-Mer).

Great Britain

Public Documents

Cabinet Papers

CAB 1/27	Cabinet. Memoranda. German Colonies.
CAB 2/6	Committee on Imperial Defence. Mandates.
CAB 5/9	Committee on Imperial Defence. Oversea Defence Committee East Africa.
CAB 7	Committee on Imperial Defence. Oversea Defence Committee.
CAB 8	Committee on Imperial Defence. Oversea Defence Committee.
CAB 16/36	Committee on Imperial Defence. Sub-Committee on Territorial Changes.
CAB 16/145	Committee on Imperial Defence. Sub-Committee on Transfer of Mandates to Germany.
CAB 21	Imperial War Cabinet.
CAB 23	War Cabinet Minutes.
CAB 24	Cabinet. Memoranda.
CAB 27/349	Cabinet Committee Minutes and Memoranda. Closer Union in East Africa.
CAB 27/369	Cabinet Committee Minutes and Memoranda. Law Officer's Opinion.
CAB 27/384	Cabinet Committee Minutes and Memoranda. Committee on Policy in East Africa.
CAB 27/410	Cabinet Committee Minutes and Memoranda. Closer Union in East Africa.
CAB 29	Committee of Imperial Defence.
CAB 32/52	Imperial Conference. Memoranda.
CAB 32/89	Imperial Conference. Sub-Committee on Mandates.
CAB 32/130	Imperial Conference. German Colonies.
CAB 37	Cabinet. 1880–1916.

Colonial Office

CO 96	Gold Coast.
CO 649	British Cameroons.
CO 537	Colonies General Supplementary.
CO 583	Nigeria.
CO 691	Tanganyika Territory.
CO 724	Togoland.
CO 822	East Africa.

Foreign Office

FO 371	General Correspondence.
FO 372	Treaties.

Private Papers

Anti-Slavery and Aborigines Protection Society (Rhodes House).
Baldwin, Stanley (Cambridge University).
Balfour, Arthur James (British Museum).
Bertie, Francis (British Museum).
Bourdillon, Bernard Henry (Rhodes House).
Cadogan, Alexander (Churchill College, Cambridge).
Cardale, R. B. (Rhodes House).
Cave, George (British Museum).
Cecil, Lord Robert (British Museum).
Chamberlain, Austen (PRO).
Churchill, Winston (Churchill College, Cambridge).
Cripps, Stafford (Nuffield College, Oxford).
Crowe, Eyre (PRO).
Cunliffe-Lister, Philip (Churchill College, Cambridge).
Curzon, Lord (India Office Library).
Davidson, John C. C. (House of Lords Record Office).
Dawson, Geoffrey (Bodleian Library, Oxford).
Drummond, Eric (PRO).
Gowers, William Frederick (Rhodes House).
Grey, Edward (PRO).
Grigg, Edward William (Bodleian Library, Oxford).
Hailey, Lord (Rhodes House).
Hankey, Maurice (Churchill College, Cambridge).
Hardinge, Charles (Cambridge University).
Harmsworth, Cecil B. (PRO).
Harris, John H. (Rhodes House).
Henderson, Arthur (PRO).
Hoare, Samuel (PRO).
Hollis, Alfred Claude (Rhodes House).
Kerr, Philip (Scottish Record Office).
Knatchbull-Hugesson, Hughe (Churchill College, Cambridge).
Lambert, Henry Charles (PRO).
Langley, Walter (PRO).
Law, A. Bonar (House of Lords Record Office).
League of Nations Union (London School of Economics and Political Science).
Lloyd George, David (House of Lords Record Office).
Locker-Lampson, Godfrey (PRO).
Long, Walter (British Museum).
Lugard, Frederick D. (Rhodes House).
Lumley, E. K. (Rhodes House).
Mance, H. Osborne (PRO).
Melville, Sarah (House of Lords Record Office).
MacDonald, James Ramsay (PRO).
MacMichael, Harold (Rhodes House).
Milner, Alfred (Bodleian Library, Oxford).
Morel, E. D. (London School of Economics and Political Science).
Murray, Gilbert (Bodleian Library, Oxford).
Nicholson, Arthur (PRO).
Noel-Baker, Philip (Churchill College, Cambridge).
Oldham, J. H. (Rhodes House).
Perham, Margery (Rhodes House).

Phipps, Eric (Churchill College, Cambridge).
Ponsonby, William (PRO).
Reading, Lord (India Office Library).
Riddell, Lord (British Museum).
Sargent, Orme (PRO).
Simon, John (Bodleian Library, Oxford).
Smuts, Jan. C. (Cambridge University).
Spender, J. Alfred (British Museum).
Tyrrell, William (PRO).
Vansittart, Robert (Churchill College, Cambridge).
Webb, Sidney (London School of Economic and Political Science).
Wigram, Ralph F. (PRO).

Official Publications and Published Primary Collections

France

Annuaire du Ministère des Colonies.
Cambon, Paul, *Correspondance* 1870–1924 (Paris, 1946).
Cohen, William, ed., *Robert Delevignette on the French Empire* (Chicago, 1977).
Commissariat de la République Française au Cameroun, *Guide de la colonisation au Cameroun* (Paris, 1923).
Documents Diplomatiques Français (Paris, 1961–).
Journal Officiel. Chambre des Députés. Debats parliamentaires.
Journal Officiel de la République Française.
Journal Officiel du Territoire du Cameroun.
Journal Officiel du Territoire du Togo.
Poincaré, Raymond, *Au Service de la France* (Paris, 1974) vol. 11.
Rapport Annuel du Gouvernment Français sur l'administration sous mandat du territoire du Cameroun, 1921–1939.
Rapport Annuel du Gouvernment Français sur l'administration sous mandat du territoire du Togo, 1921–1939.

Great Britain

Cell, John W., ed., *By Kenya Possessed: The Correspondence of Norman Leys and J.H. Oldham 1918–1926* (Chicago, 1976).
Documents on British Foreign Policy (London, 1946–).
Gooch, G. P., and Temperley, Harold, eds., *British Documents on the Origin of the War, 1898–1914* 11 vols. (London, 1927–1938).
Government Command Papers and Blue Books.
Great Britain. *German African Possessions (Late)* (London, 1920).
Great Britain. *Handbook of German East Africa* (London, 1921).
Parliamentary Debates. 5th series.
MacKenzie, Norman, ed., *The Letters of Sidney and Beatrice Webb* (London, 1978).
MacKenzie, Norman and Jeanne, *The Diary of Beatrice Webb* (Cambridge, MA, 1985) vol. 4.
McEwen, J. M., ed., *The Riddell Diaries 1908–1923* (London, 1986).
Report by H.M.G. to the Council of the League of Nations on the Administration of the British Cameroons, 1921–1939.
Report by H.M.G. to the Council of the League of Nations on the Administration

of British Togoland, 1921–1939.
Report by H.M.G. to the Council of the League of Nations on the Administration of the Tanganyika Territory, 1921–1939.

League of Nations

Minutes and Reports of the League of Nations Permanent Mandates Commission, 1921–1939.
Official Journal.

United States

Congressional Record.
Link, Arthur, ed., *The Deliberations of the Council of Four* (Princeton, 1992) 2 vols.
Link, Arthur, ed., *The Papers of Woodrow Wilson* (Princeton, 1984–1991) vols. 50–64.
Papers Relating to the Foreign Relations of the United States. Paris Peace Conference. (Washington, D.C.,1942–1947) 13 vols.
Papers Relating to the Foreign Relations of the United States. Supplement: The World War.
Papers of Vance McCormick, Michigan State University microfilm collection, no. 23028.
Scott, James Brown, *Official Statements of War Aims and Peace Proposals: December 1916 to November 1918* (Washington, D.C., 1921).
Seymour, Charles, ed., *The Intimate Papers of Colonel House* (New York, 1928) vol. 4.

Contemporary Sources and Memoirs

Alexander, Gilchrist, *Tanganyika Memories: A Judge in the Red Kanzu* (London, 1936).
Altrincham, Lord, *Kenya's Opportunity* (London, 1955).
Amery, Leo, *The Forward View* (London, 1935).
——, *My Political Life: War and Peace* (London, 1953).
Angell, Norman, *If Britain is to Live* (London, 1923).
Aymerich, Joseph-Gaudéric, *La Conquête du Cameroun* (Paris, 1933).
Barnes, Leonard, *The Duty of Empire* (London, 1935).
Beer, George Louis, *African Questions at the Paris Peace Conference* (New York, 1923).
Bell, P. M. H., *France and Britain, 1900–1940: Entente and Estrangement* (London, 1996).
Bentwich, Norman, *The Mandates System* (London, 1930).
Bertrum, A., *The Colonial Service* (London, 1930).
Borden, Robert, *Robert Laird Borden: His Memoirs* (Toronto, 1938).
Buell, Raymond, *The Native Problem in Africa* (New York, 1928) 2 vols.
Burns, Alan, *Colonial Civil Servant* (London, 1949).
Buxton, C. R., *Exploitation of the Coloured Man* (London, 1925).
Cameron, Donald, *My Tanganyika Service and Some Nigeria* (London, 1939).
Cecil, Viscount, *A Great Experiment: An Autobiography by Viscount* Cecil (New York, 1941).
Chazelas, Victor, *Territoires Africains sous Mandat de la France: Cameroun et*

Togo (Paris, 1931).
Clemenceau, Georges, *Grandeur and Misery of Victory* (New York, 1930).
Clifford, Hugh, *German Colonies* (London, 1918).
Costedot, René, *L'Effort français au Cameroun* (Paris, 1930).
Dewavrin, Maurice, et al., *Comment mettre en valeur notre domaine colonial* (Paris, 1920).
Dundas, Charles, *African Crossroads* (London, 1955).
Fiddes, G. V., *The Dominions and Colonial Offices* (London, 1926).
Fraser, Donald, *The New Africa* (London, 1927).
Furse, Ralph, *Aucuparius: Recollections of a Recruiting Officer* (London, 1962).
Gheerbrant, J. L., *Notre empire* (Paris, 1943).
Hailey, Lord, *An Africa Survey* (London, 1938).
Hall, William Edward, *A Treatise of the Foreign Powers and Jurisdiction of the British Crown* (Oxford, 1894).
Hankey, Lord, *The Supreme Control at the Paris Peace Conference* (London, 1963).
Hardinge, Lord, *Old Diplomacy* (London, 1947).
Hardy, Georges, *Histoire de la colonisation française* (Paris, 1928).
——., *La politique coloniale et la partage de la terre aux XIXe et XXe siècles* (Paris, 1937).
Harris, J. H., *Slavery or 'Sacred Trust'?* (London, 1926).
Harris, Norman Dwight, *Europe and Africa* (New York, 1927).
Hobson, J. A., *Imperialism: A Study* (London, 1902).
Hughes, W. M., *Policies and Potentates* (Sydney, 1950).
Huxley, Elspeth, *White Man's Country: Lord Delamere and the Making of Kenya* (London, 1935).
Huxley, Julian, *African View* (New York, 1931).
Jean-François, Armand, *La France et la mise en valeur des colonies* (Paris, 1931).
Jeffries, Charles, *The Colonial Empire and its Civil Service* (London, 1938).
Joleson, F. S., *Germany's Claim to Colonies* (London, 1939).
Labouret, Henri, *Le Cameroun* (Paris, 1937).
Lansing, Robert, *The Peace Negotiations: A Personal Narrative* (New York, 1921).
——, *The Big Four and Others at the Paris Peace Conference* (Boston, 1921).
Lenin, V. I., *Imperialism: The Highest Stage of Capitalism* (London, 1916).
Lettow-Vorbeck, Paul von, *My Reminiscences of East Africa* (London, n.d.).
Leys, Norman, *Kenya* (London, 1925).
Leubuscher, Charlotte, *Tanganyika Territory: A Study of Economic Policy under Mandate* (London, 1944).
Lloyd George, David, *The Truth About the Peace Treaties* (London 1938) vol. 1.
Lugard, Lord, *The Dual Mandate in British Tropical Africa* (London, 1965 edn.).
Lumley, E. K., *Forgotten Mandate: A British District Officer in Tanganyika* (London, 1976).
Lyautey, Marshal Louis, *Paroles d'action* (Paris, 1927).
Lyautey, Pierre, *L'empire colonial français* (Paris, 1931).
Maanen-Helmer, Elizabeth van, *The Mandates System in Relation to Africa and the Pacific Islands* (London, 1929).
Macaulay, Neil, *Mandates: Reasons, Results, and Remedies* (London, 1937).
Maguet, Edgard, *Concessions domaniales dans les colonies françaises* (Paris, 1930).
Milner, Lord, *Questions of the Hour* (London, 1924).
Mitchell, Philip, *African Afterthoughts* (London, 1954).

Moberly, F. J., *Official History of the War: Military Operations, Togoland and the Cameroons, 1914–1916* (London, 1931).
Morel, E. D., *Africa and the Peace of Europe* (London, 1917).
Mumford, W. Bryant, *Africans Learn to be French* (London, 1935).
Nicholson, Harold, *Peacemaking 1919* (New York, 1965).
Oldham, J. H., *Christianity and the Race Problem* (London, 1924).
Parkinson, Cosmo, *The Colonial Office From Within* (London, 1946).
Pechoux, L., *Le Mandat Français sur le Togo* (Paris, 1939).
Perham, Margery, *East African Journey: Kenya and Tanganyika 1929–1930* (London, 1976).
——, *Ten Africans* (London, 1936).
Petit, Edouard, *Organisation des colonies française et des pays de protectorat* (Paris, 1894) 2 vols.
Rappard, William, *The Quest for Peace since the World War* (Cambridge, Mass., 1940).
Robert, Stephen H., *A History of French Colonial Policy, 1875–1925* (London, 1929) 2 vols.
Sarraut, Albert, *La mise en valeur des colonies françaises* (Paris, 1923).
Schact, Hjalmar, *New Colonial Policy* (London, 1926).
Schnee, Heinrich, *Braucht Deutschland Kolonien?* (Leipzig, 1921).
——, *Die Deutschen Kolonien unter Fremder Mandatherrschaft* (Leipzig, 1922).
——, *German Colonization Past and Future: The Truth about the German Colonies* (London, 1926).
Smith, Bryan Sharwood, *Recollections of British Administration in the Cameroons and Northern Nigeria 1921–1957* (Durham, North Carolina, 1969).
Smuts, Jan. C., *The League of Nations: A Practical Suggestion* (London, 1918).
——, *Africa and Some World Problems* (London, 1930).
Symes, Stewart, *Tour of Duty* (London, 1946).
Vignon, Louis, *L'Exploitation de notre empire colonial* (Paris, 1900).
White, Freda, *Mandates* (London, 1926).
Woolf, Leonard, *Empire and Commerce in Africa* (London, 1920).
Wright, Quincy, *Mandates Under the League of Nations* (New York, 1968 edn.).
Zimmern, Alfred, *The Third British Empire* (London, 1926).

Secondary Sources

Ageron, Charles-Robert, *France coloniale ou parti coloniale?* (Paris, 1978).
——, *La Décolonisation française* (Paris, 1991).
d'Almeida, Silvi K. and Gbedemah, Seti Y. G., *Le Gouverneur Bonnecarrère au Togo* (Lomé, 1982).
Andrew, Christopher M., and Kanya-Forstner, A. S., *France Overseas: The Great War and the Climax of French Imperial* Expansion (London, 1981).
Armstrong, David, *The Rise of the International Organization: A Short History* (New York, 1982).
Austen, Ralph A., *Northwest Tanzania under German and British Rule* (New Haven and London, 1968).
Baer, George W., ed., *International Organizations 1918–1945: A Guide to Research and Research Materials* (Wilmington, Delaware, 1991 edn.).
Bariéty, Jaques, *Les relations franco-allemandes après la première guerre mondiale* (Paris, 1972).
——, *La France et l'Allemagne entre les deux guerres mondiales* (Nancy, 1987).

Berman, Bruce, *Control and Crisis in Colonial Kenya: The Dialectic of Domination* (London, 1990).
Betts, Raymond F., *Assimilation and Association in French Colonial Theory, 1890–1914* (NewYork, 1961).
——, *Uncertain Dimensions: Western Overseas Empires in the Twentieth Century* (Minneapolis, 1985).
Birn, Donald S., *The League of Nations Union 1918–1945* (Oxford, 1981).
Boahen, A. Adu, ed., *Africa under Colonial Domination 1880–1935*, abridged edition (Berkeley, 1990).
Bouche, Denise, *Histoire de la colonisation française* 2 vols (Paris 1991).
Brett, E. A., *Colonialism and Underdevelopment in East Africa* (London, 1973).
Brunschwig, Henri, *Mythes et réalités de l'impérialisme colonial français 1870–1914* (Paris, 1960).
Cain, P. J. and Hopkins, A. G., *British Imperialism: Crisis and Deconstruction, 1914–1990* (London, 1993).
Chanock, M. L., *Law, Custom, and Social Order: The Colonial Experience in Malawi and Zambia* (Cambridge, 1985).
Chiabi, Emmanuel, *The Making of Modern Cameroon: A History of Substate Nationalism and Disparate Union, 1914–1961* vol. 1 (Lanham, Maryland, 1997).
Chidzero, B. T. G. *Tanganyika and International Trusteeship* (London, 1961).
Clark, M., *Modern Italy 1871–1982* (London, 1984).
Cohen, Warren I., *Empire Without Tears: America's Foreign Relations 1921–1933* (New York, 1987).
Cohen, William B., *Rulers of Empire: The French Colonial Service in Africa* (Stanford, 1971).
Conklin, Alice L., *A Mission to Civilize: The Republican Idea of Empire in France and West Africa, 1895–1930* (Stanford, 1997).
Constantine, Stephen, *The Making of British Colonial Development Policy 1914–1940* (London, 1984).
Coogan, John W., "Wilsonian Diplomacy in War and Peace" in Gordon Martel, ed., *American Foreign Relations Reconsidered, 1890–1993* (London, 1994).
Cooper, Frederick, *From Slaves to Squatters: Plantation Labor and Agriculture in Zanzibar and Coastal Kenya 1890–1925* (Nairobi, 1981).
Cornevin, Robert, *Le Togo: Des origines à nos jours* (Paris, 1987).
Crozier, Andrew J., *Appeasement and Germany's Last Bid for Colonies* (New York, 1988).
DeLancey, Mark W., *Cameroon: Dependence and Independence* (Boulder, Colorado, 1989).
Deng, Francis M. and Daly, M. W., *'Bonds of Silk': The Human Factor in the British Administration of the Sudan* (East Lansing, Michigan, 1990).
Digre, Brian, *Imperialism's New Clothes: The Repartition of Tropical Africa 1914–1919* (New York, 1990).
Dirks, Nicholas B., ed., *Colonialism and Culture* (Ann Arbor, 1992).
Duignan, Peter and Gann, L. H., *The Rulers of German Africa 1884–1914* (Stanford, 1977).
——, eds., *African Proconsuls: European Governors in Africa* (New York, 1978).
Dumbuya, Peter, A., *Tanganyika under International Mandate, 1919–1946* (Lanham, Maryland, 1995).
Dutton, David, *Austen Chamberlain: Gentleman in Politics* (Bolton UK, 1985).
Echenberg, Myron J., *Colonial Conscripts: The Tirailleurs Sénégalais in French West Africa, 1857–1960* (London, 1991).

Eckert, Andreas, *Die Duala und die Kolonialmächte* (Münster, 1991).
Egerton, George W., *Great Britain and the Creation of the League of Nations: Strategy, Politics, and International Organization, 1914–1919* (Chapel Hill, North Carolina, 1978).
Eyonetah, Tambi, *A History of the Cameroon* (London, 1987 edn.).
Fall, Barbacar, *Le travail forcé en Afrique-Occidentale française (1900–1946)* (Paris, 1993).
Ferro, Marc, *Colonization: A Global History* (Quebec, 1997).
Feuer, Lewis, *Imperialism and the Anti-Imperialist Mind* (Buffalo NY, 1986).
Fischer, Fritz, *Germany's Aims in the First World War* (New York, 1967).
Fitzpatrick, Sheila, *The Russian Revolution 1917–1932* (Oxford, 1982).
Flint, John E., "Frederick Lugard: The Making of an Autocrat (1858–1945)" in L. H. Gann and Peter Duignan, eds., *African Proconsuls: European Governors in Africa* (New York, 1978).
Freund, Bill, *The Making of Contemporary Africa: The Development of African Society Since 1800* (Bloomington, Indiana, 1984).
Frost, Richard, *Enigmatic Proconsul: Sir Philip Mitchell and the Twilight of Empire* (London, 1992).
Fry, Michael G., *Illusions of Security: North Atlantic Diplomacy, 1918–1922* (Toronto, 1972).
Gailey, Harry A., *Sir Donald Cameron: Colonial Governor* (Stanford, 1974).
——, *Clifford: Imperial Proconsul* (London, 1982).
Gaillard, Philippe, *Le Cameroun*, 2 vols (Paris, 1989).
Gayibor, N. L., ed., *Les Togolais face à la colonisation* (Lomé, 1994).
Gelfand, Lawrence E., *The Inquiry: American Preparations for Peace 1917–1919* (New Haven, Conn., 1963).
Gifford, Prosser and Louis, Wm. Roger, eds., *Britain and Germany in Africa* (New Haven, 1967).
——, *France and Britain in Africa* (New Haven, 1971).
Glassman, Jonathon, *Feasts and Riot: Revelry, Rebellion, and Popular Consciousness on the Swahili Coast, 1850–1880* (London, 1995).
Greenhalgh, Paul, *Ephemeral Vistas: A History of the Expositions Universelles, Great Exhibitions and World's Fairs, 1851–1939* (New York, 1988).
Gregory, Robert G., "Sidney Webb and East Africa: Labour's Experiment with the Doctrine of Native Paramountcy," *University of California Publications in History* vol. 71, 1962.
Gupta, Partha Sarathi, *Imperialism and the British Labour Movement 1914–1964* (London, 1975).
De Haan, Léo, *La région des savanes au Togo: l'État, les paysans et l'intégration régional (1885–1985)* (Paris, 1993).
Hall, H. Duncan, *Mandates, Dependencies and Trusteeship* (Washington, D.C., 1948).
Haugerud, Angelique, *The Culture of Politics in Modern Kenya* (Cambridge, 1995).
Hetherington, Penelope, *British Paternalism and Africa 1920–1940* (London, 1978).
Hiden, John, *Germany and Europe 1919–1939* (London, 1993 edn.).
Hordern, Charles, *History of the Great War: Military Operations, East Africa* (London, 1941).
Howe, Steven, *Anticolonialism in British Politics: The Left and the End of Empire 1989–1964* (Oxford, 1993).
Illife, John, *Tanganyika Under German Rule* (Cambridge, 1969).

——, *A Modern History of Tanganyika* (Cambridge, 1979).
——, *Africans: The History of a Continent* (Cambridge, 1995).
James, Lawrence, *The Rise and Fall of the British Empire* (New York, 1994).
Johnson, G. Wesley, ed., *Double Impact: France and Africa in the Age of Imperialism* (Westport, Conn., 1985).
Joseph, Richard A., *Radical Nationalism in Cameroun: Social Origins of the U.P.C. Rebellion* (Oxford, 1977).
Judd, Denis, *Empire: The British Imperial Experience from 1765 to the Present* (London, 1996).
Kaniki, Martin H. Y., *Tanzania Under Colonial Rule* (London, 1980).
Kennan, George F., *The Decision to Intervene: Soviet-American Relations, 1917–1929* (Princeton, 1958).
Kent, John, *The Internationalization of Colonialism: Britain, France, and Black Africa, 1939–1956* (Oxford, 1992).
Killingray, David and Clayton, Anthony, *Khaki and Blue: Military and Police in British Colonial Africa* (Athens, Ohio, 1989).
Kimambo, Isria N., *Penetration and Protest in Tanzania: The Impact of the World Economy on the Page, 1860–1960* (London, 1991).
Kimmich, Christoph M., *Germany and the League of Nations* (Chicago, 1976).
Kirk-Greene, A. H. M., *A Biographical Dictionary of the British Colonial Governor* (Stanford, 1980).
Kitchen, Martin, *Europe between the Wars: A Political History* (London, 1988).
Knoll, Arthur J., *Togo Under Imperial Germany 1884–1914* (Stanford, 1978).
Kolb, E., *The Weimar Republic* (London, trans. edn., 1989).
Lawler, Nancy Ellen, *Soldiers of Misfortune: Ivoirien Tirailleurs of World War II* (Athens, Ohio, 1992).
Lee, M. and Michalka, W., *German Foreign Policy 1917–1933* (Lemington Spa, 1987).
LeVine, Victor, *The Cameroons from Mandate to Independence* (Berkeley, 1964).
Lloyd, Lorna, *Peace Through Law: Britain and the International Court in the 1920s* (Woodbridge, UK, 1997).
Logan, Rayford W., *The African Mandates in World Politics* (Washington, D.C., 1948).
Louis, Wm. Roger, *Great Britain and Germany's Lost Colonies* (Oxford, 1967).
Lovejoy, Paul E. and Hogendorn, Jan S., *Slow Death for Slavery: The Course of Abolition in Northern Nigeria, 1897–1936* (Cambridge, 1993).
Luckau, A. M., *The German Delegation at the Paris Peace Conference* (New York, 1941).
MacKenzie, John M., *Imperialism and Popular Culture* (London, 1986).
Maisel, Ephraim, *The Foreign Office and Foreign Policy, 1919–1926* (Brighton, UK, 1994).
Mangan, J. A., ed., *Making Imperial Mentalities: Socialisation and British Imperialism* (New York, 1990).
Manning, Patric, *Francophone Sub-Saharan Africa 1880–1985* (Cambridge, 1988).
Martelli, George, *Leopold to Lumumba: A History of the Belgian Congo 1877–1960* (London, 1962).
Michel, Marc, *L'Appel à l'Afrique: Contributions et réactions à l'effort de guerre en A.O.F. 1914–1919* (Paris, 1982).
Miers, Suzanne and Roberts, Richard, eds., *The End of Slavery in Africa* (Madison, Wisc., 1988).
McCarthy, D. M. P., *Colonial Bureaucracy and Creating Underdevelopment:*

Tanganyika, 1919–1940 (Ames, Iowa, 1982).
Moneta, Jacob, *La Politique du parti communiste français et la question coloniale (1920–1963)* (Paris, 1971).
Mveng, Engelbert, *Histoire du Cameroun* (Paris, 1963).
Nicholson, I. N., *The Administration of Nigeria 1900–1960: Men, Methods, and Myths* (Oxford, 1969).
Northedge, F. S., *The League of Nations: Its Life and Times, 1920–1946* (Leicester, 1986).
Njeuma, Martin, ed., *Introduction to the History of Cameroon: Nineteenth and Twentieth Centuries* (New York, 1989).
O'Brien, Terence H., *Milner: Viscount Milner of St. James's and Cape Town 1854–1924* (London, 1979).
Osterhammel, Jürgen, *Colonialism: A Theoretical Overview* (Princeton, 1997).
Oyono, Dieudonné, *Colonie ou mandat international? La politique française au Cameroun de 1919 à 1946* (Paris, 1992).
Page, Melvin E., ed., *Africa and the First World War* (New York, 1987).
Perham, Margery, *Lugard: The Years of Adventure, 1858–1898* (London, 1956).
——, *Lugard: The Years of Authority, 1898–1945* (London, 1960).
Persell, Stuart Michael, *The French Colonial Lobby 1889–1938* (Stanford, 1983).
Phillips, Anne, *The Enigma of Colonialism: British Policy in West Africa* (London, 1989).
Porter, Bernard, *The Lion's Share: A Short History of British Imperialism 1850–1995* (London, 1996 edn.).
Pugh, Martin, *Lloyd George* (London, 1988).
Rich, Paul B., *Race and Empire in British Politics* (Cambridge, 1986).
Roberts, Andrew, ed., *The Colonial Moment in Africa: Essays on the Movement of Minds and Materials, 1900–1940* (Cambridge, 1990).
Robinson, Kenneth and Madden, Frederick, eds., *Essays in Imperial Government Presented to Margery Perham* (Oxford, 1963).
Robinson, Kenneth, *The Dilemmas of Trusteeship: Aspects of British Colonial Policy between the Wars* (London, 1965).
Rumuia, Jean, *Le Rwanda sous le régime du mandat Belge, 1916–1931* (Paris, 1992).
Said, Edward W., *Culture and Imperialism* (New York, 1993).
Schmokel, Wolfe W., *Dream of Empire: German Colonialism 1919–1945* (New Haven, Conn., 1964).
Skinner, Elliot P., *African Americans and U.S. Policy Toward Africa 1850–1934: In Defense of Black Nationality* (Washington, D.C., 1992).
Smith, Woodruff D., *The German Colonial Empire* (Chapel Hill, North Carolina, 1978).
Stansky, Peter, ed., *The Left and War: The British Labour Party and World War I* (New York, 1969).
Stevenson, D., *French War Aims against Germany, 1914–1919* (Oxford, 1982).
Swartz, Marvin, *The Union of Democratic Control in British Politics During the First World War* (Oxford, 1971).
Tabili, Laura, *'We Ask for British Justice': Workers and Racial Difference in Late Imperial Britain* (Ithaca, New York, 1994).
Tidrick, Kathryn, *Empire and the English Character* (London, 1990).
Tomlinson, B. R., *The Economy of Modern India, 1860–1970* (Cambridge, 1993).
Upthegrove, Campbell L., *Empire by Mandate: A History of the Relations of Great Britain with the Permanent Mandates Commission of the League of*

Nations (New York, 1954).
Walworth, Arthur, *America's Moment, 1918: American Diplomacy at the End of World War I* (New York, 1977).
——, *Wilson and His Peacemakers: American Diplomacy at the Paris Peace Conference, 1919* (New York, 1986).
Weber, Charles W., *International Influences and Baptist Mission in West Cameroon: German-American Missionary Endeavor under International Mandate and British Colonialism* (New York, 1993).
Walter, F. P., *A History of the League of Nations* (London, 1960).
Whol, David, *French Communism in the Making, 1914–1924* (Stanford, 1966).
Wilson, H. S., *African Decolonization* (London, 1994).
Winks, Robin W., ed., *The Historiography of the British Empire-Commonwealth: Trends, Interpretations, and Resources* (Durham, North Carolina, 1966).
Wolfers, Arnold, *Britain and France between Two Wars: Conflicting Strategies of Peace from Versailles to World War II* (New York, 1986 edn.).
Wright, Marcia, *German Missions in Tanganyika 1890–1941* (Oxford, 1971).
Von Laue, Theodore H., *Why Lenin? Why Stalin?* (New York, 1971).
——, *The World Revolution of Westernization: The Twentieth Century in Global Perspective* (New York, 1987).
Yagla, Ogma Wen'saa, *Les indigènes du Togo à l'asssaut du pouvoir colonial, 1920–1958: l'histoire politique d'un peuple africain* (Lomé, 1992).

Index

Printed and bound by CPI Group (UK) Ltd, Croydon, CR0 4YY

13/09/2026

14961101-0004